VOLUME **TWO**

BURMA'S VOICES
of FREEDOM

In Conversation with Alan Clements

AN ONGOING STRUGGLE *for* DEMOCRACY

By **ALAN CLEMENTS**
and **FERGUS HARLOW**

WORLD DHARMA PUBLICATIONS
©2020

VOLUME TWO

BURMA'S VOICES
of FREEDOM

―――――

In Conversation with Alan Clements

AN ONGOING STRUGGLE *for* DEMOCRACY

"By dedicating her life to the fight for human rights and Democracy in Burma, Aung San Suu Kyi is not only speaking out for justice in her own country, but also for all those who want to be free to choose their own destiny. As long as the struggle for freedom needs to be fought throughout the world, voices such as Aung San Suu Kyi's will summon others to the cause. Whether the cry for freedom comes from central Europe, Russia, Africa, or Asia, it has a common sound: all people must be treated with dignity; all people need to hope."

~ **VACLAV HAVEL**, FORMER PRESIDENT OF
THE CZECH REPUBLIC

WORLD DHARMA PUBLICATIONS

Published in 2020 by World Dharma Publications
Copyright © Alan Clements 1997, 2008, 2012, 2020

Cover design by World Dharma Publications
Typography by World Dharma Publications

Library of Congress Cataloging-in-Publication Data

Clements, Alan 1951 —
Burma's Voices of Freedom:
An Ongoing Struggle for Democracy
p. cm.
ISBN 978-1-953508-14-0
1. Biography 2. International Relations. 3. Political. 4. Liberty — freedom —
Buddhism 5. Spiritual life — Buddhism— non-sectarian 6. Human rights — all
aspects 7. Social, Political and Environmental justice — all 8. Activism — all
9. Consciousness — all 10. Politics — global 11. Body, Mind & Spirit

First printing, September 1, 2020

World Dharma Publications
www.WorldDharma.com

TABLE OF CONTENTS

FURTHER CHAPTERS IN THE SERIES

Volume 1

Introduction

Chapter 1: Conversations with Aung San Suu Kyi

Chapter 2: Excerpts from Selected Interviews with Aung San Suu Kyi

Chapter 3: Excerpts from Key Speeches by Aung San Suu Kyi

Chapter 4: Aung San Suu Kyi Quotes

Chapter 5: Aung San Suu Kyi Timeline

Chapter 6: Conversations with U Tin Oo

Chapter 7: Conversations with U Win Tin

Chapter 8: Conversations with U Win Htein

Photographic Section

Author Profiles

Volume 3

Volume 4

CHAPTER 9

CONVERSATIONS *with*
AUNG SAN SUU KYI

1996

"There is no perfection in this world. Once you accept that fact, you can lead a full life wherever you are."

ALAN CLEMENTS: When you reflect back over the years of your life, what have been the most important experiences and personal lessons that have had a significant effect on your growth as an individual?

AUNG SAN SUU KYI: It's very simple. What I have learned in life is that it's always your own wrongdoing that causes you the greatest suffering. It is never what other people do to you. Perhaps this is due to the way in which I was brought up. My mother instilled in me the principle that wrongdoing never pays, and my own experience has proved that to be true. Also, if you have positive feelings towards other people, they can't do anything to you—they can't frighten you. I think that if you stop loving other people then you really suffer.

AC: How would you characterize yourself as a person?

ASSK: Well, I see myself sometimes quite differently from how other people see me. For example, all this business about my being so brave...I had never thought of myself as a particularly brave person at all. And when people say: "How marvelous it is that you stuck out those six years of detention," my reaction is, "Well, what's so difficult about it? What's all the fuss about?" Anybody can stick out six years of house arrest. It's those people who have had to stick out years and years in prison, in terrible conditions, that make you wonder how they did it. So I don't see myself as all that extraordinary. I do see myself as a trier. I don't give up. When I say, "I don't give up," I'm not talking about not giving up working for democracy. That too, but basically, I don't give up trying to be a better person.

AC: So it's this inner drive, this determination towards perfection or wholeness that most characterizes you?

ASSK: Yes. People talk quite a lot about my determination but I don't think of myself as a very determined person. I just think of myself as a trier.

AC: What is it in your life that provides you with the greatest sense of meaning and purpose?

ASSK: At the moment, of course, it's our cause for democracy. In that sense...I am very fortunate. A lot of people here in Burma are. I have spoken about this to members of the NLD: "Don't feel sorry for yourselves. Don't think of yourselves as being unfortunate because of having to live through these times. Think of it as fortunate, because you have an opportunity to work for justice and the welfare of other people. This sort of opportunity does not come to everybody all the time." You may desire it but you may not get it. So I think of myself as fortunate, because I have been able to work for something which is worth working for—democracy. I think this is what is behind the sacrifices made by so many of my colleagues. They believe that their sacrifices are worth what they are fighting for.

AC: Let's broaden the issue. What might be the common bond that allows others in the world to feel and understand that your people's struggle for freedom is not different or separate from their own pursuit of happiness? Might there be an intimate link that binds all humankind together?

ASSK: Yes, of course. Everybody understands the fundamental human desire for freedom and security. What we want in Burma is both security and freedom; freedom from want and freedom from fear; freedom to be allowed to pursue our own interests—obviously, without harming other people's interests. At the same time, we want the security that allows us to pursue these interests without fear of other people's interference. Real freedom cannot exist without security. An insecure person is never really free.

AC: What are the most prevalent fears among the Burmese people today?

ASSK: I think most people are afraid of loss. They're afraid of losing their friends, their liberty, their means of livelihood. Basically, they are afraid of losing what they have or losing the opportunity to be able to get something they need in order to live decent lives. What people want is freedom from that sort of fear. For instance, they should not be afraid that anybody at any time can take away their right to practice their own profession. This has been done in Burma. Many lawyers of the NLD, when they came out of prison, had their licenses taken from them. They must find other ways of earning their livelihood.

AC: Could you explain the variety of ways SLORC oppresses the NLD?

ASSK: The very fact that you are an NLD member makes you vulnerable. If you are active as an organizer you are constantly harassed. In many townships NLD [members] are not allowed to hold their own meetings in their own offices. In some places NLD organizers are not allowed to go out of town without the consent of the authorities. And of course, they are constantly watched and questioned by the MI [Military Intelligence].

AC: On a more personal note: Daw Suu, when you consider your life, would you say that there are distinct periods that are definable by some dramatic emotional or psychological changes?

ASSK: No, I don't think it happens like that. It's more gradual. Except, I suppose, for people who've had very traumatic experiences. Perhaps such people suddenly change quite noticeably.

AC: I don't know how you use the word trauma, but the death of your father at such a young age would be considered by most standards to be rather traumatic. Or the witnessing of your brother's death by drowning when you were seven. He was your best friend too...

ASSK: I don't remember my father's death as such. I don't think I was aware that he died; I was too young. I felt my brother's death much more. I was very close to him...probably closer to him than to anybody else. We shared the same room and played together all the time. His death was a tremendous loss for me. At that time, I felt enormous grief. I suppose you could call it a "trauma," but it was not something that I couldn't cope with. Of course, I was very upset by the fact that I would never see him again. That, I think, is how a child sees death; I won't play with him again; I'll never be able to be with him again. But at the same time, looking back, there must have been a tremendous sense of security surrounding me. I was able to cope—I didn't suffer from depression or great emotional upheaval.

AC: If I may make a personal observation...you seem so confident.

ASSK: I have never thought of myself as particularly confident. What I do know is that I want to do what is right. I don't claim that what I'm doing is always right. But I know for a fact that my intentions are good and that I don't want to hurt anyone.

AC: What has been the experience in your life that has caused you the most grief?

ASSK: I would say it was my brother's death. But looking back, it seems to me that I did cope with it very well. I've thought of it from time to time. I was not utterly devastated by it. I was grieved, but I did not go to pieces. So that seems to indicate that the family situation was such that there was enough support around for me to be able to cope with my grief.

AC: Have you ever been betrayed in such a way that it pierced your heart?

ASSK: I think all of us who have joined the movement for democracy have known betrayal. We have known people who have left our cause because it was too difficult and they just could not cope with it anymore.

But none of the really important people have done that—U Tin Oo, U Kyi Maung, U Aung Shwe, U Lwin—they have all remained staunch.

AC: From the time of SLORC's coup in 1988 up to the present, they have obsessively reiterated that their true intentions are to bring peace, tranquility and a genuine multi-party democracy to Burma. Now I am curious, why haven't these generals just come out and said: "Listen, we're a totalitarian dictatorship. It's our show. We own the banks; we have the power, the armed forces and the weapons; we have the seat at the United Nations; all foreign business contracts are with us—the SLORC. So, no more democratic jargon. No more lies." Why don't they just come out with the truth?

ASSK: They must know better than I why they have not come out with it. But basically, it's a recognition of the fact that dictatorship is wrong and democracy is desirable.

AC: So, you do feel that SLORC recognizes their shortcomings?

ASSK: Yes, of course, after all they promised multi-party democracy. That's a recognition of the fact that they see it as something good and desirable, even if they're not keen on it.

AC: Perhaps I'm naïve, but why would a totalitarian regime say they want a multi-party democracy, without believing in it themselves?

ASSK: Because they know that's what most of the people want.

AC: So they're just pandering in words to the people's desire?

ASSK: I wouldn't say that the term is "pandering to." I suppose the thing is that they can't entirely resist the will of the people.

AC: But the people utterly despise SLORC. And SLORC has proven time and again that repression of democracy is their true intention. So who is SLORC appealing to with all this democracy rhetoric? Are they trying to convince themselves?

ASSK: It's possible that they are appealing to those from whom they hope to attract investment. It could be as cynical as that. But it is a question that only they can answer. Nevertheless, sometimes there are questions that some people can't answer, even about themselves. Because their motives are so mixed.

AC: On to more evident truths. It's a well-established fact that SLORC uses corruption as both a political tactic to control people and out of sheer greed on their part. Could you shed some light on how their corruption functions and how widespread it is?

ASSK: Corruption exists everywhere throughout the country. You have to pay to get the most ordinary things done such as renewing a car license. You even have to bribe hospital workers to perform necessary little services for patients. Corruption is endemic. Whoever has the authority can do whatever they want. At the village level the authorities refuse to do what they should do, unless they are bribed. But that does not apply to everybody. I know that there are some Village or Ward Law and Order Restoration Councils, that are honest and try to help the people. This is why we need democracy. We need a system that does not depend on whether an individual wants to do what is right or not. The system should have checks and balances that prevent him from going along the wrong path.

AC: Just how pervasive is bribery in Burma?

ASSK: Very pervasive. And you can't really blame the civil servants who demand bribes, when you consider that their starting salary is about 670 kyats a month. You told me that a cup of tea at the Strand Hotel costs three dollars which is more than half that. In a system like that, can one be surprised that there's such widespread bribery and corruption?

AC: Not an easy question, but when democracy is achieved, how will you and the NLD tackle the problem of such widespread corruption?

ASSK: It will not vanish overnight. Measures will have to be taken to ensure that civil servants are adequately paid. Accountability is one of the best ways of checking corruption and a democratic system means accountable government. But corruption is also a state of mind which has been brought about by the political situation. If the people at the top are corrupt, then people below think it is all right to be corrupt. If the people at the top are not corrupt and if it becomes obvious that they are accountable, we will be able to check corruption. It's also a matter of education. We will try our best to make people understand that corruption is not a way of life and if it is a way of life then it is certainly not the best.

AC: Talking of education, what is the state of education in Burma?

ASSK: Abysmal. Education is in a very bad state indeed. The drop-out rate in primary schools has been rising steadily since SLORC seized power. In schools, pupils are forced to make donations for all sorts of silly things and are not even provided with adequate textbooks. But there is something very interesting. I have mentioned this during my weekend meetings quite often. Last week, at the end of May, the schools reopened and at least two schools, perhaps more, had big signs saying: no donations of any kind and you can buy all your books in school—you don't have to buy them outside. So I think that our weekend meetings have a good effect because they always emphasize the necessity of good education.

AC: The SLORC is responding positively to your talks?

ASSK: They always respond. Always. This is why when some people ask me "If SLORC's policy was to try to marginalize you, what would you do?" I reply that they are not marginalizing us. They are not even trying. They keep me on the spot all the time. In a way, they are my unpaid PR.

AC: Back to business. All over Rangoon there are new imported cars. There are computer dealers selling the latest models from Apple, and Toshiba and Sony outlets selling state-of-the-art televisions and sound-systems. In an impoverished nation, who is buying these things?

ASSK: I don't know...but I was told that some have gotten very rich through the drug trade and they are laundering their black money...

AC: Are you saying that a large portion of the rich in Burma today are involved in the drug [heroin] trade?

ASSK: Not a large portion...but certainly a significant portion. Of course, if you investigate those who have become very rich over the last seven or so years [since SLORC's takeover], you will find that their wealth comes not as much from straightforward business, as it does from bribes.

AC: Burma's dictator, Ne Win, has ruled Burma for well over three decades. In so doing, he has systematically suppressed almost every form of freedom. The large majority of people in Burma were born under his rule. How has this psychologically affected the people?

ASSK: One dominant feature is the lack of confidence. And lack of confidence often means lack of honesty, because you don't know whom you can trust enough to be honest with. That is connected to fear. If you don't have confidence, you're filled with fear. This lack of confidence, of trust in each other, is a real sickness.

AC: People from all over the country, and from all walks of life, come to speak with you here at your home. Do you find that some of them are reluctant, or at times too scared to speak the truth?

ASSK: They are not afraid of telling me the truth because a lot of them trust me and know that I won't betray their trust. But what they say does demonstrate to a large extent how little they trust each other. I get a lot of information on who is not reliable and who is in contact with whom and therefore not to be trusted. But a lot of it is just genuine anxiety, not mischief-making. They really are afraid that somebody might be informing on somebody else.

AC: How pervasive is SLORC's Military Intelligence network?

ASSK: It's pervasive. We know for a fact that there are informers and that news sometimes does leak out, or get to the intelligence services. That is how it works in all police states. It's not unique to Burma.

AC: Is mistrust so widespread that it has reached a paranoia level?

ASSK: I think it's going along those lines.

AC: Daw Suu, at your weekend public gatherings you answer questions that have been submitted to you during the week. Almost every one of these questions reflects SLORC's numerous styles of repression and corruption—questions that speak of pain and struggle. Do you prepare your answers the night before or are they spontaneous?

ASSK: Sometimes I look over the questions the night before, that is if I have time. If I have no time, at least half an hour before. And it's only in case there's anything technical.

AC: From all the questions that are submitted to you weekly, who decides which questions are to be answered on weekends, and why?

ASSK: We get so many letters that I can't read them all myself. So our office staff read them first, weeding out the ones which we've answered before or ones that viciously attack someone personally or the government. We don't mind people criticizing the injustices of the government from which we are all suffering, but I never read to the public letters which viciously attack anyone in particular, even if the attack is justified in the sense that the injustice they are pointing out is true. For example, if a person writes a letter accusing a particular individual by name of corruption, I don't read it out. I'm against bringing personalities into politics. We do not like focusing on individuals, this is a very low kind of politics. Such letters are removed or we adapt them to leave out the names of individuals and say the authorities said or did such and such a thing on such and such a date. Also, we verify the facts before we read out anything. We don't just accept everything as it comes. This is not a place where you air your grievances without proper evidence.

AC: What would you say are the most positive qualities that have emerged among your people through their struggle for freedom under such harsh conditions of repression?

ASSK: Well...I think the Burmese people are much more hard-working than they used to be. They have been "forced" to work hard. I think those of us involved in the movement for democracy have learned to recognize our strengths and to build on them. I think it has also created very strong friendships.

AC: Could it be said that in your movement for democracy, you are ushering in a renaissance period in Burma, which is combining timeless Buddhist values with modern political principles?

ASSK: I don't think any individual can usher in a renaissance but I hope that we're heading for one. When people face troubles, they are forced to reassess their lives and their values, and that is what leads to renaissance.

AC: You've described your struggle for democracy as a "revolution of the spirit." In essence, what does this mean?

ASSK: When I speak about a spiritual revolution, I'm talking a lot about our struggle for democracy. I have always said that a true revolution has to be that of the spirit. You have to be convinced that you need to change and want to change certain things—not just material things. You want a political system which is guided by certain spiritual values—values that are different from those that you've lived by before.

AC: What shift in consciousness has been required in order to make the struggle a "spiritual revolution" from a socio-political one?

ASSK: Because of the tremendous repression to which we have been subjected it's almost impossible for it to be either a political or a social revolution. We're so hemmed in by all kinds of unjust regulations that we can hardly move as a political or a social movement. So it has had to be a movement very much of the spirit.

AC: Have you had a parallel passion to that of a political life?

ASSK: My other passion is literature, but it seems to dovetail with politics. In Burma, politics has always been linked to literature and literary men have often been involved in politics, especially the politics of independence.

AC: Before your arrival on to the political scene in Burma in 1988, did you feel that anything was missing from your life in Oxford?

ASSK: No. I think one should lead a full life wherever one is.

AC: Do you feel pretty complete wherever you are?

ASSK: Well, here and now I'm not part of my family and a family is part of one's life. So I cannot say that my life is complete. But I don't think anybody's life is. There is no perfection in this world. Once you accept that fact, you can lead a full life wherever you are.

AC: Do you live with demanding models of perfection in your speech and behavior?

ASSK: Oh yes, I do have perfectionist tendencies. I would very much like to be perfect. I know I'm not but that does not stop me from trying.

AC: Is striving for perfection a hardship?

ASSK: No. It's just part of everyday living. One tries.

AC: In essence what does "perfection" mean to you?

ASSK: My father once talked about purity in thought, word and deed. That's what I mean by perfection. Purity.

AC: Always the perfectly pure motivation?

ASSK: Yes. I think the greatest protection in life is absolute purity. I believe that nobody can hurt you except yourself, ultimately.

AC: Your father was assassinated when you were two years old. Then when you were seven years old you witnessed your brother's death by drowning. With the loss of your most intimate male figures at such a young age was there a dominant male—a father figure—who took over that important role during the years of your childhood?

ASSK: Not really. I never felt the need for a dominant male figure, because my mother's father who lived with us was the ideal grandfather. He was very indulgent and loving. During my childhood he was the most important male figure in my life.

AC: Do you have any actual memory of your father?

ASSK: Well, I have a memory of him picking me up every time he came home from work, but I think this may be a memory that was reinforced by people repeating it to me all the time. In other words, I was not allowed to forget. So it may be a genuine memory or it may be something I imagined from what people kept telling me. But I do seem to remember that whenever he would come back from work, my two brothers and I would come running around the stairs to meet him and he would pick me up.

AC: Do you think of your father every day?

ASSK: Not every day, no. I'm not obsessed by him, as some people think I am. I hope that my attitude towards him is one of healthy respect and admiration, not obsession.

AC: All the people compare you to him, from your physical appearance, your obvious leadership roles in Burma's independence, your articulation of similar and at times identical principles...the list goes on. What are your differences? What sets you apart? Not in the obvious ways but perhaps in policy choices—ways of thinking.

ASSK: I do not think we have any major differences. He was a better person than I am, and I'm not saying this just because I want to appear modest. My father was one of those people who was born with a sense of responsibility, far greater and more developed than mine. From the very moment he started going to school, he was a hard worker, very conscientious. I wasn't like that. I would study hard only when I liked the teacher or the subject. I had to develop my sense of responsibility and work at it. I think that's one of our differences. But in attitude, I don't think there are any fundamental differences between us. In fact, when I started doing research into my father's life I was struck by our similarities. I was surprised that we thought so much alike. At one time there were some thoughts and feelings that I thought were my own, and then I discovered that he had had them already.

AC: I read the following passage from a book you wrote about your father: "He was a difficult personality. There was much criticism about his moods, his untidiness, his devastating fits of silence, his equally devastating fits of loquacity and his altogether angular behavior. He himself admitted that he sometimes found polite, refined people irksome and would long to separate himself from them to live the life of a savage." It sounds like he was a straightforward wild man.

ASSK: My father was not really a savage. He was very angular, as I said, and got irritated by the outward trappings of certain fine society people. But at the same time, he was very refined in spirit, flexible and able to adapt. This is why, I think, he was the great man that he was. But all the people, because he was the leader, made a big deal of the fact that he was abrupt, stern and not always sociable. However, he was objective enough to see that this was not the way in which a head of state should behave. And towards the end of his life he maintained the dignity and honor of the nation, taking his responsibilities very seriously.

AC: What first comes to mind when you think about him?

ASSK: First of all the fact that he was a person capable of learning and who learned all the time. He also had an innate confidence in himself. Which did not mean that he was not aware of his own faults: he was conscious of them and of the need to improve. He was a person who went in for self-improvement all the time. There was at the core of his being a wholesomeness and a refinement that kept him together and made him an integrated person throughout all the phases he went through.

AC: You symbolize and embody for millions of people around the world a spiritually infused, nonviolent approach to politics. On the other hand, your father as an army general advocated an armed struggle and used violence successfully in a revolution to free his country from foreign oppression. If your father were alive in 1988, at the time of SLORC's slaughter of unarmed pro-democracy demonstrators, and if he were a student leader—a young Aung San—how do you think he would have responded to the crisis?

ASSK: Don't forget that I was over forty-four when I entered the movement for democracy, and my father was thirty-two when he died. He entered politics when he was eighteen, and founded the Burmese army when he was twenty-six. Now, when I was twenty-six, I was not the person I was at forty-four. And it is possible that if I had entered politics much earlier I might have had a far more passionate approach and might not have followed the way of nonviolence. I might have taken the same attitude he did, that any means used for gaining Burmese independence was acceptable. That was why he founded the army. At that time he thought that the most important thing was to achieve independence. But by the time he died, he understood that the problems of the country should be resolved through democratic politics and not through armed combat.

AC: How would you characterize your relationship with your mother?

ASSK: I treated my mother with a lot of love, respect and awe, as most Burmese children are taught to do. To me, my mother represented integrity, courage and discipline. She was also very warm-hearted. But she did not have a very easy life. I think it was difficult for her to bring up the family and cope with a career after my father's death.

AC: When you look back over your relationship with your mother, are there aspects of her which were limiting to you? Perhaps values or attitudes that confined you? Or mistakes in the way she raised you?

ASSK: I think she tried her best. She tried very hard to give us the best education and the best life she could. I do not think anybody is ever free from making mistakes. She was very strict at times. When I was younger I felt that was a disadvantage. But now, I think it was a good thing because it set me up well in life.

AC: How was she strict?

ASSK: Highly disciplined...everything at the right time...in the right way. She was a perfectionist.

AC: Are you that way with your children?

ASSK: I'm not that much of a disciplinarian, but I am strict. My mother was a very strong person and I suppose I too am strong, in my own way. But I have a much more informal relationship with my children. My mother's relationship with me was quite formal. She never ran around and played with me when I was young. With my sons, I was always running around with them, playing together. Also, I would have long discussions with them. Sometimes I would argue with them—tremendously passionate arguments, because my sons can be quite argumentative, and I am argumentative too. I never did this sort of thing with my mother.

AC: What do you argue about? Your values? Your Buddhist beliefs?

ASSK: It depends. I think my elder son, being more mature, tends to discuss philosophical issues more, whereas with my younger son we don't talk about that sort of thing much—at least not yet.

AC: Before we started our interview the other day, you mentioned that your youngest son, Kim, is a bit of a rock 'n' roller.

ASSK: Yes, he's very fond of...do you call it "hard rock"?

AC: If it's electric and loud...

ASSK: He is very musical and I've learned a lot about the kind of music that he likes. I have no problems with him...it's his father who has arguments with him about the kind of music he likes. Michael objects to Kim playing his music so loudly. Whereas that never troubles me...I can tolerate it.

AC: So he's allowed to play hard rock music as loud as he wants in the house?

ASSK: Yes, I never stop him because I don't like him listening to this music on the earphones. I think that damages his ears. I'd rather put up with all that noise than have him damage his ears.

AC: Western music has invaded Burma. Music Channel V—Star TV's attempt at MTV—is beamed in by satellite. Rock concerts are now available on video for rental and purchase. There are even several discos and night-clubs in Rangoon with live music, including hard rock. Some of the cutting edge of western music with radical video images of sex, drugs and often violence, is mixing with an ancient mystical culture. What do you think of this in light of hoping to preserve traditional Burmese Buddhist culture?

ASSK: If it comes in too quickly in this way, we may end up with a very superficial kind of non-culture. I am very much for openness—people studying other cultures. But this kind of quick invasion can be unhealthy. There are many aspects of Burmese culture which are worth preserving. Foreign influences have come in so overwhelmingly and so quickly we might lose more than we should.

AC: What are the most important qualities of Burmese culture you wish to preserve?

ASSK: The Buddhist values of loving-kindness and compassion. A respect for education.

AC: Burma will soon have a major influx of tourists and along with them the "backpackers," who will inevitably bring in drugs—acid, marijuana, hashish, Ecstasy, and a loose, cool attitude towards travel. What about the incoming travelers?

ASSK: It's worrying to me that they're coming in before the Burmese people have had a chance to develop self-confidence. The economy is in a terrible state and the Burmese people do not feel proud of their country at the moment. At such a time it is too easy for young people to grab at foreign ideas and values, simply because they think foreigners are better than they are and more successful. A people who have confidence in themselves have a better appreciation of both their own culture and that of others. They are more discriminating about what they should preserve, what they should discard; what they should accept, what they should reject.

"In many ways,
the opposition is your greatest benefactor."

ALAN CLEMENTS: Buddhist philosophy explains the transformation of an apparently negative experience into its positive opposite. For example, seeing cruelty as an opportunity to love, or deception as an invitation to honesty. In other words, everything is workable. There are no obstacles, only challenges, if spiritual attitude is well-focused. To explain this point the Buddha once chastised his monks for criticizing his arch-nemesis Devadatta, upon his death. As you know, Devadatta attempted to kill the Buddha on several occasions. But if I'm not mistaken, the Buddha said that without Devadatta's aggression he would never have been able to become fully accomplished in patience. One could see this as praise for the adversary or the opposition.

In Burma today we have a nearly identical metaphor with SLORC's politics of repression being confronted by a spiritual revolution. May I ask you for your views on the transformation of negativity into freedom as it applies to your struggle for democracy?

AUNG SAN SUU KYI: In order to have a really strong, healthy democracy, we need a strong, healthy opposition. I always explain that you need a good opposition because they'll always point out your mistakes and keep you on your toes. In many ways, the opposition is your greatest benefactor. In worldly terms the opposition in a democracy plays the role of Devadatta for any legal government. It stops the ruling party from going astray by constantly pointing out its every mistake. The opposition as the potential next government keeps the current one from misusing its power.

AC: As you know, the Buddha used the concept "*Saṃsāra*" to point out existence in its totality—the whole swirl of life, with birth, aging and death, as the backdrop of all else that we think of as important. Do you ever step back from the immediacy of the struggle and contemplate your anonymity or your unimportance to yourself within the bigger picture of existence?

ASSK: Yes. In fact, it still surprises me that I'm supposed to be an important person. I don't see things that way at all. I don't feel any different now that I'm in politics compared to what I felt before. Of course, I've got more responsibilities to discharge. But I had many responsibilities as a wife and a mother too. Things may appear big and important at times but I realize they are small when I consider the fact that we're all subject to the law of *anicca* [impermanence]. To put it in more blunt terms, I do contemplate my death. Which means to me an acceptance of the principle of chance. And by reflecting upon your own death some of the problems which seem significant to you just shrivel into nothingness. Do you ever think of your death?

AC: Yes, I do, sometimes. But by contemplating death, it hasn't brought me fear of death as such, the impression that something is ending, but a greater passion for living in the present. And you, may I ask how the contemplation of death has been of value to you?

ASSK: Few people really face the fact that they are going to die one day.

If you contemplate your own death, in a sense it means that you accept how unimportant you are. It's a way of stepping back from the present, from the immediate concerns of the world in which you're engaged, realizing just how insignificant you are within the whole scheme of things—within this swirl of *Saṃsāra*. And yet, you are essential in your place, even if you may not be of great importance. Everybody is essential. But it is a matter of having a balanced view of your place in the world. Having enough respect for yourself to understand that you too have a role to play and at the same time, having enough humility to accept that your role isn't as important as you or some people may think it is.

AC: As you know the First Noble Truth of the Buddha's enlightenment was the truth of *dukkha*—the truth of suffering. A truth that was rooted in the realization that all things were *anicca* or changing; everything was in a constant flux and therefore unsatisfactory. In the ultimate sense, that there could be no "permanent" happiness in an "impermanent" world. Do you ever teeter on the edge of your own existential plight—your individual struggle for spiritual freedom and your socio-political struggle for your people's freedom?

ASSK: No. Since we live in this world we have a duty to do our best for the world. Buddhism accepts this fact. And I don't consider myself so spiritually advanced as to be above all worldly concerns. Because of this, it's my duty to do the best that I can.

AC: So you see no split or tension between your Buddhist pursuits and your political ones?

ASSK: No...no.

AC: Many years ago I interviewed Burma's former Prime Minister U Nu who stated as a matter of fact that he was a committed *Bodhisattva* [a being striving for Buddhahood]. I asked him what was it like being the Prime Minister with full control of the army and to have made the vow to become a Buddha. He said rather explicitly, if I remember correctly, that it was a major burden, a nearly constant moral dilemma. What he was saying was that being a devout Buddhist was incompatible with being a political leader who had a responsibility to use the armed forces. Don't you feel any such dilemma?

ASSK: No, I do not see a dilemma. I would not think that I'm in any position to even contemplate taking the *Bodhisattva* vow. My first concern is to abide by Buddhist principles in my worldly dealings. Of course, I do meditate. That's because I believe that all of us, as human beings, have a spiritual dimension which cannot be neglected. Overall, I think of myself as a very ordinary Burmese Buddhist who will devote more time to religion in my older years.

AC: Do you consider yourself a Theravada Buddhist [which means the school of the elders, and is practiced in Burma, Thailand, Cambodia, Laos and Sri Lanka]?

ASSK: I am a Theravada Buddhist but I respect Mahayana Buddhism as well [a school of Buddhism practiced primarily in Tibet and other Himalayan countries as well as in Vietnam, Japan and to an extent in China]. Also, I have a great respect for other religions. I do not think anyone has the right to look down on anybody's religion.

AC: What are the elements of Mahayana Buddhism that you respect?

ASSK: In Mahayana Buddhism there's much more emphasis on compassion than in Theravada Buddhism. I'm very sensitive to this, because we need a lot of compassion in this world. Of course, compassion is also a part of Theravada Buddhism. But I would like to see more of our people putting compassion into action.

AC: What motivates you to meditate as a daily practice?

ASSK: The main reason why I meditate is the satisfaction that I derive from the knowledge that I am doing what I think I should do, that is, to try to develop awareness as a step towards understanding *anicca* as an experience. I have very ordinary attitudes towards life. If I think there is something I should do in the name of justice or in the name of love, then I'll do it. The motivation is its own reward.

AC: When we consider those who perpetrate the injustices in the world, they often seem to have the assumption that they are immune to their own actions, that they are above the law, so to speak, and that their repressive actions have no real effect on themselves...

ASSK: But it does have an effect on them. I'm sure everything that everybody does has a psychological effect on them. For example, take the extreme case of a dictator who is in a position to do anything he pleases. He can just say: "Have that man executed." He may not have anything to do with the execution itself and he may not even think about it the next day. But the very fact that he's had another man executed means that his sensitivities have become much more hardened. He has been affected. Every time he does something to somebody, he is also doing something to himself. And if he's a man with any sense of a conscience, somewhere inside of him, something will make him feel uncomfortable. Another thing is that he will affect people's perception of him. To put it in the simplest way, those who are connected to the man who was executed will like him less. So every time he commits an injustice he is adversely affected, whether he realizes it or not. In fact, this dictator may die without ever realizing how much the people had hated him. But the effect remains the same.

AC: So no one is above the law, no matter how lawless they may be?

ASSK: They may be above human laws, but not above the law of *karma* because the law of *karma* is actually very scientific. There is always a connection between cause and effect. It's like the light of a star, isn't it? The light that we see now was initiated so many light years ago, but there it is. In science too, there can be a seemingly long gap between cause and effect. But there's always the connection between them.

AC: Or perhaps in the more immediate sense, like the Vietnamese Buddhist monk Thich Nhat Hanh said, "In the grain of rice see the sun." Do you see yourself as just a seed-sower of democracy?

ASSK: I'm thinking of a book I once read, by Rebecca West. She was talking about musicians and artists as a "procession of saints always progressing towards an impossible goal." I see myself like that—as part of a procession, a dynamic process, doing all that we can to move towards more good and justice; a process that is not isolated from what has happened before or what will come after. And I do whatever I have to do along the path, whether it's sowing seeds or reaping the harvest or (*laughing*) tending the plants half-grown.

AC: Do you ever feel inadequate for the role that you are in?

ASSK: I very seldom think of myself as playing a role. I always think of myself as part of a movement, so my adequacies or inadequacies don't come so much into the question. I know that a lot of people will find this hard to believe because so much media attention is focused on me it seems as though I am playing the central role.

The main role in which I have to cope alone is meeting the foreign media. The other EC [Executive Committee] members of the National League for Democracy don't do much of that. But in everything else we work together. I'm not alone. Perhaps because of that I don't feel inadequate. I do not think my role is as large as some people think it is.

At the meeting table, which is where it matters, we are very much on an equal footing. I don't have any more clout than anybody else. If my suggestions are better they will take them, but not for any other reason. Mind you, they give me a lot more work to do because I am the youngest so I think I'm rather at a disadvantage!

But it's a family feeling between us and I do feel almost a blood bond with them. There's a lot of affection between all the members of the EC, and the more we meet, the stronger this bond of affection between us becomes. We are happy to work together and are courteous to each other. I'm surrounded by gentlemen. And when we are together, even when we have enormous problems to cope with, we draw strength from each other.

AC: If I may make another personal comment about you, I would say that you're an extremely articulate woman, with a profound sense of what is right and wrong, and at the same time a very simple person. Am I right?

ASSK: Yes, (*laughing*) I have very simple attitudes and this is one of the problems. Some people want to make something extraordinary out of me, but I'm not particularly extraordinary. I suppose people think I'm extraordinary because I'm so simple they can't believe it.

AC: Do you even see yourself as a leader?

ASSK: No! I find it very embarrassing when people refer to me as "*gaungzamggyi*"—big leader.

AC: In a previous conversation I asked you whether you believed in intrinsic evil. What about its opposite? Do you believe in the inherent goodness of people?

ASSK: I believe in the inherent goodness of some people and I think there is both good and bad in everyone. It's a matter of which bits you cultivate. Also, I think some people are born intrinsically more serene, sensible and compassionate than others. And there are those who, because of their upbringing, are able to develop these qualities more than others. Then of course, there are those who have certain traits that are so strong that perhaps all training can do is curb them to some extent, but not remove them entirely.

AC: Does that mean that everyone is awakening despite appearances?

ASSK: That, one cannot say, because the seed of awakening may not come to fruition. Some people are naturally more inclined towards the good and some are more inclined towards the stupid or the bad.

AC: From where do you think does this inclination towards the "good" or the "bad" originate?

ASSK: Well, it's a combination of things. I think we're all born different.

For example, the moment my eldest son was born, he had a distinctive personality. Something about him marked him out as an individual. It's not just the loving-mother syndrome, thinking my child is different from everybody else. He was different. Even his cry was different. In fact, every mother in the hospital ward learned to recognize their baby's cry easily and quickly. In the same way when my second son, Kim, was born, I knew immediately that he was not at all like Alexander. I just had to hold this baby in my arms and look at him and I knew that he was different from his brother.

But of course, our surroundings make a difference too. I read somewhere that psychologists claim that 80 percent is nature and 20 percent is nurture. But that 20 percent goes a long way. On the other hand, I have heard of children who have grown up in the most awful circumstances and yet...

AC: Who really shine?

ASSK: Yes. They've come out of it strong and compassionate.

AC: What do you think it is in the human spirit that allows one person to rise to new heights through traumatic experiences, while someone else descends into the abyss?

ASSK: There are those who rise to a challenge and achieve great heights in the face of adversity. It can even bring out the best in them. While in others, adversity seems to bring out the worst. But it is very difficult to know what makes them different. You can hardly say that it has anything to do with upbringing. Now some psychologists and psychiatrists blame all problems on childhood experiences. But I think there are people who have something innate in them that enables them to rise above the limitations of their environment. For instance, I've been reading about an Iranian woman who became blind when she was three or four years old. The mother found her a burden and treated her badly. In fact, she told her repeatedly; "I wish you were dead. What use are you being alive?"

Furthermore, even her mother's friends would say that it would have been much better if she had died. But apparently the girl had a strong sense of her own existence. I suppose you could say that she never lost the sense of her own self-worth as a human being despite the fact that it was drummed into her all the time that she was a worthless burden to her family. This girl was totally deprived of parental love, but she became the first blind graduate in Iran.

AC: So you do believe that no matter how tragic one's circumstances may be, with courage and determination one can make it? And with wise attitude they can transform the difficulties into strengths?

ASSK: Yes. But some really thrive on adversity while others go under. You can see this with people who have been in prison. I have to say that the majority of our people who have been put in prison have come out unshaken. But others have broken and turned away because they just couldn't take it anymore.

AC: I understand that U Win Tin, the Secretary for the NLD who was arrested along with yourself and others in '89, is still in prison.

ASSK: Yes, he's still in Insein Prison, and I understand that his health is not very good. He was sentenced to four years' imprisonment. Then after he had been put in prison they added another seven years on to it. This is one of their [SLORC's] standard practices. In February 1996 he was tried again in prison, without benefit of counsel, and had yet another prison term—five years—slapped on him.

AC: But why wasn't he released too? SLORC had a personal vendetta against him?

ASSK: He's a very able man and as you said, he is the Secretary of the NLD. He works hard and is well respected. He's also extremely intelligent and he's incorruptible. I think the combination is too much for SLORC.

AC: Speaking of incorruptibility—what is it about someone that allows him to maintain his integrity and dignity, even in such extreme conditions as solitary confinement or even torture?

ASSK: I think most of the people I know who have not become corrupt have a real sense of self-responsibility. While those who become corrupt either cannot see, or do not accept, that they are responsible for the consequences of their actions. They don't understand the connection between cause and effect.

AC: Could it be that they're too frightened?

ASSK: It's self-deception. Basically it's an issue of honesty. If you accept responsibility for your actions, whether they are right or wrong, that's honesty. You're prepared to accept that your actions may have certain consequences. You may not be aware of all of them and your assessment of the consequences may not be correct. Nevertheless, you do try to see things honestly for what they are.

AC: Would you say more about the relationship between corruption and self-deception?

ASSK: Corruption is a form of dishonesty because it's rooted in self-deception. I don't think that people who are corrupt really admit it. They have other words for it. They may say, "Oh, it's what everybody is doing." Or, "There's nothing wrong with it." There're so many ways of explaining away their corruption. That in itself is a lack of honesty. A lack of honesty with oneself.

AC: So it's this quality of radical self-honesty that is the key. Which comes back to self-awareness. Have you found that meditation has been an essential force in protecting and strengthening you against any form of corruptibility?

ASSK: It has been a help. But I have to go back to my parents and the way I was brought up and taught. My mother always emphasized honesty and integrity. It wasn't just that she herself was honest and incorruptible but she was also upholding my father's values. So it does go back a lot to nurture. It's not that I didn't know these things before I started meditating. Meditation has helped me to uphold the values that I've always been taught since I was a child.

AC: What does Buddhist meditation mean to you?

ASSK: It's a form of spiritual cultivation—a spiritual education and a purifying process. Basically, it's learning awareness. By being aware of whatever you're doing, you learn to avoid impurities.

AC: How instrumental has meditation been in discovering new aspects of your interior life? Has it been a process of self-discovery?

ASSK: I don't know if it has been a process of self-discovery as much as one of spiritual strengthening. I was always taught to be honest with myself. Since I was quite young I had been in the habit of analyzing my own actions and feelings. So I haven't really discovered anything new about myself. But meditation has helped to strengthen me spiritually in order to follow the right path.

Also, for me, meditation is part of a way of life because what you do when you meditate is to learn to control your mind through developing awareness. This awareness carries on into everyday life. For me, that's one of the most practical benefits of meditation—my sense of awareness has become heightened. I'm now much less inclined to do things carelessly and unconsciously.

AC: How did you learn meditation?

ASSK: I did go to the Mahasi Thathana Yeiktha meditation center but that was long ago, when I was in Burma on one of my visits. I was in my twenties. But I never really meditated very much. My real meditation took off only during my years of house arrest. And for that I had to depend a lot on books. Sayadaw U Pandita's book, *In This Very Life*, was a great help.

AC: As a Theravada Buddhist, are you still open in your spiritual attitudes to learn from other traditions, or are they fairly set?

ASSK: I'm very interested in hearing about other people's spiritual experiences and views. I've got a lot more to learn, from as many people as are prepared to teach me.

AC: You often refer to your democracy movement here in Burma as a "revolution of the spirit" that is rooted in Buddhist principles. How much, if at all, do you draw upon the wisdom of other religions in your approach to politics?

ASSK: I have read books on other religions but I haven't gone into any of them particularly deeply. But I find that the idea of *mettā* is in every religion. The Christians say God is love. And when they say, "perfect love casts out fear," I think by perfect love they mean exactly what we mean by *mettā*. I think at the core of all religions there is this idea of love for one's fellow human beings.

AC: You and your colleagues have set up a Welfare Committee for political prisoners. What is its main function?

ASSK: We help the families with funds, medicines and food for the prisoners. Some people can't even afford to go see their husbands or fathers in prison, because they are kept in jails far away from where the families live. As you know, fares are very high now. We help all political prisoners, not just those who belong to the NLD. We don't make any discrimination. We give help to those who have been pulled in on strange cases, like celebrating my winning of the Nobel Peace Prize and so on. I think those are practically all out now, because they were sentenced to three to four years' imprisonment and it's four years since I got the Nobel Prize.

I mentioned earlier that U Win Tin was subjected to another trial in prison. Twenty-two other political prisoners were tried with him and sentenced to additional terms of five to twelve years. Our Legal Aid Committee is preparing their appeals. We want to help political prisoners in any way we can—social, financial, legal.

AC: Speaking about the Nobel Peace Prize, how did winning the prize affect you?

ASSK: My immediate thought was that people would take a greater interest in our cause for democracy. And of course, when I wrote to the Nobel Committee, I did say that I was very grateful that they had recognized our cause. But at the same time, whenever I'm given any prize like that I feel a sense of humility. I think of all my colleagues who have suffered much more, but who have not been recognized. My recognition really stems from the courage and the sufferings of many, many others.

AC: You were the first person ever to receive the prize while under detention. How did you receive word of the award, and was it a surprise?

ASSK: I heard it on the radio. And it was not really a surprise to me because they had started saying a week or so before that I was on the short-list. With President Václav Havel having nominated me, with such strong backing, it was not altogether a surprise for me that I did get the prize.

AC: Were you in any way looking forward to the results?

ASSK: No, not looking forward but of course, I was curious to know. When you are under detention alone, you are always curious to hear the next day's news. And yet, at the same time, you become much more objective. You become a little more distant from what's going on; you're not that passionately involved, in a sense.

AC: Coming back to the present circumstances in Burma under SLORC, is your party allowed to print anything?

ASSK: No, we are not allowed to print anything. You have to get a license in order to print anything as a political party and the license has to be renewed every six months. Our license has not been renewed since July 1990.

AC: What about other forms of censorship?

ASSK: Everything is censored. Look at some of the magazines. You'll find that some have silver ink blocking out passages, articles and even short stories—whether it's fiction or non-fiction. Anything can be censored. In 1993, when Nelson Mandela was given the Nobel Peace Prize, a magazine printed his photograph, and they made them ink out his picture. All because he was a Nobel Peace Prize winner.

AC: Well, that makes the picture clear...

ASSK: I think that they heard that some people compared me to him.

AC: And it's true that a Burmese writer can't even use your name as a fictional character in a novel?

ASSK: It's forbidden to even use the name "Suu" I hear. But I suppose that if that name were given to a really nasty character the censors might allow it to pass...

"What we are struggling for
is a change in our everyday lives."

ALAN CLEMENTS: The SLORC Chairman, General Than Shwe, has been in Bangkok attending the ASEAN [Association of South-East Asian Nations] conference at the invitation of Thailand. It seems that host members are seriously considering granting Burma membership status by the year 2000. If you had been there, how would you have addressed the leaders of your neighboring countries?

AUNG SAN SUU KYI: It really depends on the context. That time, I believe, they were going to sign a nuclear non-proliferation treaty, and I'm very much in favor of one. So it depends on what they are discussing.

AC: Let me ask the question in context. Often, such conferences as this one, ASEAN, neglect the role of "human rights" for the sake of economic interests, which generally means self-interest. Take for example the American administration's present policy towards China. Most educated people know of China's sorrowful human rights record, both internal and external to the country, as in the case of its genocide of the Tibetan culture.

In relationship to this, President Clinton has made it clear that despite China's disregard for human rights, it will not affect their "most favored trade status." And it seems that ASEAN countries have also separated human rights and democracy in Burma from economic involvement and co-operation. What do you think of this need of some world leaders to separate money and profits from people and human values?

ASSK: It's a totally artificial separation.

AC: But why do you think so many political leaders insist on this "artificial" separation as a matter of firm national policy?

ASSK: It's because certain systems which are not what one would call wholly democratic have achieved economic success. There has come about a school of thought that economic success is totally divorced from political freedoms. But, I think, there are other reasons for economic success. Take Singapore [a member of ASEAN] for example. I think there are two basic reasons for their economic success. One is that they have had a government which is not corrupt. Nobody can accuse them of corruption. They

29

may not be wholly democratic in the way in which some of us see democracy but they are not corrupt. Secondly, they have put a great value on education and have done everything they can to raise its standard. So I think it's wrong to equate Singapore's economic success with the fact that it's not wholly a democracy. It makes much more sense to link its success to the fact that it has an intelligent, upright government, along with an excellent educational system. I think we're getting our values and equations wrong.

AC: But Daw Suu, isn't the situation a bit more insidious? It might be true that the Singaporean government is not corrupt, in an overt sense. But when you consider the fact that Singapore is one of the largest investors in SLORC's economy, totaling nearly 770 million dollars, doesn't that point to complicity?

ASSK: Yes, of course. That's what I'm saying. Because Singapore has succeeded economically, they think their success is because they're not wholly a democracy. But my argument is that this is not so. The reason for Singapore's success is not a lack of certain democratic rights but the fact that they have an upright government that is very intelligent. That you cannot deny.

In addition, they have an excellent educational system which has made their people fit to cope with many modern-day economic issues. I think people are just barking up the wrong tree when they equate economic success with lack of democracy. There have been a couple of very interesting speeches by the Hong Kong Governor Chris Patten. He sees a belief in progress, economic freedom and free trade as the most important features of societies that have achieved economic success. He said it has not much to do with particularly Western or Eastern values.

AC: But one's complicity with the denigration of life is not "upright." I don't see the wisdom here. And by complimenting the Singaporean government as intelligent, well, it strikes me as a compliment for materialism at the least—setting aside the complicity factor.

ASSK: No. I'm not complimenting materialism at all. I'm just saying that they have what we would call in Buddhism *moha* [ignorance]. It's not the right understanding.

AC: What isn't the right understanding?

ASSK: The fact that they think their economic success is due to their lack of democracy.

AC: Let's be specific. How do you feel about Singapore's massive infusion of economic dollars into SLORC-controlled Burma? We all know that a vast percentage of these millions of dollars goes right into the bank accounts of the generals and their most favored friends.

ASSK: I don't think it helps the democratic cause and in the long run it will not help their economic cause either. Because I do not think that without a change in the political system Burma will be able to maintain its economic development. The reason why it seems as though Burma has developed economically over the last six years is that we started from less than zero, and it's very easy to show progress from that point.

AC: Can you explain how investing in Burma doesn't help the country from where the investment originates? Singapore thinks it is secure.

ASSK: The Singaporeans think that the lack of democracy is not an obstacle in the way of economic success. It may not have been so in their own country, but Singapore is very different from Burma. Here in Burma, the present system of government is such that there can be no economic progress. The system of education is such that there cannot be any sustained development. They have not looked at the factors that really matter. What they're looking at is the fact that Burma is virgin territory. Let's take the tourist industry as an example. People just want to go to a new place that others have not yet been. So they calculate that if they invest in the tourist industry of Burma they will be able to reap good returns. But as I understand it, the tourist figures are not good.

AC: Archbishop Desmond Tutu of South Africa has stressed his belief in the need for international economic sanctions against SLORC's Burma. He substantiated this "need" by pointing to the fact that it was only when sanctions occurred in his country that the apartheid government buckled.

He also stressed that "engaged diplomacy" was gibberish and in no way reliable in bringing down an authoritarian regime. May I ask your views about the issue of "engaged diplomacy" *vis-à-vis* an international economic embargo as it applies to Burma?

ASSK: It depends on what they mean by "engaged." If they were truly engaged with both sides—the democratic forces as well as SLORC—I think it could help a great deal. But some of the countries which are said to be pursuing a constructive engagement policy seem to be only engaged with one side.

AC: I have spoken with a number of political attachés in several of the embassies here in Rangoon about the issue of imposing economic sanctions against SLORC. Most of them made the argument against sanctions

31

stating that such measures would only hurt the people and not SLORC. I asked the obvious question: "How could the vast majority of the people become any more hurt than they already are?"

ASSK: Somebody said to me, "We're already crawling." There are some who think that it might have a positive effect if there were the type of economic sanctions that prohibited people from buying rice from Burma. In that case, the farmers would be in a much easier situation.

AC: So the argument that sanctions hurt the people just doesn't hold water?

ASSK: I wouldn't say that so glibly. One would have to study the situation quite carefully.

AC: Of course, you've studied the situation. Would you say more?

ASSK: For example, Burma depends a lot on imported medicines. The BPI [Burma Pharmaceutical Industry]—which produces high-quality medicines, just cannot produce enough. So there are certain sorts of imports that would really hurt the people if they were stopped.

AC: Please correct me if I'm wrong, but it seems that 99.9 percent of the cash in your country is owned by SLORC and their friends.

ASSK: Yes...

AC: Then wouldn't international economic sanctions awaken SLORC, so to speak, from their totalitarian nightmare and in fact ease the suffering for the vast majority of your people who want democracy?

ASSK: Yes. It is possible.

AC: With regard to medicines, sanctions could easily be tailored.

ASSK: Yes...

AC: So if economic sanctions were imposed it wouldn't hurt anyone except SLORC?

ASSK: Yes, I don't think it would really hurt the people very much. But I've always been very careful not to support economic sanctions without thought. Because certainly one does not want to do anything that hurts the people.

AC: The United Nations General Assembly has just issued yet another strong resolution against SLORC, citing the usual violations — forced labor, political prisoners, and so on. However, the United States

Ambassador to the United Nations, Madeleine Albright, said she would have liked an even stronger statement...

ASSK: The resolution is quite good. It's a strong resolution...and it could have been stronger. But it's always good to leave room for stronger measures in the future.

AC: The SLORC seat at the United Nations has been repeatedly yet unsuccessfully contested by Burma's government-in-exile, the NCGUB, [the National Coalition Government of the Union of Burma] based in Washington, D.C. How is it that this respected body of men and women that comprises the United Nations allows an "illegal government" to hold a seat? After all, it was your party—the NLD—that won the free and fair elections, and not SLORC.

ASSK: SLORC is not the only government in this sort of situation. They've always allowed governments which came into power by force to sit in the United Nations, with the exception of the Khmer Rouge.

AC: As the rather well-known story goes, when Gandhi was asked what he thought of Western civilization he replied: "I think it would be a good idea." As an American, my country—as you must know—was founded upon a human, spiritual and cultural genocide of the native American population. I think it's also rather common knowledge that wherever European civilization spread around that time, it did so by decimating the indigenous peoples of the countries they invaded. Of course the British also oppressed Burma for over 150 years until she gained her independence in 1947. Don't you think there's some value in questioning the West's understanding of human rights, despite the fact that they have signed the Universal Declaration of Human Rights?

ASSK: Well, isn't it precisely because they have done these things that they are aware of the need for human rights?

AC: Of course, one would like to believe so—but the examples are numerous, that point to major and consistent contradictions to the West's awareness of human rights, post signing of the Declaration. America's invasion of Vietnam is but one example. However, setting aside my beliefs—do you have a real faith and trust in the value systems of the West?

ASSK: These are not just the value systems of the West. Human rights were quite recently enforced in the West because the Western world had suffered such utter devastation from World War II and the denial of human rights. Of course, we suffered in the East too from World War II. But don't forget that our sufferings were not imposed on us by any Western power, but by an Eastern power. Because of the power of pre-war Japan there was equal devastation in Asia. Just as there was tremendous devastation in Europe because of the power of pre-war Germany. The point is that it's encouraging that peoples and countries decided it was time to try to stop the same kind of disaster from ever befalling the planet again.

AC: Recently President Bill Clinton expressed his support for you and Burma's struggle for freedom and democracy. But I couldn't help thinking how much more he could do beyond a few words of support. I spent six months last year in the former Yugoslavia, and the feeling among the vast majority of people that I came to know, was that Bosnia was of "no strategic interest" to the West, and therefore expendable. Do you ever feel that Burma has been placed in the same category by some world leaders and therefore seems to them unimportant to defend?

ASSK: We are not depending on either the West or the East to help us through. But we know that in this day and age the opinion of the international community cannot be ignored. No country can survive by itself. No country can be an island unto itself. We know that. And we want to live in a world where each country is linked to the others through bonds of humanity. We will always try to promote such an atmosphere.

And yes, it is true, that in the old state of the Republic of Yugoslavia, the international community could have done more. And yet one asks, what more? Come in with arms? Of course, that's violence again and would not resolve the hatred between the Serbs, Croats and Bosnians. That is something they will have to address.

AC: But certainly armed intervention by the West would have stopped the atrocities perpetrated against the civilian population by the soldiers of each side. Are you saying that under no circumstance would you advocate armed intervention, or the use of arms at all?

ASSK: I would not say that. I never said that we do not need an army in Burma. I do accept that the situation of the world is such that there is still a need for military forces. But in their own place. And with regard to the former Yugoslavia what I'm saying is that of course the international community might have taken more positive action. But are you not saying rather that America should have taken more positive action? But then one asks why America? Why not Europe? I'm just being the devil's advocate. Because what some Americans say is, "Why didn't the Europeans look after their own backyards? Why America, when there were many European countries quite capable of taking more positive action in former Yugoslavia?" And that becomes a difficult question to answer.

AC: Are you disappointed in America's response or role in Burma's struggle for democracy?

ASSK: No. I think in recent months the United States has been very firm in its support for democracy in Burma. We might want firmer action—depending on what happens. Not just on the part of the United States, but from the international community as a whole.

AC: Which might be?

ASSK: As you know, I never discuss our future plans.

AC: Some time ago, Mr. Burton Levin, the US Ambassador to Burma during 1988, sent me a video that showed some of the pro-democracy demonstrations that occurred in front of the embassy. Banners and placards held by the demonstrators clearly showed their enthusiasm for American support. Were the demonstrators at that early stage in the movement looking for American-style democracy as a role model?

ASSK: Some of them seemed to be. I think really one should depend on oneself, first of all. That's very Buddhist, isn't it? Whom do you have to worship but yourself, as it were?

AC: A fleet of American warships was just off the coast at that time. Was there any place in you that was hoping for intervention?

ASSK: No, no, I knew perfectly well that the American warships off the coast had nothing to do with our situation. I'm not that naïve.

AC: So the fleet was there only to potentially evacuate Americans?

ASSK: Of course!

AC: I was watching an interview on BBC with a Rwandan refugee who said, "Because it was a genocide in Rwanda it meant nothing to the international community. But if we were gorillas it would have moved heaven and earth to intervene."

ASSK: I'm not sure that remark is absolutely accurate. If gorillas were massacred, there are animal rights associations which would have worked very hard to stop the massacre. It's just that the issue of genocide is so much more complex that the international community hesitates to get involved.

AC: I know that it's a complex issue, but the reality remains that genocide occurred and the world community only watched. The "hesitation" was at the price of 700,000 deaths. Don't you think that some leaders of powerful countries rather consistently wobble when it comes to assisting the power-less in their time of need?

ASSK: It depends on the country. There are some countries that are always ready to speak up for human rights and others that hesitate much more.

AC: Are you disappointed by the international response to Burma?

ASSK: No. Of course, we always hope that it will get better and there will be more sympathy and support for the principles and values that we're struggling for. However, we should consider the fact that very few people in the world even knew where Burma was before 1988.

AC: Do you feel that it is ever appropriate or justified for one country to intervene in the internal affairs of another country whose powers are creating hell for the population? Is it the duty of a powerful country to help the weaker one in such instances?

ASSK: I think it is better that the international community carries out this responsibility as a whole. There are far too many complications that arise when one country is given either the responsibility or the right to interfere in the affairs of another country. But I do think that the international community as a whole should recognize that it has got responsibilities. It can't ignore grave injustices that are going on within the borders of any particular country.

AC: Back to the issue of foreign investment in Burma. Hundreds of millions of dollars are pouring into your country, with more waiting in bank accounts. I assume that many of these businesspeople want the truth. What would be the most appropriate way for these potential investors to cut through SLORC propaganda, and get to the facts about what's really going on in your country?

ASSK: They could always start by talking to us. We could give them a good idea of what is going on…if they're interested in finding out the truth. But I think a lot of people just don't want to know.

AC: So potential investors should seek appointments with you?

ASSK: Not necessarily with me. They can also seek appointments with other people in our organization and other people in the democratic forces who would be in a position to explain to them what is really going on in this country.

AC: Certain businesspeople and politicians argue that investment in Burma is good because it creates a middle class and therefore the most expedient way to usher in democracy. How would you respond to this argument?

ASSK: Investments in Burma during the last seven years [from the time of SLORC taking power] have done nothing to create a stronger middle class. There are a few people who have gotten very rich, and a rapidly increasing pool of the very poor. The great majority of civil servants, who should normally be part of the middle class, are struggling to get on with their lives. Their salaries are so low compared to the cost of living they have to choose between corruption and starvation.

AC: SLORC presents a grotesquely inaccurate picture of reality in your country to its own people. No one believes SLORC's newspaper or television reports. The vast majority of the population today rely on your weekend talks for the truth and an analysis of the facts. Are tapes and videos of your talks getting out into the rural areas?

ASSK: I believe so. But people can learn the truth in a variety of ways. For example, everybody was very grateful because the official Burmese media broadcast the whole speech of their Ambassador to the United Nations. It gave them a chance to find out what was actually in the resolution (*laughing*). Otherwise, they would not have known. So truth "won out" in some way or another.

AC: What happens if someone is caught by the authorities listening to one of your tapes or watching one of your videos?

ASSK: In some instances people have had their television sets and video decks confiscated. While in other places the authorities have actually issued orders that no one is to watch my videotapes.

AC: What are your feelings about the use of nonviolent demonstrations in Burma today? Are you advocating them? Considering them? Discouraging them?

ASSK: At the moment I'm not advocating anything. I've always said that one works according to a changing situation. You cannot have one fixed policy for all time.

AC: Are you aware of any radical, left-wing militant groups within the country that advocate urban guerrilla tactics as we have seen in Northern Ireland or in the Middle East?

ASSK: I'm not aware of them. But there are probably individuals who would like to work along those lines.

AC: Do you have students who plead with you to engage in an armed struggle with SLORC?

ASSK: Not just students, there have also been elderly men who have advocated armed struggle. They think this government is so lacking in good intentions that the only way to get democracy is by crushing them through force of arms. I think it's sheer frustration that drives them to this conclusion and the fact that the attitude of the authorities is so extreme. Extremism begets extremism.

AC: I can easily understand their attitude. In Nigeria, Ken Saro-Wiwa [a writer, human rights and environmental activist] summed it up bluntly in a letter that was smuggled from his prison cell several months prior to his execution: "Do I think I'll be executed? Yes. I expect it. We're dealing here with a group of Stone-Age military dictators addicted to blood."

What turned your father away from the use of weapons to overthrow fascism and imperialism towards a nonviolent political solution? Did he study Gandhian principles?

ASSK: He didn't advocate a nonviolent, non-cooperation movement the way Gandhi did in India. My father was very intelligent and he used it in an extremely practical way. He was also quite ready to admit his mistakes. For example, he acknowledged that it was because of his—not just his—but a general political immaturity of the younger people involved in the independence movement that made them look to a fascist military power [Japan] for help. But he was quick to learn and decided later that the best way to go about achieving independence was through a political solution that hurts no one.

AC: Do you consider yourself more of a Gandhian-styled political leader? Or does your approach to nonviolence come more from your understanding within Buddhism?

ASSK: I don't think of myself as either a Gandhian or Buddhist politician. I am Buddhist of course, and I would be guided by all the Buddhist principles that I have absorbed throughout my life. The fact that I admire the men who led Burma's "first independence movement" also means that I'm influenced to some degree by their principles and actions. But primarily the reason why I object to violent means is because I think it would perpetuate a tradition of changing the political situation through force of arms.

AC: All of your most intimate colleagues—the EC members within the NLD—are ex-military men, mostly retired or sacked generals with a long history of appreciating the combatant's role in life. Do you find in your discussions together that they struggle perhaps to understand or appreciate your conviction in the use of nonviolence in achieving a political solution?

ASSK: For me it's very practical. If you want to establish a strong tradition of democracy in this country one of the basic principles of achieving it is that you bring about political change peacefully through consulting the will of the people via the ballot box and not through force of arms. If you want democracy you must demonstrate its principles; you need to be consistent in politics.

AC: Would you say more about consistency in political policy?

ASSK: If you say that you want to change a system where might is right, then you have to prove that right is might. You can't use might in order to bring about what you think is right and then still insist that right is might. People are not fooled by that. I was told a story by a monk in the Inlay Lake area when I went up there in 1989. Have you ever heard of U Po Sein? He was a very well-known dancer in a Burmese theater troupe. There was a comedian in U Po Sein's troupe who would say before the beginning of a performance: "Look here, U Po Sein, nobody in the audience can dance as well as you. But there is nobody in this audience who will not know if you make a wrong move." It's like that in politics too. People may seem apathetic and indifferent but they know if you make a wrong move, or that you've been inconsistent.

AC: Do you ever feel, perhaps in one of your more private moments, overwhelmed in your position of nonviolence, say in relationship to the global addiction to violence? Do you feel like a lone star, so to speak, in the midst of the darkness? Leaders the world over generally believe that "might is right" and the greater the might usually determines who wins in the end.

ASSK: I don't think I'm the only one who does not believe that weapons are the way to change. But yes, if you really conjure up an image of all the weapons in the world it would be much higher than Mount Everest, don't you think?

AC: I have heard an image used to describe the number of nuclear weapons on the planet. If you were to translate nuclear warheads into TNT, you could fill successive train cars that would extend to the moon and back eight times.

ASSK: I really wonder why people waste so much time, energy and money on producing that kind of stuff.

AC: Do you know specifically where all the weapons are coming from that SLORC consumes?

ASSK: I know that the government buys a lot of arms from China. But I think it buys arms from other places as well. There was a rumor some time ago that some high-ranking officials in SLORC were going around to various countries—including some in Europe—trying to buy arms.

AC: What would you say are the main qualities of consciousness that you try to foster in yourself and encourage others to embrace, as the foundation of your struggle for democracy?

ASSK: First of all, what we would like is vision. We would like the people to see and understand why a political system is tied up with our daily lives. Why we cannot ignore politics and just concentrate on economics, as the authorities would like us to do. We want them to understand that our struggle for democracy is a struggle for our everyday life, that it's not removed. It's not something that you do when you have a bit of free time, or when you feel like it. You have to work at it all the time, because it affects your life all the time. You can never separate the political system of a country from the way in which you conduct your daily life. This is basically the spirit that we want—an awareness that what we are struggling for is not some distant goal or ideal. What we are struggling for is a change in our everyday lives. We want freedom from fear and want. There are people today who enjoy materially secure lives, but they can never be sure when this will be taken from them. There must be a sense of security that as long as we're not doing harm to others, as long as we are not infringing the laws which were brought about so that we should not harm each other, we should be able to rest secure in the knowledge that we ourselves will not be harmed. That the authorities cannot remove you from your job, kick you out of your house, throw you in prison, or have you executed, if you have done nothing to warrant such actions.

AC: SLORC seems to have a fetish for forcibly evicting people from their homes and relocating them to more "desirable" areas. I know that in 1990, the *New York Times* reported that the authorities "forcibly relocated over 500,000 people from Rangoon alone" and trucked these people to their "new towns," that turned out to be nothing more than malaria-infested swamp land. Apparently this happened all over the country and I'm told that it continues today. Could you explain what's behind these current SLORC evictions and confiscations of property?

ASSK: Whenever they [SLORC] think they need a particular piece of land for a building project, then off these people go...

AC: These people have no rights whatsoever?

ASSK: No. People have no rights.

AC: So they are simply told by the authorities to get out of their homes on such and such a date and that's it?

ASSK: That's right.

AC: Where do they go?

ASSK: Most of them are just dumped in fields and told to put up their huts.

AC: How widespread is this today?

ASSK: It happens all over Burma.

AC: And the reason?

ASSK: Forced relocations are mostly carried out with a view to making a place more attractive for tourists.

AC: I know that the American government has a two-million-dollar ransom on the Burmese citizen Khun Sa, known by most people as the world's most notorious heroin drug lord—supplying approximately 60 percent of the global heroin supply. And just recently SLORC cut a deal with him; however, the nature of the deal remains somewhat of a mystery. Which leads to my question. Khun Sa's 13,000 soldiers are seen every day on SLORC-controlled television handing over their weapons, but where is the beef, in other words—the tens of thousands of tons of heroin?

ASSK: I've absolutely no idea where the heroin is. Let's wait and see, perhaps the heroin will emerge...

AC: Is it as simple as the SLORC having cut an amnesty deal with him? I mean this guy makes Noriega look like a drug-store cowboy.

ASSK: Well, you've seen photographs of Khun Sa. Does he look like a man who is in fear of his future?

AC: He looks like a pretty happy camper to me.

ASSK: Exactly. He does not look at all nervous. He's on equal terms with the [SLORC] ministers and commanders. He seems very much like a man who has got nothing to worry about.

AC: I guess I've once again been outsmarted by SLORC's stupidity. I could never have imagined that they would go public with it.

ASSK: It comes back to that same old question we were talking about, are they really that stupid? Or is there some deep thought behind it? Tell me what you think. Everyone is absolutely mystified as to why they've done something so silly.

AC: How would the NLD go about resolving the opium and heroin problem in Burma? And would you in fact grant America's request to extradite Khun Sa to stand trial in the US?

ASSK: Let us talk about the drug issue—how we are going to try to eradicate this problem. Those people who actually grow opium poppies are not that rich. The reason they grow poppies is because they have no other means of income or because they are afraid of the drug runners who force them to grow them. If we provide them with alternative sources of income, then they won't be so keen to go on. It is all a matter of education. They have to understand why it is better for them not to continue growing opium. We don't believe in just telling people to stop doing something. We want them to understand why they should stop. We, at the NLD, are great believers in education. We want to make the people understand that they do not need to grow opium poppies. So we will give them practical help and also educate them so that they will not want to go on with opium production.

AC: As we know, habits run deep, it'll take quite some time...

ASSK: It will take time but perhaps it will not take as long as people think it will, because do not forget that in these days of international communications revolution, you can get across to people very quickly if you really want to try—if you are really intent on doing so.

AC: And regarding Khun Sa?

ASSK: We shall have to go into that very carefully. We are not the government of this country. We are not in a position to do anything about him and we do not believe in making premature comments.

AC: What do you think would be Burma's unique expression of democracy?

ASSK: I don't know because we have not started our democracy yet. But I would like to think that it would be a democracy with a more compassionate face. A gentler sort of democracy...gentler because it's stronger.

AC: Would it be a capitalistic form of democracy?

ASSK: We've never thought of it as a capitalist democracy as such. We do not see why democracy should be made a part of capitalism or vice versa. We think that democracy means the will of the people. It means certain basic freedoms, which will have to include basic economic freedoms that would allow for capitalism. But that does not mean that the state would not have the responsibility for other aspects of the nation, such as education and health.

AC: Last year His Holiness the Dalai Lama said that what the Chinese are doing to his people "is a kind of cultural genocide and that time is running out." He went on to say that if the Chinese continue this, "there will be no Tibet to save." Could the same be said of Burma? Is time running out? Is there a time limit to how...

ASSK: No, of course not. Why should there be a time limit?

AC: I don't know, perhaps the desperation level of the people will peak and exceed their fears and they'll rise up again like in 1988...

ASSK: There's always a limit to what people are prepared to take. That doesn't necessarily mean that they'll express their discontent through demonstrations. But I don't think people will go on forever accepting injustice.

CHAPTER 10

CONVERSATION *with*
U KYI MAUNG

1996

Deputy Chairman of the National League for Democracy U Kyi Maung is regarded as the man most singly responsible for leading the National League for Democracy to overwhelming victory in the elections that took place in Burma in May 1990, while Daw Aung San Suu Kyi and U Tin Oo were in detention. In his youth he joined the struggle for independence from Britain, suffering head injuries during a demonstration in 1938. At the outbreak of war, he joined the Burma Independence Army and later rose to the rank of colonel. He was strongly opposed to the military takeover of 1962 and was therefore forced to retire in 1963 from control of the South-Western Command. He was twice imprisoned, for a total of seven years, and in 1988 on the outbreak of the democracy movement he was imprisoned for a third time but released after a month.

In September of that year he became one of the twelve members of the Executive Council of the NLD and it was in that capacity that he led the party to victory in the 1990 elections after the leadership of the party had been arrested. In September of that year he was tried by a military tribunal and sentenced to twenty years in prison. However, he was released in March 1995 and soon resumed his work for democracy as Deputy Chairman of the NLD. A cultivated man with a great love for literature and music, he is known by many for his immense courage and his commitment to the freedom of his country.

ALAN CLEMENTS: How did you first meet Aung San Suu Kyi and what were your impressions of her?

U KYI MAUNG: Well, by chance, at the home of a mutual friend here in Rangoon. It was back in 1986. But let me tell you it was completely uneventful. We spoke for only a few minutes. My most lasting impression was how shy and reticent she was. She seemed like a decent girl who had no interest in frivolous talk or gossip. In fact, I remember thinking how peculiar it was that I never saw her laugh at that time, or it could have been that she didn't want to communicate with strangers *(laughing)*. Anyway, the point is that she didn't impress me at all. Except by how young she looked. She must have been about forty-two at the time but she could have passed as a girl of seventeen.

AC: And from there?

UKM: Then about a year later my friend U Htwe Myint came to see me. He's now in prison. But at that time, he was a close associate of Suu's. He said, "Aung San Suu Kyi is interested in getting involved in politics. She wants to know if you're willing to consult with her." I told him that I had no interest at all. None. I had no plans to get involved in politics. Twice he returned with the same request and twice I gave him the same reply. So the subject stopped there.

AC: Was it because re-entering politics meant a most certain return to prison?

UKM: No, not at all. Under a totalitarian regime, whether you are in politics or not doesn't matter, there is always the possibility of arrest. You might call it an occupational hazard. There's no law here. When the authorities don't enjoy their meal they snap someone up just like that. So I don't base decisions on whether I would be re-arrested. I couldn't care less. I operate on the assumption that I could be nabbed at any moment. That's life with SLORC. However, I always consider myself a free man. I've been in prison four times for a total of about eleven years and I don't consider it a special matter to waste my energies on.

AC: Were you surprised that Daw Suu was interested in entering the cauldron of Burmese politics?

UKM: Well, she had a lot going for her. Of course, she was the daughter of *Bogyoke* Aung San—a "warrior-statesman" as she might put it—our national hero. Furthermore, Suu was a Burmese citizen. If entering politics was her interest, so be it, that was her right. But I was surprised she was taking an interest in me. That is to say, we were total strangers. I didn't know her nor did I know her capabilities. But about a year later, at the end of July 1988, I was hauled off to prison for the third time. I was taken in with nine others and kept for twenty-eight days because of my longtime association with Aung Gyi, a veteran politician who wrote a lengthy letter to Ne Win, our resident dictator, asking the old man to step down. But an hour or two after my release, U Htwe Myint came to my house again and said, "Aung San Suu Kyi would like to see you." So I thought to myself, well, let's see what this lady is up to...now is the time, a revolution was stirring. So I drove over to see her. The essence of the meeting was this: I said "Suu, if you're prepared to enter Burmese politics and to go the distance, you must be tolerant and be prepared for the worst." She listened attentively.

AC: What was Daw Suu's interest in you?

UKM: I was a veteran jail bird *(laughing)* and well over twenty years her senior. Later on I learned that she was watching people, looking in all directions for people who could be trusted—candidates you know, for the struggle. She was born with revolution in her blood but she needed all the help possible to see it through. So from then on we began to meet frequently, until later that year we all formed the National League for Democracy. This is a concise version of the facts.

AC: So Daw Suu trusted you as a veteran of the opposition voice?

UKM: She showed me respect and was fond of me, I think. She trusted that I could be relied upon. I was given the task of writing the NLD party manifesto, which I did, and after presenting it to the party it was accepted. Also, Suu trusted that I could be sensible and talk sensibly. Whatever thoughts, impressions and attitudes she might have, she could gauge them against my own. In other words it was a good working relationship.

You see the whole concept of us forming the NLD was simple. There was a massive vacuum in Burma with this one-party system, and all we did was fill the hole. After some reshuffling, U Tin Oo became our Chairman, Suu our General Secretary and I took charge of research. But when U Tin Oo and Suu were arrested on 20 July 1989, I became the spokesman for the NLD, talking to foreign journalists, handling the press, that sort of thing.

AC: It's curious that you of all people were not imprisoned along with Aung San Suu Kyi and U Tin Oo. You were the man articulating the views of the NLD to the world, the voice of Burma's struggle.

UKM: Well, they did make a mistake. They underestimated my capacity for making myself a nuisance to them. Then I became the *de facto* Chairman of the NLD until the elections were held on 27 May 1990. On 6 September I was hauled away to jail.

AC: But how did you manage to avoid prison for nearly fourteen months after Aung San Suu Kyi and U Tin Oo had been arrested?

UKM: You see, I was constantly followed and harassed. But I didn't make any fiery speeches. I didn't harangue people overtly for one thing. It's not my nature to throw my weight around, you know. I'm quite happy to live anonymously. I keep reminding myself I'm nobody. Maybe that is my asset, I think, maybe my only one *(laughing)*...

AC: There must be others. You seem free of political ambition...

UKM: Yes, I'm prepared to leave politics at any time—on the spot. I always say if any member of my party is dissatisfied with my work, I'm prepared to quit without conditions. I said to my colleagues: "Look, it's a game and we're players in the game. So let's play it without so much ego—without nonsense." If you don't like my decision and you are not in favor of it—if you are dissatisfied with it—if you want me to leave, well then, I'll leave the League. I'm prepared to leave the whole business to you. I think my colleagues are convinced of this. And since my house is a few minutes' walking distance from Suu's, well, I'll just walk home without a fuss. I consider this attitude an asset.

AC: Sir, a simple question: why did SLORC hold their free and fair multi-party elections for the establishing of a democratic nation when in fact as the results came in they imprisoned the majority of elected MPs, tortured to death a few, forced others into silence...

UKM: They thought they were going to win.

AC: That's shocking. SLORC had just massacred thousands of unarmed pro-democracy demonstrators and created a "terror state" using such means as institutionalized torture to control people, and you say they actually thought they would win.

UKM: SLORC thought we as a party were broken. They went as far as to say, "Now that the head is chopped off, the limbs are useless." Now you can deduce for yourself the kind of people we are dealing with.

AC: They miscalculated? Let me ask you, sir, isn't it possible that SLORC's real intention was to weed out from society all people with popularity and political ability and to eliminate once and for all the democratic apparatus from Burma? Isn't it possible that Ne Win himself concocted this whole multi-party democracy business as a diabolical ruse to further his dictatorship? To continue your image, not only to decapitate the democracy movement, but to dismember it piece by piece.

UKM: Well, they were shocked and angry when they realized that they had lost in their own places—in all the military areas. They were so utterly sure that their own people at least would vote for them. You see, we were told that SLORC's Military Intelligence made a rough secret survey to determine how the voting pattern might turn out, and they didn't realize until it was too late that the majority of people would be voting for the NLD. They were really shocked when the results turned out to be so contrary to their own expectations.

AC: There's something very devious about the whole affair...

UKM: There's a lot of credibility to your hypothesis but I did hear reports that some of the ex-BSPP people, higher-ups, actually broke down and wept when they heard the results. We heard that in some places banquets were even prepared to celebrate victory. We heard this from many sources. They're not very good actors, you know, so these reports are credible.

AC: But still, from what I've learned about Ne Win he only broaches his schemes to a few. Anyway, with the election results coming in and the elected MPs being imprisoned, you must have considered that your hours were numbered.

UKM: I was prepared for anything because the MI were following me everywhere. But I've never considered that my freedom is theirs to give or to deny. I just do my business with that knowledge, always.

AC: Then on 7 September 1990 they came and took you away—may I respectfully ask you, sir, to share your impressions of that moment?

UKM: It was after midnight. They always come after midnight for me. They came to the gate and were shouting like anything to open it up. I got up and dressed, all the while knowing that, "Here comes Insein." I already had a rather lengthy prison record, I'm what you might call the habitual offender *(laughing)*. My wife and I looked out of the window and saw they had jumped the fence. Perhaps a platoon or more of armed soldiers had surrounded the house. Then a major from Military Intelligence reported to me with a warrant for my arrest. After that they started ransacking our cupboards and drawers. They searched the whole house, turned everything upside down, just like in the movies. This took quite some time. I think they were looking for guns or heroin or it might have been pornography...

AC: Did they even bother with a trial?

UKM: Oh, of course. That's just where the party begins. Everyone was brought to court, charged and sentenced. Mind you, they don't just go through the motions. They take their non-judicial system quite seriously. They paraded me before some brass with seventeen others; all were chained together except me, with handcuffs no less. In the party were engineers, lawyers, artists—democracy folks. Then a SLORC superstar witness stood up and said, "We raided the NLD headquarters some time ago and seized this document." Ironically, it was an excerpt from a small booklet outlining the negotiating principles of how to achieve mutual agreement between opponents. They bungled through a stream of witnesses—policemen and other MI goons—trustworthy types. By this time I was getting a bit bored so I asked the judge, "Would you allow me to cross-question them?" The judge was not the least bit amused. He snarled at me like I had spit on him. So I sat down and smiled. He asked me, "Are you guilty or not guilty?" "Not guilty," I replied. One by one we pleaded "Not guilty." One by one each of us was told to stand up to be sentenced. One by one the SLORC judge gave us ten years for those lined up in front and seven years for those behind. Then I was whisked away to my solitary abode to continue the struggle from within.

AC: One wonders how these people sleep at night...

UKM: Oh, let me tell you a short story. We had some visitors over at Suu's house this morning who had come down from the Karen State. The Karen elder proceeded to tell us his story of incarceration. During his trial for his non-offense the judge called him up close to his desk and said, "Brother, you have done nothing. You are absolutely innocent. But my superiors have ordered me to give you a seven-year sentence. However, I will reduce your sentence to only three years." Now the Karen elder told us how pleased he was to hear that, especially after having already waited well over a year for his non-trial. He thought to himself, well, I only have to serve less than two years more. After the sentencing was over and he was on his way back to his cell the judge came over to him and said, "I'm sorry about what I just did. They just sacked me and sentenced me too." "Why?" the elder asked. The gentleman replied, "Because I gave you three years instead of seven which the higher authorities had ordered." So Suu, hearing this, asked the elder, "Please, sir, could you give us the name of that ex-judge? We must find this man and look after him. We must treat him as a very special person."

AC: You know Aung San Suu Kyi as well as anyone. How would you characterize her?

UKM: One of the great things about Suu is that what you see is what you get. She's genuine, she never play-acts. She's not a pretender. She speaks her mind straight and frank. Another wonderful quality in Suu is that she genuinely loves people. She flourishes from her contact with people. She listens to them, learns from them and she's patient. You see her on weekends, look at the rapport she has with her audience. They're her family. Also, Suu is funny. She has an abundant sense of humor. When we're together as a group, say in meetings, she is always telling jokes. Always. We all do. There's always a genuine feeling of love among us, we are all a family. This is the atmosphere we work in.

Now Suu is always Suu, in private or in public. But one thing is that she's not one for suffering fools. You have seen her at the center of a number of big press conferences. If a journalist asks her a crude or pointless question, she puts it right back in his lap. Suu responds to sincerity and whether someone is intelligent or feeble, doesn't matter to her.

Also, she's a fanatic in carrying out her duty to her country. Look at her work schedule. She starts at 8:00 or 8:30 a.m. and sometimes will not stop until 7:00 or so in the evening. It's one long talk-quest. People from all over the country come to see her, from all walks of life—farmers, students, laborer's, rickshaw drivers—Suu wants to know! She wants the truth, the facts. She wants to hear how people feel, to know what's going on—their day-to-day lives, their hopes and concerns, their struggles, the cruelties, the inhuman behavior of SLORC. We all know that politics are about people, so with that in mind, it is really quite simple—Suu makes people her priority. However, Suu has got a devotion bordering on fanaticism, to the point of fault, I think. She is a real workaholic. Now, I have some influence with her in these matters so I will say it, and she would readily admit it. As you know there is a near-endless stream of journalists coming to see her from all over the world. For example, during one pool interview there were a lot of cameras focused on her and hot blinding lights blazing down on her. Then came the questions—a barrage of them being asked simultaneously. She was fielding them as fast as they were fired. I felt pity for her. It was punishment. It was an inquisition, not an interview. I just stood by and observed. But at the end of the session, I told her I wouldn't allow such a thing to happen again. See, Suu is like a daughter to me. I didn't appoint myself as such. She has a high regard for my wife and I and we consider it an honor.

AC: It's really touching to feel your care for her...

UKM: Suu needs all the help she can get. For instance, when Suu was under house arrest she took no provisions from the authorities. She sold much of her furniture just to survive. There were times when she had barely enough to eat, and was so weak she could barely walk or get out of bed. Her hair was falling out. And she pretty much refuses to talk about this—it's not her way. And I respect that—we all respect her way of handling hardship.

Now when she was released, there was no medical care. None at all. So we arranged for someone whom we could trust. Others would help her too. The main point here is that Suu needs a lot of help.

AC: For seven years now SLORC has criticized and slandered Aung San Suu Kyi in every way imaginable. Their two most consistently used criticisms are that she doesn't understand her own people through having lived abroad for over twenty years and that she is married to a British citizen. May I ask for your objective impressions of these?

UKM: It's really silly. No, it's downright pathetic. The SLORC's criticisms of Suu come from one of five motivations, all of which depend on how much fear and insecurity they feel on any particular morning: it's jealousy, envy, anger, greed, or childish stupidity. In SLORC-speak these are known as the Buddha's five moral precepts. Suu is intelligent and brilliantly conversant in her mother tongue, Burmese. She has studied classical Burmese literature and poetry. So when her enemies criticize her as an absentee citizen or a carpetbagger, I feel sorry for them. Obviously, she was absent from Burma for a long time, but look at the people who were here for all those decaying years under the dictatorship. What did they do for the country? They must really ask themselves this question.

Clearly, Suu's years abroad were a great gift to her as well as to her country. It was her time of education. To live and learn and to absorb democracy. To get freedom into her blood so to speak, to get it flowing through her veins. She had the rare and wonderful opportunity of serving at the United Nations under one of Burma's great statesmen, Secretary-General U Thant. She's lived in so many different cultures—America, England, Nepal, Bhutan, India, Japan; she knows diversity. Suu's absence from Burma was not an absence at all. It groomed her, matured her into adulthood, into womanhood, so that she could come back and serve her people, to help them to help themselves to challenge the deadening cruelty of authoritarianism. At least that's my way of seeing things. Perhaps I'm trying to interpret her destiny. But the situation speaks for itself.

Even her critics are dumbfounded at how she delivers her talks as she does without talking over the heads of people. I have learned from her in this way. Suu speaks practically in everyday language. I have seen her talk to farmers in the delta, rickshaw drivers, laborer's, the ordinary people— and they fall in love with her. Suu is always making friends. That's her spirit, her power—she loves people.

Nor does she play the role of a saint either (laughing). There is nothing saintly in Suu. She would readily admit that as a child she was afraid of the dark and ghosts and that she has no exceptional courage in her, only that her sense of duty drives her. "Even though you may be afraid," she says, "you have to face it, get over it, and do your work." That's Suu's simple message and she delivers it every time. And as for Suu having married a foreigner—he's a very nice man.

AC: Sir, on 16 July 1989, the SLORC announced regulations allowing military officers to "arrest political protesters at will," and administer one of three sentences on the spot: three years' hard labor, life imprisonment, or execution. Then on 20 July, the SLORC "arrested" Aung San Suu Kyi. Would you take us back to the moment?

UKM: Oh it was nothing special, really. Yet another of SLORC's absurdities. But we expected Suu's arrest. She knew it—we all knew it. Nor was their show of force the least bit surprising. The prisons were filling up faster than there was space. SLORC was on the hunt and the voice of freedom was their prey.

As for Suu's arrest, well, I'll explain. Around 6:30 or so that morning, many armed SLORC troops surrounded Suu's compound. When I arrived it was the oddest sight…all these soldiers poised like robots with their guns pointing at her house. They were still; frozen in a state of siege. And all for what? Just one lady! Arrest was imminent, it was obvious. Oddly the commander, a SLORC officer, let me into the compound. Now, by the time of my arrival all of our NLD Executive Committee Members were there except U Tin Oo. Troops had also surrounded his compound. For a moment I thought they were going to imprison us all. But we carried on, had a casual lunch and joked a lot. See, none of us is the least bit concerned, nor the slightest bit intimidated by SLORC. So, we just laughed the day in.

AC: A casual lunch, with laughter and joking? You describe a party atmosphere more than a state of siege. You were all about to go to prison. How is it possible to be so jovial under such conditions of oppression?

UKM: Oh, there's no secret about it. I know it sounds strange to you that we were joking and having fun with all those soldiers surrounding Suu's compound, but you have to realize that Suu is really funny. Ask U Aung Shwe and U Lwin (NLD EC Members). We were cracking jokes the whole time. Of course, we did a few practical things like deciding who would fill the vacant places of the NLD's Executive Committee and made a short agenda to carry on into the future.

AC: It's refreshing to feel the flesh on a myth rather than to keep it imprisoned inside a sacred dream.

UKM: Well, that's good, isn't it? Ideals can keep you wondering, you know. They might keep you full of hope but hope is contrary to our policy of action. We're much more down to earth about such things. Politics are about work and pragmatism. Democracy is an earth-based endeavor. So all this business of ideals and hopes has to be put into action. But let me come back to Suu's arrest. No doubt, it was an ugly moment. But it was inevitable and we accepted it…that is what I'm saying. It wasn't as tragic or grave as many people might assume it was…there was no melodrama in other words.

AC: Sir, you had been to prison three times by this point—a total of seven years. You knew well how notorious Insein Prison was, with torture and sub-human living conditions. However, Aung San Suu Kyi had never been imprisoned. Did you counsel her in any way about how to handle prison life or deal with solitary confinement?

UKM: Well, in all seriousness a lot of our discussion was about Suu's arrest. I did think she would be taken to Insein—house arrest was not on the cards. But there was nothing mentioned, at least to my recollection, about how she should handle prison life. You have to understand, Suu is determined, she can handle herself. Of course, we knew the soldiers would walk in at any minute. Remember that we had been surrounded by soldiers for months by this point. So having them outside Suu's compound was simply SLORC's logical next step. So at about 2:30 or so we said, "All right...they must be getting impatient outside waiting for our meeting to adjourn." So we said our goodbyes, and we all left. That's all...

AC: What about the arrest itself?

UKM: Oddly, the soldiers didn't enter Suu's compound until 4:00 or 4:30 that evening. Ten hours hardened like statues. Well, they may have waited so long because there were a lot of our NLD youth activists in her compound—twenty or so. They were Suu's security. In fact, the whole day they played Suu's speeches and democracy songs loudly over the speakers. Let me interject here that as a matter of policy, we believe that the most effective weapon to unveil ignorance and repression is a nonviolent education. So our NLD youth gave the soldiers an all-day scolding with freedom songs and Suu's words on courage and human dignity. All those things they love to hear.

Well, when they finally raided her compound, which was our NLD headquarters, of course, they placed Suu under arrest. Also, they took our typewriters, cameras, video equipment, tape-recorders and all our NLD registration cards—files that listed the names and addresses with photographs of every NLD member nationwide. Now put this in context and you get a clear picture of the absurdity of it all. All this occurred during SLORC's "free and fair multi-party democratic election campaign process." After Suu and U Tin Oo's arrest, U Aung Shwe and I carried on the work.

AC: Sir, you were the last person to see Daw Suu on the day of her detention and from what I am told, the first person that she asked to see upon her release. It must have been quite a special moment to see your dear friend and colleague after such a long separation. The struggle resumed?

UKM: Well, it never stopped you know. But yes, we too were happy that Suu was free. I'll take you there. It was Monday, 10 July 1995. There's one SLORC security man—a chap who has been at Suu's gate for several years now. Well, this same officer came to my house that afternoon. My two dogs started to howl. I was in my study doing political research, reading a crumbling old book on the collapse of some fascist regime or other when my wife calmly walked in and said, "There's an intelligence officer at the door." We looked at each other with that uncertain kind of silence. Well, I put down my book and went to the door and I asked the obvious, "What is it?" He replied with a very straight face, "Daw Aung San Suu Kyi wants to see you." Well, my immediate thought was that something had happened to her. "Is she seriously ill?" I asked. "No, she's not ill," he replied. That's all he would say. I still had no idea that she was released. So I deferred myself to his hospitality, "Are you here to give me a lift?" "No," he responded, "come in your own car." Only then did I know it wasn't a re-arrest. Then he said, "Daw Aung San Suu Kyi would like to see your wife, too."

We arrived at about 5:00 in the afternoon. SLORC guards let us in, and as we drove up to Suu who was standing on her doorstep she quipped, "Uncle, what took you so long, six years to drive a mile?" Only then did we know Suu was free, that she had been released. So we went inside, the three of us. We exchanged stories, filling in the blanks, so to speak. Suu was unscathed, untouched, her mind as free as a bird. I had never doubted it and seeing her again after six years just confirmed my instincts. We laughed and joked at the absurdity of it all. I know from my own incarceration that prison never weakened my spirit; rather, it strengthened my resolve. The same with Suu. Her convictions had always been strong but nothing like what I saw that day. She was Suu with a free heart, an iron will and a lightning-bolt mind.

But just as we were about to leave U Tin Oo arrived with his wife. The news had spread like wildfire. He said that outside Suu's front gate was a swarm of camera-crews and journalists. Then our current NLD Chairman U Aung Shwe arrived. Now the party was warming up, we had tears in our eyes from laughing so much. Then by nine that night the front gate was fully packed with foreign journalists and photographers. The main point I would like to make is that the struggle had never ceased for any of us. Nor was it dormant. We all had a lot of time to think during our detention and now that we were all united again the energy together was stronger than ever. But it was time to settle down and get on with practical work. One party was over, and another one was about to begin.

AC: How does one maintain freedom in prison and not succumb to anger, bitterness and thoughts of revenge?

UKM: Freedom in a sense means absence of fetters which restrain you physically and mentally. A person thrown into prison immediately feels the impact of loss. It's difficult to pin it down to any single factor as it comes out of so many factors, such as: the loss of contact with one's family and friends; termination of the normal daily life that one is accustomed to;

denial of access to books and radio and companionship with people living in one's close proximity; having to contend with difficulties just to carry out simple chores beneficial to yourself and others who are in more dire circumstances than yourself, etcetera.

I was put in prison for the first time at the end of May 1965. On the third day of my incarceration I overcame the feeling of loss in a flash, and quite unexpectedly at that. It was as if someone advised me to stop thinking about anything at all.

Later on I paraphrased that idea at length to guide my conduct throughout the eleven years' duration of my life in Insein Prison. It says: "In your present state of isolation you are denied all data to serve as premises for your thinking, and based on which you have to draw appropriate conclusions. So go on thinking about anything if you are determined to make your life miserable." Ever since, I believe I have been able to manage my life, to live with a degree of success on a path free from excessive anger and frustration.

AC: I know that arbitrary arrests are commonplace in Burma. May I ask you for your thoughts about this SLORC tactic?

UKM: Arbitrary arrests are mean, irresponsible measures designed to crush political opposition and therefore are much to be deplored. These arrests are ruinous to political organizations working for democratic change in a number of ways. In a one-party state such as we have been accustomed to in our country for over three decades, arrests of political activists in the capital cities create ripples all over the country. Lower echelon security men in district towns—eager-beaver types—might initiate arrests on their own, even without specific instructions from their headquarters. Families of political activists are the worst hit because, more often than not, they lose their principal breadwinners. Impositions of extremely harsh sentences by the surreal courts have been the standard custom throughout this period. Treatment meted out to political prisoners since the inception of the SLORC regime is noted for its extreme brutality.

AC: The numbers of people attending your weekend public talks are noticeably increasing week by week. Do you ever anticipate armed SLORC soldiers advancing on the crowds and arresting the whole group in a major crackdown?

UKM: Several things to consider. One is that reconciliation could come about at any moment. They are allowing the weekend talks for a reason. We can only speculate why. Suu, Tin U and I—all of us at the NLD—really hope, what I mean to say is that we really want to believe that there is an opening here. Maybe allowing our talks to continue indicates something genuine in them. If so, it's a start. Maybe they are learning something from our words. Maybe it is that they feel the *mettā* among the people. Maybe they yearn to have that *mettā* directed towards them rather than it being forced or coerced from people. It could be that this *mettā* that is being generated among the people is having an effect on them. *Mettā* does that you know. Maybe it is opening them to a new way of treating people, seeing them as human beings to be honored and served rather than oppressed and robbed. It could be that they are moved by the people's courage. People who are not only willing to defy them but who are also ready and waiting to forgive them. It's all possible.

Secondly, we wish we could provide decent accommodations for our people that come and listen. As it is now, they are forced to sit on newspapers or plastic bags or directly on the dirty asphalt. And it's sweltering, without shade. We know the risk they are taking. This is unpleasant for us to see. Troops could come in at any moment, block the sides and say, "Don't move." But the people are following their conscience. They're committed to freedom. That is special. Call it dignity in action. The courage to live freely and not wait for freedom to be delivered. So I'm not worried. Nor am I worried for the people. We are in this together.

Now one day, perhaps soon, I don't know—we never know, do we?—I'll be incapable of taking a few steps outside. I'll be infirm and feeble. At that point I'll just lie down on my bed and die. I don't have any illusions about my worth, you know. Someone younger and stronger will replace me. I encourage that. But for now this work is my duty, and no one is imposing it on me. I too am following my conscience. So as long as I am needed I will stand and speak. I don't have any fears or worries, nothing at all.

Thirdly, I'll answer your question. I believe that at this point the SLORC would not want to arrest the weekend crowds. Their international image is being scrutinized and this intolerable act would surely be counterproductive. And all the foreign journalists with their video cameras would be thrilled to shoot SLORC soldiers for posterity. The sad spectacle could then be seen worldwide on CNN and BBC. That would be ample evidence of the kind of people we have to deal with.

AC: Several months down the road there could be ten thousand people attending your talks. How do you think SLORC will respond to this?

UKM: Well, we've learned that the authorities are quite disturbed about our "happy hour." But some of them must be enjoying them or they wouldn't be happening. But you see, they want us to behave like subjects in the old days of monarchs and Burmese kings. To kowtow like frogs. This is their mentality. Perhaps they see us as beggars in defiance of their almighty throne of superiority, and we're like "things" to be used and abused at their whim. They can't stand the fact that we're happy—those of us at the core of the NLD. But of course, at any time they're welcome to join the party, so to speak.

AC: Just how repressed is free speech in Burma today?

UKM: You can answer that yourself. Practically. I suggest that you put my words to the test, if you have the courage to do it. Go into the city to a corner teashop and stand on a box and say a few words about democracy. Now see what would happen. You would no sooner get the word "justice" out of your mouth than you would be grabbed and put on the next plane out of here. And for a Burmese to do that, it's a one-way truck-ride to Insein. This is why I say Suu's compound is the only liberated area in Burma. From there we say all sorts of things. We joke about the SLORC and tell them how much happier everyone would be, themselves included, if they would just talk to us. Suu was telling the crowd last weekend that "One day if you look back at these long days of struggle and fear—when you reminisce on the situation—you and us—who are gathered together in this place, you behind the barbed wire, and we peering over the gate, you will laugh at the absurdity of it all. Yes, it is really inconvenient, though one day, that day might come—that day must come. That is one privilege that dissidents all over the world have had so far. When they reflect back upon their courage in the struggle they feel elated. And you too, all of you will surely feel that way one day. The time is near, it's coming."

AC: But why are the authorities allowing the weekly talks despite having banned them?

UKM: Call it what you will—a concession or a tactical maneuver—we believe that this action of the SLORC is not without pluses for them. Just to list a few: the scene of the weekend talks over time has fast changed itself into a tourist attraction. This is good for "Visit Myanmar Year 1996." Also, it could very well help soften the perception of people whose knowledge of SLORC acquired through the Western media had the SLORC projected as being a brutal and repressive regime. Furthermore, SLORC benefits from the letters to Suu written by her followers about what current gripes there are against the SLORC which need to be attended to. And lastly, these talks enable SLORC to maintain continuous assessment of the state of mind of the NLD leadership whom they consider their adversaries.

AC: And the benefits for the NLD?

UKM: Well, viewed from our angle, these weekly talks offer the NLD leadership an opportunity to dispense their views on the current political situation for the benefit of its followers with whom communication by means of printed matter is impossible [printing rights having been denied to the NLD since July 1990]. Under present conditions, this is the only place in the country where dissidents can counsel, confer, express, exchange and propagate their convictions among themselves with a degree of impunity. One cannot help but include a third factor into this bargain. By this, I mean the crowds who, braving SLORC's disdain, congregate regularly at Suu's gate to listen to her talks. The police and security details regularly raid their homes by night to check the night-visitors' list. [If anyone is staying overnight the law requires that the matter be reported to the Local Law and Order office early in the evening, or the host risks being fined or even imprisoned.] The ward security men then ask people to stay away from the weekend talks to keep themselves out of possible trouble. Half a dozen [SLORC] photographers take pictures of the people in assembly for identification purposes. Yet, undaunted, people come crowding back week after week.

AC: Are you a religious man?

UKM: It is a difficult question for me to answer. I live by a few precepts taught by the Buddha. If I were to tell you what these precepts are, I'm afraid you might be confused; so I'd rather not elaborate. Be it sufficient just to say that whatever they are, these few precepts have enabled me to get on well with my life.

For example, you were quite surprised when I told you how much we laughed together on the day of Suu's arrest or again in some grim episodes that we covered together. It can be explained by the fact that the narrator had no regrets at all for what had happened in the past. The "I" and the "me" of the past are dead and gone. By the same token, the narrator of the present is not worried about what might happen to "him" of the future. In fact, "he" is not status-conscious at all. What I strive for is to live a life of complete awareness from moment to moment and to provide the best service I possibly can to all living beings without discrimination and with a detached mind. Does religion serve politics? I do not speculate. I just try to do my best.

AC: Sir, you follow the teachings of the Buddha which is the path of non-attachment. May I ask, how does your understanding influence your leadership in your people's struggle for democratic freedoms?

UKM: Drive around the city streets and you are bound to come across big red billboards at road junctions on which are written slogans reflecting the current thoughts of the authorities. These billboards are representatives of the forces we have to contend with. Someone once wrote that "the kindest of men had to watch their words."

One of the things that Buddha taught us was to step outside ourselves and see our own stupidity—as often as we can. We regard the teachings of the Buddha as an inner compass to keep ourselves on course. Actions geared to the mood of the moment and not related to the overall strategy could prove to be disastrous.

AC: Sir, before your resignation from the Burma Army you were a respected commander. You were in combat, you've faced bullets and I suspect that you've killed people—the enemy. As a Buddhist can you kill with love in your heart?

UKM: Yes, I have killed men in war—the enemy. But with love in my heart? You can't lie truthfully, can you? So no, I wouldn't call it love in the real sense. I'll explain briefly. I was not fighting out of hatred for the enemy who was attempting to crush us. It's just honest combat. I had a job to do and I was doing it.

AC: Would you as a leader of the democracy struggle instigate an armed struggle against the SLORC if you had weapons?

UKM: No. I don't believe in armed struggle to bring about political change.

AC: You fought against fascism in the '40s, so why not fight it in the '90s?

UKM: Don't get me wrong. The only reason I joined the army was to fight for independence. That's it. If this war had not come to Burma I would have been more than content to pursue my real interest which is music and drama. I love the arts. But you see, we were kids. Just like leaves lying by the roadside, when the strong wind of revolution came we were swept away. My involvement in the army was quite incidental and not by design. We had no choice but to fight for independence. You don't doubt such choices…you just do it. But given a choice, I would never have opted for arms. All right, have I cleared myself?

AC: No, sir, you haven't. I'm just trying to understand your views on nonviolent activism as a principal leader of the freedom struggle.

UKM: As for that nonviolence business, I don't condemn it, but I'm not a Gandhi. If I see the need for force, I would tackle it head-on, without hesitation, if that is the only means available to me.

I was trained to fight and if somebody attempted to manhandle you,

I wouldn't tuck my tail between my legs and run away, listening to you scream with my back to you. That's cowardice. It's despicable. Nor would I sit there in meditation, trusting that my mettā would dissolve the ordeal. I'm no saint. I would try and defend you. Now I don't like the use of force, but I could never tell you that I would completely abstain from it. But Gandhi said that too.

AC: Will the struggle for democracy in your country be successful without much stronger support from the United States and Europe?

UKM: We are not relying on external support alone. It's a people's movement. That is our focus and our strength.

AC: So it's just an issue of patience and nonviolent perseverance?

UKM: Yes, patience. We don't need to run away. If they imprison me again, fine—I'll go to prison. I am as free in prison as I am in my own home. But putting me back in prison doesn't solve anything.

You see, another thing is that they [SLORC] think they cannot talk with Suu on a one-to-one basis. But a streetcleaner can talk with Suu on a one-to-one basis. Why do they doubt that a big general could have his say? So as you see I may be living in a fool's paradise but I'm happy where I am. I am not worried. The problems they [SLORC] are dealing with are of such magnitude that unless they cooperate with us they won't be able to secure the cooperation of the entire population.

AC: I remember a story that St. Augustine describes. I am not sure where I read it. Alexander the Great caught a pirate and asked him, "How dare you molest the sea?" The pirate retorted, "How dare you molest the whole world? I have a small boat, so I'm called a thief and a pirate. You have a navy. So you're called an emperor."

Here in Burma, SLORC takes the perversion one step further. They subjugate the whole country and for this they call themselves magnanimous leaders and the upholders of justice. While you at the NLD lead a nonviolent "revolution of the spirit" and are labeled "subversives," essentially political terrorists.

Now SLORC has cut deals with Burma's armed insurgents, and more recently with Khun Sa, the world's most notorious heroin drug-lord, but ironically SLORC won't talk with the NLD. Perhaps you could clarify these so called "ceasefires" once and for all?

UKM: First of all, these fifteen insurgent groups should be called by their true names. They are ethnic minorities who have taken up arms against

SLORC. These people—men, women and children—are citizens of Burma. They are human beings. That is the first point.

Secondly, these ceasefires are in no way an end to ethnic problems in Burma. In my view, they are nothing more than an R&R device. Take just one example, that of the Wa people of Shan state, in the Golden Triangle area. The ceasefire is nothing more than a cooling-off period for them to regroup and train even more of their population. In Wa villages every household must produce one male to undergo military training.

Now, this applies to the Kachins too. It applies to every one of the fifteen groups. They've all retained their weapons and what is called a ceasefire is just a retraining and regrouping period. So it's fair to say that these ceasefires cannot guarantee long-term peace.

And there's another problem. The SLORC every now and again announces a period of public money laundering. They even publicize it in their newspaper: 75 percent return on undeclared cash—no questions asked. So it's no leap of the imagination to understand why heroin production has radically increased in Burma since SLORC seized power. There is clear, hard evidence for this. Of course, the black money then goes directly into real estate. Some of the finest land in Rangoon and Mandalay has been purchased by black money. Mansions with swimming pools are built and in some cases left empty. The black money is getting into the tourist business through hotel constructions. It's going into jade, sapphire and ruby mining.

AC: Sir, there is a twist of irony to the fact that George Orwell was a police chief in one of Burma's major cities during the 1920s and then to hear you at Sunday's public talk explain and decode a few Orwellian concepts from his book, *1984*. As you had said, "all under the watchful eye of Big Brother." Were you inferring that Orwell's *1984* was similar to SLORC's "1996"?

UKM: Of course, all the elements of *1984* are here in Burma today. Perhaps slightly watered down, but they are here. Thought-control is the bulwark of a totalitarian regime, although not confined to that system alone. It can operate even in democratic societies, at more subtle but equally effective levels. The manipulation of the public mind through propaganda and disinformation is a vast, fascinating topic. It's important for us all to understand how control occurs; control of the masses through tortured terminology and abstruse concepts used by governments, PR firms, advertising agencies and hidden censorship. There's control through educational systems and within religions. We have to learn to question…to learn ways of protecting ourselves and to be vigilant in peeling away the layers of distortion. Not to be imprisoned, in other words, by propaganda. But let's stay here in Burma with our SLORC's brand of Big Brother.

AC: Would you explain how Big Brother operates in Burma and also explain who this Big Brother is, SLORC?

UKM: SLORC is a clique of twenty-one generals. That's it. With a bunch of subordinates who dare not defy the brass. These generals control every aspect of life in this country. Totalitarianism by function is Big Brother. So all these Orwellian terms, "thought-control, brainwash, Newspeak, the Ministry of Truth, the Ministry of Love," all of them, exist in variations within all systems of control. They are not as sophisticated as Orwell depicted them, but nevertheless they are here, and for the same reason—to deny life!

AC: How does "Big Brother SLORC" enforce their will upon political dissent or even ordinary Burmese citizens?

UKM: SLORC has shown repeatedly that they will use any means within their grasp to crush dissent and even the suspicion of dissent. They go about this in a variety of ways. Harassment is a mandate, so it seems by the frequency with which it occurs; they axe a person's work, confiscate land and property, public beatings, force the young and old to build roads, bridges, dams, without compensation. They'll snatch people in the middle of the night. Suu said it before her arrest seven years ago, she says it now, we all say it—"Nothing has changed, let the world know, under this regime we are prisoners in our own country."

AC: Does that mean that this "Big Brother SLORC" is so maniacal, so cunning, so perverse, that for some yet-to-be-known reason they are allowing you, Daw Suu and U Tin Oo to speak publicly on weekends to serve their own devious self-interest? Or are they truly opening to a new way of being, a micro-step towards authentic reformation?

UKM: A new way of being? Authenticity? These concepts are not within SLORC's vocabulary as of yet, that is unless they study our weekend talks. And yes, anything is possible. Anything could occur—even the dinosaurs became extinct. All I am saying is that their repressive habits are so fossilized that I seriously doubt that their thought is thawing or that they are on the road to an authentic democracy.

Now as for them allowing our public talks. This is yet another Orwellianism. At our public talks, you see, we have SLORC's version of the two-way television system. There are SLORC MI men out there mingling with the crowds. Watch those Burmese who video row after row of people. Why? We all know that Big Brother SLORC will be watching us close up within an hour or so. And since Suu frequently criticizes SLORC's repressive tactics brought to our attention by individuals who write to her, some must be using the information to maintain a grip on others within their own ranks. That's the nature of fear-based regimes: no one is safe, no one can be trusted...even if you happen to be at the very top. That is except Big Brother himself. Whoever that fiction is.

AC: Václav Havel has written about the effects of the secret police in Czechoslovakia. He called them, "That hideous spider whose invisible web runs right through society...[creating] a dull, existential fear that seeped into every crack and crevice of daily life...and made one think twice about everything one said and did." Is this the general atmosphere created by the SLORC's MI?

UKM: Yes. The clan of the spider is watching us right now. MI are at the corner of my street. They are outside the gate. On the main road. Wherever I go they follow. They have cellular phones and transmit information instantaneously to headquarters. The whole country is webbed and wired. And you can be sure they followed you here. They are at your hotel. They have most likely searched your room and tapped your telephone.

AC: You're not the least bit concerned about the "hideous spider"?

UKM: No, I'm not. Not in the slightest. In fact, the more the SLORC observes and listens the more they will be able to trust us, because our intentions are sincere. After all our struggle for democracy doesn't exclude them, it includes them. And all this MI business, well, they use it as fodder for character assassinations and all that SLORC-speak.

AC: I have to admit, for research purposes I have forced myself to watch SLORC-television and read their newspaper. What a chore, and rarely a day goes by without a malicious and slanderous half page commentary about Aung San Suu Kyi, U Tin Oo and yourself. But who reads this? Who are they appealing to? Does anyone believe what they print? Do you ever read the newspaper or watch television, perhaps for no other reason than to become more acquainted with your enemy to perhaps give you further insight into how their minds work in order to bring you closer to dialogue and hopefully reconciliation?

UKM: Listen, the irony is that they don't believe any of it themselves. They know it's all nonsense. We know that. The whole country knows it. Everything they say and print is trash. It's rubbish. Even if you tried reading it, most of the stuff they print is unreadable. It's written in such a long and rambling style with so much distortion that you can barely locate the point. It's like trying to watch television when it's out of focus. We have a boy scout version of Big Brother.

AC: I understand that you're a playwright banned by the regime? Do you still write underground?

UKM: No, no, no...that's not accurate. I am nowhere near a Václav Havel, if that's what you mean. I just happen to love good drama; a good story in other words. Even if I could write, it's no use my writing because if the authorities saw my name my work would immediately be burned or used for toilet paper. There's absolutely zero chance of my work being published. None.

AC: Does SLORC tolerate even the slightest whisper of political satire, say, buried deep within the pablum of a magazine article, or hidden on page 911 in the nightmare of the novel's protagonist? Are they that scrupulous?

UKM: Everything original, provocative and intelligent, anything with an inspired dimension to it is censored by SLORC. Almost every writer in our organization refuses to write or create, or is forced out of the profession. Now if any of us published something, the authorities would immediately find out who the author was and would ban it. Or the writer would be harassed or detained. All our artists, musicians, writers, actors, anyone belonging to our side—the NLD—it's blanket treatment. We're banned. So a great resource of intelligent and creative talent has been absolutely removed from society. Except the puppet show SLORC puts on, which is bad comedy.

AC: Would you give a few examples of how SLORC censorship operates?

UKM: There was a theater piece that was performed at the recent 75th Film Diamond Jubilee here in Rangoon. One actor came out on to the stage after the curtain fell and pointed a finger in the direction of SLORC's MI Chief [Khin Nyunt] repeating the final words that he as the Burmese hero of the play said during the final scene of the show: "You, sir, think that because you have the guns, you are superior." Something to that effect. Of course, the MI Chief couldn't bear the free publicity and sauntered out of the audience in disgust. Soon thereafter the actor was banned from acting for three years, or maybe it was five.

Then on Independence Day, we held a celebration for our NLD members within Suu's compound. You were there. Well, that theater piece mid-way through the celebration was a brilliantly executed, witty and intelligent piece of political satire. There was nothing base about it at all. In fact, the actors were just repeating old jokes—some had even been used in the shows on SLORC television. Well, those actors and musicians, eleven of them, were arrested on their return home to Mandalay. All but four were released after several weeks of interrogation. The two main actors will likely be sentenced and imprisoned [they were both sentenced to seven years' hard labor]. This is the price of free speech under SLORC. But you see, those actors knew the score beforehand. One had been imprisoned a few years before and they knew it could very well happen again. Nevertheless, they stood up, delivered their jokes, and performed boldly and courageously. This is why I said to you, Big Brother SLORC is always watching.

I'll give you another example. A well-known young musician recently produced a tape titled Power 54, which was in reference to his 54th recorded song or something like that. He put the piece up to the SLORC censorship board and they passed it. Immediately it received wide distribution because of his fame, that is until the SLORC thought that 54 was in reference to Suu's house number, which is 54 University Avenue. The authorities hit the roof and removed every tape from every store in the country within days. Are the SLORC scared of Suu?

Sometimes fifteen, twenty, or even forty or more pages may be torn out of a one-hundred-page magazine. This could create problems. The stories are numerous. This censorship board has been in operation for three decades or more. Dictators loathed free thought. Their idea of society was tailored after places like East Germany.

AC: When a dialogue does occur with SLORC, may I ask, what will be the first item of business on your agenda?

UKM: The first thing we want to do is listen. We would like to hear what it is they want. It is my belief that every time you talk with your enemy it must be your genuine wish not to destroy him. It's a mutual deal, a reciprocity, a give and take. It can't be one-sided. As you advance your interests so too must you advance the interests of your enemy. Sincerity is the key and sincerity takes courage. Why? Because to be sincere requires openness—a genuine willingness to listen, to be willing to reflect upon opposing views to those of your own. I believe that within everyone, buried beneath the distorting layers of pride and fear is a heart of goodness, it's the natural state of humankind. All this egoistic subterfuge—greed, arrogance, insecurity, racism, domination, all of it blocks the living daylight out of the intrinsic sincerity of the human heart.

In reality, I don't see SLORC as the enemy, really. Sure, on a conventional level of speaking I use the word. I use strong words to describe my disdain for them because of their behavior. I say, call a spade a spade.

We're grown-ups talking. But under it all they're human—they bathe, eat and sweat like the rest of us. Equally, they have hearts. They have good-will. It's in them, I'm sure of that. We just want more of it. So much more that they make it the predominant expression of their speech and actions.

Now they publicly state that they are working non-stop for the benefit of all the people and with magnanimous intentions. Well, if it's genuine, then put it across to us. If it's real then we'll do our best to greet their sincerity with our own. In that spirit, I have no doubt that we can work it out, happily.

We do not want to hurt them, humiliate them, nothing, that is if they cooperate with us in the endeavor. I say let us stop wasting time. People are suffering. So they should put their heads together and count back from ten. When they get to one they should say one nation for the people, by the people, and make haste to University Avenue with the good news. We're waiting for their invitation but we can't write it for them. They must show some genuine goodwill.

AC: How do you think the NLD and SLORC could start working together?

UKM: It would be important to confirm the results of the May 1990 elections as a first step. Let me explain why. The military's anti-democratic sentiment seen during the mass demonstrations of 1988 and in its aftermath had focused on the National League for Democracy. Its intensity had grown in proportion to the NLD's popularity with the people and found expression when it decided to place U Tin Oo and Suu under house arrest on 20 July 1989. When the NLD won 392 electoral seats out of the total of 452 seats in the election held on 27 May 1990, the SLORC issued an edict on 28 July 1990, known as Notification 1/90, obviously to obfuscate and delay the process of democratization. Prompt rejection of Notification 1/90 by the NLD leadership and its call for the SLORC to convene the first Parliament in September, 1990, further aggravated the situation.

In the first week of September, the SLORC decided to launch a major campaign to annihilate the NLD organization. Mass arrests of NLD activists and elected MPs were carried out throughout the country and various charges were made against them resulting in long-term prison sentences. In the meantime fresh directives were given to the NLD to stop recruitment of new members. We were not allowed to replace those organizers who had been removed by death or disability. And if the numbers in any organizational unit fell below five, that office had to be shut down.

In January, 1992, the SLORC ultimately embarked upon the process of holding a National Convention under their own direction and tight surveillance, setting their own agenda and handpicking non-MP members whose strength approximated a 6 to 1 ratio with elected MPs forming the minority. The NLD tagged along with the SLORC while insisting from time to time upon its objections to various irregularities in the conduct of the National Convention. The breaking point came on 29 October 1995 when the Chairman of the National Convention Convening Committee [a SLORC general] decided to ignore an important request made to him by the Chairman of the NLD [U Aung Shwe].

I believe that so much misery, suffering and wretchedness imposed upon the people of Burma had their genesis in the military's denial to respect the will of the people as illustrated in the result of the election held under their auspices in 1990. By tracing this history I mean to show the linkage between the excesses that have developed from one source: namely, the military's misguided concept of democracy. To untangle the problem, I suggest that they accept the result of the election held on 27 May 1990 as the first priority.

AC: Sir, it is not easy for me to ask you this question. Military Intelligence observes every move you make. Does re-arrest concern you?

UKM: You don't seem to understand that imprisonment is not a concern of mine. The spider, that "hideous old spider," so what? His web is dirty and dusty, filled with the empty shells of his victims. But I am not afraid. Of course, re-arrest is possible. It's there at any moment of the day or night. Burma is lawless. Without justice. Everything's arbitrary. So what I am saying is that the seriousness of the situation is balanced by the absurdity of it. I defend myself with irony and humor. That poor old spider, despite his nasty ways, is trapped in his own web. And I'm happy while he's confined to hunting. Now imagine the mind of a hunter, always looking, suspicious of every sound. Always at odds with his environment. He wants to conquer and kill. That is a very, very, sad state of mind. It's pathetic. I'm in no hurry. My freedom is not tomorrow, it's today.

AC: Peace accords and settlements are occurring in Bosnia, the Middle East and possibly in Northern Ireland—once bitter enemies are talking, in some cases, after decades of horror and bloodshed, even genocide. But why not in Burma? After all you are all Burmese, you're family, really. Furthermore, SLORC has a magnificent chance in the palms of their hands, the most precious of opportunities. I use the word with hesitation, but they can redeem themselves, gain worldwide respect, and more importantly gain the respect they so desperately crave from their own people. Arafat, De Klerk, even Kissinger have won the Nobel Peace Prize. Is Khin Nyunt next?

UKM: Good question. That's exactly what we want to know. Why? Why is it that they are waiting? Why are they so angry with us? Why wait? Tell us face to face. We can handle it! But Khin Nyunt as a Nobel Laureate? Well, in the way that you put it, who knows?

AC: But, sir, surely you must have some idea of why they are waiting?

UKM: Maybe they're not waiting. I told our people this morning that actually we are in a dialogue with SLORC. I'll explain. Read SLORC editorials about us in their newspaper, the *New Light of Myanmar*. They're talking to us. Are they not? Then, we talk to them through our weekend talks at the gates of Suu's house. SLORC videotapes the talks. The only problem is, we are talking back to back *(laughing)*. What we need is someone to come and help them by saying, "Come on boys, you face this way" and they'll listen. But this is a dialogue. They call us clowns, subversives, heaping insult upon insult. That is no way to put food in the mouths of malnourished people. That's not the way to unlock the cells of political prisoners. That's not the way to honor the results of the 1990 elections. But who can say that it's not a beginning? Maybe it is their way of opening to us. My mindset is different from theirs. They're so unpredictable. Except, that is, for their policy of repression. That's consistent.

AC: Let me ask the same question in another way. You have made it quite clear that SLORC's desperation roots in one thing—fear of losing power. What does that mean in reality?

UKM: Fine, I'll tell you. What's biting them is fear. Fear of revenge. Fear of persecution. Fear of losing face. Fear of losing their property, their mansions, their cars, their motorcades, all these privileges—it's the fear of losing power. These generals know they have done wrong. They fear for their security, they fear for their own families, for their sons and daughters. But I can assure them. Listen. The past is the past. What is done is done. We will not take up this matter anymore than to the extent that it is permissible to the majority of the people.

Almost everyone is aware of the indictments and legal proceedings going on against South Korea's two former presidents. Almost everyone is aware that in South Africa Desmond Tutu is heading a Commission for Truth and Reconciliation. Some people will not be able to escape blame for deeds done nearly two decades before. But our Burmese people are by nature compassionate and I think the people will forgive them. That is my belief. Forgiveness will win. This will strengthen our nation and not weaken it. The generals must understand this. And if they want to talk to us, we're ready, now!

AC: Sounds like a message worth repeating at next weekend's talk.

UKM: Such words we will reserve for our initial talks. You see, they don't believe us. They don't believe that the people are forgiving. Even if Suu had such a mindset, I could correct it. "Well Suu, that won't serve the purpose of benefiting the people of Burma." But that's not the case. We don't operate from a policy of revenge or vindictiveness. We want truth and reconciliation, not deceit and persecution. Forgiveness will be the bedrock of Burma's democracy. But each day that SLORC delays means yet another day of suffering for a lot of people.

AC: Perhaps what's needed is an appropriate mediator to get SLORC to the dialogue table; President Carter comes to mind. Or perhaps a mutually agreed upon team of mediators; people from both sides.

UKM: I think this is a fabulous idea. Please help us to turn SLORC's face towards someone who really inspires faith from both our sides. If there was an outsider that SLORC selected to mediate between us it would be a godsend.

AC: Do you think the SLORC would be open to this as a possibility?

UKM: No, not at the moment. They don't trust anyone to be impartial.

AC: There're ways to remedy that. Perhaps they need an incentive, like loans from the World Bank or International Monetary Fund, or aid from the US or the European Union...

UKM: Anyone who could help nudge SLORC to the conference table would be just fine. We will give them our full guarantee that they can be abusive, they can say anything to us, as long as they sit down with us face to face. If they really need to scold us, go ahead, howl if they want to. As long as they don't do us physical harm, that's all.

AC: Speaking of physical harm, how could these generals ever trust that they will go free?

UKM: Many people who have suffered. I mean really suffered much more than myself...more than U Tin Oo...more than Suu, are laughing and joking about their experiences as we do. You look a bit shocked...

AC: Yes, I am. It is hard to understand your humor and laughter in the face of such overwhelming suffering. I've talked with Daw Suu about this very point. But I'm beginning to see the value of turning the whole ordeal around and making it work in one's favor. Otherwise, as Václav Havel said, "One tends to petrify into one's own statue." A very uncomfortable image. But please, back to you...

UKM: Well, that's a good point and it relates to what I'm saying. If we harbor hatred towards our oppressors we instantly turn into that statue. Which is the opposite of compassion and forgiveness. Now, if need be I'll go out into the streets to persuade people who have really suffered. I'll ask them personally to show their mercy, to align themselves with our way of thinking. I'll speak from my own experiences—I've survived prison, many times—and here I am. It should go without mention but I'll say it. Certainly some grieving is needed. A loss has occurred and grieving is human. It's needed for some people. But dragging up all the evils of SLORC and others won't give us any real relief at all. Now I'm confident that the vast majority of our Burmese people want freedom, not revenge.

AC: I certainly respect your confidence and convictions nor am I one who espouses absolute justice. But sir, it is true that causes have effects. When cruelty has been inflicted upon people mustn't some form of justice prevail? What is democracy without the rule of law?

UKM: That is why Suu said, and we all agree with her, that we will be quite happy if some responsible people on their side would just say yes, we have done such-and-such and we are sorry and we'll see to it that others belonging to our side do not repeat such things. We would be quite happy to hear something like this. We won't cut off their salaries or imprison them. This is our attitude.

AC: Do you envision some role for the SLORC in a democratic Burma?

UKM: They need re-orientation. They are completely uneducated in matters of democracy. These men cut their political teeth under a totalitarian regime. What is the political concept behind that? Follow the leader...

AC: I would like to ask you a personal question if I may. You live on the radical edge of uncertainty moment to moment, never knowing when or if you will be taken away at any time of the day or night. How does this "great unknown" affect your marriage?

UKM: No...please ask anything you would like. In fact, I am glad you asked the question. My wife is my friend, my best friend, and in so many ways. She too is dedicated to the struggle. In so doing we are both under constant intimidation and scrutiny. Now I've said quite enough about the MI outside our compound. They follow us everywhere we go. These things do affect us, but my wife seems to have gotten used to it. I heard her talking to friends the other day about the possibility of my re-arrest and she said, "From the moment when Suu asked us to come see her on the day of her release, we knew that we would be liable for re-arrest again." She is aware of the situation. But she too jokes about it. Little things like, "Well, you know eleven years are missing from our marriage," or that "We have to stop meeting this way," meaning when she would visit me in prison. That is this reality in SLORC-controlled Burma. Democracy, marriage and imprisonment all walk hand-in-hand. I think for all of us in the struggle our idea of marriage has expanded to include separation from our family and loved ones as inevitable. We accept that fully. It's a choice we've all made.

AC: Sir, if in fact you were re-arrested, what would you say to the people of the country, should this be your last opportunity? What message would you like to leave with them to carry on the struggle?

UKM: For the coming generations I would encourage them to emphasize two most important things; education, and to enrich themselves with a sense of history. Knowledge is essential. They should learn about Burma, our history, our people, our own world, as well as the world at large. This will assist them in shaping their own lives, freely.

To grasp history is to grasp the importance of interrelatedness; where, why and how, the causes, conditions and the consequences of thought and action and how they affect the development or demise of civilization—human existence at large. Everyone plays a part and the gift of life is to play that part with profound responsibility. Furthermore, the twentieth century has taught us great lessons in all aspects of human involvement. There have been some advances which humankind could never have imagined. In this century we have seen the folly of ideologies, such as Fascism and Communism, that are inconsistent with creativity and the flourishing of the spirit. From the nineteenth century came the rise of the British Empire that sent a plague of exploitation around the world. Yet it too was humbled. We have witnessed all types of war from urban violence to global wars, from bolt-action rifles to the nuclear bomb, typewriters to cyberspace, a revolution in music and dance, there's just so much, and within it all have come a few good men and women with vision, that remarkable gift to see our tomorrow today. Gifts that are shifting our thinking about the future of the planet, our survival as a species. It's all about interrelatedness. So I would like to encourage all generations to explore this fully. From this I believe there will be the flourishing of civilization, and not its untimely demise—I hope.

AC: How would you encourage specifically the present generation in Burma and their children, and their children's children, if need be, to further your vision of a free and democratic Burmese society?

UKM: Do everything humanly possible not to live in fear. That's all.

AC: On the possibility that this book—your words—might find its way into the Burmese language and smuggled into one of Burma's many prisons, would you care to say a few words to the many prisoners of conscience?

UKM: I would like them to remember that the collapse of the Soviet Union was unpredictable and that once the deterioration started, it continued at lightning speed. While our democracy forces are strong, gaining momentum day by day, the people will not rest until freedom is secured. Know that.

AC: Sir, if I may, I would like to ask you a personal question. How would you like to be remembered after you pass from this life?

UKM: Oh...I don't want to leave anything behind, nothing at all, no landmark, no gravestone, no books, nothing—just like a bird flies out from the water, traceless. I would want to be burnt. I want to be buried in an unmarked grave. Nor do I wish to leave any message for you or for anyone. But I will say, when you look at your life, it's ridiculous, really. And to build a monument over one's bones is even more ridiculous. I don't believe in monuments. Look at the amount of brass they wasted for Stalin's statues...

AC: You seem absolutely immune to SLORC intimidation, nor do you have any fear of re-arrest or imprisonment. But you're human. Doesn't it get to you sometimes?

UKM: I couldn't care less. What I do care about and practice off and on throughout the day is to be aware. That's all. To be aware. See, I have pieces of paper in my pockets which I carry with me, quotes, inspiring reminders. They refocus my mind on the here and now. That is the most important thing to me. To be present. Awake. Aware. Because you know, my life in prison was not a bed of roses. But I used the time to my advantage. I never forget that what I am seeing now—that pale green line streaking across the pond, or the shadow of the tree across your leg—all these things disappear the moment I turn my face to the other side. This is life's simplicity. Just the here and now. Aware that nothing is permanent, and all of it, as empty as a shadow. That barbed-wire fence across the back of Suu's compound that we see, why worry about the presence of such an irritant. It's insignificant. Now if I worry about anything, it's that I might lose this sense of awareness. So I guard it as something precious. Things pass...that I have seen. Life is what you make it, now. Nothing profound, very basic, you see. So let us put our energies into life. In this way I try not to lose my perspective.

AC: Do you ever contemplate your own death?

UKM: Yes...when I stand up there speaking to the people on Sunday, I sometimes visualize myself with a projectile piercing my heart, the blood, and my fall to the ground. But I don't worry. I'm not worried at all. I don't care. If it is coming, let it come. But what I do fear is that I would be so weak that I would choose the easiest way out, lie around in bed all day and read some book on the collapse of yet another totalitarian regime...

CHAPTER 11

CONVERSATION *with* NINE NLD MPS

February 2014

- "Meditation was part of our prison life. We meditated every day."
- "The generals thought that they were superior to ordinary humans."
- "They tried to get legitimacy internationally, but it was not successful."
- 'Two things kept him alive—reflecting on his integrity and contemplating the *Dhamma*.'
- "Peaceful revolution is the norm of future revolutions."

Conversation with 9 NLD MPs in Naypyidaw, in a Q&A led by U Win Htein and organized by Aung San Suu Kyi. Provides readers with an exclusive account of the party's progress and obstacles since 1996, a portrait characterizing the spirit of revolutionary freedom that sustained all of its members through years of persecution. Five of the prominent political figures served decades behind bars as prisoners of conscience, including Daw Phyu Thin, founder of a successful HIV/AIDS clinic and member of the House of Representatives; Dr Zaw Myint Maung, now Chief Minister of Mandalay Region; U Ohn Kyaing, a teacher, journalist and MP; Dr May Lwin Myint, a former medical doctor who became an MP following the uprising of 1988; and Phyo Min Thein, now Chief Minister for Yangon. In this discussion, the interviewees talk at length about the principles of democratic freedom, political integrity and national reconciliation that paved the way for an NLD government in 2015.

Participants

1. DPT: Daw Phyu Thin
2. DrMM: Dr. Zaw Myint Maung
3. DTN: Daw Than Ngwe
4. DKT: Daw Khin Thanda
5. UKTH: U Kyaw Thi Ha
6. PMT: Phyo Min Thein
7. DrLM: Dr. May Lwin Myint
8. UOK: U Ohn Kyaing
9. UWH: U Win Htein

"Meditation was part of our prison life.
We meditated every day"

U WIN HTEIN: Alan, please sit down. The reason we are meeting today is that our chairperson, Daw Aung San Suu Kyi, asked the nine of us to speak with you, in support of your work on behalf of our people. She instructed us that whatever questions you ask, to oblige in answering them, fully.

ALAN CLEMENTS: I'm honored. Thank you all.

UWH (to the group): Alan regularly visited Daw Suu at her home in Yangon in 1995 and 1996 for nearly six months (after her release from her first six years of detention). Earlier, in the late 1970s and 1980s, Alan was at the Mahasi Sāsana Yeiktha Meditation Centre in Yangon, living as a Buddhist monk, ordained by the late Venerable Mahasi Sayadaw. Alan was among the first Westerners to ordain as a monk in our country. He went onto to write a number of books on our country's struggle for freedom, including *Burma's Revolution of the Spirit* and *The Voice of Hope,* a book of conversations with Daw Aung San Suu Kyi, and our NLD co-founders, the late U Kyi Maung, and U Tin Oo.

DAW THAN NGWE: Oh, I've read your book. I've still got it.

AC: That's an honor. Thank you. I keep reading it at least once a year. Your leaders have so much insight that applies far beyond your borders— to all people who care about freedom, nonviolent struggle, and respect for global human rights.

Just recently I saw a copy of the book in a Yangon bookstore. It was the first copy I had seen in Burma. I think it was banned for nearly 15 years. There it was—a single copy with Daw Suu's image on the cover—in full view for all to see as you walked into the bookstore.

UWT: There are cases of people going to prison for having a copy of the book. I know of at least one person, and there must be others.

AC: My God. The cost of freedom! As you all know so well.

Besides Daw Suu, along with U Kyi Maung, U Tin Oo, U Aye Win and U Aung Ko, U Win Htein was most responsible for making the book a reality. Talking with him so frequently at Daw Suu's house gave me precious insight into your peoples' aspirations for freedom. As for me, it was among the greatest gifts of my life, to have been involved in this small way in your country's ongoing struggle for freedom. Thank you again for your own courageous expressions of caring for the freedom of others more than your own.

UWT: If you would, please explain more of your background.

AC: Well, as U Win Htein said, I was blessed to be a Buddhist monk under the guidance of the late Venerable Mahasi Sayadaw, and later, his successor, the Venerable Sayadaw U Pandita. As you may well know, Daw Suu and Sayadaw U Pandita are very close. He's her spiritual advisor and meditation teacher. Perhaps there are others too, but he has played a significant role in her *Dhamma* life. He also has a deep sense of *mettā* (loving-kindness) for her and equally a great *karuṇā* (compassion) for the plight of your people. My first love in Burma was and remains the *Dhamma* (insight meditation and the quest for freedom). Burma is my spiritual home and my *Dhamma* teachers are my spiritual parents. I would not be who I am without them. And you, as it were, are my extended family—mentors in peaceful revolution.

In 1980 or so, I was doing slow walking meditation at the Mahasi Centre when a procession of cars came into the monastery grounds. It turned out to be the former Commander-in-Chief of the Defense Forces, General U Tin Oo. I learned that he had just been released a day or two before after five or six years of imprisonment, by his boss, the dictator, Ne Win. Inspired to practice intensive mindfulness meditation, he ordained as a monk and was given a room near mine within the monastery.

Progressively, throughout our months of intensive meditation practice, U Tin Oo explained to me the truth about your country's political sphere, primarily giving me an insiders historical perspective on the politics, the plight of your people, and moreover, the psychology of totalitarianism under the dictator, Ne Win. At the time, I was fairly ignorant of such matters. Frankly, all I wanted to do was be quiet and meditate—in breath, out breath, month after month—with the intention of realizing progressive stages of insight and hopefully, *Nibbana* (enlightenment) itself. I knew almost nothing about the politics of Burma or the psychology of dictatorship or moreover, the intense *dukkha* (suffering) of your people.

Dr ZAW MYINT MAUNG: Yes, *dukkha*; suffering, such suffering.

AC: Just terrible... Although I had met the former Prime Minister U Nu while he was under house arrest, I had little understanding of Ne Win, but, when U Tin Oo came to the centre, he talked actively and openly about his former boss. I would say this was my first foray into the machinations of totalitarian doctrine. U Tin Oo and I became very close over the following years. Even today, 32 years later, he remains as my Uncle, mentor and true *Dhamma* friend.

Only in 1988, at the time of your nationwide nonviolent uprising, did I start to become active in your peoples' struggle, as an outsider, of course.

My colleague, Leslie Kean, and I formed The Burma Project, a non-profit foundation dedicated to bringing awareness of your struggle to the world through all means possible. During the next two decades, we produced many articles and books, along with media appearances, public events and participated in the creation of a feature film depicting your country's "revolution of the spirit," based, in part, on my book Burma: The Next Killing Fields?, written back in 1990.

Then, when Daw Suu was released in 1995, I came to Burma immediately. Of course, the whole world wanted to know who she was, having been awarded the Nobel Peace prize while under house arrest. It was U Tin Oo who introduced me to Daw Suu. In fact, I just spoke with him yesterday at the NLD Union Day in Yangon. I also interviewed your NLD co-founder, U Win Tin (who spent 19 years in solitary confinement).

By way of saying, again, that my first and greatest love here in Burma has been, and remains, the *Dhamma* and the freedom that develops based on studying how we so often create our own internal suffering. But I had very little understanding of how this *Dhamma*, how this inner freedom, intersected among the people in daily life, in social and political interactions and with outer freedom. It was Daw Suu and U Tin Oo, U Kyi Maung and U Win Htein who revealed to me their knowledge of how the *Dhamma* operated within politics. As Daw Suu said, "It is our freedom. No one is an island. And everyone can do their part." It was the intersection of the *Dhamma* and timeless spiritual principles with politics and the everyday lives of the people that has motivated me the most. And because your struggle was clearly stated as a nonviolent revolution of the spirit for democracy, I was inspired to learn all I could about this new frontier of *Dhamma*-inspired, spiritual-political activism.

At this point, I invited Daw Suu to meet for a series of conversations to explore peaceful revolution. I asked her if we could record the conversations for the world to understand the full meaning of what she and your people were trying to achieve. She agreed on the condition that U Kyi Maung and U Tin Oo were an equal part of the project. Those conversations became *The Voice of Hope*.

And now, nearly twenty years later, it seems as if almost the entire world is focused on Myanmar, looking carefully at what will unfold here during this complex struggle and transition towards democracy.

Backing up a bit. Daw Suu and I spoke in San Francisco recently. It was the first time we had seen each other or spoken since I was thrown out of the country back in 1996 and subsequently banned from re-entering Burma for 17 years. At that time in San Francisco, Daw Suu was awarded the Vaclav Havel Award for Creative Dissent. The next day she spoke to 5,000 or so people at San Francisco State University. Most of the people in attendance were Burmese. If I recall correctly, she explained, in essence, how your country's ongoing struggle for democracy was unfinished. She also explained how so many people had suffered but this wasn't the time to process that *dukkha*. Rather, it was a time of renewed action. She emphasized, to all those who care about freedom, "Do what you can to support the aspirations of our people." I was moved. I explained to her that President Thein Sein had un-blacklisted me after 17 years. She encouraged me to return to Burma to carry on with my work.

And so, here I am, to listen, observe, ask questions, reflect, learn and mature my understanding of nonviolent struggle. And do what I can to bring the truth of your struggle to the world. That is why I am creating a new set of books—a four volume series—as a sequel to The Voice of Hope, as well as a feature documentary film on your country's ongoing struggle for freedom. In both the books and film, U Tin Oo, U Win Htein, U Win Tin, U Aye Win, and all of you and many others will be featured. We will call it Burma's Voices of Freedom and it will include as many voices as possible. I am asking what should we know about Burma? How should we understand what is going on here, now? What is reality versus propaganda? How to know the difference? How do you keep hope alive? How did you keep it alive in prison? And what can the international community do to help your people? So many questions. With that said, I would like to take a few minutes today to talk about these issues and whatever else you may wish to share. And most of all, share my love and respect for you all. Thank you for your courage. Thank you for caring. Thank you for speaking with me. And thank you Daw Suu for making this remarkable meeting possible.

Dr.MM: Thank you. So, you are practicing meditation?

AC: Yes, I'd say that silent meditation is my lifeblood, but I'd like to add, my greater interest—my true passion—is in taking meditation and mindfulness out of the monastery and integrating it as fully as possible into everything I do, my speech, my actions, especially in my interactions with other people. Daw Suu told me back in 1995 that she called this practice "active *mettā*" (loving-kindness) and "active *karunā*" (compassion); active *muditā* (sympathetic joy); active *uppekā* (equanimity); something I've been calling the practice of "*Dhamma* intelligence, or mindful intelligence." So that my *Dhamma* life becomes an expression of interactive meditation, or the development of *pāramī*, the active cultivation of beautiful and liberating states of mind.

DrMM: Yes, it's called *pāramī*. So very nice to hear you speak this way.

AC: Thank you. Allow me to ask a long-awaited question: Has your peaceful revolution succeeded?

UWH: We have a long way to go but things are very much different.

AC: There have been so many atrocities. You have been tortured. Do you seek revenge?

UWH: No. Revenge is not in our agenda.

AC: I forgot to ask if you are okay that with the cameras? Our goal is to create a feature documentary film for the world to have an intimate look into the nature of your peoples ongoing struggle for democracy, from those at the center of the revolution. This film will be important at this time when the power of violence is the predominant measure of a nation's worth.

DrMM: *(Laughs)* Our military intelligence took our photo so many times in prison!

AC: *(Laughs)* In other words, your face is well known? May I ask, how many of you were political prisoners?

DrMM: In total, five of us.

AC: What was your crime? And how long were you in prison?

U KYAW THI HA: I served three years in prison because in Mandalay University--

UWH: He was a tutor at Mandalay University, in the history department.

AC: Why was teaching history a crime?

UKTH: It was not for crime. It was because my students and my colleagues, all of us went to the revolution about the USDP party, the socialist program party. We didn't like that administration. We didn't like the army dictator. We did not like the administration. We were against it and organized a strike. I got three years' in prison for that strike.

AC: Courageous! [to DKT] And what was your crime?

UWH: At that time, she was a young girl. She was not politically active. She received only the occasional interrogation. She was most fortunate.

AC: [to UWH] Why did you go to prison in '97?

UWH: It was their necessity. See, in 1997, the military was supreme and General Khin Nyunt conducted all kinds of political agendas. At that time, in May to be exact, we tried to organize a big event celebrating the

1990 "free and fair" election. Daw Aung San Suu Kyi and our staff invited all remaining MPs, all elected persons, to come to Rangoon and discuss our future. When they arrived, all were rounded up. Even one man, after hiring a car to Rangoon, was stopped on the way and turned back to his hometown, either taken to prison or to the police station or an army unit, then imprisoned. No one was spared. Everyone was rounded up. That's why this is their necessity, not our crime! *(Laughing)* We can laugh it off!

AC: You can, can't you?

UWH: Yes, and quite easily.

DrMM: The military regime thought that freedom of expression and freedom of speech were crimes.

UWH: Not only that, freedom of thought, like in George Orwell's *1984*.

DrMM: Anybody who revolted at the time, it was seen as a crime.

UWH: And we were all punished for our evil thoughts, so to speak, against Big Brother. Because in *1984*, Big Brother is watching you, everywhere—even in your toilet!

(All laugh).

AC: The first rule of revolution: keep your sense of humor?

UWH: Indeed. And we have done all we can to keep our sense of humour. We tried to keep it all the time in prison. In fact, it kept us alive, mentally and physically. Still, many broke down; changed their mind; changed their belief. Some gave up their political life. Those who remained—committed to the struggle, to the revolution—were less than 50 percent.

DrMM: Along with humor, meditation was an active part of our prison life.

UWH: Yes, we meditated every day.

DrMM: Yes, every day. To overcome our stress, to release our stress, while suffering so many sufferings. The conditions were horrible. We were apart from our family. When I was detained, my youngest daughter was only 18 months old. She couldn't even call me papa or father. When I was released from prison, she was a medical student.

AC: What we take for granted.

DrMM: When she saw me the first time, she did not call me Papa.

UWH: He was a stranger.

AC: How many of you have children?

DrMM: Everybody here except those three, they're unmarried.

AC: And how long were you in prison?

DrLM: For 11 years.

AC: And may I ask, what was the charge against you?

DrLM: I was sentenced due to my NLD Youth organization. The authorities came to our offices--

UWH: The problem was she was sentenced to seven years, but when the time was up, she was questioned again. When they discovered she wasn't broken—that she hadn't lost her convictions in the NLD—she was put under what they call Section 10. Without any decision by the judges, she was given an additional one-year detention. They did this four times in a row.

DrLM: For a total of 11 years in prison. And for what? Organizing the youth to participate in active democracy and our nonviolent struggle for human rights.

AC: The contrast is so striking: a nonviolent struggle for freedom versus violent authoritarian to subjugate freedom.

UWH: Definitely.

DrMM: There is simply no rule of law in this country.

UWH: That's why last week we had a symposium in a hotel, organized by the UN and EU, where the title of the discussion was 'Rule of Law.'

AC: It's so helter-skelter here. Or should I say, psychotic. I met a woman recently at U Tin Oo's home who had been picked up and later imprisoned while walking around the Shwedagon Pagoda, and this was done six months after she announced to a few people that she had made a *dāna*, a contribution, for Daw Suu's birthday.

UWH: When they tried to organize the youth, they rounded up hundreds of young people. They were put in the back of lorries and dispatched east, west, south, north—everywhere out of Rangoon city. When far out of town, they were ordered to get off the trucks and onto the road. Then they were told to start walking back to their homes.

AC: To torture them?

UWH: Yes, to torture them.

DrMM: It's a form of mental torture and of course, physical as well.

UWH: Many were dumped off in the cemetery.

DTN: Later at night, when they were in bed, they came and arrested many more.

AC: Who was behind this barbarity? Who orders this cruelty?

(All laugh).

DTN: Who else—dictator Ne Win.

UWH: At first it was all organized by U Ne Win, it was believed, and later U Ne Win and Than Shwe fell apart. He was the reason for Than Shwe's captivity, and later he was the authority who could just say, "smash them."

AC: Who put Ne Win under house arrest?

UWH: General Than Shwe.

DTN: First was U Ne Win; in 1998 it was U Ne Win.

*"The generals thought that they
were superior to ordinary humans."*

ALAN CLEMENTS: Almost everyone in the world knows that human rights violations have occurred in Burma. We also know the different types of torture that have been used against your people. They have been documented by human rights organizations. And you all know those techniques as well as anyone. You have been tortured. But what we don't know or know very little about, is the mind of the dictator, the mind of the torturer. Why do dictators and torturers torture? Why do they commit atrocities and gross violations of human rights? Why? The only way to stop it, perhaps, is to address the core issue within human consciousness. That is one question. Another question that I am asked all the time is, 'Why did the people of Burma treat their own people so cruelly?' And lastly, how did Burma get this way?

UWH: Yes, important questions. And it's a very, very sad chapter in our history.

AC: Was it the oppression of your people by British occupation for 124 years?

DrMM: No, it has little to do with the British.

UWH: It's our own mentality. I remember us talking about this back in 1995 when we were at Daw Aung San Suu Kyi's residence. It's like when there was apartheid in South Africa—whites against blacks. But in our country, it was the military who thought they were superior and the rest of us must listen to them, must obey them. That's why here, what is happening, is the ideology of apartheid. Do you remember those discussions?

AC: Yes. I remember that—*ideological apartheid*—where people are divided and oppressed based on race, gender, class, and so on. But that was 20 years ago. And now?

UOK: In our case, the generals think they are superior to us ordinary humans.

AC: Where did this thinking originate?

DrMM: Be clear, it did not originate from General Aung San (Daw Aung San Suu Kyi's father and founder of Burma's army). It came from General Ne Win.

DTN: Yes. From Ne Win. From the 1962 coup d'état onwards.

AC: So, he got ambitious and then became utterly corrupted?

UWH: Yes. Power corrupts. Absolute power corrupts absolutely.

DTN: And after him, U Than Shwe is even worse.

AC: We're only a few miles from his bunker? Or is it palace? Perhaps it's both?

UWH: It's a palace, a huge one.

AC: Has anyone seen him, spoken with him, been to his home?

UWH: No, we met some people who've been to his residence, paying homage by doing chores. This is our tradition, to pay respect to elders. Some ex-generals and some ex-ministers were there.

AC: Is he still in control of the country and the military?

DTN: We think so.

U OHN KYAING: Yes, we think so.

AC: Does it concern you that he may still be in control?

UWH: No, not a bit.

AC: Do you take it into consideration when you have talks in Parliament?

UOK: No, nothing.

AC: So, it's there but it's irrelevant? When I was here in '95 and '96 I asked the same question to Daw Suu, U Tin Oo, U Kyi Maung, and to you (U Win Htein) and to others as well: "Is the old man (New Win) across the lake still in control?" Everyone would say similar things to what you just said. And it turned out that he was still very much in control. He put all your leader and several of you back in prison.

UWH: Yes, that's true.

AC: If that was true today but we could learn from the past, what would be different today, in your thinking or behaviour or in your way of making decisions, or going about the actions of bringing about democracy to your country? What would you do differently knowing the past? It happened in '95, and '96, and '97—he appointed Than Shwe and look where we are today. We still think Than Shwe is in control. What would be different? How would you behave differently knowing the past could reoccur, as it's said?

UWH: Well, what we say today, whenever we speak to the foreign correspondents or the political MPs from England or Australia, is that we have definitely answered that question: we are cautiously optimistic. We haven't abandoned trust in the system because we have perceived it for so many years and in so many forms—still, we still cannot believe them and trust them 100 percent.

AC: Let me ask you this: I know that I've been wronged in life by certain people, and, as a result, I felt upset and hurt. Let me put it this way: I have a daughter. If someone harmed her, I don't know how I could control my anger. How do you control your very human impulse for revenge and how do you control your anger, if you even feel it at all?

DrMM: We take refuge in our *Dhamma*, in cause and effect, in birth and death. These facts of life are firmly with us. There is no doubt that Than Shwe will be suffering now for what he has done in the past. He has done many evils. Unless he is devoid of conscience, which I doubt, he will be suffering from what he has done in the past. We do not take pride or joy in this. It is simply the effect of his evil. This is a *Dhamma* principle.

AC: So, it's with that knowledge you can relax your *dosa* (anger)?

DrMM: Yes. Through that reflection anger ceases.

AC: Do you take it even further? For instance, do you hold the Buddhist belief that because of his *karma*, that when he passes away, he'll take a lower rebirth as a *peta*, a lower being, a hungry ghost, destined to live in one of the hell realms suffering for aeons of time based on his evil behavior in this life?

DrMM: Yes.

DTN: The truth is simple: we've suffered, most of the people have suffered, and we have suffered for so many years—50 years. We've been overwhelmed by suffering.

DrMM: I met with another trial while in prison. In total my imprisonment was for 37 years. But in 1988, many students came to prison with 65-year sentences. And they were treated much more severely than me. This was another case of *pāramī*—mindful of their pain while encouraging patience and compassion. A challenging situation.

AC: Daw Aung Suu speaks of restorative justice, not punitive justice; is there a Truth Council on the horizon?

UWH: Not yet.

AC: Is it taboo to talk about it?

UWH: It's not taboo, but we're still not advising or making formulations to set up a truth council.

DrMM: In South Africa they set up a truth-finding commission, not for retribution, not for revenge, but for the truth.

AC: Why don't the top people just come out and say, 'Listen, we made mistakes; we were deluded; we apologize.'

DrMM: Too early to apologize.

UWH: Most of us don't put emphasis a need for apology. Let bygones be bygones.

AC: Is that a Buddhist thing, or simply skilful political reasoning?

UWH: A Buddhist thing.

DrMM: The path of patience, of tolerance for what they have done to us; this is the proper path in Buddhism. Yet, our leader Daw Aung San Suu Kyi has said that while she can forgive what they have done to her, she cannot forgive what they have done to our country.

AC: Interesting.

DrMM: That's important. For what they've done, they must apologize to the country.

AC: And you all feel that way?

UOK: Yes.

DrMM: They've destroyed the mindset of our people. The primary objective, the top crime of the military, is to maintain their power lifelong, forever, eternal.

UOK: U Ne Win was furious after the 1988 uprising—he wanted to hold power for his whole life. After the people revolted against the military dictator, he became furious. Therefore, he punished the people *intentionally*. He intentionally tortured the whole nation. There were very bad events in our country after the 1988 revolt. He crushed, intentionally, the NLD and the leadership of the NLD.

For me, I became the second-in-line leader after 1989, after Daw Aung San Suu Kyi, U Win Tin, and U Tin Oo were arrested. I became a close assistant to U Kyi Maung. In 1990, after the elections, we asked Khin Nyunt to abide by his promise to convene Parliament and transfer power to the elected body, but he refused to abide by that promise. We said, 'You lied to the people.' Therefore, U Kyi Maung was arrested. Then all of us were arrested. They had no evidence of crime. He lied to the people and we accused him of being a liar. Therefore, I was arrested and sentenced to 17 years in prison.

DrMM: Our military government set up the basic principles to write the Constitution. The sixth principle is that they will lead national politics in our country—the military has a leading role in our national politics. They wrote it according to that principle, so that the 2008 Constitution states that the military has a leading role. The chief-of-staff is superior to the president.

AC: So, this is not a constitution.

DrMM: Yes, this is not a constitution. It's like a prison ward.

"They tried to get legitimacy internationally, but it was not successful."

U WIN HTEIN: In our party's manifesto, we have three objectives. The first objective is to establish rule of law. The second objective is to gain a permanent peace with the ethnic people. The third objective is to amend the Constitution to suit a future democratic nation. We're going to amend it, sooner or later. That's our objective.

You'll be interested in why the change occurred. When the election was held in November and they formed a new government in early 2012, they tried to get legitimacy internationally, but it was not successful. They found out that without Daw Aung San Suu Kyi's participation, they won't go far in their objectives. That's why, at the same time, Daw Aung San Suu Kyi was seeking ways to have communication with them, to have a dialogue with them.

Then the one thing that occurred was that our party was made illegal, so we didn't recognize the Constitution, and we didn't participate in 2010 election. That's why our party was illegal. And then in July, the Ministry of the Interior wrote to our headquarters, stating that our headquarters was conducting political propaganda, issuing pamphlets and doing certain things that were not proper for a registered party. They asked us to stop our activities. So we wrote back, stating that we were acting as a legal party since we are the party who won the 1990 election. And in the last paragraph we included Daw Aung San Suu Kyi's suggestion that we ask the government authorities to meet with her.

After a few weeks, they appointed a minister as a liaison officer between the government and the NLD. After meeting with Daw Aung San Suu Kyi and U Aung Gyi, President Thein Sein invited Daw Suu to meet in August 2011. That was the opening of the gate from all the oppression. After that, our political activities became easier and they agreed to amend the election law. Because of these amendments we agreed to register our party legally. Then we participated in the by-election. So, they changed their attitude to us, as well as to Daw Aung San Suu's ability and value to grasp the moment.

ALAN CLEMENTS: Let me ask you this: even if the amendment takes place in the Constitution and, say, Daw Aung San Suu Kyi becomes president, still the military is above the president, and they can act in any way the general of the army wishes, right?

UOK: They can dissolve the Parliament.

AC: So, this is clearly not a democracy. This is the pretence of a democracy by a dictator or disguised totalitarianism. Let me ask you this; how to get the military to belong to civilian rule and not to the commander-in-chief of the military?

UWH: Well, according to Daw Aung San Suu Kyi's ideas and her suggestion to us, we are making friends with a lot of USDP MPs, as well as the military MPs, with the intention of changing their mindset. So, NLD people are not revolutionary, we are here to help rebuild the mindset of country.

AC: Revolutionary psychologists? *Dhamma* in action? It's back to the ideological apartheid issue—how to overcome that? How to evolve that meme out of the soul, so to speak?

UWH: Exactly. That's the challenge!

AC: So, it really is the next phase of Burma's revolution of the spirit. It really is a heart/consciousness opening, the building of a liberation ideology that frees the spirit from the bondage of fear and greed driven control.

UWH: Yes. We're keeping it simple at the moment. Some of them are now realizing that we've come to Parliament with the intention of doing good for the country. We're not there to make trouble or seek revenge. For instance, two months ago, there was a crisis in Parliament, a constitutional crisis concerned with the constitutional tribunal. That tribunal was appointed by the president, and the problem occurred that all the parliamentary communities must have authority as union-level ministers. But the tribunal banned the decision of the president and other people. They decided it is not union level. It was before our arrival in Parliament, when the USDP MPs were furious and demanded to impeach the constitutional tribunal. When we joined Parliament, this debate was brewing, going on.

So, we studied the law and we found that the decision of the constitutional tribunal was against the law. That's why we agreed to go along with the USDP MPs. However, at the same time, Daw Aung San Suu Kyi would like to have a solution, a negotiation of a settlement. Yet the USDP refused.

Still, when these ideas were discussed in Parliament, many MPs, especially from the military, found out that we were not against anybody. We were on the side of which is right or wrong with the law. They recognized this, and we gained a lot of prestige because of the crisis, although the agreement was passed and the tribunal, the whole bunch, was kicked out of the system. Now we have to rebuild the constitutional tribunal.

Another thing was that, according to the Constitution, those people who are in the high echelon of government must not have political appointment. But, three months ago, the USDP had a national conference. At that conference, many of them agreed that their chairperson should be Thura Shwe Mann. But on that particular day, President Thein Sein arrived and announced himself as the chairman. This is against the law. So, we put that question to Parliament: 'Please make a revision of the Constitution whether a president should be the chairperson of the USDP.' So, this question will be put to a constitutional tribunal which is not in existence yet! *(Laughs)* It is still to be formed.

'Two things kept him alive—reflecting on his integrity,
and contemplating the Dhamma.'

ALAN CLEMENTS: If there's a single most important thing that you've learned as a freedom fighter and a peaceful revolutionary, what is it? And how have you learned to cope with difficulty? Where does your source your resilience? Or if you prefer, what is the single most important piece of advice you wish to give future revolutionaries, from the unthinkable lessons that you've learned from your many years of struggle for freedom and democracy?

Dr MYINT MAUNG: The most important thing for me is meditation. The *Dhamma*.

AC: What does meditation mean to you? What does the *Dhamma* mean to you?

DrMM: It means practicing birth and death in daily life, every day, every hour, all the time. Just birth and death, all the time. It also means practicing compassion. Our oppressors also have suffering. They won't easily escape their suffering. Further, they are faced with death. Everybody is. We must have compassion for them, as they are conditioned creatures, like all of us.

UWH: U Kyaw Thi Ha took part in the 1988 strike and when he was put in jail, he kept his faith. He knew that what we did was right. And he knew what the government did was wrong. He kept his confidence intact and that kept him alive. The meditation came later.

AC: So, reflection on his convictions in knowing right from wrong. An abiding faith in his integrity, his *sīla* (right conduct)?

UWH: Yes. And Phyo Min Thein here lost his youth in prison. He was arrested at the age of 20 and released at 35. Two things kept him alive: one thing was keeping his integrity intact, like U Kyaw Thi Ha said. The second thing was contemplation on *Dhamma*, on the character of the situation, the consequences that everyone must deal with in being human.

When the young students marched in front of the hospital, Dr May Lwin Myint came out to observe them. Someone, a doctor, remarked that "those children are more courageous than us." That remark incited her to participate in the struggle. Then she became elected in the 1990 election, but only then she was arrested, and only then did she realize that she was dutiful to the party, to the politics of freedom and democracy. But on the other hand, she was not dutiful to her husband, to her children, and to her parents. That's why she had remorse. During the day she could reflect about what should be done to the family, but during the night she dared not think about them. Otherwise, she'd lose her mind. But, like the other gentleman said, there are two things: belief in political duty and belief in karma.

UOK: I have three points I'd like to share. One is my practice of meditation. It allowed me to survive the pressure from the jailers. Another thing is to have a totally clear conscience. I have no guilt because there was no crime. I worked for my people. I worked for my leaders, I worked for freedom. I was dutiful. Principled. Another thing is I'm a journalist. In prison I released news bulletins weekly! *(Laughs)* I worked hard for my journal. I stealthily got a radio transmitter in prison.

DrMM: Me too!

UOK: With the help of my friends I built one into the wall. At night I took out my transistor, a digital radio (a small one). We kept it hidden in the day and took it out in the night to listen to the news. As such, we were punished to another seven years!

UOK: *(Laughs)* Another seven years!

UWH: After two years they found it.

DrMM: They found it and we took the pamphlets we'd made and put them under the table.

AC: Where did you get the parts to make it?

DrMM: Smuggled them in. Some of our sympathetic jailers brought them in, after we bribed them.

UOK: We gave them bribes!

UWH: *(Laughs)* Corruption!

AC: Anti-corruption corruption.

DrMM: At that time, a digital radio cost 10,000 kyats, and we bribed them with another 10,000 kyats for them to pick it up. We paid 20,000 kyats in total!

UWH: We encouraged nonviolent corruption and bribery!

DrMM: *(Laughs)* But it was for the betterment of the people!

UOK: And then every Monday I released a news bulletin, news pamphlet, for my revolutionary comrades.

DrMM: We were in touch with the outside world, what they had done, what our party had done, and what our leader was talking about.

UOK: Therefore, I was always busy!

UWH: We didn't have time to worry about anything.

DTN: Only news for the pamphlet.

AC: So, you lived a dangerous life in prison?

UWH: Yes. We were walking on the edge.

AC: What do you do with your fear?

DrMM: We are familiar with a dangerous life. The greater the risks, the better the day was in prison! *(Laughs)* This is true.

AC: Revolution in action, even behind bars.

DrMM: Yes. We are always struggling for freedom and democracy.

UOK: I have to say one thing. I was released in 2005, after 15 years in prison. In 2008 I was arrested again and sent back to jail. But I have no fear—the prison masters became my friends. When I arrived back to the old jail, they welcomed me back again! There was no fear at all. I felt like I was returning to my nephew's home or something like that *(laughs)*.

DAW PHYU THEIN: [Burmese]

UWH: Daw Phyu Thein's detainment in jail was not very long, only a few months. But since she was quite young, she felt very agitated and angry. She could not right the captivity of the jail. But later she considered her political belief, plus she tried to convey loving kindness to those people, to everybody. And at first it was not successful. Gradually when it became successful, she felt very peaceful in her mind. Another factor was that when she was in jail, she found out there were so many people like her in the women's ward and men's ward, thousands and thousands of people 'all suffering like me,' so why not her? These are the consideration that right the captivity. That take fear and anger out of the situation.

AC: How did she practice *mettā* in the prison? What did she do?

UWH: At first, she thought about the most undesirable people in her mind's eye. Then she would send them loving-kindness.

DrMM: Sending *mettā* is also a *pāramī*, one of the ten *pāramitās* in our *Dhamma*.

AC: In South Africa, the Robben Island Prison, where Nelson Mandela was incarcerated, was turned into a world heritage site. Why not, in Parliament, recommend closing Insein Prison and turning it into a heritage site?

DrMM: If you want to make a heritage site, consider multiple ones—all the prisons in the entire country!

UWH: That's correct!

DrMM: You agree! *(Laughs).*

UWH: I went to five prisons!

*"Peaceful revolution is the norm
of future revolutions."*

ALAN CLEMENTS: Clearly you and your colleagues are nonviolent revolutionaries. You're now members of government but you know revolution. It's in your blood. There are many young girls and boys around the world who feel a growing discontent with some aspect of society, with their governments, and their politics. My question, similar to before: If you were to pass on a single piece of advice to people who watch this film and read our new books, to the new revolutionaries around the world in all cultures, what would you encourage them to remember as they proceed down the path to confront injustice and ideological apartheid, and perhaps dictatorship itself, nonviolently? What would you say?

PMT: [Burmese]

UWH: Violent revolution will not prevail. Peaceful revolution is the norm of future revolutions.

AC: So, always remain peaceful in your mind regardless of how violent the resistance may be?

UWH: Yes.

AC: And how to keep this peace in one's heart when they are hurting, torturing and killing your people? How do non-Buddhists keep this peace in one's heart under cruel circumstances?

PMT: [Burmese]

UWH: He personally experienced, as an NLD leader, seeing people shot down and dying in his own hands. Yet, his faith was such that he understood only peaceful revolution can rebuild our nation, only peaceful revolution will succeed in ushering in democratic norms. He said that if he had participated or asked people to participate in violent revolution, he would not get anywhere. That's his understanding.

DKT: [Burmese]

UWH: To look at the things that are happening and try to find out what's correct or right, and then try to organize people with the same belief. Only then will one be able to proceed, for the future. She's a lawyer. She's offering lawyerly insight.

AC: Thank you. Others?

UKTH: [Burmese]

UWH: His way is that whatever cause one may believe in, bring people together, bring everyone in the country together. Never abandon them. What he didn't mention is that he doesn't have respect for the people outside the country. The thing is that the struggle can only go on within the country, not from outside. As precedent, Daw Aung San Suu Kyi can go anywhere at any time, but she refuses to leave. She continues her struggle inside the country. That's the main point. And be with the people all the time. Stand in solidarity with people.

DTN: [Burmese]

UWH: At the moment we have the 2008 Constitution, whether we like it or not. Before that we didn't have any paper, any contract, any constitution. Because of the Constitution, we, part of our governing body of the country, are to be punished because of the election. So there are still struggles to be waged in the future, a lot of political space to move around in. But she will put emphasis on the point that those who stayed away and live in other countries try and give assistance, morally and physically, materially, to the people who are suffering inside the country.

AC: Are you also saying you would like the people from your country who are living overseas to come home?

DTN: No. They can stay where they like, that depends on them. But they must participate as much as possible.

AC: Others? The world wants to know your revolutionary advice.

DrMM: Every young person has a revolutionary spirit, but don't use that revolutionary mind in every situation. Use your revolutionary mind for the betterment of the people and the betterment of the country. Then be prepared for transition.

DrLM: [Burmese]

UWH: She said we have to suffer for the future. It may be a quite a long way away, but the main thing is to get the support of the Myanmar family.

AC: When I became a monk, Mahasi Sayadaw said to me, 'You have now given up one family, and now you belong to the *Dhamma* family, to the *Saṅgha*.' And Sayadaw U Pandita, when we saw each other the other day for the first time in 17 years, he said, 'We're family in four ways, by shared humanness, by *Dhamma*, by birth and by *Saṃsāra*.' My question is that when I saw Daw Suu and spoke with her in '95, there was the belief that she gave up one family—Michael, Kim, Alexander—or rather that she chose not to give it up, but put it in perspective of the family of people from her country. And then, even more, the family of her shared values, freedom, democracy, human rights, integrity. Is that graduation from nuclear family to political democratic family something that you talk and think about?

UWH: This happens automatically, because in Parliament, since we're involved in our struggle since 1988 or 1990, we consider ourselves part of a family. We've in-got jokes and everything, and we treat people like our own brothers and sisters. People were astonished with how we were so close.

UOK: For me, the history of mankind teaches us that anarchy and tyranny are quite dangerous for mankind. We must take a very balanced pathway to democracy. Every day we must move carefully against tyranny and against anarchy. If someone introduced anarchy into society, automatically a tyrant will come. I believe that. Therefore, our leader is practicing a very balanced path to democracy.

AC: Let us close, please. May your democracy become a bright shining example of a spiritually infused compassionate expression of peace and goodwill. May the everyone come together in national reconciliation. As you said, let the past be and may everyone move boldly into the future. May all forms of freedom thrive and be respected by rule of law. May forgiveness prevail. And thank you all for taking time from your busy lives to speak with me and to the world through our books and film. From my heart to yours, thank you. *Sadhu, Sadhu, Sadhu.*

UWH: If we can ask, what is the real impression you have after talking with us today?

AC: That's a beautiful question. I feel like I have met members of an expanded family of nonviolent freedom fighters. I feel inspired. You've given me hope to live more freely, more compassionately, more forgiving, more dedicated to the well-being of others. You have given me one of the greatest gifts of my life.

UWH: It's our turn to say *Sadhu, Sadhu, Sadhu.*

CHAPTER 12

CONVERSATION *with* U AYE WIN

February 2013

- "You can chop the branches off the old tree..."
- "What I did was meditate—my teacher was U Win Htein."
- "We never thought we'd betrayed our country."

Conversations with U Aye Win, Aung San Suu Kyi's cousin and one of her closest colleagues in the National League for Democracy. U Aye Win managed Aung San Suu Kyi's foreign press engagements and worked as her secretary and aide. Many view his later arrest as an emotional intimidation of Aung San Suu Kyi. He served seven years, and, like many other political prisoners, his health suffered greatly as a result. Despite such hardship, he has remained a staunch advocate of democracy. In this candid interview, he recounts his time with the NLD and his time in prison.

'You can chop the branches off the old tree...'

ALAN CLEMENTS: I'm happy to see you. It's been 17 years; a long time. I have many memories of your calm, joyous and dignified presence. You helped me so much. You are a courageous man. I hope your heart and health and spirit are good and strong. How long were you in prison?

U AYE WIN: I was imprisoned for five years. There were five of us arrested under the same section, Section 10(a), and 10(b). Under 10(b) you can stay in your own house, under house arrest, but under 10(a) you must go to prison. I was 10(a).

AC: What was the charge?

UAW: No charge—with this section there's no charge.

AC: Yet another arbitrary detention under dictatorship?

UAW: Yes. They do as they wish. The section itself is to prevent so called danger to the state, or something like that. There are no charges and you don't go to court.

AC: From home to prison without charge or trial?

UAW: Yes. First, they took me to military intelligence.

AC: A dark hole for interrogation?

UAW: Yes. Then after about two months they took me to prison.

AC: What did they want from you? As you were the media liaison for the international press, a prominent position in the NLD, surely they must have already known everything—every phone call you had was tapped?

UAW: Yes, of course.

AC: They wanted to punish you for your commitment to freedom and democracy?

UAW: Yes. Daw Suu called it 'emotional blackmail,' against her.

AC: This is what she said to you?

UAW: Yes. Those who are near her, those who help her, they punish us to punish her.

AC: How did your wife and family get on without you? Who took care of them?

UAW: The person who gave support was my sister. She was brilliant.

AC: Are things different in Burma now, politically speaking?

UAW: I hope so. But like you said, they know everything. They know absolutely everything. But see, I'm not involved in the political sector anymore. I looked after finance and some domestic administration, and, of course, the liaison with foreigners. That's the reason what I was imprisoned. But even back when we met, the authorities knew that I was not involved in political activities.

AC: Just to get back at Daw Suu. So wrong to treat those around her this way when, in fact, all she has ever called for is rule of law and peace and harmony among all. She has never sought revenge or persecution. To the contrary, she is often criticized for her kindness to the military.

UAW: We, the Burmese people, have a saying, 'you can chop the branches off the old tree.'

AC: In other words, this originated from Ne Win?

UAW: Everything came from Ne Win, in recent history.

AC: How long has it been since you were released?

UAW: About 11 years. I was released in 2001. I was arrested on May 26th, 1996, then taken to MI (military intelligence), then transferred to prison on June 15th and released five years later.

AC: When did you see Daw Suu again?

UAW: When she was released from detention, I forget the year, she visited us because my mother is her aunt. At that time, we spoke. Then, yet again, as she was doing her political activities, she was rearrested and put under house arrest, under 10(b). You know that affair. I forget the name of the incident. At that time, she was nearly killed.

AC: The Depayin Massacre?

UAW: Yes. I think so.

AC: Were you allowed visits in prison?

UAW: No. My family could not visit. Because of this special section, I was supposed to be a very dangerous person. Therefore, I was forbidden contact with my family.

AC: You saw none of your family for five years?

UAW: Yes, for five years. When the ICRC were allowed to come to the prison for the first time, they made a list of all the political prisoners and their basic question was, 'When were you charged, sentenced, and how many years?' I said I was never charged, and I was never sentenced. We were categorized not as prisoners but as detainees. Because of this I was not allowed visitors. But there was some consolation, like I didn't have to wear a prison uniform.

AC: I guess there is always some good in everyone.

UAW: Nor did I have to follow the rules. I was just locked away.

AC: They just locked you in and left you there?

UAW: Just locked you in. Just like that. Like an animal in a zoo. We always thought about it like that, in our little cell. Just like a caged animal.

AC: Your friends, were they near?

UAW: Yes, all five of us, the group, under 10(a).

AC: Who were they?

UAW: One was Kyaw Min (he was an architect). He died. Another was U Thein Tin. You may not know him.

AC: All were NLD (National League for Democracy)?

UAW: Yes. He also died during the detention. And another was U Moe Thu. He was a film director, writer and editor. He's still alive. And another was U Soe Thein. He's alive. And U Wun Tha. He was a journalist and quite prominent. Unfortunately, he got lung cancer. But he's surviving, for now. All five of us were in the same cell. And all other political prisoners they arrested and paraded through court and sentenced were moved on. Our cell block was a transit deeper into Insein, the prison complex.

AC: Of course, based on the accounts of all of you—as political activists—the prison is notorious worldwide for its despicable conditions, violent abuse of inmates, and lethal use of mental and physical torture. My heart breaks listening to you. So, all five of you were in one cell?

UAW: No, not one cell, but one cell block. According to their logic, you see, we were never allowed company in our cells.

AC: No company and no visitors?

UAW: Family could give food parcels. But we could never meet with them, see their faces.

AC: You didn't see your wife for five years?

UAW: Not exactly. Because I was hospitalized twice, and at that time they allowed my family to visit me in the hospital. Other than these short hospital breaks, I didn't see my wife or children for five years.

"What I did was meditate. My teacher was U Win Htein."

ALAN CLEMENTS: The courage you folks have to fight for freedom is awe inspiring. I think it's fair to say that many millions of people worldwide—those who have been following your nonviolent revolution from '88 onward—are cautiously celebrating your country's transition from dictatorship to democracy. Let me ask you directly: what should we believe about Burma today? Is this the true emergence of genuine democracy? Or is it yet another disguise of dictatorship, totalitarianism with a facade?

U AYE WIN: It's not what it was, but we're not sure what the future will bring. There is visible progress, but the future is unknown. Not even Daw Suu can say exactly.

AC: Are you active in politics?

UAW: Not active, because of the health problems I have. I cannot go to Daw Suu's house alone. I must have help to walk. I can't move much. My vertebrae are fused. Not only in my neck. Pretty much my whole side, more or less.

AC: This is a result of your time in prison?

UAW: Yes, because of my time in prison. If I had medical attention soon enough, it wouldn't be like this. There are many people with the same problem, but if they get attended to there is no problem. It's a very simply thing, you see. This problem I have was only identified the second time I was hospitalized. If you keep your limbs moving, it won't happen.

AC: Oh, the cruelty. I often think of how to get dictators and those who work for them to see the blindness of their ways? Perhaps putting themselves in prison for a stretch would awaken them. Or better yet, a three-month intensive meditation retreat would humble them. If they could only see the value of it. Oh well. Do you speak with Daw Suu very much?

UAW: No, not much. She's so busy it's almost impossible to get time to speak with her. When she was released, this last time, we did meet occasionally. But afterwards, her schedule became somewhat overwhelming.

AC: I'm told Desmond Tutu is here visiting with her today.

UAW: I didn't know that. Due to my health crisis, I've had to step way back from day-to-day involvement. Back when we worked closely together, prior to prison, I had breakfast with her five days a week, and was with her every day of the week.

AC: Do you talk to your brother, Dr. Sein Win (the former Prime Minister in exile)?

UAW: No. He's still in Washington.

AC: Do you think he'll come back to Burma?

UAW: That I can't say. I think it's all very complicated.

AC: How many brothers and sisters do you have? And how many are alive?

UAW: Altogether there are six of us, including me. And five of us are alive. My eldest brother passed away only about five months ago.

AC: And the others are living in Burma?

UAW: Yes, except Sein Win.

AC: And the others, they're politically active?

UAW: My sister lives here for about six months of the year, and the other months in the States, because her children are there.

AC: How do you get your news about Burma, and about your cousin, Daw Suu?

UAW: All the usual ways—television, radio, newspaper. There is also a weekly published by the NLD.

AC: U Tin Oo; I was asking him about you, and he says, 'Please go see Aye Win,' and of course I was going to see you. And I went to see U Win Htein in Naypyidaw. I met him and eight other MPs; he said, 'You must see U Aye Win, you must see U Aye Win.' He's also very different now, you know? He walks with a cane. He also had a hard time in prison.

UAW: We are all old now, you see? I'm now 74.

AC: When did you join the freedom struggle? Were you with Daw Suu from the beginning, in 1988?

UAW: I only joined the movement in '96. You see, we had some under-standing before she was arrested for the first time. I resigned from a post, I was a director at that time, in the government service. I resigned so that I could help her. But the very day she was arrested, on July 20th, I got my release from active service, so we didn't have any contact. Then in the 1990 election, the day before the election, the NLD CC requested me to act as her representative and I accepted. But she was disqualified by the commission. So that was the end...

AC: The end of that career?

UAW: *(Laughs)* Yes, and when she was released, I immediately joined her. Because at that time I was no longer a government servant. I had my own practice—I'm an auditor—and when you're self-employed you can do what you like.

AC: I know that what you did for me—providing appointments to speak with Daw Suu—you also did for other journalists. But I never asked you what you did the rest of the time.

UAW: I stayed at her house, pretty much full time. At that time, I was fully immersed in activities at her house. I never went to my office. I still had an active audit practice, and I kept my office in downtown, but it was run by my staff.

AC: What did you do for the NLD and for Daw Suu?

UAW: One part of my job was finances and accounting, expenditures and things. I also did all the cheques for her, then converted them into Burmese Kyats. Of course, making sure everything was above board. And another thing was arranging appointments with journalists.

AC: You're sort of smiling now...

UAW: That was a full-time job. The telephone was ringing all the time, and at that time there was no Internet, you see?

AC: That's right, I remember. And no mobile phones either.

UAW: Letters and the telephone. I usually went to her house at about 8:30am, had lunch with her, then returned to my home about 6:30pm or 7pm. As I said, my business was run by my staff, but once I was arrested it went to shambles.

AC: So, all of Daw Suu's appointments were done through you at that time?

UAW: Yes, all done by me. Foreign press, diplomats, everyone. Everything foreign was my responsibility. Everything local was handled by U Win Htein. But we were in the same room, and the appointments I made I had to tell him, and the appointments he made, he had to tell me. We had a very good working relationship and great coordination.

AC: You two are as good as it gets. What you have had to deal with to bring freedom to your country. What a challenge.

UAW: There are many, many people who sacrificed more than me.

AC: How did you occupy yourself in prison? Were you allowed books? Could you write?

UAW: No, no one was allowed to read or write. But I was an exception. I was allowed a Buddhist book to read, but nobody else was given that facility. I could at least read a religious magazine, but it was an exception given to me. But what I did was meditate—my teacher was U Win Htein, because I had no experience at that time. He gave me advice, and then I read a few books on meditation that were sent by my family.

AC: Who was the author of the books?

UAW: My school of meditation is Mogok. My wife sent the books, by Mogok Sayadaw. They were very clear.

AC: Did you have lights to read by in prison?

UAW: Funny you should ask. They were on 24 hours a day! *(Laughs)*.

AC: Oh, my!

UAW: They wanted to look into our cells at any time and see if there was something going on.

AC: Did you have windows in your cell?

UAW: Yes, there was the main door and a single window very high up. But you couldn't see out.

AC: Could you hear anything from outside the window?

UAW: No, but you can hear your cell mates in other cells close by. We often talked, U Win Htein and I. Later, he was sent to the main prison but for two months we stayed together, and we talked about everything, including you. But if it was a faraway cell you couldn't hear or communicate.

AC: How disappointing. How mean. He came as your dear friend and then they took him away. Human behavior can be so despicable. If only more people in power would understand the *Dhamma*.

UAW: Yes, of course. The whole cell block was a sort of transit. We were never transferred, but when people were arrested, they were brought there and then transferred to wherever else.

AC: Could you see anyone, or just hear them?

UAW: We were all on one side, so you could only see the wall, and, at times, the ordinary prisoners doing their jobs.

AC: But not your friends? No faces, only their voices?

UAW: Yes, but when we were taken out for bathing, we could see each other. My cell was in the middle, cell number three. When I went out, I could see cell numbers four, five, and six.

AC: Were you able to talk freely in front of the guards?

UAW: No—well, it would depend on the guard. If he was good natured, no problem. If he was not good natured, he would request 'no talking.'

AC: Did you have a chair in your cell?

UAW: No chair. No cushion. For the first year we slept on the concrete floor. But eventually they gave us a bamboo mat, and you could put on top of it a blanket, if one was brought in. But no pillows. No cushions. Nothing.

AC: Mosquito net?

UAW: No mosquito nets. That was a problem. We wanted to avoid them, especially in the hot season. Our blanket was thin, so we used it to block mosquitoes. You just stay under it, but regardless, you're still exposed. About a year later they gave us a small wooden cot for our cell. They gave us nothing else. But, fortunately, because I'm a management type of person by training, I thought there was always possibility that I would have to go to prison, so I prepared.

AC: How so?

UAW: When I was in the military intelligence interrogation center, I asked my family to bring blankets and everything. But when they took me to prison, I was told there was nothing allowed. Still, they kept them for me and eventually gave them to me. For others, those who were arrested on the street, they had nothing but the clothes they were wearing when taken to prison. They had nothing in prison. It's inhuman, in the literal sense.

AC: And if I may, what did you think about when you were in prison? Was there a central theme or a set of reflections? What went on inside of your mind?

UAW: I tried not to think, at all. No thoughts, at all.

AC: You meditated, regularly?

UAW: Yes, I meditated regularly. And I also prayed and exercised. As I was saying before, the section they use to imprison us is very clear: When you arrest a person, you can release him in two months, or five months, or eight months, or you can keep him in for five years. So there's always an unknowing, and always the possibility that you may be released.

AC: At any time?

UAW: Yes. This point is a bad point. Some people would think about 'release' all the time. I, on the other hand, told my friends 'that's not my affair.' They will release me when they do. Otherwise, it's not my concern.

AC: You just let go, surrendered?

UAW: Yes. The most important thing is meditation. Then reading religious books. They only allowed religious books. No pens. No paper. Nothing. Very inhumane. That's why, when the ICRC came, sometimes we laughed when talking to the interpreter. And she's saying to me, 'Oh, you can laugh?' And I told her that if you don't laugh what will you do? You'll have to cry. Why cry when you can laugh? So, I laughed.

AC: Amazing. How cool is that! So, you kept your humor, your ability to laugh?

UAW: Oh yes, very much so. We'd often make jokes and laugh heartily.

AC: U Win Htein was telling me that he found his ability to withstand these conditions through humor, and Par Par Lay (Burma's most well-known comedian) said the same thing.

UAW: Most of the people—the political detainees—are prepared, psychologically and mentally. In contrast, Khin Nyunt's people (the head of MI, military intelligence), when they were arrested, they became angry, depressed, and fearful.

AC: You were never tortured?

UAW: Not physically.

AC: No one in you cell block, no detainees, were tortured, in your area of the prison? None of the other four or five in your block? The conditions are torturous, of course, inhumane, really, so it's torture by function of being here.

UAW: Well, you see, they're very clever. They're very well trained, the intelligence people. They're highly trained. They have different categories—if you are of old-age they leave you alone. With the young, during the interrogation, they know how strong headed they can be. We heard they were severely tortured.

"We never thought we'd betrayed our country."

ALAN CLEMENTS: I've travelled around Burma for nearly a month now, by buses, trains, horse carts, taxis, and by foot. I have walked the streets of the most affluent areas of the country, and the homes—they're massive; they are more like palaces than residences. The wealth is staggering. I'm told that many of these owners are either military or cronies, those intimately connected to the dictator, the generals and former generals. I'm also told they looted the country and continue to do so. They've taken control of the oil, gas, jade, sapphire, trees, construction and land confiscations. My question: How will this disparity between the corrupted rich and the general population be balanced?

U AYE WIN: I don't know. It's a difficult question, unless we prosecute them, which is not possible at the present time. Sometimes I wonder what will happen to the country, to them, in 10 years. In South America, the dictators were brought to justice after 10 or 15 years, when they were very old and feeble. People speculate that Than Shwe (Burma's former dictator) and America made some agreement that he won't be prosecute them by the ICC, the International Criminal Court, if he really changes, if he lets the country change.

AC: May it be so. Back to prison life. How did you cope, how did you not fall into despair?

UAW: Well, I never fell into despair. Not at all. One reason why, in my opinion, is that we were all prepared to be arrested and imprisoned. This allowed us some degree of emotional and psychological preparation. In addition, it was like Daw Suu said at the time, that she never thought that she was detained. Something along the lines that her freedom was not theirs to take or determine. We too did everything to keep our minds free, despite being caged in like animals.

For me, personally speaking, of course, I was afraid at time, worried about my family. As I said, I had no contact with my family for the better part of five years. My youngest son was about 12 and in 7th standard, and I was worried about him. But you don't have any means of knowing whether everything is alright with him. At that age children can get swayed or withdraw. That was what was worrying me some of the time.

AC: Of course. It is only natural.

UAW: This is the first time I've talked about these things. I've never shared them before.

AC: I'm humbled. And honored. We can stop, if you wish, please...

UAW: I thought about him a lot of the time. He's a good boy, goodhearted, sincere. As a Buddhist Burmese family, we asked him to become a novice monk. He said, 'No, not this year,' so we conceded, 'Oh, ok, ok,' and then the next year, 'ok, ok.' Only in the third year did he agree to do it. There's a monastery nearby and he was ordained as a novice monk. He willingly stayed there for 12 days. He learned basic *Dhamma* culture. And he participated in morning alms round. What do you call it?

AC: Walking on alms round through the villages for food? We call it *Pindapata* in Buddhist Pali.

UAW: Yes. In the second year he voluntarily said he wanted to become a novice, for the second time. Maybe that's a psychological way of coping with this worry. I am not sure. When we travelled, in Bagan and Monywa, there's so many Buddha statues, and he told me that he wanted to donate a statue, asking, 'How can we give a Buddha statue?'

AC: He's got a strong *Dhamma* heart.

UAW: Yes, yes, he does.

AC: You didn't see him, was it for five years?

UAW: I saw him only during my hospitalization. And when I did, it was clear that he had a good heart and was coping. That's the conclusion I made. With that, I felt he was safe and secure, and my heart relaxed. And another thing, as I mentioned, was the value of meditation. And you know for yourself, its value. Also, prayer. I love prayer.

AC: In a way, you were in a culture of activists, revolutionaries, former prisoners. You were well educated about the role you were in with your cousin, so your mental and emotional preparation, your psychological preparation, allowed you to have the strength to make it through?

UAW: Yes, I think so.

AC: Another key thing that people are concerned about is that for years you've had no freedom here. It's a culture of 'do this, do that,' essentially, and, if not, you're imprisoned or tortured, or you lose your home, or all of these combined. And your brother fled the country to form the government in exile—I met him in Mannerplaw, in Karen State, deep in the jungle, in 1990 (I have a very interesting story about that) and afterwards, in America, we became close friends. But you had no access to freedom, so people around the world want to know how you kept hope alive in prison?

UAW: I think that in the first place, we were sure that what we were doing was right. That we we're doing nothing wrong to the country. We knew that without a doubt. Not only me, but U Win Htein, U Win Tin, they are much more aggressive than me, they didn't care a bit! We never thought we'd betrayed our country. We never thought we'd done anything wrong to the country or our cause. Psychologically, emotionally, we had no guilt. But, in a practical sense, you still have some worries about your son, your family, or your finances, those things. Then another thing, I think, is the Buddhist culture. You can do nothing about the situation, at that time, so why dwell on it? And I also had faith in my family, that if they had problems, they would try to cope with them, especially my sister (she supported the family).

AC: Most every former political prisoner, ones I've interviewed and others that I've met, has told me the same thing. You all say, 'We had our conscience on our side,' 'We knew we were doing the right thing.' 'Conscience was our freedom.'

UAW: Yes. So true.

AC: And the eight or nine MPs I spoke with in the capital with U Win Htein, they had so much integrity. They also had their meditative ability. They had their *Dhamma* culture, and they also had their families. One woman specifically had difficulty with her family and that was a tremendous challenge for her in prison. But the strength of the family; I think Nelson Mandela said that his ability to maintain his stature had a lot to do with his relationship with his family. This is a very powerful thing for all of you, as former political prisoners. I have to say, I'm a tremendous fan of your brother. I respect him. He's done so much good for your country— you must know this better than me. You know that, right? And you have these intimate relatives, you're like families within families; and then you have the family of democracy. You have lots of levels of interrelated power, concentric circles of families, so to speak, to draw strength from.

UAW: Yes, we kept going in these harsh conditions. But not only me, all the friends, because you can speak only about two cells to the right and two cells to the left (the others we couldn't hear). We knew we were doing nothing wrong. They were the ones doing the wrong.

Very late in the day, maybe five or six years ago, Khin Nyunt's people got into trouble. They were unable to keep their composure. We heard how they became depressed, and in some instances, they became suicidal. For our group, yes, at times they worried, but not nearly at that level. And never showing others how they'd become afraid. We had our conscience on our side.

AC: I'm concerned not to take more time because I know it's not good for you to sit for long. I'm so happy to see you. Can I come back and speak with you again, at a later time?

UAW: Yes, yes, please do.

AC: By the way, Michael (Daw Suu's husband) and I became quite close when we are altogether at their house. Did you ever see him again?

UAW: No. Nor did Suu. I only heard about his death in prison. A doctor, at that time, said he'd heard of it on the radio. Sad.

AC: Yes. He was such a good man. And your life sir, is a huge gift. Thank you for your time. Thank you for your courage. That you for caring for the freedom of others as essential to your own freedom. Thank you for safeguarding universal human rights. I will take leave now. I'll call you again soon.

UAW: Thank you. When you called me the other day, I explained to my daughter about you. I told her about you being a monk for almost four years with the Venerable Mahasi Sayadaw, as well as your good work for our people from '88 onward, and about this book. You see another thing is, when I was arrested, I was a member of the international accounting committee, the British Institute of Accounting and Management Association. I was obligated to give an annual membership fee which was quite high. But because when I was arrested my practice was halved, they tried to salvage it, and my sister also helped. She's also an auditor. But she's not living here. She's living abroad and came here to help me. By way of saying, her daughter, who is also named Suu, read about your book—*The Voice of Hope*—and in your book you mention my name.

AC: That's right.

UAW: And she quoted you to the institute. And as result, the institute gave me exemption for annual subscription fees.

AC: How wonderful.

UAW: Yes. A good thing. Thank you. But I haven't read your book.

AC: I'll get a copy for you, soon, and give it to you. I found one copy in a bookstore in Rangoon recently. But if it is gone, I know someone who has a copy and I will get it copied.

UAW: I also told my daughter about why they were trying to kick you out of the country and having to arrange interviews to finish the book.

AC: Yes, that was very complicated, at the end. MI came to the hotel and told me to get out immediately.

UAW: Everything is him. He was the one who personally ordered our arrest. And only he can release you.

AC: You have no anger towards him?

UAW: Not to the degree of Suu. She has no bitterness towards them at all.

AC: You are an inspiration. Great to see you, an honor. Sadhu, Sadhu, Sadhu.

UAW: Great to see you as well.

CHAPTER 13

CONVERSATION *with* ZEYA THAW

April 2013

- "I decided to clear up my mind."
- "If you want change, you will need to become a politician."
- "Trust your own feelings and your actions."
- "We rely on Daw Aung San Suu Kyi."

A conversation with Phyo Zeya Thaw, NLD MP and former rapper with the activist-inspired hip-hop band Acid, and a former political prisoner from the younger, second generation of activists. He co-founded the pro-democracy band and youth movement Generation Wave, shortly after the Saffron Revolution of 2007, the name a tribute to the 88 Generation group whose activism he pledged to continue. As Ko Ko Gyi and Min Ko Naing had done before him, he organized many nationwide campaigns, championing the right to freedom of expression and association before going on to become an elected NLD MP and Aung San Suu Kyi's assistant. This interview provides an intimate and definitive account of his activism, from the formation of his band, to the Saffron Revolution and his election as an NLD MP, in the military stronghold of Naypyidaw. He makes plain the country's need to move forward through inspired action and shares how Aung San Suu Kyi influenced him and their political party, providing an inside look at the politics of Burma's revolution of the spirit as it plays out in Parliament.

"When I realized that you need to do the right thing,
I decided to clear up my mind."

ALAN CLEMENTS: You're known, not just in Burma but worldwide, as a founding member of the hugely popular hip-hop group *Acid,* as well as the *Generation Wave* activist movement here in Burma. You are currently a member of Burma's Parliament, elected in Naypyidaw, of all places, the capital of the country which is primarily populated by high-ranking military and mega-wealthy cronies. By way of saying, you—a hip-hop singer, a radical activist and former prisoner of conscience—won a parliamentary seat in the epicentre of power, essentially the seat of dictatorship. In the home of the somewhat-former dictator himself, former general Than Shwe. Now, if that isn't progress, what is?

So straight away, I want to ask, 'please explain that,' and maybe you will throughout our conversation, but if we can, let's start with your roots: How did you emerge as an artist in a totalitarian terror state? And what are a some of your philosophical, spiritual and musical influences?

PHYO ZEYA THAW: It's really quite simple. I was a hip-hop artist. I did lots of concerts and travelled to many places. I meet with many people.

Because I was close with the public, I could feel their pain. I could feel their suffering. This moved me, very deeply. It changed my way of thinking. At first, we tried to entertain people, but only until we realized that they couldn't feel joy because they were suffering. When this perception of suffering became acute, I knew we needed change. Big change!

If my artistic concept is true, then to my mind, my role as an artist, in being dependent on my audience for my livelihood, is defined by a need to do something greater than provide entertainment. Something much greater. We must do our best to try to educate the people. We must help them understand what is right and what is wrong, to be a role model for our people. We needed to help the understand that they have their own rights and responsibilities. And they have the freedom to choose those rights, and responsibilities.

But you see, under the military regime they didn't know anything about those rights. Nor did most people know right from wrong. That's why we, as artists, took a stand and began to educate and encourage the people to know their rights. We switched from being hip hop entertainers to hip hop activists.

AC: You've lived your entire life under dictatorship—severe, unremitting tyranny. The prisons were filled with dissidents. The tortures and human rights atrocities are well documented. What we don't know, or know very little about, is the mind and the motivation of the activist artist here in Burma, and how he and she emerged from within this tyranny—this ever present threat of imprisonment and torture—to find the courage to voice your freedom, and to care so much for your audiences, and your country, that you were willing to go to prison for voicing your truth, your principles, your freedom of expression. Would you please speak about your journey artist and how it all began for you, pre-hip hop, pre-fame?

PZT: It's a bit complicated to explain because, at first, I was just a regular guy. I lived under suppression, like everyone else, so I had some level of fear. But when I realized that you need to do the right thing, I decided to clear up my mind and abandon this fear. My thinking was this: if I want to do more for the people—the people, the public, and our audiences who gave us their money to attend our concerts—you need to tell them just one very simple thing: 'You have the power to choose what you like and do not like. You can choose.'

AC: You can choose your state of mind? You can choose your actions?

PZT: At the time, I couldn't go quite that far. See, at that time I could only speak to younger people. If someone offered you drugs, you can choose to take it, or you can choose not to. You have your right to like or dislike such things. I could only say very simple things at that to the public. I couldn't go any further because, to tell you the truth, as much as I tried to abandon fear, I still had a lot of fear in my mind. Because, during those early years, when you are involved in politics, you end up in prison. It's a 90 percent certainty. Knowing that, I had fear. Prisons, as you know in Burma, are … well, let me leave it at that.

AC: Courageous, you are. When did you start *Acid*, your band?

PZT: We started singing hip-hop around the end of '96. I was 17 years old. I'm 32 now. At that time, both for me and my band, we couldn't touch politics. We could only sing about our young people's hopes and dreams. But the military regime, especially the censorship board, they nevertheless thought we were criticizing them. But it wasn't like that, at all. We were just expressing our hopes and dreams. Sometimes we sang about how the youth felt a sense of hopelessness. Frankly, the majority of people did not have any opportunities. And we sang to that fact.

AC: Which led to prison?

PZT: Yes, to prison. Around 2005 to 2006, most of the '88 Generation student leaders were getting out of prison, and I was in touch with them. I was also participating in their movement. I was taking very small steps, engaging in the Signature Campaign or White Campaign, and so on. In August, we knew that the regime had raised fuel prices, and so most of the '88 Generation students and some of my friends as well were participating in street protests about the fuel price increase. At that time, most of the '88 Generation leaders were arrested again. And this was also when the Saffron Revolution had just begun. I was participating in that movement. We knew we wanted change. We knew that we could not live with this level of oppression any longer. It was unacceptable. That's when the regime came out and brutally cracked down.

See, most young people rejected the government. They wanted to get rid of them. But we didn't know what to do. We did not know how to get rid of them. So we started to organize the youth, those among us who had the same dreams and the same hopes. This is when we started Generation Wave, our young activist group.

AC: Generation Wave emerged out of the Saffron Revolution?

PZT: During the Saffron Revolution, we initially started to organize. But at the time we didn't want to put a name on our organization. After the Saffron Revolution we thought that if we wanted to act with a common purpose, we needed to build our group with a very strong sense of commitment. That's why we named our group Generation Wave.

*"If you want change, you will need
to become a politician."*

ALAN CLEMENTS: Why were you imprisoned?

PHYO ZEYA THAW: As I mentioned earlier, if you're involved in politics in Burma you'll likely end up in jail. Knowing this, you need to decide if this is something you are willing to face, before you get involved in politics. So, I cleared my mind and decided that I wanted to be involved in politics. I wanted change. We all did. We wanted to move our country and our politics forward. So, my thinking was like this: if I'm involved in this way, it will result in prison. It was a clear decision with almost certain consequences.

AC: There is such a thin line between what is political and what isn't. How to understand the differences—what is deemed political in Burma and what isn't? What are some of the distinctions?

PZT: For me, this is hard to describe, because I was involved in politics with a great deal of emotion. We wanted to get rid of the regime. That's why we participated in a movement doing political activities and undertaking political campaigns. We were activists. We not only wanted change, we wanted to get rid of the government. And that is when they arrested me and put me in prison. Once in prison, I had a lot of time to think about how I wanted to change my country, how I wanted it to move it forward, and how activism wasn't enough.

That's my point of view. It may be right, or it may be wrong. If you want change, you need to become a politician. Because in activism you do things task by task, issue by issue. You cannot scope out all things needing to be done. For the politician, you can scope all of the things you need to build up the country, to move it forward towards a better future. That's why I decided to become a politician.

Right now, in Parliament, I'm learning the way of politicians. This is because in our country, we've lived under military rule for nearly half a century. So, our mindsets, all of our thinking, is revolutionary. Right now, to be a politician, to be the opposition party, we need to change our mindset. For me, this is the most important part: developing an entirely new way of thinking.

AC: You are an artist, former activist, youth leader, former prisoner of conscience, and a politician; you work intimately close with Daw Aung San Suu Kyi and members of Parliament. There are numerous dictatorships around the world. You have lived your entire life under one of the most militant ones in modern times. Would you share some of the key points of learning of what it meant to come of age under totalitarian rule?

PZT: I don't want to express hatred, so let me share something that's a little bit funny. For example, when I was an artist, if you wanted to publish an album it needed to pass through the censorship board. Now, the censorship board controls all media, all journals, all music albums, and so on. The funny thing is, in my lyrics, I used the word "rose" and the censorship board told me I could not use the word "rose." I asked them why I couldn't write about a rose. They told me that "The Rose" was the alias of The Lady, a code name for Daw Aung San Suu Kyi. And if you use the word "rose" this would be a dedication to The Lady. It's a funny thing—if they didn't tell me The Lady's code word was "rose," I wouldn't have known The Lady's code word was "rose."

AC: What were they afraid of, the rose's fragrance?

PZT: *(Laughs)* Yes, I think they are afraid of her love of nonviolence.

AC: Once politicized, when you wrote lyrics, did you consciously try to be political?

PZT: No. At first, we were just expressing ourselves. Hip-hop is writing a rhyme, expressing ourselves and our environment, that's all. But when we released our album in 2000 and had created nearly 20 songs, when it passed before the censorship board, they cut one third of them. So we only published 11 songs.

AC: Did the censorship make you angry and further radicalize you, make you even more political?

PZT: Of course. I was only 20 at that time, and I felt that the young people, all of us, were not doing what we could be doing politically. At the time, we as a group were more concerned with business—distributing an album is business. Because we were trying to make it in the mainstream, we approached our music as a business, the music business. So, when they cut so many of our songs, we were somewhat outraged. In some of those songs, they wouldn't even let us change a word. If they did not like a word, they just banned the whole song. So yes, because of the censorship we became politicized. It actually worked against them to censor us.

AC: How long were you in prison?

PZT: Not long—three years and three months. I was in Kauta, a very remote prison in the southernmost part of Burma. This prevented my parents from making the trip to see me only two or three times a year.

AC: Few people in the world can imagine the life of a political prisoner. You, for the most part, knew you would go to prison for your act of conscience. You didn't really take a risk, so it seems, as much as you made a conscious decision to not sit by and let dictatorship further embed without revolutionary resistance.

PZT: I wanted change. I could no longer live under that kind of government. That's why I made my choice. Enough was enough.

AC: Did your choice to activate come quickly or was it like a slow building fever?

PZT: My emotions came slowly, step by step. At first, I didn't know much about politics. In Burma there's a lot of censorship. You can't buy a book that hasn't passed through censorship. Almost everything has to go by censors. For example, The Lady's father—General Aung San—you couldn't buy a book of his speeches during that time. That book was published very long ago, but under the military regime you couldn't buy a single book. And the worst thing, the old bank notes, already banned by the government, printed with General Aung San's picture on them—you can't keep those notes in your pocket or wallet because they're banned. You can't use them. This is our national leader. But you can't even keep them as a souvenir, or a reminder of better times.

AC: You would go to prison if caught?

PZT: Perhaps not, but you would be under watch, because you have some sort of revolutionary mind.

AC: Big Brother-like.

PZT: Of course. For example, if you're walking in the street and someone's looking at you, staring at you, you think, 'Who is this? Is it military intelligence? Is it the police special branch?' You might be burned by it. I think you already know about our party's uniform, a Kachin longyi. You can't wear it with a white shirt. If you're wearing this, MI could be watching you.

"If you trust your own feelings and your actions, you can pass through, not easily, but a little bit easier than the worst."

ALAN CLEMENTS: As I was saying earlier, few people understand—and

I'm one of them—what life is like as a political prisoner in your country. What does a day in the life of a political prisoner look like? What do you do? How do you think? How do you relate to your cellmates? How do the wardens treat you? Do you long to escape? How do you speak with yourself? What is the *Dhamma* that keeps you resilient, non-bitter? Anything you would care to share, please.

PHYO ZEYA THAW: I always say that around the world, a prisoner's situation will be much lower than the country's situation. The lower the country's situation, the lower the political prisoner's situation. In our country, the living standard is already so low, our prison situation will be far worse than that. But if you have a clear mind or if you are confident in the right way, you can pass through it.

Of course, you face challenges every single day. That's because prison life is unstable. For example, one day you can get books, and then the next the warden changes and those books are banned. Then after the next warden change, things change again. There is no stability. No continuity. It can be crazymaking. And because of the corruption in prison, the rules are not fixed. For example, some criminal prisoners get far more access than us political prisoners. That's because they can pay the wardens. Money gets you whatever you want. But for us they were very strict.

AC: Did you always think of your freedom, the day you would leave prison?

PZT: It wasn't like that. My prison days were short. Although I was sentenced to six years, I served just three years and three months. Compared with others, it was very short. Plus, I shared my cell with other political prisoners, so that was good.

AC: If you were to give some simple advice to a young girl or boy who's made the same decision you made—enough is enough of living under dictatorship—and I know that if I voice my mind, if I become a nonviolent revolutionary, I'm likely to end up in jail, what would you say to them to help them get through prison?

PZT: From my point of view, the main thing is to empower your strongest commitment to your revolution. If you don't have strong commitment, and if you're not confident about what you're doing, your imprisonment will be hard. But, if you trust your own feelings and your actions, you can pass through, not easily but a little bit easier than the worst. In other words, conviction and conscience are essential. Know the rightness of what you've done. Believe in it.

AC: Take refuge in your conscience.

PZT: Yes. Because we met people who were only partially involved, not strongly committed. After the Saffron Revolution, lots of people were arrested. They were beaten and dragged away and put in cars; lots and lots of people arrested. Some were strong, and some were not strong enough. The people who weren't strong enough, their imprisonment was hard. So, if you decided to act, at first you need to clear your mind and ask yourself if it's true—do you want to act or not? Know yourself. Get clear. Know what's moving you. That is essential.

AC: When you look back over the years of your life, do you have regrets? 'I wish I could have done this or should have done that; I should have stayed as an artist'?

PZT: What I regret most in my life is that when I first became involved in politics, I choose not to use my real name. Because at the time, as an artist, I had some celebrity, and if I used my real name the whole Generation Wave crew would have been arrested. Most of my friends thought this way about me as well, that if I used my real name the regime would arrest us all as soon as possible. So I regret not using my name.

AC: You wish you did use it?

PZT: Yes, I wish I did. At that time, when I was arrested, most people didn't know why they were arresting me—I was participating in the Saffron Revolution, that's all they knew. They didn't know about my political movement and political activities.

AC: You were an underground, subversive movement?

PZT: Yes, very much so. See, four of us founded it. At that time, we knew almost nothing about politics or about political activities. But our commitment was clear: we did not want to live any longer under an oppressive government. So, we made a firm commitment to go against the government and we undertook many campaigns against them. For me, as an artist, I did my activism in my own way, doing musical things and graffiti, and so on. Some other members of Generation Wave were poets, so they were writing and distributing poems, and so forth.

AC: Generation Wave was born of a vision to use your mind, use your freedom, use your art to overthrow dictatorship?

PZT: Our activism was not only using the arts, but in many other ways as well. The main thing we emphasized was self-expression and educating the people. We had our own slogan; it means, 'The activist is the left hand of the boxer.' On the right hand are the people—they provide the knockout punch. But activists only jab, agitate, annoy. That was our goal—to annoy the regime.

AC: What were the circumstances of your arrest?

PZT: During a meeting with the other five guys at a tea shop, military intelligence came and took us to the nearest police station. At that time, our meeting was on Saya San Road, so they took us to the Bahan Police Station. We spent the night there. The next night they blindfolded us and took us away. I don't know where. I could vaguely see some lights through the blindfold, so I tried to memorize all the streets. After my release from prison three and a half years later, I went straight back to that place. I think it was some sort of military base.

AC: They interrogated you?

PZT: They linked me with the '88 Generation students and the student union. Since a number of their leaders were in hiding, they wanted to arrest us all. They thought we knew where they were hiding.

AC: How rigorous was the interrogation?

PZT: Let me say it this way, there was 'a little blood shed on the decorations,' that's all. I don't want to talk about it because we can't go forward with hatred. Right now, we need to build up our country and move forward into a positive future. Our country is very far behind.

AC: You are a leader now. A politician, A member of Parliament. How do you encourage your people to overcome bitterness? What should they do with their *dosa*, their anger? As we know, it's only human to feel hurt, abused, violated. The Special Rapporteur for the United Nations was here recently. As you know, he's calling for full accountability for these crimes. He's saying those responsible should be tried. He's not calling for 'amnesty.' He's not encouraging 'forgive and forget.' Let me ask you this way: What is the way forward with addressing these abuses? What is your recommendation? Should the abusers and those who ordered them be held accountable? Should they be tried and if found guilty, go to prison? Should there be a public apology? Or should it all be let go of and move on?

PZT: It's hard to say because, for me, as I told you, my imprisonment was a very short period. But I don't want to talk about 'forgive and forget.' Rather, I want to say I can ignore what happened. The past is the past. Let it be.

AC: As others have told me, let bygones be bygones?

PZT: Yes. Our very good example is The Lady, because you can see her sitting beside the very person who sentenced her to house arrest, the former Minister of Home Affairs, General Maung Oo.

AC: Interesting. I didn't know that. All I knew was that he was the regional commander of Rakhine State for some time.

PZT: Yes. He's the one who ordered her house arrest. And if I am not mistaken, he's also the one who came to her house to announce the extension of her house arrest.

AC: Why are they sitting next to each other?

PZT: It's because he's also the head of one of the committees in Parliament and The Lady is also the head of the Rule of Law Committee. All committee leaders sit together. For me the key message here is the importance of giving priority to our country and the next generation's future. If you are filled with hatred, you can't move forward. If your mind is not clear, if your mind is filled with anger or some sort of disturbance, you can't think clearly. That's why if your heart is filled with hatred of your enemy, or hatred of somebody, your judgment or your thinking will be wrong. It will be tainted.

AC: When one has been imprisoned, taken from family, beaten, and tortured, hatred is expected. How to overcome it?

PZT: This is my opinion, my own point of view, it may be a good example or not, I'm not sure. For me, at first, I was involved in politics with strong emotions, as I said. At that time, I became involved in politics because of hatred, because of wanting to get rid of the regime. I was doing lots of things with hate in my heart. But, for me, hate doesn't bring positive results. It's just you expressing hate. It didn't have much to do with consciously building our country. And for effective political work, you can't do it with negative emotions. They distort and misguide. That's why if you want to be involved in politics or help your country move forward, or if you want to build a brighter future for future generations, you need to develop a positive state of mind.

AC: What do you do for fun?

PZT: For fun?

AC: Naypyidaw seems to be devoid of fun things. Maybe I'm wrong. It seems like a big surreal Disneyland.

PZT: Some people think of Naypyidaw as the new capital, with 20 lane roads and shining like a Christmas tree, but the reality is not like that. I was elected because of the people who live in the villages voted for me.

AC: So the massive buildings, mega-hotels and Romanesque ornamentation are only one element of Naypyidaw? There are rural villages all around?

PZT: Yeah, lots and lots of villages. The Naypyidaw which was built by the regime is only a small part. Before they built their version of Naypyidaw there were lots and lots of villages.

AC: Villagers were relocated?

PZT: Yes, they were relocated, and 80 percent of their farms were seized by the government.

AC: Naypyidaw was built by confiscating the land of the farmers?

PZT: Yes, of course. That's why most of the former villagers have strong feelings.

AC: And they, of course, voted for you...

PZT: Yes. Since Naypyidaw is a very new city, most of the new people who live there are mostly migrants from other townships and other cities. They're not native to the town.

AC: Of course, they want their land back, right? I hear this all over the country. People are demanding their land back. Do the people of Naypyidaw ask this of you as their MP?

PZT: Yes. Because all of them are farmers, their livelihood depends on the land. Right now, they don't have any land and they don't know how to live their lives.

AC: What do you tell them?

PZT: The main problem is the unemployment. That's why we need to create more jobs for the younger people.

AC: But the unemployment in Naypyidaw was caused by stealing. They're not unemployed, their livelihoods were taken from them.

PZT: Of course.

AC: Why should they get a job?

PZT: Right now, most of the land is gone, they've already built the roads and buildings. According to the new law, most of the former farmers can demand exceptions to government projects, but when the government project is already built, they can do nothing.

*"We rely on Daw Aung San Suu Kyi because she's
the one who can move our country forward."*

ALAN CLEMENTS: We've talked about being a political prisoner; what is it like to be in Naypyidaw as a Parliament member? What is it like to sit with the former generals, side by side?

PHYO ZEYA THAW: It's quite simple. This is the life we chose, because we decided to become politicians. But, for me, my own opinion, spending so much time in Parliament is a bit of a waste. Because it's like seven to eight months of the year spent in Parliament. It's too much, because we need to be in touch more with our own constituents. We need to spend more time with the people. And we need more time to organize our own party.

AC: Digressing a bit; do you socialize with the former generals in Parliament? Do you chat? Does everyone say 'hello,' 'good morning'? Do you have coffee together? Are they nice to you?

PZT: At first, I think most of the people—not the military representatives; some of the office staff—were afraid to speak with us, because they thought we are outlaws. But after a couple of months they understood what we stood for, because we were not criticizing everything and everyone. Our party is very restrictive. We have strict party rules and regulations.

AC: So, the former military people, the ones who put you in prison, do they ever ask you questions privately or socially? Like, 'I want to say it's really good to get to know you, my opinion of you is very different'—anything human like that ever happen, or is it much more formal?

PZT: Right now, it hasn't reached that level, but they do show respect to the NLD.

AC: But no personal conversations?

PZT: Not the higher rank; the lower rank military representatives or ex-military, and some representatives from the USDP, we have a close relationship with them.

AC: I know that you've travelled with Daw Suu around the world. We see how hard she is working.

PZT: Most people think that our party, the NLD, relies too much on her. Yes, we rely on her. But we don't worship her. We rely on Daw Aung San Suu Kyi because she's the one who can move our country forward. She's the one respected abroad and respected by all the people. That's why she's the one who can make change. We give all of our efforts to her. Because we want change, we do are parts and equally support her, fully. But some of people criticize us for relying on her too much.

AC: Are you relying on her too much?

PZT: No, it's not like that. Everyone does their part. And we rely on her, support her, because she's the one who can change our country. If we have a great leader, for us, for me, we support the one who is most effective. Not the one who is less effective. That's why we're focusing our support on The Lady.

AC: The dictator, former general Than Shwe, seems to be living in Naypyidaw. How should we regard him?

PZT: From my point of view, we need to neglect if he exists or not, because sometimes, if you think about your number one enemy, you can't do better in your present activities, because you live under your past. You might be filled with hatred. So, for me, his house is within my constituency, but I don't know if he lives there or not. I'm not sure, and I've never seen him. For me, neglecting him is best. If he exists or not, it is not the important thing for us.

Right now, some of the people think Burma's situation is not stable, it can turn back or something like that. Yes, maybe; I don't know whether that's right or wrong. I don't want to comment on that. But the main thing is that if Burma turns back there will be no more Than Shwe. It will be another Than Shwe. There will be a new Than Shwe. It's systemic. So, for me, neglecting him is best for the country.

AC: A final question: many millions of people are holding Myanmar in their hearts today. They want to believe in your country's democracy, in this flicker of freedom. Yes, there is the Muslim/Buddhist conflict, the unraveling of totalitarian decades, all these symptoms of decades of repression and tyranny. Yes, those are there. My question is this: millions of people will visit your country this year. They're already coming. The hotels are filled. What would you say to the tourists who are coming to have a more emotionally rewarding experience? How would you encourage them? What advice would you give them to better serve your emerging democracy?

PZT: We need more exposure from the tourists, because, as I already said, when I became interested in politics, I didn't know what my own rights were, what were the things I could and could not do. The people of the US and so on, you have your own rights and you often take those rights for granted. But most people don't understand or don't think about it. I mean, your life is free, so you can do whatever you want, and you can say whatever you want. But for the people in Burma, it's not like this. People from the US, sometimes it's a little funny because they do things their own way. For example, back in the old days, '93 or '94, a road was not blocked but it was guarded by the police—I was only 13 or 14 at the time. When the police block the street, from my point of view, I think we don't have the right to pass through it. But when one of the tourists was coming down the street, he tried to get through the barricade because he said his hotel is at the other end and he needed to go straight there. This was a very good example for me, because you have your own rights and you have the right to negotiate or compromise with the local authorities. But for us, we didn't have this confidence at the time. It was a good example for me. Same as The Lady. Sometimes she is doing her own thing in her own right way and it is a good example for us.

AC: Thank you. Thank you from my heart.

PZT: Thank you. And thank you especially for supporting the freedom of my people.

CHAPTER 14

CONVERSATION *with* ZIN MAR AUNG

March 2013

- "We knew that people across the country were supporting our movement."
- "In our Constitution, they do not prescribe women's rights."
- "My definition of democracy doesn't just concern elections."

A conversation with Zin Mar Aung, Member of Parliament, recipient of the International Award for Most Courageous Woman presented by Hillary Clinton and Michelle Obama in 2012. An NLD MP for Yankin township and a prominent activist from the time of the 88 uprising, she spent 11 years in prison, nine of those in solitary confinement. Since her release, she has founded a cultural-studies impact group and a self-help group for former political prisoners at Yangon School of Political Sciences, as well as a women's empowerment group. In this chapter, she shares what inspired her to pursue activism at such a young age, how *Dhamma* and meditation helped her endure her time in prison, and her views on the nature of dictatorship and how it can be addressed, paying particular attention to the role of women in the peace process.

"We knew that people across the country were supporting our movement. That made me stronger."

ALAN CLEMENTS: As a former Buddhist monk in your country and a long-time student of your freedom struggle, I'm interested in the psychology, the emotions and wisdom of nonviolent revolution; of hope, of freedom, of resilience and empowerment, especially from women. I asked my friend, Kyaw Thu's wife, 'Please, who are the women in the struggle that I should speak with?' She immediately said that I must speak with you. By way of saying, I'm both grateful and honored to have the opportunity. Thank you for taking the time to connect.

ZIN MAR AUNG: The honour is mine. And thank you.

AC: When did you get involved in the movement for democracy?

ZMA: In 1998 I joined the '96/'98 Student Union and was arrested that same year, in 1998. We were a new wave of student activists, post '88 Generation.

AC: And how many years did you spend in prison?

ZMA: I spent 11 years in prison.

AC: What was the charge against you?

ZMA: At that time, we delivered a statement, and also poems, that supported the NLD and The Lady (Daw Aung San Suu Kyi). During this period, the NLD announced its decision to implement the 1990 elections and to call for Parliament. We supported the statement. If the NLD convenes Parliament, the students stand with the NLD. We delivered such statements to the public, at the cinema, in the middle of Rangoon, in busy markets, on streets.

AC: The prisons were filled with activists at that time. Surely, you knew the risk of your own political and provocative actions, that you too would likely end up as a prisoner of conscience?

ZMA: We knew, absolutely, that many students were still in prison, as well as activists and other political party members, especially from the NLD. We did know that. But what we believed was that we needed to do the right thing. It was not enough to just let the elders take responsibility. Our generation also needed to step up and take responsibility. And we did.

AC: You knew you would go to prison but despite that, you did it because it was right. It was an act of conscience?

ZMA: Yes.

AC: Just like that?

ZMA: Just like that.

AC: Your mother and father, what did they think? Did they intervene and ask that you not act in this way?

ZMA: Yeah. Actually, my mother passed away a year earlier (in 1996), and later my father was really very worried about me doing such kinds of political activities. He didn't want me to be arrested. Even though he didn't like the military regime, as my parent he worried. In fact, he'd forbidden me from taking part in such activities. He said, 'No.' But I had to do it. And I did.

AC: And the consequences—11 years in prison. One stretch?

ZMA: Yes, one stretch. My original sentence was 28 years, but after 11 years they released me. During my imprisonment, even though my father had forbidden me from committing political activities, when I was arrested, he fully supported me.

AC: Many millions around the world also supported you. You folks are so brave. So principled. So beautiful. So, you were in Insein Prison?

ZMA: Thank you. I was sent to Insein Prison, and six months later I was moved to Mandalay prison. It's an awful prison. Horrible in every sense.

AC: I assume they're all horrible. But this one is notorious? A real hellhole?

ZMA: Yes, exactly.

AC: I don't like asking the question, but I feel it's important to ask for the world to know the truth, to possibly learn and heal and outgrow such barbarism: were you tortured?

ZMA: Not physically, but mentally. For example, firstly they didn't allow political prisoners to have slippers or shoes, like the others, the ordinary inmates.

AC: Barefoot.

ZMA: Barefoot. And our families didn't even know where we were.

AC: Dictatorship.

ZMA: Eventually, they came to find out. And gradually, my family followed.

AC: They came to visit?

ZMA: Yes.

AC: How old were you when you were arrested and sent to prison?

ZMA: I was 22. And I came out when I was 33. In 2009.

AC: Just one day, unexpectedly, they set you free? While thinking you had 28 years to serve?

ZMA: Yes, exactly.

AC: Prison life; how did you cope with under such horrendous prison conditions? Also, how did you keep your activism close to heart during your many years of incarceration?

ZMA: The main thing is that we believed in ourselves, that we were doing the right thing. And also, I felt that I was not alone, that there were a lot of political prisoners, still are, across the country. And, also, our student leaders—people like Min Ko Naing and our democracy leader, The Lady, Daw Aung San Suu Kyi—were still struggling. And we knew that people across the country were supporting our movement. That made me stronger. Also, we had time to reflect, and we had time to meditate. We had time to think and imagine our future, so I liked thinking about these things.

AC: Would you describe what your day-to-day life was like for those years in prison? What did you do? Who was in your cell? Did you have blankets? What was the air like? What did you eat? How did you bathe? How were you treated? What did you feel like in your heart? Can you describe whatever moves you to share about your experience?

ZMA: It was different at different times. The first period of prison life was the most horrible period. This was true for almost all political prisoners. It was our first experience. Also, the prison guards treated us badly. Gradually we tried to learn. Tried to survive, without giving up our belief in democracy and freedom and human rights. That's a very important thing. Gradually, six months later, our family visited once a month, after I was sent to Mandalay prison. Also, in 1999, the ICRC, the International Committee for the Red Cross, was allowed to visit the prison, and we got permission to read religious books and things like that, at that time.

AC: Would you care to share more?

ZMA: Sometimes, if the prison officer changed and a bad one came, the good things were withdrawn. The thing is that we were hoping for good things, for betterment, but we realized that we also had to prepare for the worst. That helped me cope. On the other hand, when I read books and recited and reflected upon the motto that I'm really fond of—they can imprison your body but not your mind—when I meditated, I realized that truth. This motto, this single line, made me stronger, and when I'm enjoying meditation, I feel free.

AC: If I am not mistaken, that is a line by Daw Suu. You are in the lineage of greatness. I think it was Gandhi who said, "You can chain me, you can torture me, you can even destroy this body, but you will never imprison my mind." But even Mandela said he thought frequently of the day he would be set free during his decades of imprisonment. Surely you too must have had thoughts of being released?

ZMA: Yes, during my first period of imprisonment I thought about release. Sometimes one of my case partners would be released and so I hoped that 'oh, when will be my turn?' But gradually I realized that if I'm to be released or not is not my job, it's their job. Further, I realized that the only thing I should do is try to live and try to survive successfully during my prison period. I meditated every day, from three years after I was arrested, trying to learn meditation, and also reading.

*"I have the opportunity to express 'we are human beings
and human beings do not want to accept injustice and tyranny.'"*

ALAN CLEMENTS: You are the recipient of the prestigious International Award for Women of Courage, given by the American government. When you travelled to Washington DC to receive the award, who actually presented it to you?

ZIN MAR AUNG: Both US Secretary of State Hilary Clinton and First Lady Michelle Obama.

AC: Congratulations. You know, you and your activist friends are amazing. You must know that. Let me ask this: you are recognized internationally for your strength of heart and conscience, doing the right thing at the right time in the right way. There are many boys and girls, men, and women, around the world, wanting to rise up in their own way against tyranny, against injustice, against fascism and dictatorship. If this film were seen by someone or this book read by someone who is deliberating, 'Should I? Shouldn't I?', 'Should I join the movement and recite a poem,' should they join their Lady, whoever that is in their country, and they think, 'If I do this I might go to prison'—would you talk to those people; what would you encourage them to think at that moment of decision? Should I act, or should I not risk it? What would you say to them?

ZMA: I would like to encourage them just to do the right thing. What I believe is that I have, based on my experience, the opportunity to stand with the people who are doing the right thing for their society. And I have the opportunity to express 'we are human beings and human beings do not want to accept injustice and tyranny.' In our country, and in our society, that will be a good example for other human beings. That is what I believe. If you believe that, and dare to face any difficulties, you can overcome the difficulties. I believe that.

AC: Many people have focused and continue to focus on the injustices in this country. Human rights organizations, NGOs, and leaders in many governments have documented the atrocities, the abuses, the systematic use of forced labour, the raping of women. You know all this from your association with a women's empowerment organization that you've started. In other words, the tortures are well known. What do you think, having suffered under the hands of these oppressors, these torturers for 11 years, what motivates them to do what they do? What motivates the tyrant? What motivates the torturer? Why do human rights atrocities exist in the first place? Why?

ZMA: In my point of view, such people also have fear—they do not want to give up their power. They do not want to lose their positions. They do not want to lose their privileges. Further, many of them are blind and indoctrinated. They do what they are told without questioning 'why' they should follow such a command. Why they should abuse their fellow man. Since they do not know how to cope with this fear, they commit crimes. It's all about a mindset.

AC: Do you think that they're aware that they're frightened? Do you think they actually know they're feeling fear? Or is the mindset of indoctrination set in stone?

ZMA: Unconsciously they know.

AC: You are an active member of the political transformation process here in your country. You are active in numerous organizations, specifically the big ones dealing with ethnic conflict in all the ethnic areas, correct?

ZMA: Yes. Actually, we've started to raise awareness of Kachin State, specifically of Kachin, because one and a half years ago, after the government handed over power to the new government, the fighting between the KIA (Kachin Independence Army) and new government troops started. What we realized is that Burma has one of the world's longest civil conflicts happening in our country. Our concern was that if the fighting goes on longer, we will lose the trust of the ethnic people and our Burmese people. That's our concern. We try to raise this awareness and we try to show that the fighting is just between the armed groups, not Burma and the people. We try to draw a distinction.

AC: I've asked this question to numerous people and had many informed responses about President Thein Sein's army—he's the president; our president in America controls the army, the army doesn't control the president. In Burma, the army controls the army, and seems to have nothing to do with the president. This is maybe a simplification. My point being that the Burmese Army, at least what's stationed in Kachin State, is harassing, raping, burning and killing civilians, even though it's armed conflict between the Kachin army and the Burmese army. It's the lay and civilian populations of the Kachin who really suffer. Why are they killing the Kachin people? Why don't they stop, as President Thein Sein has ordered them to?

ZMA: I think this is our kind of political culture. The military always keeps the upper hand in our political scenarios for the last half a century, and so they would like to shore up their power, even though the government changed. And on the other hand, this is a weakness of our Constitution.

AC: Old habits die hard.

ZMA: Yeah.

AC: Would it be a simplification or a completely wrong belief to say that Kachin State is resource rich: huge stands of teak wood, the finest jade in the world, gold mines? Is this blood-teak, blood-jade, blood-gold? Is this the fight for those gems, resources, and timber?

ZMA: Theoretically that is right. On the other hand, we *can* solve this problem. We'll manage it through power sharing. We don't have proper power sharing written into the Constitution. We cannot practice federalism very well. If we can understand federalism and power sharing well, we can solve this problem properly, I think.

AC: So, it comes back to dialogue?

ZMA: Yes, exactly, political dialogue.

AC: We must learn how to talk. You're a woman; you're receptive; you have an organization that empowers women; how should we learn how to talk together? It's a worldwide problem. What would you suggest?

ZMA: Regarding the peace process, especially in the KIA and government dialogue, there are no women yet, so they don't realize, and I think they still don't believe in, the value of listening to the voices of the women who are most vulnerable in every conflict, every war. The first thing is that the military is a male dominated institution and they don't realize that. On the other hand, the dialogue between the Burmese government, the military and the KNU (Karen National Union), the women leading the KNU team, compromise and negotiate, so we can compare the benefit of involving women in the peace process. That's one major issue.

AC: You're doing women's empowerment; how should we understand the role and the crisis women face in your country?

ZMA: The thing is that women themselves do not realize there is a glass ceiling in our society that they cannot overcome. Firstly, we need to know, and we need to realize, that we don't have a written law that prohibits women from participating politically and economically, but we still have unwritten social norms and cultural practices like that. We need to realize that. Women have their potential. The other issue is the consequences of the military. We, our country, was governed for almost half a century by a military regime, so during this period the ideology was dominated by male chauvinism.

AC: A worldwide problem.

ZMA: Yes *(laughs)*.

"In our Constitution, they do not prescribe women's rights,
so we urgently need to recognize and promote that."

ALAN CLEMENTS: What is most urgently needed in your country?

ZIN MAR AUNG: We need to amend the 2008 Constitution, but it will take time. On the other hand, currently, we need more women in Parliament, in parliamentary seats, so they can balance the 25 percent military personnel. That is our urgent need. If more women get parliamentary seats, we can balance the sense of the military dominance, its ideology. On the other hand, we need to amend the Constitution urgently.

AC: Let me ask you this: imagine you're invited to Naypyidaw to address the members of Parliament; it's likely coming soon, you could even be president...

ZMA: *(Laughs)* But not without amending the Constitution...

AC: ...no women either?

ZMA: Yes, because the criteria they mention to be president, a candidate should be understanding and familiar with the military point of view. There is a clause in the Constitution.

AC: It's so interesting that you don't have any enemies in this country, except one. In my country, much of the world is perceived as an enemy. And we both aggressively export those weapons and use them whenever we wish; Vietnam, Iraq, Afghanistan, to name just a few. Burma, on the other hands, only attacks their own people. If you were going to Naypyidaw to address Parliament, to hear how you think the Constitution should change, what would you suggest? What should the constitution be that's most favourable to the people as you see what the people need?

ZMA: The Constitution should guarantee human rights and also citizenship rights, and also, in our Constitution, they do not prescribe women's rights, the role of women, so we urgently need to recognize and promote women's rights.

AC: Women are not recognized at all?

ZMA: Not at all. They've simply prescribed 'the states will treat all equally, regardless of gender and religions,' something like that. Regarding job opportunities, the government and state do not discriminate based on gender, but on the other hand, the state defines jobs that are only appropriate for men, should only be the place for men. Such a clause is very vague. How do we identify the jobs that are only suitable for men? That's a problem.

AC: So, the problem is not just dictatorship, it's really also very connected to gender.

ZMA: Yes, for sure.

AC: Men have failed the job, here in Burma, and elsewhere too, for that matter. But focussing on Burma, the country is a hellhole for human rights. And the Constitution enshrines a lie—this is disguised dictatorship, not a democracy. It's not a constitution.

ZMA: Yes. The role of the president and commander-in-chief is crucial. As it is now, the civilian government cannot interfere in military affairs, to judge or reveal crimes by the commander-in-chief, so that's very controversial. And, also, the commander-in-chief can stage a coup at any time for security reasons. That is a weakness. Another thing is we need to nurture and teach the military about the role of a professional military, on what the role of the military is in democratic countries. They also need to learn.

AC: The whole country is in need of an education on the meaning of democracy?

ZMA: Exactly, yes.

AC: Let me ask you this: What does freedom mean to you?

ZMA: Freedom means somebody's freedom should not assault or disturb another's freedom.

AC: You've been violated by people who would easily be seen as an enemy. How do you not see people as the enemy? You've been tortured, you've been imprisoned, you've lost a big chunk of your life. You're a woman; many of your womenfolk have been raped. How do you overcome feeling someone is your enemy?

ZMA: The people who arrested me are also the prey of the system, a bad system. They are also the victims of the system. They are indoctrinated.

AC: This gives you compassion?

ZMA: Yes. They do not understand or realize what they're doing and for whom. They are blind. And most people lived in fear in the past under dictatorship. They also lost their conscience. They lived in fear, acted in fear, fear dominated their lives. It was a dark age.

AC: People are looking for leadership, almost to the point where they look to the leaders as the people who will solve the problems as they live out their lives. But Daw Suu, one of the things that I most respect about her, is that she incessantly tells the public, 'We cannot do it alone. Everybody must do their part in bringing democracy to Burma.' What can people do that is their part? What are some of the ways that the population can bring democracy to their lives and to the lives of other people in this country? What does it look like to bring democracy into daily life?

ZMA: The only thing is that we still need to learn what democracy is, in practice. We need a practical understanding of the meaning and the application of democracy in our day-to-day lives. When I give trainings, we assess our attendees understanding of democracy. They answer that the majority rules, it's about human rights, and the rule of law. They answer with things related to democratic society. But almost no one speaks of 'political tolerance.' We need to learn what political tolerance is and respect each other's politics. Because democracy is originally very diverse, and in our country, we are also a very diverse people. We need to respect each other, especially our differences.

AC: I forgot to ask you, and if I may, what did you and Michelle Obama and Hilary Clinton talk about? And what was it like to meet them?

ZMA: Like a dream! *(Laughs)* Mrs. Clinton is one of my role models, so that was amazing. And they encouraged me, and their recognition made me feel that I have more responsibility than before. And Mrs. Obama was very interested in Burma. She too was amazing. She couldn't believe that I spent 11 years in prison. That was very amazing for her. Overall, she encouraged me to do good things, that the United States will stand with Burma now and in the future.

AC: What does courage mean to you?

ZMA: I think there are two types of courage: physical and moral. I prefer moral courage; it's more important than physical courage.

AC: And what does moral courage mean to you?

ZMA: Honesty. And tolerance.

AC: Many millions of people are focussed on your country right now. I think over a million tourists have come to Burma this last year, and many millions more will come. They're building a new Hilton Hotel along with many other luxury hotels as well as dozens of high-rise condominiums and massive Singaporean and Hong Kong-like shopping malls. And the price of everything has skyrocketed. And when you think of the grinding poverty, 25 percent of the population live at ground zero level, 37 percent unemployment; my question: millions of people are coming, billions of dollars are being put into this country by just a few corporate leaders, money that is primarily going into the hands of a few present and former military leaders and cronies. If you would give advice to those investors, and all those freedom-loving tourists arriving, what would you like them to know about your country before they invest and before they visit?

ZMA: The thing is not to just focus on money and economic development but focus on human rights and how we need infrastructure and to amend a lot of rules and regulations regarding foreign investment and economic development. I think international business and cooperation should focus on emerging small and medium size businesses. That's how we can develop and nurture the people in Burma, the ordinary people who have potential to develop their businesses. If not, the money will go to the cronies, not to the people. That's my suggestion.

AC: 'Let your investment serve the people, not the rich'?

ZMA: Yes. That's it. Serve our people, please.

"My definition of democracy doesn't just concern elections and the government but focusses on society."

ALAN CLEMENTS: Have you met Daw Aung San Suu Kyi? And if so, would you be willing to share your impressions for the benefit of others around the world? Especially for young revolutionaries seeking inspiration and guidance in their respective struggles for freedom?

ZIN MAR AUNG: Yes, I have. After she was released, I met her four times. See, before I was arrested, I had been going to the front of her home on University Avenue, where every weekend she gave a public talk (along with NLD co-founders, U Tin Oo and U Kyi Maung) on some aspect of democracy, freedom, and human rights. For many of us, it was our political training, while inspiring insight in nonviolent activism and the power of *mettā*-in-action (loving-kindness). This was in 1996. Her talks were a great gift to me and to so many others, as we had the opportunity to learn from her experiences and depth of insight. In addition, I studied her book, *Freedom from Fear.* There is so much important information in that book. And the more I learned about her—her way of thinking and behaving and her compassion and caring for the future of freedom—the more I admired her, especially her determination and courage, her moral courage. There was a deep sense in her of not to ever give up. Keep your conscience. Keep it active in your heart. And keep going forward, no matter what. Those reflections helped me to keep my spirit high during my 11 years in prison.

AC: Thank you. And thank you for your life, your own dedication. You are an inspiration to me. I'm a guest in your country. I have a tremendous love of your people, and I have a great love of human rights, and even more now that we have met. So, thank you again, for giving me a chance to speak with you, listen to you and learn from you and moreover, participate in my own small way in your country's revolution for freedom, the next phase of it, that is.

ZMA: And thank you for caring for our people and our struggle.

AC: The honour is mine. May national reconciliation come soon, one person at a time.

ZMA: Yes, let bygones be bygones, one person at a time.

CHAPTER 15

CONVERSATION *with* NAY PHONE LATT

March 2013

- "I wanted to be a writer, but I didn't have a chance to be a writer."
- "They arrested me because I have so many connections with politicians."
- "They didn't know the word 'blogger.' They thought I was a 'blocker.'"
- "Where you are is not important. What you are doing is what is important."
- "The real cause is in my heart, not outside myself."
- "When we are thinking about rights, we should think two things: my right and your right."

A prominent blogger and activist, Nay Phone Latt, 33 years old, was arrested in January 2008 for his involvement in the Saffron Revolution. Released from his 20-year sentence in 2012 by mass presidential pardon, he now serves as an MP in Thingangyun Township, Yangon. He is a recipient of the PEN/Barbara Goldsmith Freedom to Write Award and was included in the 2010 Time 100 list as a "hero." Here he talks about what motivated him to keep writing during years of threat and Orwellian repression, the role of the Internet in opening up the country to democracy, and about how he survived his time in prison.

"I wanted to be a writer, but I didn't have a chance to be a writer."

ALAN CLEMENTS: You were political prisoner for four years. What was the charge?

NAY PHONE LATT: They charged me under three articles. The first was 33(a) of the Electronic Transition Act. Another one was 32(b), the video act. Number 3 was 505(b), because I participated in the Saffron Revolution. For all three articles they sentenced me to 20 years and six months. At first, they put me in Insein Prison for nearly one year. After that, they sent me to Pan Prison in Karen State.

AC: I understand that you have training in computer technology, especially digital media and citizen journalism. What is your real passion?

NPL: I want to be a writer. I'm very interested in writing. So, I write many articles, short stories, and poems. In the early days, it was difficult to get published in local magazines or journals, because of strict censorship. Another obstacle was the editor. If you wanted to publish your artwork or article in a local magazine you had to pass through these two big walls. But naturally as a writer and a Myanmar citizen growing up under a totalitarian regime, I wanted to criticize the government in some way, so those feelings were often included in my stories and articles. The censorship board did not like it nor allow it.

AC: Would you take me through the process? You're a writer of short stories, a blogger. I assume you communicate based upon the inalienable human right that you have to freely express yourself. What was the process prior to your imprisonment that you passed through in order to publish, print or digitally deliver your truth in any and all forms of media?

NPL: For example, I write a story and send it to a magazine. After that, the editor must choose my story for publication. After the editor, he asks permission from the censorship board to have it published. If he does not receive approval from the censorship board, he can't have it published. That's the process. It's black and white. So, to begin with, it's difficult to get chosen by the editor. That's one huge difficulty. After that, you had to pass through another wall—censorship. Most of my short stories and articles were rejected by the censorship board.

AC: What did they find offensive in your writings?

NPL: They're extremely sensitive. For example, on our website we had a "Contact Us" button. If you wanted to contact me, click the icon. So, I wrote about the website and used the words "contact us." But they didn't allow those words. Why? Because they thought it was a message to contact the US (United Sates).

AC: Clever bunch, they are.

NPL: Obviously, they didn't know the meaning of "contact us." They thought I wanted to give messages to the USA. They thought that "us" meant "U.S." As I said, they're very sensitive.

AC: What other things would they censor? What words, particularly?

NPL: We can't use "88," or "Daw Aung San Suu Kyi," or "democracy." They're sensitive to every word. So, you have to be clever. If we wanted to criticize the government, we couldn't do it directly. We had to use metaphor and simile.

AC: Can you share an example of something you would write that would be critical of the government?

NPL: 'That the role of the military is not to govern the country. It's to protect the country. I don't want to see the military in a position of government.'

AC: And you said such things, just like that, directly?

NPL: No *(laughs)*. I couldn't! I couldn't say those words directly. If we said those words you could be arrested.

AC: Why were you arrested? What did you write or do?

NPL: Well, before I was arrested in 2007, just before the Saffron Revolution, I created a blog. I created it because I wanted to be a writer and write whatever I wanted to write, which I could do in my blog. There would be no censorship or editor—you are your own editor. So, I created a blog and I wrote anything I wanted. In time, I got something of an audience. Most of the people who are online in Myanmar know of me and my blog. After that, I went back to Yangon and we bloggers connected with each other and organized MBS (Myanmar Bloggers Society). Our purpose was to introduce people to this new technology. On September 1st, 2007, we held a seminar in the MIT (Myanmar Institute of Technology) department. The name of the seminar was "Why Do We Blog?" We invited many people. Over 500 attendees came, and we introduced them to what a blog was, along with what we were writing and why we were doing it.

AC: You ushered in the first wave of digital revolution in Burma?

NPL: I created my blog in 2007, but there were a few pioneers before me, by a year or two. In fact, I was inspired by them, and when I went to Singapore a friend introduced me to blogs. My friend also had an online magazine and told me that to take the responsibility of the editor is a key feature of an online magazine. So, I worked as one of the editors. After that, they also introduced me to the idea, "Here is a blog. You can create freely. No need to pay anything. Just write what you want to write."

AC: Must have been liberating to know that you could relate directly with the world, free of censorship?

NPL: Yes. But you know, in our country, to use the Internet is not easy. It's expensive and slow. I went to Singapore to find a job. That was the first turning point of my life. Singapore is a developed country and to use the Internet is easy and the Internet speed is fast. In the morning, when I woke up, the first thing I did was open the Internet to update my blog. That was one of the first turning points of my life—I arrived in Singapore and I got a chance to get familiar with this new technology. As such, I created a blog and became a blogger.

AC: That was your first inner revolution, so to speak, with digital technology and using the blog to communicate your views? What was the name of your blog?

NPL: "The City I Dropped Down." I simply wanted to be a writer but didn't have a chance to do so.

AC: And you came back to your country and started tech trainings?

NPL: No, not trainings. When I returned to my country, I opened an Internet cafe. Then I organized some bloggers through the creation of the Myanmar Bloggers Society. That was not for training. It was just a way to introduce this exciting new technology to the people.

"They arrested me because I have
so many connections with politicians."

ALAN CLEMENTS: You mentioned organizing a blogging seminar back in 2007 with 500 people in attendance, sharing with them the virtues of digital media. That's almost a full-scale demonstration.

NAY PHONE LATT: *(Laughs)* Yes, September 1st, just before the Saffron Revolution.

AC: That began September 28th. Could you feel it coming?

NPL: Yes. It was in the air.

AC: Censorship in Burma was Orwellian. One wrong word and your entire manuscript is rejected. Pretty harsh. And if you're a flagrant user of the 'wrong' word you could be arrested. And here you are, just weeks before the world knew of Saffron, and you assemble 500 young people and say, "Hey, this new technology that I become acquainted with in Singapore allows us to bypass editors and the censorship board and communicate freely and directly with anyone in our country and around the world with access to a computer. We are no longer prisoners of dictatorship." You then opened up an Internet cafe to give everyone access to censor free digital expression. In a way, motivated to do so or not, you're a ringleader in the awakening of freedom and conscience. You're one of the original Saffron Revolutionaries—an online version, a digital activist.

NPL: *(Laughs)* But I didn't have that intention.

AC: Please allow me; you were clear about how much you liked criticizing the government. And then you go and assemble 500 young people—who are likely, like yourself, creative and frustrated by censorship—and probably yearning, as you were, to express their pent-up criticisms of dictatorship. You were telling them to use this new technology to speak their minds? Am I right?

NPL: Yes. We didn't have freedom of expression in Burma at that time, but you could use this new technology to express yourself, express your feelings, if you were so moved.

AC: Today, March 8th, is Burma's Human Rights Day. As you know, this is when the young student Phone Maw was killed, the first student shot in the '88 uprising. And here you are, 15 years later, four of those years in prison, and the revolution continues. You paid a heavy price for blogging, for speaking your mind.

NPL: Not just me. We have a bloggers' society, a bloggers' collective.

AC: How many of them went to prison?

NPL: Nobody.

AC: Just you?

NPL: Yes.

AC: Why only you?

NPL: At the time they didn't know about blogs. See, they didn't arrest me because of blogging. They arrested me because I had many connections with politicians and I'm also a member of the NLD. I also helped politicians. At that time, I helped members of '88 Generation and also Zarganar (a popular Burmese comedian, film actor, and a film director, as well as a fierce critic of the Burmese military government and a political prisoner). If they needed something that was connected with technology, they asked for my help. And I gave it to them, as much as I could. That was the real reason I was arrested and went to prison.

AC: And so, the Saffron Revolution takes place, and the country is sealed, and the world learns through smuggled video and photographs how the monks and people took to the streets. And as in '88, the military comes out with orders to shoot, and they do, killing many and injuring many more. May I ask, where were you at the time and what were you doing?

NPL: At first, I participated in the marching, and then I helped the monks as much as I could. I also had two cyber cafes at the time. And not only me, but some of my friends participated in the Saffron Revolution. During that time, most people knew me and also knew my blog.

With the bloggers, we had to differentiate two groups. One group were bloggers based in Yangon, and the other group were bloggers based in foreign countries. For the bloggers in Yangon, they didn't post anything about the Saffron Revolution in their blogs. They didn't post photographs or news because everybody knew who the owners of the blogs were. But we had connections with foreign based bloggers. Some of our people who could use the technology took photos and videos and sent them to foreign-based bloggers, and they posted the photos and videos in *their* blogs.

AC: From your cafes?

NPL: Not only from my cafes; everybody with access to a computer and an Internet connection sent things abroad.

"They didn't know the word "blogger."
They thought I was a 'blocker.'"

ALAN CLEMENTS: And why did you go to prison? Your crime?

NAY PHONE LATT: I didn't do anything wrong, but the reason they could sentence me was that they had a CD that was in my possession, one that had been censored. They found censored caricatures and cartoons on it when they checked my email inbox. And then also because I participated in the Saffron Revolution. These are the reasons they sentenced me to 20 years and six months.

AC: Where did they arrest you? At home, in a cafe, on the street?

NPL: In the cafe. I had an appointment with my friend. She had a connection with the '88 Generation. The '88 Generation asked me if they could see the CD. It was a performance show of four comedians—the people of Zarganar. The name of the CD is *Four Fruit*. In it, they criticized the military government.

AC: And, of course, you had their CD?

NPL: Yeah, I had it. At the time, '88 Generation members were hiding because the government was trying to arrest them. This was just after the brutal crackdown by the military of the monk-led Saffron Revolution. The '88 Generation members were in hiding, and they asked me for the CD. I made an appointment with my friend to meet in a cafe to give her the CD. MI got that information and arrested me and my friend.

AC: How did they know? Hacked your email? Telephone?

NPL: I can't say for sure. I don't know.

AC: There you are, your friend comes, then military intelligence arrives. Do they handcuff you?

NPL: No handcuffs. They took me straight away to the police station.

AC: Then what?

NPL: They knew I had a connection with the '88 Generation, so they asked me where they were. At that time, they didn't know about me; they didn't know I was a blogger. After I was arrested, my friends all over the world got this information and they sent out the news, "The Blogger Nay Phone Latt was arrested."

At that time, the government didn't know the word "blogger." They heard and thought I was a "blocker" *(laughs)*. The truth is b-l-o-g-g-e-r but they thought b-l-o-c-k-e-r, so some of the senior members said to their men, "He's a problem, he tried to block overseas investment coming to our country." Because they thought I was a "blocker," they thought that I was blocking investments into the country.

AC: The irony, when in fact, they're the blockers.

NPL: Yes. So, I said, "No, it's not like that." I had to explain what a blogger meant.

AC: You also introduced them to freedom of expression. Did you know where the '88 Generation leaders were hiding?

NPL: No. But they didn't believe me. They thought I knew where they were.

AC: Were you beaten?

NPL: Yes. At first, they interrogated me at the police station. Then they took me to another place, and at that place there were four of five people— they hit me and asked many questions. I told them that I really didn't know where they were hiding, and I couldn't say anything more about it. I told them what I had been doing. That I had made a seminar. And I had plans to make another one. They had also known about this and asked many questions about it. I explained that my intention was not to protest the government. Rather, it was about education and for sharing the new technology. I explained it like that. I had the advantage because they didn't understand what I was saying, and what I was saying was not what they were afraid of. So, this was very surprising for me.

AC: You provided them with their first access to digital media?

NPL: I don't think they knew about the Internet and those kinds of things at that time.

AC: After the interrogation, was there a trial? Or did you go straight to prison?

NPL: I got a trial.

AC: What's a trial like for a dissident under dictatorship?

NPL: There's no local trial. The trial was within Insein Prison. At first, my parents could come, and we could talk, but as the trial proceeded, I was no longer allowed to see my parents. The trial, of course, was just for show, you know? Nothing but show.

AC: Why do they even go through the motions?

NPL: The main thing is that they wanted to sentence me to as many years as possible as a deterrent, to set an example for other people. They wanted to show people that they'd sentenced a blogger to so many years so that other bloggers and anyone else interested in ICT (Information and Communications Technology) would be frightened by such a long sentence. That is their thinking. The trial is just show. They had already said that they would sentence me before the trial.

"Where you are is not important.
What you are doing is what is important."

ALAN CLEMENTS: Not many people know the day to day life of a dissident inside one of Burma's many prisons. Would you take us there? Share anything you wish. For instance, what does it look like inside your cell? What do you eat? How do you behave? What goes through your mind? Who are your cellmates? How do you resolve conflicts? How do you keep your health? What are the guards like? Can you receive visitors? Can you read books? How do you stay active in the struggle? Do you get scared? Do you get depressed? How do you keep hope alive? Do you meditate? Anything that you care to share would be a gift to all dissidents worldwide—now and forever—those good folks willing to risk their own well-being and freedom, risk even their lives, to support the freedom of others. What would you like to share?

NPL: In Insein Prison, I was moved from one cell to another many times. Only in some cells did I have a chance to speak to others, and I don't know why they moved me from one cell to another so frequently. During the final three months in prison they sent me to one cell and didn't allow me to go outside or speak to anyone the entire time. When they moved me to Pan Prison in Karen State, it was not as difficult as Insein Prison. It's far from Yangon. In Pan, we had some degree of freedom. My parents came every month, and we could meet for 45 minutes or so. They also gave me food, and books and journals. That was a big change from Insein Prison.

In the earliest days of our struggle, political prisoners were given no chance to read. But in 2008, things changed, at least for me. They allowed me to read some books and journals. Even so, at first, they didn't allow English books. They only allowed Myanmar books. I asked them why they wouldn't allow me to read English books and they replied that they didn't understand English and so couldn't check their suitability. Therefore, they did not allow them. But I didn't accept that. I said to them, "If you can't understand English, I can, and would like to read English books to learn English. So, please, you must give me the chance to read in English." After struggling with them in this way, after a few months, they allowed me to read English books.

AC: Were you alone in your cell or did you have cellmates?

NPL: Only one to a cell. But in the morning, at 6am, they opened the doors to our cells, and we could speak with each other. At 5pm they closed the doors again.

AC: Did you have blankets, a bed? Water? A toilet?

NPL: There's no toilet in the cell. Only a bucket. There's no running water. And our food—they supplied rice and soup every day, and fish or meat two days a week. On the other days, we had to eat food given to us by our family.

AC: How did you spend your days for those four years?

NPL: I had a timetable. In the morning I paid homage to the Buddha's, and after that I had breakfast. After that I read books and I also had a chance to write to my family. In the morning, most of the time I was reading and writing. In the late afternoon, we got together in the room and had discussions. At first, we chose a topic and then we read about the topic. We then discussed it as a group. All political prisoners did this at Pan. There were nine of us.

AC: Do you remember their names?

NPL: Nyan Lin was one of the '88 Generation. Another one was Nanda Say Ah, a member of the student union. Ne Chaw was working in the D-Wave journal. Another was Won Ah Soe. Then there was Ko Ni Kyaw— he had served almost 12 years at that time. And there was Pyi Phyo Aung. He was imprisoned for distributing pamphlets critical of the government.

AC: Daw Aung San Suu Kyi once said, "Although they can imprison your body, they cannot imprison your mind, unless you let them. We must always remember to keep our mind free." I ask you: How did you keep your mind free in prison? How did you practice freedom?

NPL: They arrested me and sent me to prison because they didn't want me to do anything beneficial for the country. They wanted to silence me. That was their purpose in sending me to prison. But I didn't want to cooperate with them in fulfilling their desire. I didn't want to be quiet in prison. I didn't want to be inactive behind bars.

Do you know the words of '88 Generation leader, Min Ko Naing? He said, "Where you are is not important. What you are doing is what is important." Although the situation is tight, it doesn't matter. What we can do in any given situation is what matters. I was in prison, and there I found out what I could do in such a tight situation. I read. I talked with the other political prisoners. We learned English. And I also taught them English. We chose a book title and we had discussions. I also taught some of the other political prisoners ICT. I found out what I could do in prison and I practiced those things. I stayed active.

AC: What were some of the subjects you discussed?

NPL: We discussed so many things. Sometimes we discussed rights and responsibilities, and genes and the environment, and values—"What are values?" We discussed so many things.

AC: Did you discuss anything to do with Buddhism or the *Dhamma*?

NPL: We did not discuss Buddhism directly, but we practiced it. I'm lucky to have been born a Buddhist. Both my parents and grandparents are also Buddhist. During my childhood, I grew up with many Buddhist books through my grandfather. That was a foundation for me. And, in prison, I had a chance to read so many books, perhaps as many as 13 books a month. I'm not so free to do that now *(laughs)*.

"The real cause is in my heart,
not outside myself."

ALAN CLEMENTS: What do you love about Buddhism? What are some of the features of Buddhism that touch you the most? Let me say it this way: You've had a rare opportunity to practice *Dhamma* in an extreme circumstance—in prison and under dictatorship. Not many people have practiced meditation or Buddhism under totalitarianism, under threat of imprisonment, and in prison itself. You're a rare disciple of the Buddha.

NAY PHONE LATT: You know, I learned the basic concept of the

Buddha, about cause and effect. After learning that, I tried to find out what is the real cause. Okay, I was in prison. What is the real cause? The real cause is not the government. The real cause is not the lawyer. The real cause is not the judge. I tried to find out the real cause. Because the real cause are not those things. And I wanted to know the real cause. At that time, I felt anger arise. Okay, somebody criticized me, said rude things to me, and then I feel angry. Okay, I find out the real cause. He is not the real cause. What is the real cause? The real cause is in my heart, not outside myself. Whatever I learned of Buddhism in prison, I tried to practice this truth: freedom is not outside of my heart. The real cause is found by tracing it back to oneself. In that way, as it has been said, 'my freedom is not there for another to take.'

AC: Beautiful.

NPL: I know you understand this. We must all try to understand this. The real cause of suffering and the real cause of freedom are not in the outside world. The real causes are in ourselves. If we can control ourselves, if we can control our minds, then everything is quite okay. I practiced these things daily in prison. In this way, I didn't get angry with others.

AC: Sadhu, sadhu...

NPL: Sometimes we had problems with the authorities in prison, but I didn't get angry with them. I focused on the problem and I tried to solve the problem.

AC: When you meditate, may I ask, what do you do?

NPL: When I meditate, I focus on the breathing. The sensations that arise from breathing. And, as you know from your years with Mahasi Sayadaw, meditation is not only in the position of sitting still. Whatever we do, we can be mindful of it. That is also meditation. Okay, sometimes I write something. My mind is really focused on this writing. My mind is not anywhere else. My mind and my mindfulness is just really concentrated on the writing. That is another type of meditation. I practiced this way during my time in prison. Whatever I did, I tried to make it the object of my concentration. I also tried to do this when eating, but not nearly as much as when I was writing and speaking.

AC: Sounds like you were a dissident prison yogi. How did you practice meditation while talking in prison?

NPL: The main thing is to know what you are talking about. You could also call that basic intelligence, though, right? *(Laughs)* I'm sure you have noticed that sometimes people say things, but they don't know what they're talking about.

AC: *(Laughs)* I've noticed. Like Big Brother announcing how he's ushering in democracy and simultaneously arresting anyone expressing anything critical of the government?

NPL: *(Laughs)* Hypocrisy meditation.

AC: *(Laughs)* My teachers would always encourage us to 'know what you know and know what you don't know,' and to 'know how you can know what you don't know—that's meditation.'

NPL: Yes, good. We must try to have an awareness or to have mindfulness of knowing what we're actually talking about. To know what I'm saying and equally, if I don't know what I'm talking about, to know that—I can take responsibility for my words. To know the truth or the falsity of my speech. Also, to know our motivation while speaking. Yes, to 'know,' to truly know, to mindfully know, is so important.

AC: Perhaps what you are saying will become the basis of democracy in Burma—open, mindful, compassionate dialogue and the respectful evolution of ideas. And you must have also had a lot of experience in prison learning to listen to each other mindfully, meditatively?

NPL: Yes, we did this as well. Learning to concentrate on both our words when speaking as well as on the listening process. This too is meditation. You concentrate on what other people are saying, and you hear them more fully and clearly. And you also hear yourself inside when they are talking.

AC: And so, to be clear, while in prison, when having discussions, would you talk about doing it meditatively or was it just your own discipline? Did all of you practice mindful speaking and mindful listening?

NPL: I'm not sure how deeply it was practiced by the others. But I certainly encouraged them to do that kind of practice. But most of all, we really loved our discussions. I learned so much. Gained so much.

AC: What does freedom mean to you, and why is it important for you, such that you and many of your colleagues and friends have knowingly gone to prison, and, if I'm correct, are willing to go to prison again?

NPL: What we contemplated was that we had a military government and because of that, there's no democracy in Burma. And whatever we do to make that point is seen as a crime, according to their assumptions. Now the government is trying to change the system from a military government to a democratic one. Under rule of law and under a democratic government, our actions would not be seen as criminal. We cannot have this kind of situation in our country. For one, we did nothing wrong, and further, what we were doing was right. Our actions were for the benefit of the people. So, in a democratic country, with real rule of law, we would not go to prison for exercising our freedom of mind, freedom of conscience, and freedom of expression. But to answer your question, if I need to, if I must, I can go back to prison. I can endure. Yes, if I go back to prison unexpectedly, I can endure it. No problem. Because freedom is not outside of us. Freedom is inside me.

AC: Are you angry at anyone?

NPL: No. I don't feel angry.

AC: Because you practice *Dhamma*?

NPL: Yes. And I focus on the future, you know? I have so many things to do for the country and for the people. I don't have time to feel angry. If I feel anger towards them, I can hurt myself and my health.

AC: Do you have hope for the future of your country?

NPL: Just hoping is not enough. Yes, I have so many hopes. But we must try ourselves. Just hoping is not enough. If you want to fulfil your hope, you must try yourself. You must be active.

AC: What do you do that you most respect in bringing democracy to your people?

NPL: I do as much as I can. I also write in the local magazines and local journals.

AC: And you can write freely, without fear of censorship and or imprisonment?

NPL: Yes, freely. Now there is no censorship.

AC: None?

NPL: No.

AC: So, you can write, "I hate you, Than Shwe!"

NPL: Yeah, you can! If you read some journals, you can see those kinds of words.

AC: "Than Shwe, you should give all your money back to the people and become a Buddhist monk." You can say that?

NPL: Yes, you can.

AC: No problem?

NPL: But now the government is trying to control freedom of expression by using some new laws.

AC: Please explain. I haven't heard this.

NPL: Now the Minister of Information, U Aung Gyi, published a draft Print and Publishing Law to Parliament. Most of the journalists don't accept the Print and Publishing Law. In it, they want to control freedom of expression.

AC: What does the law state?

NPL: You must get permission whenever you want to publish.

AC: Sounds like the censorship board is coming back?

NPL: *(Laughs)* Yeah, most of the journalists think it is replacing the censorship board. We cannot accept this law.

AC: The law is in discussion, or already passed?

NPL: Hasn't passed. U Aung Gyi put this law to the Parliament to discuss. They haven't discussed it yet and haven't passed it. But it is there before the Parliament.

"When we are thinking about rights,
we should think two things:
my right and your right."

ALAN CLEMENTS: You've organized your people. You've opened cyber cafes, opening your country to interact with each other and the world. Not only do you like digital communication, you clearly want others to enjoy it as well. You've gone to prison for your beliefs, your love of freedom and universal human rights. My question: If you had five minutes to address Naypyidaw—the whole of Parliament to speak to, and Myanmar TV will broadcast your talk throughout the country, and to all ethnicities—what are some of the key points you'd like to share with your people? From your heart, what would you want to say to the members of Parliament, to Daw Aung San Suu Kyi, to President Thein Sein, and even the former dictator Than Shwe?

NPL: I want to say, "Give us freedom," and, "We can take responsibility for what we are writing." We don't want a situation in which somebody or some group is above us and they try to control us in everything we do. We don't like that. We want freedom and we will take responsibility for what we are writing. We don't need any restrictions or any control—state restrictions or state control from the government or any other group. That is what I want to say to the government sector.

Then, what I want to say to the people, and to the bloggers: I want you to take responsibility. Sometimes some people think that we are free, and we can do whatever we want, and we don't care about other people. Sometimes some people think this way. I don't like that thinking. You cannot be so free when there is such an oppressive environment all around you. Think of freedom for the whole, the greater good of everyone.

In other words, think before you act. Think before you hit "enter." In online environments, some people don't think. They see something, and they share it quickly. They see something, they feel emotionally very strong, and then share this information to everybody very quickly and without thinking. So, think before you hit "enter."

AC: Be mindful?

NPL: Yes. Be mindful. Think carefully. We need to take responsibility for what we are doing. Democracy does not mean total freedom. It doesn't mean not caring about anything. That is not democracy. Democracy means that we have rights, but we also must take responsibility for what we are doing. Know what you are doing and what you are saying, how it effects other people, how it effects the environment.

AC: So, think carefully before you hit "enter"?

NPL: Yes *(laughs)*. That's my message.

AC: My mediation teacher, Sayadaw U Pandita, once explained to me the importance of knowing one's impact on oneself and others. He said, "If you throw a rock in the pond, you can see that it impacts both the place of contact and sends ripples outwardly, that may affect the whole pond and all life in it. Maybe it's something that even pollutes the pond, as well as impacts the face of the water." He went onto explain how important it was to be conscious of one's words and actions like a stone thrown in a pond. I heard this as illuminating a concept I've used for decades, called "shared freedom." A freedom that isn't individual but a freedom that's shared. Call it the oxygen of civilized existence. So, as you were saying, the importance of understanding cause and effect—a freedom that's interrelated.

NPL: Yes, well said. Sometimes we make a small mistake but that can be a cause for very big effects. In other words, we unknowingly cause a big problem.

Most people today are talking about their rights, but they are primarily thinking about their own rights. They don't necessarily think about the rights of others. When we are thinking about rights, we should think two things: my rights and your rights. Not only my rights.

AC: It brings up another question. Your country, for nearly 50 years, has had a succession of dictators. Ne Win. Saw Maung. Than Shwe. We pray there's not another one, but it may be. When you look across your people's consciousness—the collective psychology of your country and culture, their inner typography, so to speak—what would you say is the cause that precedes dictatorship? Why do dictators arise out of this predominantly Buddhist culture? What is the cause for dictatorship? What does this country or any country need to look for, to avoid the arising of dictatorship? What are the seeds of totalitarianism? And how can it be avoided?

NPL: If we are thinking about the real cause, we must define two causes. One cause is the cause from the past, not the near past, but the earliest life, what we were doing in our previous life. It can be a cause in our current life. That kind of cause we cannot amend, but we have the current cause in our hands. We are talking about causes, and we must differentiate two things: past cause and present cause. Sometimes our past causes are very bad. But we can create, in the present, good causes. Sometimes, our past causes are good, but in the current situation, you do many wrongs, many crimes, and your present cause will be very bad. As a result, you get into a mess.

Okay, let's say with our country; our past cause is not good. We were under the rule of the military government and dictatorship, and it is because of the past cause. But, in our hands, we have the present cause. We have to try to create our present cause to be better and better. To the extent that our past cause is bad, if we can create our present cause to be better and better, we can hope for a better future.

AC: And what would that cause be? What cause are you looking to cultivate? Present causes right here: what will it be? "Dear Than Shwe, I'm a blogger who you imprisoned. I'd like to write you a letter, sir." One man's mind shifts and the whole country changes, right? Ever written a letter to Than Shwe?

NPL: Interesting you would ask. I want to write to him.

AC: What would you say?

NPL: I have many questions to ask him, and I want to show him the hope of the people. I also want to assure him that we don't have any intention of revenge.

AC: No retribution; no one way flight to the War Crimes Tribunal in the Hague?

NPL: I can assure him for myself. I'm not sure for everybody. But I can assure him that I don't have any intention of such an action.

AC: What do you want to tell him? You spent years in prison because of him, your country has gone through hell because of him. What do you really want to say?

NPL: For my imprisonment, I don't think he was the real reason. Personally, he did it. But if we find out the real reason according to *Dhamma*, according to *pattana* (conditioned relations of cause and effect), he's not the real reason.

AC: *Moha* is—one's fundamental ignorance.*

NPL: *(Laughs)* Yes. You asked, what do I really want to tell Than Shwe? I would like to know if he has control over the military. I would like to ask this question to him. And if he does have control of the military, I want to say to him that I don't want 25 percent of Parliament to be military members. I would ask him to "please withdraw this 25 percent from Parliament."

AC: What if he says, "Okay, I've read Nay Phone Latt's letter. He wants me to remove the military from parliament. Everyone wants me to—Daw Suu does, they all want me to remove the military." Why, though? Why?

NPL: It's not the democratic way, you know?

AC: But he says back to you, "I can't trust you—I can't trust that you won't put me in jail, or you won't call me to go on trial. This is the surest way that I can live in peace and read books." Isn't that what he's thinking?

NPL: Yeah, he's probably thinking that way. He put this 25 percent in Parliament because of fear. That's why we must assure him that there is no problem. We must assure him that he's safe and his family is safe. If we study the Constitution, we easily see his fear. He's clearly afraid of revenge. We can see this fear all throughout the Constitution. If so, we can assure him of his safety, the 25 percent can be withdrawn.

AC: I wonder if he will surprise everyone and make a public announcement that "Now that I've retired, I've had more time to meditate and I apologize for my cruel actions. Please forgive me." I wonder if he would say this. He would likely win the Nobel Peace Prize, or at least be nominated, perhaps even by his 25 percent in Parliament.

NPL: *(Laughs)* King Ashoka of ancient India redeemed himself. Why not Than Shwe?

AC: It would be a remarkable moment. Very healing not just for Burma but for all peoples worldwide

NPL: Yeah, yeah, for sure. But now, most of the military guys continue to think that what they are doing is right. They think they are doing it for the country, and for the people. So, I don't think he will apologize. They didn't accept that we were political prisoners. But we should send letters to Thein Sein and Than Shwe.

AC: Perhaps consider a nationwide campaign, with all people writing letters to Than Shwe.

NPL: But we don't have a channel to Than Shwe *(laughs)*.

AC: Just put "Than Shwe, Naypyidaw" and he'll get it, right? Just make sure you put enough postage on, or you might go to prison for trying to cheat the government.

NPL: *(Laughs).*

AC: Maybe if the people simply sent him *mettā*, thoughts of loving-kindness, just loved him so much that he might break down and cry. Maybe the whole country could stop work for a day and send him *mettā*. Maybe the whole world could join in. International *Mettā* Day for U Than Shwe. Maybe when he saw and felt millions of people worldwide sending him loving thoughts, he would soften his heart. Angulimala who tried to kill the Buddha became enlightened and gave up his evil ways, why not Than Shwe?

NPL: Best for him to have an awakening through his own reflection and for our people to keep pressing for a change in the Constitution. But I do like your idea. Maybe some combination of both.

AC: The democratic approach. I like that. Thank you for your time and thank you for your courage. And thank you for your humor. May true democracy flourish in your beloved country. May there be genuine national reconciliation. May all beings enjoy peace.

NPL: May it be so. And thank you for caring about our people—our freedom. Until we meet again.

CHAPTER 16

CONVERSATION *with* U NYAN WIN

March 2018

- "Everyone understands that the NLD government does not have the power to balance the powerful military."
- "[The NLD is] trying to change the culture of politics."
- "[Despite] limits and restraints on the government, the government has done a lot."

U Nyan Win is a Central Executive Committee member for the NLD, Aung San Suu Kyi's personal attorney, NLD legal adviser and party spokesperson. In this conversation with Alan Clements, he gives his take on the transition as it stands in 2018, on the limitations of the elected government and on its success so far.

"Everyone understands that the NLD government does not have the power to balance the powerful military."

ALAN CLEMENTS: What is your role in the NLD?

U NYAN WIN: Member of the Secretary Committee and spokesperson for the NLD.

AC: How long have you been the spokesperson?

UNW: For five years.

AC: Can ask you any question I want?

UNW: Yes. If there is something else, we will tell you off the record.

AC: The first question I'd like to ask is what are the main obstacles, the main challenges, that the NLD and the people of Burma face in their ongoing struggle for democracy?

UNW: The greatest challenge is the NLD party's members are not as united as they should be. But, the NLD is not unique in this case. This happens everywhere. It is the nature of politics.

AC: How could they be more unified? What do you see as a good next step?

UNW: If we can install peace quickly, and as successfully as possible, the members of the party will be united. The quicker we get peace, the faster there's peace in the whole country.

AC: But this is a distant reality? There's war in Shan State, war in Rakhine State, war in Karen State. There's war all over the country.

UNW: This is distant to reality because our civil wars started from

166

1948. Because of this there is mistrust in our society, and this mistrust has become the culture of our Burmese people.

AC: Your country has made international news very recently with the Rakhine crisis. When you look back, what could the NLD, the present government, have done differently to have handled this crisis?

UNW: As you know, the Rakhine problem is a long running one. The difference between the NLD government and the other government is that under the NLD leadership, we have a definite policy to accept people who return to Burma, plus the NLD government's commitment to the development of the conflict area. In the past, nobody focused on that.

AC: What could have been done differently to have not had one of the world's biggest humanitarian crises ever?

UNW: What do you mean by "humanitarian crisis"?

AC: There's 665,000 Bengali's in Bangladesh. Many of them speak of rape, and the murder of children by Burma's military. This government is run by Daw Aung San Suu Kyi and many NLD ministers. The whole world has criticized, in the media, this government and this military for one of the worst cases of "ethnic cleansing" we have seen in recent decades. Now it's months after that. My question is: What have you learned from this that could, in the future, be done differently?

UNW: In this country, Burma, we have an unprecedented constitution, an unprecedented constitutional error. The NLD has kept fighting against the 2008 Constitution, from the start until now. Because of this constitution, the NLD government cannot control all the government and all states.

In Burma, everyone understands that the NLD government does not have the power to balance the powerful military. That is the point that made the international community make a wrong approach, because the international community sees it as a whole, the NLD government as a sovereign government. But the government, which is led by the NLD, has never supported any kinds of arbitrary oppression.

AC: So, what we should understand is that, in Myanmar, there's the military, there's the government, and there's a constitution that the NLD and the government does not support. Is that what you're saying?

UNW: First you have to think about the Constitution. Because of the Constitution, the NLD cannot take the power of the whole government.

AC: Meaning the military, the police, homeland security?

UNW: Yes. So, now, as the NLD, we negotiate with the military on every issue.

AC: You're negotiating now?

UNW: Yes. We always try to negotiate with the military.

AC: What is the experience so far? What are they saying?

UNW: The military always claims that everything must be done in accord with the 2008 Constitution. Anything that is against the 2008 Constitution is unacceptable.

AC: So, the military runs the country? They do what they want when they want to? That's how we should understand the situation?

UNW: The military is now exercising all the power which has been given by the 2008 Constitution.

AC: So, this country is run by the military?

UNW: This is pretty true, even though it is not completely true.

AC: But the government cannot control the military? That's the main thing.

UNW: Yes. They cannot control them. And I would like to mention one example to promote your understanding of Burmese politics. In a very recent attack in Rakhine State, ARSA launched offensive attacks on the 30 police posts. At that point, you should notice that the civilian government has no military power. Military power is in the hands of the military. So, of course, the military took a revenge attack against ARSA, and many things happened to the area. But then, the Muslim people fled to Bangladesh. As soon as the Muslim people fled to Bangladesh, the NLD government announced that the war is over. Because of saying this, it made the military stop fighting against ARSA.

"[The NLD is] trying to change the culture of politics."

ALAN CLEMENTS: How would you describe general Min Aung Hlaing? What are your feelings about him?

U NYAN WIN: We don't know him.

AC: Do General Min Aung Hlaing and Daw Aung San Suu Kyi have tea, dinner—do they talk?

UNW: Yes, Daw Aung San Suu Kyi and General Min Aung Hlaing meet occasionally, but I've never joined the meeting and I've never seen General Min Aung Hlaing face-to-face.

AC: Even if this government had a different constitution, the military seems to have a mind of its own. These boys are deeply indoctrinated in do what-you-are-told behavior. Would it really make a difference, would they even listen to this government, with a new constitution? How would a new constitution change their way of thinking.

UNW: Burmese politics is more complex and more difficult than you would ever think. The NLD and the current government is trying not only to change the Constitution, it's also trying to change the culture of Burmese politics. That is a very big issue. On that point, if the Constitution is not really difficult to amend or is flexible, that would be very good.

AC: That's a very interesting point. Would you explain, in brief, the culture of Burmese politics, and what you would like to change?

UNW: I don't know the proper English word, but you know the elephant, and then the man who controls the elephant with a whip?

AC: With the stick?

UNW: Yeah, with the stick. Taps the head of the elephant, it sits.

AC: This is the culture of Burmese politics?

UNW: Yeah. Let's call the man "master of the elephant." The master of the elephant never thinks about in what way he will tame the elephant. His focus is the result. The result is the elephant must be controlled by him.

AC: And the man on the elephant is the NLD and the government?

UNW: Yes. I like to think of it this way.

AC: Daw Aung San Suu Kyi, when she took a role in government, and when the NLD won the majority of seats in the Parliament, she made it clear that the number one focus was national reconciliation and rule of law. These two things. But national reconciliation: how many years now? Hasn't it been four years? What is the progress towards national reconciliation? Do you see any? Point two: What are some of the ways that we could understand that it's actually developing?

UNW: The most obvious process of Daw Aung San Suu Kyi promoting national reconciliation is that Daw Aung San Suu Kyi goes to the peace conference, to the Panglong. Another point is that, based on national reconciliation, the NLD government organized the government, and Daw Aung San Suu Kyi appointed nine NLD ministers. This is a very puppet process of national reconciliation. Even though I cannot tell what the progress in the government is, I know well that there is progress in the peace issue, in the peace process.

AC: The peace process with ethnic minorities?

UNW: The peace process within the whole country.

AC: The whole country? With the military? With ethnic minorities? So, there's clear development in these areas?

UWN: So, you hold criteria to assess the improvement of the peace process. The criteria should be based on what's happened before the NLD and what's happened with the NLD. Before the NLD, even though there was work for the peace process, nothing changed. After the NLD, even though it cannot reach to the international requirement, there have been a lot of changes. For example, many agreements have been reached by all parties in the peace process.

AC: It's clear to you that good things are developing, slow as they may be, for Myanmar?

UNW: Yes. No doubt.

"[Despite] limits and restraints on the government,
the government has done a lot."

ALAN CLEMENTS: Many people in the world—leaders, governments, ordinary citizens of most countries—are looking carefully at Burma. Your people have successful gone from 1988 to today, through 30 years, to have gotten here peacefully. Daw Aung San Suu Kyi and the NLD, by and large, have been devoted to nonviolent political change. Amazing in this world.

I'm an American. In my country, we don't seem to have any belief in a government of nonviolence. We kill many people around the world with impunity and often celebrate this strangeness. What are some of the ways that you as leaders in this country would like leaders of the world, and people of the world, to best support democracy, human rights, peace and reconciliation for your people? If you were speaking to the United Nations, if you were speaking to the people of the world, what would you tell us about how we can support you?

U NYAN WIN: Maybe you know, or you don't know, but before the NLD came into power, some leaders of the West put huge pressure on the NLD over one issue. That was to pick at opposite definitions of law which have been written and attacked. To pick opposite definitions of written law.

AC: What law was that?

UNW: Rohingya. We have never had "Rohingya" in Burma. It's a Rohingya issue because we've never had this word in Burmese history, "Rohingya." The West pressured us to accept this word as an ethnicity. Actually, this is completely against the existing law.

AC: And yet Western governments put pressure on this government?

UNW: Even though I can't mention the exact name of the Western leaders, or who put pressure on the NLD to accept the Rohingya as an ethnicity, we saw, obviously, there was pressure on us. That is why Daw Aung San Suu Kyi didn't talk much about this issue.

AC: Last question: What do you see in store for the 2020 elections?

UNW: We, the NLD government, won a landslide victory in the 2015 election because the NLD is the most popular party in Burma. The NLD will keep its popularity until 2020, because the people of Burma completely understand the challenges and limits of the NLD government. Even though there are a lot of limits and restraints on the government, the government has done a lot, and people understand that. As long as people understand this point, the NLD will be the top popularity in the country.

AC: The whole world, for many, many years, loved Daw Aung San Suu Kyi. They loved the struggle that she and the people represented here. It gave them hope. You know Daw Aung San Suu Kyi very well. No one in the world, by and large, except a few leaders, have met her or know anything about her. If you don't mind sharing, what are some of her qualities that you have grown to respect and appreciate?

UNW: Firstly, she always delivers on promises she's made, without thinking about popularity. And then she is direct and open, she has no secrets. Very honest.

AC: Thank you.

CHAPTER 17

CONVERSATION *with* NLD CHAIRMAN

March 2018

"If you want to criticise us, please wait one or two years."

NLD Chairman: We're Burman. I'm Burman. Burmans have ourselves as our own history. We have our own very different concept of history, different from that of the Rakhine, or the Shan, because they too have their own history. Rakhine was once a big empire, and Rakhine people were once a dominant race in the Bay of Bengal. Those things you already know. Same with the Mon. They have their own history, and their perception of history is quite different from ours.

Because of that, whenever we talk about something, everybody wants to go backward. Especially with Rakhine. They want to go back to 1784 or something like that, [when Rakhine was the seat of an empire]. And then not only relating to the Burmese this way, but because they also treated people like the Bengalese, like the Chittagonians, as their subjects, whenever they go back into their history, they think that that is the main reason. The Shan, they also suffered; they had their own king also.

I want to say that we, especially Burmans, are trapped in our history. We cannot look forward. Whenever we try to look forward, there are people among us who want to look backward. That is the main reason.

ALAN CLEMENTS: That's the main struggle. You need something like a national psychiatrist.

NLDc: Yeah, yeah. That's the main thing, I think.

AC: That's a very interesting point. Another point: clearly the 2008 Constitution separates the government from the military, from the police, from homeland security and so on. How do you ever see a way of bridging this chasm? Is it only going to come from a change in the Constitution? Because it seems as if you've got two separate countries, or a disproportionate parallel government—a civilian government and the military, who hold the power.

NLDc: When you work together or solve a problem together you come together, whether you have been divided by law or something like that. In a practical sense, as far as I know, in the regional governments and those things, I think there is some cooperation between our people and the people from the military, especially in the police or in security affairs. Yes, I've found that there have been conflicts, because of those procedures and laws and those separations, but there is also cooperation in those areas. Especially on Rakhine State.

Now, in the emergency state, we have been accused of being very close to the military. But what's happened is that when you have to solve a problem together, you think together, you become likeminded, you see? You have very similar thinking about the same things. You may have a very different background, but the thinking, the pattern of thinking, comes together. So, I think that by working together we can overcome some of the difficulties, some of the obstacles, of being divided by the Constitution.

AC: You are hopeful this is happening?

NLDc: Yes, somehow it is happening. The main obstacle is not at the ground level. At the top level, sometimes, when the regional minister for the security comes from the military and has a very close relationship with the regional government, they used to be transferred. It has happened twice in our times.

AC: You've made international news the last several months with the crisis in Rakhine State. I won't go on about this. The country, the military, the government, it's hard to decipher whom they're pointing their fingers at. But Daw Aung San Suu Kyi's been severely criticised as leader of the government, of being complicit with ethnic cleansing. This is stated all over the news, worldwide. You know it better than me. Here it is, January 16th, 2018; looking back, could you, as a government, have done things differently? And if so, what would you have done differently?

NLDc: I would do the same thing, because there are so many constraints imposed by the Constitution, and also imposed by past deeds, and because we have inherited everything from the previous government. The thing is, for the past half a century, we didn't have any say because of the lack of transparency in the whole country. The viewpoint, from the perspective of the Rakhine or the Burmans relating to that particular problem, has not been known by the international community. The only perspective is from the side of the Rohingyas.

So, the ethnic Rakhine especially, they're a minority if you look at the whole country. Or, they are about to be a minority in their state. Their perceptions of that problem are very different, but everybody thinks that they are just irrational or something like that. They have very valid and rational concerns and worries, and these worries and concerns were not recognised by the international community. The ethnic Rakhine are a minority. The international community thinks they are a majority oppressing the Rohingya peoples. They are accusing them of this. But, especially on the ground, the opposite is true.

AC: The Rakhine Buddhists are the minority?

NLDc: In the conflict areas.

AC: In those three townships.

NLDc: In those three townships they are only 10 percent of the population. They are a minority there. Nobody knows about that because of the blackout of our information system for the past half a century. Nobody knows about that, and everybody thinks that when you talk about Burma the Burmans are everywhere, and the Burmans are the majority, and there are a million Rohingyas and there are 49 million Burmans or something like that. That's what they think. The real situation is not like that.

AC: You know Daw Aung San Suu Kyi very well, I assume. The media has criticised her; leaders have criticised her; Nobel laureates have criticised her for not, so-called, "speaking out" for the Rohingyas, the Bengalis, and speaking out against the military's operations which have resulted in people saying, "ethnic cleansing!" How would you respond to that criticism?

NLDc: "Speaking out," I think, was effective when we were in opposition. It was effective because we were in opposition. But when you are governing together with the military, speaking out against the military is not very effective. It's not very useful. If you want to speak out against them, she might speak out privately, not publicly. By speaking out publicly, it will show a clear division in the government, and it will be very difficult to govern.

AC: Last question: many people around the world, leaders, ordinary people, have adored your country. They loved Daw Aung San Suu Kyi. They have loved your leaders, who've gone to prison for freedom and human rights, for 30 years since 1988. Here it is, early January 2018. If you were to talk to the people of the world, what would you want them to know on how best to support your country's struggle for democracy and freedom today? What can they do?

NLDc: I think they should wait patiently for I think one or two years. One or two years more is quite a short period, compared to the past 30 years or so that we have been struggling. We have been struggling for a very long time, more than half a century, and if you want to criticise us, please wait for one or two more years.

AC: Thank you.

CHAPTER 18

CONVERSATIONS *with*
KO KO GYI

2013 & 2018

2013

- "If we didn't firmly commit to challenging the government, nobody else would."
- "They can only imprison your body, not your mind."
- "It's easy to talk about *Dhamma*, but it's very difficult to practice *Dhamma*."
- "Our good will, our cooperation, is mainly intended to benefit our people."
- "They're talking about the minority and the underdog, which is unwittingly to … highlight the divide in the country. We must give more attention to their grievances and their unequal status".
- "We need to provide general [human rights] knowledge, even in childhood."

2018

- "Peace is the fundamental problem of our country."
- "They've noticed the importance of public opinion and support."
- "We need to promote the role of the ethnic political society and the ethnic civil society."
- "We're trying to elevate their way of thinking as much as we can."

Ko Ko Gyi is board member of the All Burma Federation Students Union and a prominent activist in the 88 uprising and later protests and campaigns. He is a close colleague of Min Ko Naing who also served two decades in prison for his activism, refusing release as a matter of conscience. Together they caught the world's attention and mobilized unrest into a coherent movement that threatened the dictatorship, and inspired a new generation of artists, campaigners, citizen journalists, protesters and pro-democracy activists. In this interview Ko Ko Gyi discusses Burma's early student movements in detail, from the formation of the ABFSU to the formation of the DPNS, sharing what inspired his activism and why it was so important. He outlines his relationship to *Dhamma,* sharing the meditation practices that supported him in prison and the principles of compassion and forgiveness that helped him to survive the hardship of prison life. He relates this to the broader issues of freedom of expression and Burma's need for transparency and accountability.

"If we didn't firmly commit to challenging
the government, nobody else would."

ALAN CLEMENTS: Ko Ko Gyi, an honor to meet you after all these years, and thank you for taking the time to speak with me through our set of books, *Burma's Voices of Freedom.* You are an inspiration to both the people of your country and to freedom loving people worldwide. As a former political prisoner and a revolutionary dissident, you are poised to be a future leader of government, and perhaps even president of your country, at some point. With your wealth of experience, I'd like to explore your insights and lessons learned from your decades of nonviolent struggle, not just for the people of Myanmar but for a new generation of dissidents worldwide.

You spent nearly 19 years in prison. What was the reason you were jailed?

KO KO GYI: Frankly speaking, it was because of a song perceived to be against the government. See, for most of my life the government suppressed our people. They've taken advantage of us for decades. Even though our country has an abundance of natural resources and our people are talented and readily adapt to new technologies, despite this, in 1987, Burma was placed on the UN's list of Least Developed Countries. And the truth is, we couldn't accept this. We felt shame for allowing it to happen, especially in intellectual circles, with university students, artists, writers and poets. We asked ourselves, 'Why? How could this have happened?' At that time, we were criticizing the government in secret.

AC: Both you and Min Ko Naing were the student leaders at that time?

KKG: Yes, that was in 1987. Then another coincidence occurred, in that, as our country slid down into the UN's list of Least Developed Countries, the government demonetized our currency. Because of this violent delusion, the 25, 35, and 75 kyats notes became worthless. Instantly, our people were looted of their honest earnings. These were provocative events in our country. They ignited the conscience of our people. We wanted change.

AC: What was it like to confront the totalitarian military machinery of U Ne Win's dictatorship?

KKG: At the time, along with some of our elders, as I said, we were actively criticizing the political and economic systems of U Ne Win's authoritarian oppression. And in so doing, we knew with absolutely certainty, they wanted us leaders dead. Yes, we knew it was dangerous. Yes, we knew we should not try to bend the brick wall of dictatorship. But we were determined. So, we met and talked in secret, all the while knowing it could lead to the end of life.

See, some of the dissidents—the activists and artists and singers—always tried to make Than Chat, our traditional form of Myanmar poetry that is similar to hip-hop or rap. Whereby one person sings, and the group shouts back. And they go on like this—back and forth—satirizing the faults of the government. Every year this is done in the Thingyan Festival. This is our Myanmar tradition. Than Chat is just one of the traditional forms of spoken word poetry, and Min Ko Naing is one of the poet-singers, making jokes about the government.

AC: Very courageous knowing it would likely land one in prison.

KKG: There comes a point when the cost of living in servitude no longer outweighs the desire for freedom. But our behavior was not taken lightly. From 1988 onwards, cracking jokes about the government—on the ministry level upward—was banned by the authorities. *Than Chat* at the Thingyan festival was also outlawed. Now we're revitalizing the *Than Chat* spoken word activist culture.

AC: Where were you on August 8th, '88, the day of your country's uprising?

KKG: Many of us student leaders called for a nationwide demonstration for that day, August 8th, 1988. As we did, we gathered downtown Yangon around the Sule Pagoda. And let me be clear, it wasn't just Min Ko Naing and myself calling for the uprising. There were so many other student leaders as well. See, we tried to form a student union at the University in secret, and at the same time, we tried to contact each other as an underground movement. In so doing, we were hiding here and there. As I said, we knew it was a dangerous situation.

AC: What were you hoping to achieve with the uprising?

KKG: Honestly, I dared not hope too much at that time. But I realized that if we didn't firmly commit to challenging the government, nobody else would dare to try to topple it.

AC: So that was your intention—to topple the government?

KKG: At the beginning we dared not try to topple the government. We wished only to express our feelings, our sufferings to them. Very simply, we opposed the government. Especially after March 13th, 1988, when Ko Phone Maw was killed in the Yangon Institute of Technology compound. This incident spread quickly to the Arts and Science university, so we, the people, demanded to know what was happening at that time.

See, the government is always lying to the people, and the Government Investigation Commission were singling out the student community mainly because of what the students *thought*. We were very angry with their investigation commission report.

AC: You had no real hope of toppling the government? All you wanted was to express your *dukkha*, your sufferings?

KKG: That's how it was at the beginning. We dared not attempt to topple the government. But gradually we sped up our movement, and realized we needed the uprising to get more support in calling for multi-party democracy.

AC: Had you any idea that the entire nation would rise up?

KKG: No. At that time, there was no media coverage on our side. Only the government media, their newspaper and television, and of course, only from their side. The only foreign broadcast media at that time was All-India Radio, VOA and BBC. In the beginning, all we had was each other, really.

AC: When did you get arrested the first time?

KKG: The first time was after the military coup on September 19th, 1988. I was arrested in 1989. But I spent only two months in custody. At that time, I'd written a paper in favor of an interim government, challenging the present situation. The title was *Interim Government vs. The Present Situation*. My opinion was that most people, especially our comrades, were calling for an interim government after the military-coup, as a practical, intermediate measure. The government had already announced multi-party elections during the seventeen-month spectacle, but mostly they decided not to honor it in the election.

My view was that we needed an interim government, but that we can't call for an interim government simply by shouting and demonstrating. We needed to overcome our challenges through an election. The election result had the same status as the interim government. It would be just a steppingstone to come through in the election, and because of this most people were against the election. The government, they were willing to believe the election procedure, but most of the people were against the elections. So, my paper, advocated rising up through the elections. This, to me, was the proper way to have progress.

AC: You were 27 years old at that time, and, as I understand it, were studying International Relations at Rangoon University. Because of this, you had a solid understanding of international politics, diplomacy, and justice.

KKG: Yes, and in my paper, we called for the interim government during the socialist regime. This was a legal demand, because at that time, the socialist government, whether we liked it or not, was the *de jure* government, according to the 1974 Constitution. Calling for an interim government from the socialist government was legal, but it was only after the military-coup by the military-government itself, which was essentially the face of a defective government. Only then did we call for an interim government. If we could remove the military government, we could form our own government, that's all. If not, we would have to accept the election. This was the first step in establishing an interim government.

AC: Why did they release you after two months? Did they underestimate your conviction and desire for change? In other words, how did they not see you as a huge threat? Or did they have an ulterior motive, and want to keep you under surveillance?

KKG: Good question. But I think it was solely because of my term paper. I think they just wanted to control us because they feared our power.

AC: What happened after those two months?

KKG: After being released from prison I tried to create the student union. We made a joint statement with the new power there, the DPNS (Democratic Party for a New Society), especially with one of our main branches of the student union. Because we didn't want to accept a student union under the military government, we never tried to get the union officially recognized. But this was a separate branch of the student union, this Democratic Party for a New Society. Also, there was the formation of the National League for Democracy Youth wing.

AC: Please say more.

KKG: The NLD Youth wing was the fever pitch, so to speak, of our '88 generation movement. That's why we tried to unify the tripartite: the ABFSU, the DPNS, and the NLD Youth. We joined together to publish our political views about the crisis. We had only four points. One point was that we would have to progress through the multi-party elections. The second was that we needed to assure ethnic equality for our future. The third was that we needed to recruit from the students and youth sectors, we needed representation in Parliament. And the final point was that our objective was to win in the election as an expression of a whole democratic process, not simply as a banner or a party. Our view was that the democratic process should win in the election. Because of those four points, we joined together the student union—All Burma Federation of Student Unions and then the Democratic Party for a New Society, and then NLD Youth—and then we announced a tripartite statement to the public.

"They can only imprison your body, not your mind."

ALAN CLEMENTS: When were you re-arrested and put back in prison?

KO KO GYI: The next time was in 1991. From '89 to '91 I was out of prison, for those two years. During that time, we organized the student groups and called for student unions.

AC: You were free during the infamous "free and fair multi-party elections" in 1990?

KKG: Yes, I was out of prison at that time.

AC: What did you do that irritated the regime so deeply that you were re-imprisoned?

KKG: Right up to the point of the 1990 elections, there weren't many problems. Because we accepted the general elections, that's why we needed to campaign so much to win the elections, especially advocating for a pro-democratic process. Because the greater problems started after the 1990 election result. The election was held on May 27, 1990, and then in September, very close to the Gandhi Hall Declaration—it was a head-on confrontation between the NLD and the military government.

The night before the Gandhi Hall Declaration, the military government announced the 1/90 Notification—a direct challenge to the political trend. The Gandhi Hall Declaration called to convene a parliament, but the 1/90 Notification stipulated only drawing the Constitution, not convening Parliament by the end of it. After that, many MPs were arrested. And likewise, we student leaders were also arrested. We were taken to Insein Prison.

AC: And interrogated?

KKG: Yes, I was interrogated. My next arrest occurred after the International Human Rights Day protests and celebrations on December 10th in 1991. This was the day when Daw Aung San Suu Kyi was awarded the Nobel Peace Prize. The Yangon University students gathered to honor Daw Aung San Suu Kyi at the campus, demonstrating and shouting protests. Because of that, we went to prison. Because we were arrested again on December 10th, we called the movement the 10D Movement.

AC: And this time they imprisoned you for, how long?

KKG: Almost 14 years, which brings up another interesting aspect of our country's story. At the very beginning I was given a life sentence. The government then ruled that all sentences over 10 years would be reduced to 10 years. So, I benefited from that, so to speak, and my sentence was reduced to 10 years. The interesting point is that all prisoners were to enjoy this remission, generally speaking, so if you were to suffer three years in prison, you only had to serve two years, one year being the remission. But in reality, political prisoners had no chance to enjoy such remission. We had to suffer the full terms.

Ordinary criminals, the other prisoners, on the other hand, enjoyed the remission. But our political prisoners, they had to spend full terms in prison. So, in 1999, the prison superintendent informed me that it was my release date. But when speaking with me about it, he seemed upset. The next thing he said was that 'the superior authorities, in accord with the State Security Act, have extended your sentence without taking you to court.' According to the State Security Act, they could extend my sentence by 60 days up to three times consecutively, which meant an extra 180 days added. Then they extended it by 1 year five times—altogether five and a half years. I spent an extra five and a half years in prison after my release date.

AC: Very Orwellian. Many millions of people around the world are deeply moved and humbled by the conscience and courage of a political prisoner, that they've chosen, as you have, to empower their integrity, conscience, compassion and dignity, and stand up to injustice and dictatorship. How did you keep freedom alive under such harsh prison conditions?

KKG: As a devoted Buddhist, I see mind and body as different phenomena. Every person, obviously, has a body and a mind. So, any dictator, any government, any aggressor, can only imprison your body, but not your mind. That is, unless you allow them to imprison your mind. We had to see our minds as free and unshackled, even though we were confined in a tiny cell. We had to see that only our body was imprisoned. But not our mind. And the most important thing in keeping our mind free was to never regret our actions. Why? Because we never committed a wrongdoing. To the contrary, we acted in conscience. We acted from compassion. We tried to liberate our people from injustice, cruelty, and unfair treatment.

AC: How inspiring. And no anger, no blame?

KKG: As ordinary people, we have so many personal feelings, but our personal suffering is our sacrifice and our contribution to the 50 million people suffering in our country. Our actions are *the* investment that we make in our future. That's why we always tried to remain calm in prison. We had enough time in prison to think of our country and our people. And to always to think of a brighter future.

Another point is that, as Buddhist philosophers, we have to ask ourselves what reason we have to be upset about being confined in such a small cell. When we think back to the beginning of our human life, we see that we are all former prisoners—you and me—in our mother's womb, confined, as it were, for the first nine months of our lives. We can't stretch out our hands or feet. Now, I'm living in a small room. But even 8' x 10' is quite enough for me to walk about seven steps, and then go back seven steps. It's plenty enough. Whereas, in our mother's womb we cannot even stretch out our legs. This is how we reflected in prison. We used our mind to keep freeing our mind. Further, we reflected that every human being has to die one day, and so we asked ourselves, since everybody has to die, why would we be afraid of a prison term or punishment. Of course, no one knows how or when they will die, but death is certain. Our lifespan is a very precious time, from the womb to the tomb. How will we use that precious time? We felt honored and strengthened by our actions to support the well-being of our people and the future of our country. This, as you know, is the role of the nonviolent activist. He and she must be prepared to go to prison for their beliefs and actions. We found that these basic reflections empowered us in keeping our conscience and minds bright and free.

AC: The beautification of the mind. This was a daily meditation of yours in prison?

KKG: Yes, every morning we brought out our Buddha and meditated for an hour or so, reflecting in these ways. And this would help us to keep these *Dhamma* qualities active in our hearts throughout the day. We then exercised before taking a bath. Eventually we rejoiced when we were given permission to have some books. This was a great improvement in prison life.

In 1999, after the ICRC's (International Committee of the Red Cross) visit to Insein, prison life was slightly better than before. For the first nine years we slept on the concrete floor. There were no wooden cots. No mattresses. No pillows. No paper, pens or books. This was extreme punishment. This was the worst we could endure. And the quality of the food was almost unimaginable. Then there was the isolation. It was bleak. Yes, there were times that we felt like we were losing our minds. The military

185

authorities tried desperately to not only to imprison our bodies but destroy our minds in prison. But we were steadfast in our resolve.

AC: You courageously challenged their ignorance, their *moha*, with *Dhamma*.

KKG: Yes, we resisted with everything we had. And we kept our freedom of mind. We also had to use our ingenuity. We consistently tried to get reading materials one way or another, mostly in secret. If we got caught even with even a single piece of paper, we would suffer severe punishment. But after the 1999 ICRC visit to the prison, they provided some medications and drinking water. As such, some parts of the prison improved. Out of those improvements we were interested in just one thing: books.

AC: I pray as a species we learn how to decode the mindset of evil. And did you get books?

KKG: Yes. At first, only religious books. And then gradually sports.

AC: Buddhism has gained considerable popularity in the Western world, especially *satipaṭṭhāna* (mindfulness meditation). But as Americans we can easily practice in safe and aesthetically pleasing settings. You on the other hand, have had the terrible beauty, if you will, of practicing the *Buddhadhamma*, this mindfulness, in some of the harshest conditions known in the world. Nine years without furniture, running water, a toilet, and sleeping on a concrete floor in a tiny prison cell is unimaginable. Was there any other element of the Buddha's teachings that you have not yet explained that was valuable to you in safeguarding both your sanity and your freedom?

KKG: What I previously explained was an inexhaustible refuge. I felt empowered by reflecting on human life. For instance, I'd go through my own past experiences and feel their ethical and *Dhamma* significance. Then I'd think of certain leaders, especially our country's military generals: 'What are they doing now? What do they think about? What really matters to them, really?' General Ne Win passed away. U Sein Lwin, his successor, passed away. Doctor Maung Maung, the last president of the socialist regime, passed away. Then the military coup leader, General Saw Maung, passed away. And then the secretary too—he died in a plane crash. One after another they passed away; what was the use of their human life? What was it for? How will they be remembered? These people lived as humans obsessively greedy for power, always trying to preserve their position and their status. They had no conscience to look back at what they'd done, to reflect. In this light, I'm a lucky man in prison. I have plenty of time to review my past experiences and I'm proud of my duty as a prisoner of conscience. And those leaders? Gone. And their legacy? They are universally seen as devoid of moral wisdom.

AC: And you stand in the power of you *silā*, your virtue.

KKG: Yes, yes indeed. It is a source of self-respect. A refuge I trust in fully. You may ask, how did I survive the hardship of prison life? Generally speaking, there are only three points. The first point is that we never regretted any of our actions. I found this not only in myself, but I always encouraged it in others, especially, our younger people, the newcomers in prison. I always said to them, 'Don't regret your deeds. You sacrificed for your country. Use prison life to improve your knowledge and your understanding of the *Dhamma*, or ethical human relations and the importance of democracy.' You can do this very well from within prison. Also, learn a second or third language, like English. And gain other forms of knowledge, such as history. We always tried to share our experiences and our knowledge with the younger generation. This is the first point: never regret, and devote yourself to learning. The second point is to joke about suffering. Use humor as a self-defense against fear and doubt. We always tried to be happy, to make each other laugh and to be happy. Each time we encountered bitterness we made jokes with each other. The third point is Buddhist philosophy. Use *Dhamma* reflections to help yourself. Just like the womb to the tomb, this is the extent of our lifespan. So, we continue to think of how best to use our time, how best to spend our lifespan, for our own benefit and the benefit of our community and country. This is our choice. That is how we survived and overcame bitterness in prison.

"It's easy to talk about Dhamma,
but it's very difficult to practice Dhamma."

ALAN CLEMENTS: It has been said in the Buddhist tradition that when the ruler or a leader has strong *Dhamma*—courageous respect for ethical and mindful intelligence, who embody a compassion for shared freedom, and practice *dāna, silā, and bhāvanā*—that the people are inspired, they feel safe and thrive. You are a leader. You obviously have *Dhamma* in your heart, but your country is presently ruled by former military generals, people who, from looking at their behaviors over decades, seem to have little or no regard for *Dhamma*. They go as far as imprisoning *Dhamma* inspired dissidents, including monks and some nuns. Of course, they put you and your comrades in prison. My question: What advice might you offer your country's military rulers, both present and past rulers who have returned to civilian life, to increase their regard for the *Dhamma*? And more specifically, how would you encourage the dictator—former Senior General U Than Shwe—to increase his understanding of the *Dhamma*? The same with Shwe Mann? Frankly, please include the same with Daw Aung San Suu Kyi. How might you advise her to increase her regard for *Dhamma* and bringing that *Dhamma* more actively into her political life? How would you encourage them? How would you inspire them?

KO KO GYI: *Dhamma* is subtle. It's easy to talk about *Dhamma*, but it's difficult to practice, as you say, ethical and mindful intelligence. You can show off your charity to the poor or so on, but your actual intention is: what? Do you want to donate to the poor to uplift their lives or do you donate to the poor to show off, to boost your ego?

According to our Buddhist *abhidhamma*—*abhidhamma* means 'the Great *Dhamma*'—our Buddha's *Dhamma* is complicated and subtle. With the highest most purified good deeds—good deeds surrounded by good deeds—we have no attachment to our charity; we have no expectation to get something in return from our charity; we totally detach from our property to give to the poor. This is the highest most purified expression of charity. On the other hand, if we want other people to know how generous we are, how much we wish to be recognized, that is not a pure motivation and the good deed becomes tainted. We have expectations of receiving something in return for our property, from our donation. This is a second good deed, and not the highest or most purified deed. That's why *Dhamma* is easy to talk about, and why it's so subtle and challenging to put into purified practice.

AC: In other words, the ego gets in the way and one becomes a spiritual showman rather than a humble servant of the *Dhamma*.

KKG: Yes. As you know from being an ordained Buddhist monk here in our country, *Dhamma* is only a name. It is a label. A designation. You can pronounce it easily: *Dha-mma*. But as you know, one cannot easily practice *Dhamma*. But we must try. In this way, democracy is very close to the Buddha's philosophy, to the *Dhamma*.

AC: Can you say more?

KKG: The Buddha, even in his time, encouraged his *Dhamma* followers to choose their opinions freely. He openly advocated 'freedom of thought,' especially among *Saṅgha*, the community of Buddhist monks and nuns. As you know, the Buddha's *Kalama Sutta* outlines very clearly the importance of freedom of thought and freedom of inquiry. One must choose freely and of course, wisely, what is good and what is bad. There's no need whatsoever to depend on a superior or the scriptures or the elders, on anybody for that matter. Only depend on your own direct experience, your own mindful intelligence, your own wisdom, and only then, choose your way. We must always keep aware of whether our thoughts, speech and actions relax greed, relax anger, and relax delusion, and whether our thoughts, speech and actions enhance generosity, loving-kindness and freedom. This too me is the intersection of *Dhamma* and democracy.

AC: People tell me that you are running for president. Is that true?

KKG: In our country, there is no such presidential direct election. Well, from the beginning we never thought about what should be or what should occur, especially in the sense that I had no personal ambition in my political activities. We just wanted to serve our people as best as we could. The main thing here is that holding a political position is very important in serving the people. That's why we've committed to taking part in parliamentary politics, and as such, we are openly speaking with the people. But I've not yet made a public statement about my political intentions.

AC: If I may; I love your country. Your people have given me so much. And you have succeeded, against all odds, in confronting this unjust group of men and their wives, called dictatorship. The world is watching. You have elections coming up in early November. We want to see Burma have its Mandela moment, a victory through nonviolence and through dialogue and national reconciliation. My question: What's required to truly have a democratic president and a truly democratic Burma at the end of these elections? A country, I might add, that is no longer run, overtly or covertly from behind-the-scenes, by a dictator and those who collude with him?

KKG: There are two aspects. One is the common people. The second aspect is the elite-level, particularly the military leaders and former generals (not the leaders Parliament or the political parties). Within that you have the responsibilities of the democratic leaders, and the ethnic leaders. So, in brief: the people and their leaders. The role of the people is being upheld quite responsibly. In 1988, from all walks of life, we took to the streets to nonviolently demonstrate for a better life. And then in 1990, and the 2012 by-elections, the people proved they were ready to vote for a democracy. So, the role of the people is quite enough.

The role of the leaders on the other hand, is how can they make deals with each other? The election is a simple way to come through the process, but beyond the election they must negotiate. They must know how to share power, and positions, among the generals and among the political leaders and ethnic leaders. This is more important rather than the role of people, I think.

AC: People in power tell me the country is totally corrupt. What would you say to this statement?

KKG: I agree. It's quite visible.

AC: So, by agreeing that Myanmar is "totally corrupt" we mean that the former generals are corrupt. The cronies are corrupt. The regional authorities are corrupt. The regional division military leaders are corrupt. I ask this question not to point out corruption alone, but to ask, 'what does corruption mean to you?' And how can one change this corruption as a leader? Without radical change, we may see a few new players, but it would be business as usual, so to speak.

KKG: The people have a saying, "the same man and a new policy." We should approach such a design. We can't remove those old guys, which is why we need to improve things with those old guys. We will have the same guys under a new policy, and not much will be achieved after the five-year term. That's why, beyond the elections, we need to make a coalition—the old guys and the democratic leaders.

AC: The old guys are ...?

KKG: Old guys; I mean the army-backed political parties.

AC: You're hopeful they can change?

KKG: That would be the better way.

AC: Let's return to the issue of corruption; how to end corruption in your country?

KKG: Just like with the practice of *Dhamma*, it's easy to say but very difficult to end corruption. The government formed an anti-corruption committee, but the people do not trust them because they themselves are not reliable.

There is a relationship between anti-corruption and reconciliation because if you handle the corruption too heavy-handedly, it will affect the people who are in power and it will have a knock-on effect on truth and reconciliation. Finding out the truth is difficult at this time. To handle both things at the same time is delicate. You must handle it carefully. You must schedule the transition, and after a certain day you must transfer power. But, before that, the question is how to handle the things that have been happening. That is another thing. After that, through transparency, there must be no corruption. That warning must be issued, but how to handle it is another thing. For example, there was a motion put to Parliament to openly declare all properties owned by government officials and parliamentarians. The motion was rejected by Parliament. The whole Parliament did not accept it.

AC: A challenging question, if I may: Do you think that the former leaders who tortured and imprisoned you and your friends and colleagues should be tried and, if found guilty, go to prison, and have their wealth and land confiscated and returned to the people?

KKG: Personally, I can forgive everyone, and, if it is beneficial, people can forgive the atrocities done to them. However, there must be a record of what happened. The truth must be discovered and recorded properly. We must do that for the lessons learned to be handed down to future generations. In this way, we can prevent corruption within future generations, and more importantly, the next generation. Our sufferings, our sacrifices, have to be recorded.

AC: You recommend a Truth and Reconciliation Council, like in South Africa?

KKG: Yes, having a truth and reconciliation council is the proper way to overcome our suffering and to build a new nation. If we cannot find the truth in the past, we cannot look to a brighter future.

AC: You truly think that former Senior General Than Shwe should voluntarily come before a truth council, as in South Africa, where it was chaired by Archbishop Desmond Tutu, and admit his atrocities?

KKG: Yes, absolutely. "Yes" to a Truth Council in Myanmar. But the problem is that we need to find a balance between truth-finding and reconciliation. So, now, some of our comrades are making their experiences of prison public, in writing books and talking to the public. This is the truth-making process.

AC: A number of Buddhist monks and nuns that I have spoken with, along with leaders in other religions, including Christians and Muslims, have explained how they would like to see former Senior General Than Shwe, and many of the other former military leaders, make a formal public apology on national television and link it simultaneously to the UN General Assembly and cable networks worldwide. It may well be one of the most pivotal moments in human history. What do you think?

KKG: May it be so! And you are right, some of our people talk like that, but the problem is that it's not easy to make them apologize on TV or the radio.

AC: No doubt, it would not come easily. But perhaps if they had the right council it could happen. Maybe one of senior monks they see could inspire them. Or for that matter, their own wives, or even their children who may be motivated to safeguard their wealth and safety; and who knows, perhaps a number of them are desiring to attend an Ivy League School in America. Of course, it could be coupled with a legal agreement not to pursue criminal charges. After all, redemption is the soul, so to speak, of the *Dhamma*. It could happen. And no doubt, they know in their heart of hearts that killing, stealing, and torture are not virtues listed in the Buddha's Eight-fold path of *silā*, *samādhi* and *paññā*. They must be mindful of this, right? And if they did make such a public apology, there would be little doubt they would win the Nobel Peace Prize. It may well be applauded as the Greatest Peace Prize of all time. Perhaps all the people of Burma would win a Peace Prize for the oppressed and the oppressors alike, for national reconciliation.

KKG: *(Laughs)* Yes! I like it. But this begs the question: how are they thinking of their remaining life?

AC: What do you think they are thinking? Are they afraid of going to prison?

KKG: Personally, I feel that if we can create prosperity for the people, imprisonment of the wrong doers is not the best solution. Rather than punishment we must focus exclusively on creating a better life for the people, security through rule of law, reconciliation and the thriving of the *Dhamma*. And of course, inspired tolerance, for all faiths. In this way, any wrongs will be righted, naturally and peacefully.

> *"Our good will, our cooperation,*
> *is mainly intended to benefit our people."*

ALAN CLEMENTS: Has there ever been a period when dissent was tolerated by the government? You are stepping out again. Do you trust that you will not be put back in prison?

KO KO GYI: Nobody knows. Is it possible? Yes. But doubtful.

AC: What could you imagine saying that would cross the line, would provoke them to re-imprison you?

KKG: I have cooperation and good relations with some government officials. That's because I am one of the members of the Rakhine Investigation Commission, and I am also a member of the Scrutinizing Committee for Remaining Political Prisoners. Because of those roles, we have goodwill and trust with some officials. And when there is opportunity, I openly talk with them. Because of our friendly relations, I'm not concerned with re-turning to prison. Frankly, whatever others think, especially those in high power, I'm unconcerned. What I care about is doing good by my people, helping them to improve their lives. In that sense, we're seeking cooper-ation from everyone for just one reason: to benefit our people and to make a smooth transition to democracy. That is my only motivation. I seek no personal gain. I seek no special opportunity. I openly talk to the people with *Dhamma*, peace and reconciliation, in my heart. I learned the import-ance of this in prison and it is more natural and more important to me now than ever.

AC: So, you are putting reconciliation into action, so to speak—winning the hearts of a few government officials?

KKG: Yes, to some extent. But in so doing, I'm not always serious. I'm always making jokes about prison life—"Hey, never threaten me with prison, it's my second home! *(Laughs)* I know very well how to live in the prison. It's much easier to keep clean than a mansion!" *(Laughing)* And don't worry about sleeping on concrete, the ants and fleas are better than a purring cat! *(Laughs)* We had a lot of time on our hands. There was nothing that we did not joke about.

AC: People often say that they wish that you and your comrades from the '88 Generation—Min Ko Naing, Ko Jimmy, and all others—would stand in unity with the NLD and Daw Aung San Suu Kyi. I often hear how the people hope you will put your full weight behind the NLD to become one large unified organization. What do you say to that? And why aren't you doing that? Or maybe you are considering that?

KKG: We have a very good relationship with the NLD, and also with other democratic parties in Myanmar. We also have very good relations with the ethnic parties. Because we are not formal NLD members, we have an opportunity to interrelate with the other parties, including both the ethnic parties and the government. Because of this independence we act as a go-between. That's why we have such a good relationship with the ethnic armed groups. We are in a strong position to have a cease fire agreement with them and to then go through the peace process together. Our goal is to work in harmony with everyone, especially the NLD and Daw Aung San Suu Kyi.

AC: What do you see as her political strengths?

KKG: She's popular with the people. She's the daughter of a national hero. And because of her womanhood, her femininity, in the eyes of the people she's more sympathetic than a man.

AC: Would you like to see her as president of Myanmar?

KKG: This is not only a matter for those concerned, but for the public also. Some of the people, many in fact, want her to be president. And some people are worried about the alien status, you know?

AC: What do you mean by alien?

KKG: Section 59(f) of the 2008 Constitution. What I mean is that I cannot accept Section 59(f). The 59(f) is totally awkward in the sense that it's a personal focus. That's why I don't want to accept 59(f). Each and every country sets the qualifications required to be a president, that's one thing, but the 59(f) is totally unfair. Daw Aung San Suu Kyi is barred because of her husband, or her son-in-law, or daughter-in-law, or just very funny things. In the 1947 Constitution, it is clearly stated the qualification for the MPs, and through Parliament the president could be elected.

AC: U Win Tin, the NLD's co-founder, was telling me that it was not smart to try to negotiate with a criminal body—the military. This is one of the arguments of why, if all of you were unified in your opposition to the military, there's a much better chance to have a democratic country. What do you think?

KKG: *(Chuckling)* So the terminology itself we need to rethink.

AC: Please explain.

KKG: First of all, we need to rethink of ourselves after the 2012 by-election. Which way do we want to go through, evolutionary or revolution? We know very well about the old guys, but so what? To have reconciliation we need to make a deal with each other, over the short-term and also for the long-term. It also needs to be timely. We should have a plan to go through the timeline of the first five-year term and the second five-year term, and so on.

AC: So, you are hopeful for your country that democracy will prevail.

KKG: We must try. And I will try my best.

AC: Another topic. I'm told that the former military leaders, and perhaps some current ones too, and their legions of corrupted cronies—about 1,000 men and women—own almost everything in this country. Is this fair to say?

KKG: Sure.

AC: Along with their sons, grandsons, cousins and friends—another 4- or 5,000—own multiple billions in revenues, live in mega-mansions, are decorated in jewels, have dozens of luxury cars, and so on. On the other hand, I've seen in Hlaingthayar untold numbers of people living in squalor. And this is just one township in Myanmar, albeit massive. In other words, the rich are getting richer, and the poor are getting poorer. And you're talking about negotiating with criminals who have looted the country and bludgeoned the people. I, speculating here, as a citizen of your country, am finding that my income is going down, the cost of living going up and up, while pollution is increasing by the minute. I feel worn down, every day, more and more. I ask you: how can I keep this up? You are a courageous man who's suffered, along with many of your colleagues. I'm putting my hope in you, but tell me, as a citizen, why should I have hope? I don't see where hope is to be found.

KKG: Actually, no one can sort out these problems on their own. We need to have cooperation between each other. Democracy is cooperation, a very natural form of harmonious competition. But, at the same time, we need to find that harmonious common ground to cooperate with each other. We don't want to exploit the divides for our own benefit. We need to reduce the gap between the defeated, in regard to the religious tensions, and the obscene inequality between rich and poor, and all the ways we try to take advantage, to exploit those social divides and the political divides. But the problem in their way of thinking is to use the larger part of the divide, the majority. This way they can win. This is the conventional way of thinking. But, actually, we need to reduce the gap between each other, as you say, between the rich and poor. So now the government is talking a lot about 'development, development, development,' but no equitable development between this region and other regions, between the poor and the rich. That's the problem in our country that will lead to radical social unrest.

*"They're talking about the minority and the underdog,
which is unwittingly to... highlight the divide in the country."*

ALAN CLEMENTS: There are leaders around the world; President Obama, the leaders of the EU, the Prime Ministers in Australia, Canada, and Japan, and the Presidents of Russia and China and so on; if they were to read your words, what would you want them to know and do in support of your people?

KO KO GYI: Firstly, I would like to express my appreciation for their contribution to our country's democratic development, in pressing for the unconditional release of political prisoners, and in both investigating and criticizing the human rights violations in our country. For those reasons, we deeply appreciate their contribution to our country. But now the situation is much more subtle—the revolutionary period was just one phase. After that, a liberalization period such as this has begun, and is a different from the revolutionary period. That's why they need to focus very carefully on our political process, such as the political dialogue and the election.

At the same time, they need to know more about local contexts. Now they're talking about the religious conflict in our country, especially the Rakhine issues. Sometimes, although they have the good will to help us solve our problems, unintentionally—intentionally or not—they're talking about the minority and the underdog, which unwittingly highlights the divide in our country. We must give more attention to their grievances and their unequal status. With this religious issue, they create a bad image for us, not the leaders of those countries but the international media. When they use such words as "Buddhist Terrorists" and "Genocide" and so on, this is extremely detrimental for our country.

In addition, we need to find and develop a moderate and devoted Buddhist community to promote our peoples' goodwill both in the country and worldwide, while reducing radical elements. It's easy for the international media to stick labels like "Buddhist Terrorist" or "Genocide" on us, and, as such, many people, including ordinary Buddhists, are upset. They want to clear up the international misunderstanding in our country, which only serves to increase the tension between sides. Actually, our general public, the common people, are afraid of the situation. Many of them think, because former Buddhist regions became Islamic states, that the same thing might happen in Myanmar. The people think that Myanmar is one of the only countries in the world that stands up for its Buddhism, a defender of *Dhamma*, so to speak. This is the opinion of the common people. And they site the demographic issue in that our country lies between some of the most populous Islamic areas in the world. Bangladesh has a population of about 160 million. India has 200 million Muslims. Malaysia, 30 million. Indonesia, 260 million. This is the demographic reality of our region of the world. And with successive governments here in Myanmar, they've had no proper policy to preserve the boundary or the citizenship of our peoples. This includes the migrant issues and the economic ones as well. Our country runs an informal economy much bigger than the formal economy. There are many problems in our country but the international media and some of international leaders don't notice the diversity of and magnitude of our actual problems. So, they stand for the minorities. And in so doing, they sometimes ignore the views and feelings of the majority.

Just like with the Rakhine issues; actually, the Rakhine residents are very upset about the international stance. Let's say the terminology wrongly interprets the situation and is highly inflammatory and controversial. Our people don't accept the terminology but the international community, and some international leaders, forcefully use that terminology, which equates to interference and or intervention of the international community. This is how our general public sees it.

For that reason, some of the elements of the former dictatorship promote and increase nationalism, head-on against the international community, and head-on against the democratic process. They're trying to preserve that nationalistic supremacy. We are beginning to see this in different places around the world and not just here in Myanmar. So, those democratic forces, or the human rights activists, they ignore the national cost, deliberately, to promote the nationalistic views. Of course, this is not good. But the international community, by and large, doesn't notice the impact of their misrepresentation.

I'm a Myanmar citizen. That's why I will always be loyal to my country, and to my people. In addition, I fully honor International Human Rights Day every year. But such a transitional situation as we have here in Myanmar is extremely subtle and fragile. And nationalism and patriotic sentiments are easy to provoke among the people, especially with a 150-year long subtext of colonization by the British. But the international community and some leaders don't seem to notice the real problem, namely the jagged transition from decades of oppressive dictatorship to democracy. It's just easy to blame and attack. And they do. What we need is support and compassion.

AC: I'm thinking about the people all over the world who will want me to ask this question of you. So many of our youth today are moved to be activists, whether it be environmental, political, or human rights focused. They are all so intertwined today. They want to stand up for the truth, to have a future to believe in. Yet, as courageous as they may be, they often look up at the powers that be and feel intimidated and somewhat powerless. What advice would you give to the young activists around the world today to find their courage, to not lose hope, and to carry on with revolutionary fortitude in their respective struggles?

KKG: We ourselves have proven, by our sacrifices, by the conscience required to nonviolently fight injustice and unfair treatment, by imprisonment itself, that remaining calm and steadfast, regardless of the consequences, is the key to successful revolution, as slow as it may seem a lot of the time. With this new generation of activists, this is an empowering sign of hope and freedom in action, not only for the support it gives our own people here in Myanmar but for oppressed populations around the world. We must remind ourselves, keep active in the struggle and be rewarded by the joy that comes each day, the certainty of knowing that you are acting in dignity and conscience for the betterment of all people. And one day we will all win, we will overcome. Upset and hardship may be there, but never be disappointed with the rightness of your actions. Although you may be struggling for the time being, ignorance will be vanquished, and injustice will fall. In the long-term, we—us freedom fighters—shall overcome and win. I believe this to be a *Dhamma* law: freedom overcomes fear.

"We need to provide general [human rights] knowledge, even in childhood."

ALAN CLEMENTS: I was reading an article in your newspaper the other day about former political prisoners (Bo Kyi was quoted in it), about 10,000 of ex-prisoners, and how so many of them are homeless. Many are without assistance. Many are depressed—traumatized from torture. I've also heard from a number of former political prisoners that a number of these heroes and heroines are angry and suffering with blame. My question: What *Dhamma* medicine would you suggest to them, to your fellow former political prisoners, to use to heal, to move forward and take it higher?

KO KO GYI: For each individual former political prisoner, *Dhamma* medicine is one of the best treatments for facing trauma, but this is only for one hour, or half an hour, every day. At the same time, the problem is also a physical one. Many suffer chronic disease. Overall, the community must recognize our former political prisoners. See, most of the people, they're busy with daily duties, and sadly they can't do more. If they have a chance to visit with a former political prisoner, they are, of course, very sorry for them and help them as best as they can. But after their meeting they must return immediately to their daily routines. And most of our former political prisoners are working extremely hard to survive, each in their own way. It's a challenging situation and one that we are aware of. In fact, one of the main problems we are faced with is convincing the authorities that these special people should be supported in their need for rehabilitation as former political prisoners. On the other hand, some of these activists are making demonstrations and always trying to blame the government. So, while taking steps to make a deal with the government, at the same time, there are too many demonstrations against the government. So, we are trying to create an understanding of each other that collapses the radical elements on other side. Extreme elements come from both sides, with no space to stand in between in a moderate way. We are trying our best to support moderation and transitional thinking. But it is a challenging situation.

AC: I have a proposal for you to consider in *Dhamma* support for your revolutionary brothers and sisters, all former prisoners of conscience in Myanmar. I think you know that I was previously a Buddhist monk in your country, ordained at the Mahasi Sasana Yeiktha Meditation Centre here in Yangon under the guidance of the late Mahasi Sayadaw and his successor, Venerable Sayadaw U Pandita. I did not live there very long, perhaps a total of three and a half years, but it was among the most transforming experiences of my life. The other day, I asked Sayadaw U Pandita (who passed away in April 2016 at 95 years old) if he would hold a special ten-day silent *Vipassanā* (insight) meditation retreat for former political prisoners at Panditarama, his center in Golden Valley. He expressed his full support, 'so long as it was not political in nature.' Since he would be leading the retreat and not me, I assured him that he and the administrators at the center should control everything. His Yeiktha, as you may know, is large and can accommodate 1,000 or more meditators. All of you could practice the *Sathipattana Vipassanā* method of meditation under his guidance. Of course, it would be offered freely, without charge. Both NLD co-founder U Tin Oo and Daw Aung San Suu Kyi have practiced there. I think it would be very healing for those who were inspired to join the retreat. There would also be a *Dhamma*-based psychologist, doctor, and psychiatrist on call, to support the yogis, along with Sayadaw U Pandita's daily *Dhamma* talks. Would you have interest in participating in this retreat and, if so, encouraging your fellow former political prisoners to attend as well? It would be my honor to initiate the retreat with Sayadaw and then step aside.

KKG: Yes, indeed. Excellent idea. I agree. This would be a very good experience for everyone. On another note, I often speak with colleagues about U Thant—the former Secretary General of the United Nations from 1961 to 1971 from our country. He was a busy man, perhaps one of the busiest in the world, but every morning he set aside an hour for silent meditation. And as for the retreat, please let me know how I can assist you in making this happen. It would be a great opportunity for my fellow former political prisoners, as well as their families and overall, for the betterment of our people. But in some instances, perhaps with a number of them, they have no earnings for their family. They spent so many years in prison, and now that they are released, what are they doing today? They need to make an income for the family, so there is a lot of pressure on their shoulders. They have given so much to our country, to our people. They must be helped.

AC: I spoke with NLD co-founder U Tin Oo about this very issue and he explained that he would be honored to bring the proposed retreat up with NLD and offer support to the former political prisoners for their 10 days of meditation. He even mentioned making offerings to their families during that time. I also have several Burmese friends who I will ask to be donors for the retreat, to offer the yogis their daily meals and medicines, and even maybe some additional money to the families, to give them a chance to take time off.

KKG: Wonderful. Allow me to tell you an experience. I celebrated my fortieth birthday in prison. Many people talk about 'life begins at 40.' Well, I celebrated my 'life begins' birthday in prison. From then on, every Sunday, we tried to hold a talk in prison. The first topic discussed was *'Dhamma* and Politics.' I just mentioned former Prime Minister U Nu. He was a devoted Buddhist. He was the most important person to celebrate the *Six Sangayana,* to purify the Buddhist *Dhammas.* Of course, this is my own personal opinion for his life. I met him in 1983. At that time, he announced publicly that he was taking back his power from the military government, to declare the parallel government in 1988. This was because the military violently took power from him in 1962. He then used public power to take back state power from the government. Some people criticized him saying he was hungry for power, and so on. But not so, he promised to hold a multiparty election again.

We had two different types of military coup—the first was in 1958 when the army tried a coup d'état, but Prime Minister U Nu knew their plan in advance. That's why he called General Ne Win and asked, 'Are trying to take power?' To which the reply was 'No.' But nobody knew whether he was honest or not. There were so many problems in our country at the time. Because of the independence movement, some of the political reforms occurred in the name of robbers, robberies and or some deaths. And that's why there are so many insurgents in our country now. They were highlighting these problems and U Nu said he was ready to hand over the power, but only according to the constitution—not wishing to dissolve Parliament and not wishing to dissolve the constitution. So, it happened according to the constitution, with General Ne Win as head of the government and accountable to Parliament. Within the framework of the constitution, he agreed to hand over power to the army. This was the first time in our country. This was the first type of coup.

The second type was the military coup in 1962. General Ne Win dissolved the Parliament and dissolved the constitution. So that now, the

2008 Constitution legitimizes the first type of military coup, anytime. Yes, any time! According to the Constitution, they can seize power any time! This is the '58 type of military coup. They've already written that into the 2008 Constitution.

So, U Nu announced his parallel government in 1988, and many people said that 'he was also hungry for power.' But he didn't respond, other than saying, 'No, I'm getting old—over 80 years old now. This is not for me, but for the next generation.' Nor did he get upset. He didn't get angry. He stood in *Dhamma*. He was not greedy for power. He empowered *Dhamma* as his responsibility, not greed for power. He gave us an example of fine leadership.

AC: The people of your country have been repeatedly violated for decades, under Ne Win, Saw Maung, Than Shwe and their close associates and cronies. You know very well the sufferings of your people, and your own personal sufferings. It seems to me that presently, the mindset of totalitarianism has morphed into the general population. Corruption and fear are rampant. Sometimes it's hard to know what one stands for and what one stands against. Yet, ordinary people by and large fear repetition of the past. They fear losing their homes, their jobs, their incomes. They fear incarceration and torture. They fear for their children, their families, their future. You are a new generation. You'll have children born of a new generation. What is your advice to practice everyday democracy? What does it look like to practice democracy and freedom of mind in the tea shops, the schools, among old and young people alike? How do you advocate to your people to practice universal human rights—to safeguard democracy and freedom today— in order to avoid the need for revolution in the future? Essentially, how would you encourage the people of your country to safeguard universal human rights?

KKG: Informal education is one way. We talk to the public about democracy, on how to practice democracy, and on the international norms for human rights and so on. This is very informal, among the public. The important thing is that we need to provide general knowledge, even in childhood, in schools, of the importance of human rights and democratic principles. Just a little at a time, bit by bit. We need to put that into the curriculum of every school. If we learn to respect the freedom of others as equal to our own from an early age it will become second nature. At the same time, we need to reduce the unfair treatment of people, especially the gap between rich and poor. Generally speaking, rich people must declare their property. I know they'll never declare *all* their properties, but perhaps a reasonable amount of properties! *(Laughs)* You know what I mean?

AC: And collect past taxes and fines on them?

KKG: Exactly. Collect property tax and revenue for the state budget. We then need to know how to use it. How to reinvest it in the community for education and health services and so on. This is an important issue. Then, our government and ethnic armed groups are trying to agree on a cease-fire. They are attempting to engage in political dialogue. So, resource sharing and a modern power sharing is crucial here to understand. We need to power-share. We need strong leaders and one's firmly grounded in *Dhamma*.

Conversation with Ko Ko Gyi, 2018

"Peace is the fundamental problem of our country."

ALAN CLEMENTS: I'm with Ko Ko Gyi, and my long-time friend [Anonymous], and we're discussing the current state of affairs in Myanmar, politically, socially and spiritually. The good, the bad and the ugly. We know what we've read in the media, but you live and breathe your country. You know the fine print that rarely if ever gets published. What are the central issues today essential to be resolved in order for your country to move forward? And what are some of your insights and actions to make good on those issues for the betterment of your people? Secondly, as a long-standing activist, now a politician-activist, I'd like to speak with about your personal vision, your own hopes and dreams, and those for the people of your country. So, first: What are the good things happening in Burma today?

KO KO GYI: First of all, we are looking back at our near past. In 2012, I was released from prison, and I am now out of prison for about six years. The first thing, after the 2010 elections, was that U Thein Sein's government tried to initiate a reform process, releasing political prisoners, including our '88 Generation leader, and then allowing the exiled activists to come home. After that, to a certain extent, the media sector became more open, and they tried to initiate a nationwide ceasefire agreement. But, at that time, the winning party was the army-backed party, and the NLD didn't contest the 2010 election. That's why the USDP dominated Parliament and the cabinet. In the 2012, the NLD decided to contest the by-election, so we endorsed the NLD's decision to run. This was the turning point for our political vision. Before then, we stood by the 1990 election result. The NLD's decision to run in the by-election meant forsaking the 1990 election result, and that, whether we like it or not, we must now accept the 2008 Constitution. So, this was a breakthrough of the political deadlock, through a very narrow path, a tough situation, and a very practical decision to go on with our democratization. In so doing, the NLD had made a promise to the voters, to the public. By choosing the hard decision to run in the by-elections, the main purpose was to amend the 2008 Constitution. That's why we, our 88 Generation, joined the NLD hand-in-hand to make a public campaign all over the country, advocating for constitutional change and collecting signatures from the public. We got over five million signatures to amend the Constitution. But we did not achieve our aim—to amend the Constitution.

After that, in the 2015 elections, the NLD campaigned all over the country, and people voted for them. About 80 percent of the elected seats were won by the NLD, a historical achievement for our country. Now, many people are talking about the 25 percent non-elected MPs and the three key ministries still controlled by the military, that is, only talking about the 2008 Constitution. We know very well about these challenges that we're facing. But, at the same time, if we look at the bright side and from the perspective of opportunity, we've got a majority of parliamentary seats. Having 80 percent of the elected seats means over 50 percent of the elected seats, all MPs.

Apart from the constitutional amendment, we can do other things to revise the existing laws and regulations, especially regarding health and education, or infrastructure or investment, mostly the development perspective. We can do that alone. We can amend the common laws and regulations. We can dissolve existing laws. This is from the perspective of opportunity.

At the same time, the peace problem is the fundamental problem of our country, ever since Independence Day, now seven decades ago. We've suffered a lot from the civil war, and our civil war problem is mainly because of two reasons. One is the ideological issue. At the time of in-dependence, our independence leaders were leaning to the left in ideol-ogy—communism, socialism. That's why the Burmese Communist party went into the jungles to take up armed revolt against the government. The second reason is ethnic equality and federalism. Now, the ideologic-al armed conflict is almost finished. U Thein Sein's government started the Nationwide Ceasefire Agreement, but only eight ethnic armed organ-izations agreed to sign the Nationwide Ceasefire Agreement. Then, the existing government, the NLD government, tried to continue the peace process, and another two ethnic armed organizations have agreed to sign the NCA (the New Mon State Party and Lahu Democratic Union) bring-ing the total to 10 signatories. But, at the same time, the Northern Alliance, the Wa, Kokang, Kachin and so on, are still fighting the government army, especially the KIA and the Arakan Army. This is the general situation of our country.

Another prominent issue is the Rakhine issue, and the international media has highlighted it. It's complicated. Many of the international organizations are only talking from a human rights point of view. We agree. We have also suffered from human rights violations and for many years. I spent nearly 20 years in prison. My family also suffered from human rights violations. Like me, many of our citizens suffered from human rights violations. Not only the Rakhine issue—some other ethnic areas as well, like the Karen, Mon, Shan and Kachin regions. Everywhere the people have suffered. But, now, the Rakhine issue is the offshoot from other ethnic problems. Although different from other ethnic armed conflicts, the Rakhine issue is, for the time being, about those people who have fled their villages. This is a humanitarian issue. This is one thing.

But, the more remote cause of the problem is the historical aspect, the political aspect, and the economic aspect. They are all intertwined. Not least the terminology—they call themselves "Rohingya," but our native people don't accept this terminology. From the native perspective, it's not only the term that's the problem, but that they have a hidden agenda, which is to create an indigenous ethnic identity. This is the native people's perspective. So, from a human rights point of view we agree that we can provide humanitarian assistance to whoever suffers. But this is one of the existing problems of our country, and then there are economic problems as well. We used to speculate that after international sanctions were lifted, many foreign investments would come in, but in reality, it didn't happen. So, we need to review the existing banking system, the financial system and investment laws, and the infrastructure problems also. There are so many things to examine and resolve. This is the general scenario of our country. Regardless, because of the 2015 elections, our people are happy with the victory. We now have the first elected president after nearly five decades of authoritarian rule. Apart from the three key ministries, all of the other cabinet ministries are in the hands of the elected government. This is the bright side of the situation.

AC: And the three key ministries not in the hands of the government?

KKG: Home Ministry, Defense Ministry and Border Affairs Ministry.

AC: Appointed by General Min Aung Hlaing?

KKG: According to the existing Constitution, the commander-in-chief nominates those three key ministers, and the president has to agree with those nominees.

AC: You know as well as anyone in your country the unbridled violence brought to bear on you and your people, primarily by your country's military, under General Than Shwe and the people near to him. From one perspective, those men and their wives and their children and their intimate cronies, they're still there, they are still in control. They made the Constitution, they run the military, they run border affairs, they run homeland security, they run the country outside of these other ministries. How do you see that anything has really changed? Clearly, the military does what it wants to when it wants to. We see the protracted wars in Kachin and Shan State, and then the Rohingya massacre as a military generated response to terrorism, as they call it—disproportionate or not. So, you've got a parallel government. Is that right? On the one hand you've got the military, and on the other hand you've got elected civilians who really have no fire power at all, nor do they have any voice among those who have firepower. How are things different? There's the military who uses violence and the threat of whenever desired. And a de-facto non-violent elected government without a weapon at their disposal.

ANON: To be clear, what we were fighting is militarism, not these military people. Militarism, in principle, is not there anymore. Although, due to the Constitution, we are being controlled by these army bodies, the system as a whole has become democratic.

AC: But, regardless of the terminology—militarism or the military—the country's controlled by senior leaders, and those senior leaders are still deeply entrenched in this country, in this system. They do what they want, when they want, without regard for anything else. Is that an inaccurate assessment?

ANON: Their institution is strong, and our civilian institutions are weak, so they can interfere whenever they like. It is not because of the principle but because of the existing situation. We cannot build our civilian society to be strong enough to control the situation yet. We are trying.

AC: Do you think it's fair to say that the military would like to become a civilized body and respected by the people? Or do you feel that they're just manipulating the country and the people and using the word "democracy" as a pseudonym for hidden agendas and dictatorship? Is there an ill motive in the military? Is it still being controlled by forces behind General Min Aung Hlaing? Or is there some good will there? None of us really know what the dialogue is like in Naypyidaw, between the elected leaders and the military elite.

KKG: We all agree about the constitutional constraint within the 2008

Constitution, especially from the security point of view. But if we look from the bright side, the military men realize they cannot go on like this. They will have to change.

AC: Are you confident of that?

KKG: Because the 2008 Constitution and the Seven Steps Road map itself, which is their exit strategy from the de-facto government to the constitutional government, step by step, they want to change. They just want to hold the controlling power in their hands—that's quite clear—but they know they will have to change. The difference between the civilian politician and the army man is how to change. Which priority has to change? The timing and the priority: how to change.

AC: Is that the meaning of reconciliation?

KKG: Sure. The reconciliation is that we are only now talking between the civilian and the army men. "Civilian" means understanding that this is the majority Burman but also including the minority ethnics. This is the federalism issue. At the same time, there is civil and military relations. This is the tripartite problem in our country. The army took power in 1962 giving the excuse of federalism—not to disintegrate the nation but to save the country. Now we can discuss federalism. Previously, this was illegal terminology. But now the army themselves agree with federalism. But which type of federalism? How to share between the minority ethnic and the majority, and so forth. They need to think this way in private and in public. Just acting that way in front of Parliament and so on is just showing off.

"They've noticed the importance of
public opinion and support."

ALAN CLEMENTS: Imagine Senior General Min Aung Hlaing were here right now, and he openly said to you, "You've given so much of your life to our country. You are going to develop a political party. I may well have to deal with you in Naypyidaw, soon. I want your advice openly, please: What are my shortcomings? What would you advise me to do differently that I'm not doing? What do I lack?" What would you say to General Min Aung Hlaing?

KO KO GYI: Its a matter of trust. We want to go beyond words. Sometimes personal interest is disguised as national interest. Personal security and national security are easily mixed together. If we can believe each other, openly say what we want to each other, and at the same time, share our real concerns, we have trust. If your concern is genuinely for the benefit of the whole country, for all people, okay, let us work together.

My perspective is this: let us be concerned for each other. Let us seek each other's welfare. Let us put aside personal gain and compassionately embrace all of our people as a whole, the military, the civilians and the ethnic populations. In other words, we the people, in *Dhamma* we trust. And please, before you ask your next question, let us remember, yes, compassionate concern is not necessarily the psychology of a senior general in Burma's army. They're trained to be the sole authority. But everything is changing. And yes, they are well trained from a security point of view, to obey. This is not only the Myanmar army; this is military training worldwide. But our civilian politicians, our liberty and our democracy—these perspectives are quite different from each other. Now, they are sitting in Parliament and at least listening to some other dialogue and debating each other. And then, because of the election result, they've noticed how important public opinion and support is. They know, one way or another. That's why they cannot go on like before. Before the 2010 elections, they thought they could go it alone: "do this, do that" anytime they wanted.

AC: But correct me if I'm wrong, any public opinion that doesn't cower to their totalitarian ways they suppress, take what you own, put you in prison, silence you. They are strident totalitarians. They don't care about public opinion, do they?

ANON: No. It's not because they care. On March 27, 2010, General Than Shwe gave a speech at Armed Forces Day in which he said that we must now realize that our country is lagging far behind many other countries because we are not yet practicing the democratic system. Democracy is the only way forward for the country to develop, he declared. Quite a statement coming from the dictator himself. And he made it clear that we must change to a democratic system for the betterment of our country. He inevitably realized that our country was lagging behind every other country. All this came after so many years of hardship for the people and trying in so many ways. And all the time, they thought they had sacrificed whatever they could. Their personal gain is another thing altogether. Let's leave that for another book. But they did as much as they could, as misguided as it was. And yes, it just so happened to be a colossal error of judgment on their part. It went nowhere except into the abyss. So, they came to the belief that they must change their ways. How? As last resort, they choose to implement a democratic system. And clearly, our democratic institution is weak. They don't even practice democratic principles in their own so-called democratic institution. Even the civilian government, our present

BURMA'S VOICE OF FREEDOM / VOLUME TWO

government, neither practice nor empower democratic principles. So, for the military institution, who has no idea whatsoever about administration or politics, or anything about leadership for that matter, we are in a fragile position. They are being guided by wrong ideas of what to do and when do it. All they know, or perhaps they've been told by some secretive think tank or PR firm in some other country, is that a democratic administration can move the development of our country forward. And that is where we are today, slow as it is and misguided as it may be, there it is. Which is far better than continuing to live under the totalitarian nightmare of decades past.

AC: Oh my, what a complex scenario. Let us go into this a bit deeper, if we can. I assume Senior General Min Aung Hlaing is a Buddhist?

KKG: Yes.

AC: Don't you think as a fellow Buddhist there's some way to reach his conscience and his heart, his *Dhamma*? Do you think there is a way to speak with him about the power of *hiri* and *ottapa,* moral shame and moral regret—the twin guardians of decency and peace in the world? The Great Indian King Ashoka apparently embodied these qualities. Again, Burma's Army would likely be nominated for the Nobel Peace Prize if Senior General Min Aung Hlaing made a public statement saying, "I'm going to dedicate myself to peace with all peoples in Burma, all ethnicities, and further, I'm going to apologize to my people for the errors we have made. From this time forward I am dedicating my life and leadership to national reconciliation." It would be so simple. I am hoping he will grant me an opportunity to interview him for our books. And the same with U Than Shwe.

ANON: If he was smart enough, yes. Those would be a great few words for him to share with the people of our country, people, for that matter, who have been brutalized by decades of militarism. Our people are ready to forgive. Our people want peace. May he find the moral courage in himself to make history and bring lasting peace to Myanmar.

KKG: Although I strongly believe in *Dhamma*, sometimes we cannot easily separate our ego and our *Dhamma*, our Buddhist teaching.

AC: My teacher, Venerable Sayadaw U Pandita, encouraged me not to demonize or condemn even those who commit atrocities. Rather, he said, 'speak to their shortcomings but don't vilify them as people.' And the question always came up, "How do you skillfully reach the conscience of the oppressor and try to illuminate their shortcomings, without highlighting their person?" Maybe there's a nugget of truth that you would care to share that would inspire him to question his delusion, question his blind obedience to a belief that doesn't serve him or his people or his family?

KKG: Everybody has their preconceptions. The army does as well. So, we are trying to set up a new political belief, and a new political ideology. Why are they taking part in politics? They love their country. They are nationalist and patriotic. Whether we agree or not, this is the hardcore ideology of the army man: "We are protecting our country; We are preserving not to disintegrate our country." That's their ideology. Previously, in my childhood, just like with the Burma Socialist Program Party or the Army, they were out only for their own self-interest. They were extremely selfish. They have their own ideology. They believe in their ideology, defending the country, serving, sacrificing their lives and so on. It's a self-serving ideology. We need a renewed and dignified Army, the way that General Aung San intended. And frankly speaking, I'd like to see our Army rooted in *Dhamma* principles. A noble army that serves the people, elevates their well-being. It's there if we try.

AC: Do you think the military leaders of your country, deep down in their minds, do not believe or have faith in democracy and are only using the word as a psychological scam so to speak, to avoid international criminal charges? To protect their wealth, their mega-mansions, their private jets and so on? Look at it another way, I'm American; although we have many freedoms, there's a palatable oppression in our country. And my country, I'm not proud to say, is violent. Afghanistan: bombed into the stone age. Iraq: a lie, the mass murder of a population, and also bombed into oblivion. Our involvement in Libya. Look what's going on in Syria today. I grew up in a predatory corporate culture of propaganda and lies under a surveillance state, with a long history of wrongful wars, toxic discrimination, and overall violence. Call it democracy but it often feels fascist, albeit somewhat disguised. Maybe Than Shwe, maybe General Min Aung Hlaing and other senior military leaders look at his word "democracy," they look at Daw Aung San Suu Kyi having lived in England for so long, they look at the United Nations and the biases that go on there, they look at our cultures and they just say, "I don't want it. I don't like it. I don't like what we see as democracy." We see violence, we see deception, we see cronyism, and 'okay, we'll take on our version of it, but by and large keep that other one away from us.' Point one.

Point two: These people have committed atrocities to your people. They put you in prison for nearly 20 years. Look at all the horrors they have done. Now, if they're going to wake up, they have to feel shame for the misdeeds that they have done. If I were them and if I were their wives, wouldn't you be fearing that they're going to be taken to the Hague, tried and put in prison, like Milosevic from Serbia? A mistrust of democracy as they see it and a terrible fear of punishment if they openly declare their weaknesses. It's like an iron wall. My point: What do you think about my assessment? And what could you possibly say or do, should you feel inclined, to inspire their *Dhamma* and soften their fears, if they have fears at all?

KKG: The historical assessment is also quite different on our side and from the military side. The 8-8-88 revolution, from our side: an unconscionable atrocity committed by the military and those who ordered it. But from the military perspective, their historical assessment is that it was in defense against anarchism, against beheadings and lootings of properties. They saw us democracy activists through the lens of violent anarchists, a highly destructive element. That's why. The vast difference between perspectives is not only about the future but about a historical assessment as well.

AC: Historical revisionism or a denial of truth. Big Brother in Burma.

KKG: Yes. They've revealed their own version of history saying that before the 1988 revolution Ne Win was trying to reform the country economically and politically. Further, they said that they already had a plan in place to change the country from the old system to a new one. That changes are not at all connected to 8888 Revolution. This is their propaganda. They see themselves as saviors, as having saved the country. They do not realize that decades of dictatorship was wrong, and we the people said, "Enough."

ANON: I know how these generals think. I know the mindset of the army. I've also talked for decades about these matters with other teachers. I've also discussed the principles taught in military training schools. By way of saying, the military's way of thinking is not unfamiliar to me. Colonel Tin Maung, a very prominent writer here in Burma, once told me, "In our military academy, we don't teach many things. And if something is exposed, paint it white (so that enemy cannot hide). If there is more than one thing, line up." He was the principle of the military academy for nearly five years. He trained these people. This is their mindset.

In addition, I've seen military trainings on television these days, how other schools train military personnel. Fact 1: Our country does not want you to think. Fact 2: Our country does not allow people to think. Fact 3: If you think, it will cost you your freedom. It is a rancid mixture of Japanese and British styles, with a militarized Big Brother.

When at a university training, we once had a military exercise for a few weeks. On one day we visited the deep jungle, and there we saw one very precious *Nalingyaw* root which can be used for medicine. Four of us were decided to dig it up. One pulled it this way, another pulled it that way, until the root was shaking. It took everything we had to stay with it. The root was deep, and we did again and again to extract it. We kept shaking and digging. The roots went deep. Soon into this process, we stopped thinking. We then sat down and pushed with our feet. We stood up and kicked it. Only after about half an hour we all fall down and start laughing, saying, "This is absurd. We have ceased thinking. We just keep doing without thinking." I think you get my point. The army trains people not to think, just to follow orders—do as you are told. That's the practice of our army. The people are not allowed to listen to VOA or BBC. They're not allowed to talk among close friends. If they talk, they will start to think. That's not what our army, the whole army, was trained for. And there were many brutal practices that our army has been doing. 'Bring no prisoners,' that's one unwritten policy. 'On the front line, there are always prisoners, and always wounded people. They're all to be killed, every time.' No one exposed that reality. You just did what you were told. All the wounded people were killed in cold blood, and whenever they confront someone that they suspected, they asked questions of them and then they are killed without a thought.

AC: Orwell meets Mad Max... sick.

ANON: They're still practicing this. And due to a lack of funding, the quality of our army is going down and down to the lowest level ever, including the generals and colonels. They don't think. I knew many high-ranking officers. I know how they think, and I know how they don't think. I have no suspicions about their sincerity or their good words, but they are more like robots and violent one's at that.

AC: I don't think I've ever heard anyone describe the mindset of the military in such terms before. You are a dissident. A free thinker. I'm inspired.

ANON: In the past, maybe 30 years back, the army was very strict. But these people who had a personal relationship with me were close friends, so we talked, openly. Somehow, they found out about it, and these people were warned. Later action was taken against them, just because of talking to me. Whatever the matter is, they do not allow people to talk. And those people admit that if we hate military intelligence, they hate them more, because they dare not talk among each other just because of the military intelligence. That's the way of their thinking. They have to follow orders. Once they are committed to military service, freedom of thought is finished.

AC: This is all because of the pathology of Ne Win? Is that where the denigration of human rights first started?

ANON: Actually, during Ne Wins time, more than 400 of his highest-ranking officers were trained in the United States. And some of them were trained in Myanmar by American instructors. There were no officers not trained by the United States. But after socialism, relations between the US and Burma deteriorated, and things ended. After, there may have been some intelligence training from Israel or the Soviets or whatever.

*"We need to promote the role of the ethnic political
society and the ethnic civil society."*

ALAN CLEMENTS: We've talked only briefly about you forming a political party. What will be the name of it?

KO KO GYI: The election commission hasn't responded yet. They referred our party founders list to Home Affairs. Now, the special branch, CID, and the immigration department are scrutinizing the backgrounds of our stakeholders. After that, they will submit us to the election commission and then the election commission will reply. The name of it will be the 'four-eight party.' 8888; August 8th, '88.

AC: And what will be your role in that party?

KKG: I'll be responsible for the leading committee.

AC: And do you anticipate running for political office in the 2020 elections?

KKG: Sure.

AC: Do you have an idea of what role you would like to run for?

KKG: As a registered political party, we will have to run for at least three constituencies. Not only in the general elections, but some by-elections also.

AC: The '88 revolution captured the awe of the international community, what we could see of it with the country sealed. And you and your dear friend Min Ko Naing were two of the main leaders of that struggle. You both suffered nearly 20 years in prison. And today, you and Generation '88 are hugely popular within your country. Everywhere I've gone in Burma over the past five years, since I was un-blacklisted by the authorities, you cannot meet anyone who doesn't smile and rejoice when asked about the 88 Generation. The people have a lot of hope in you. My question: Many millions of your people will read your words here in this book, months before the next election. What do you want them to know that makes it important for them to know what the 8888 party stands for? Also, how you are different from the NLD? Why should they vote for you and 8888?

KKG: Generally speaking: multi-party democracy, open market economy, open door policy, federalism, democracy, human rights—it's all the same. The difference between us and others is how we implement our objectives, and which issues we prioritize. This is quite different from some other parties. Another important thing is that we strongly believe in an ethnic alliance policy. For example, in the 2015 elections we were all happy, because we could remove the old guys from power. But at the same time, one of the side effects of the 2015 elections was that the ethnic political leaders got side-lined. So, if we try to find a proper solution to solve the ethnic problems—a very prominent one is the Rakhine issue—we need those well-known politicians from their ethnicities. That's why we believe in the alliance policy with like-minded democratic parties, especially the ethnic political parties.

AC: What would the 8888 party give the people that the NLD today, is not giving them, especially in regard to ethnic political parties?

KKG: We are only talking about peace, while they are focused on the armed organizations. We agree with the peace process and talks but at the same time we need to promote the role of the ethnic political society and the ethnic civil society. By doing so, we can create trust between each other. I mean administrative decentralization, financial decentralization, resource sharing and so on. We can do that bit by bit.

See, one of the main problems to peace is that previously the Burma Army itself was composed of some ethnic regiments other than Burmans. But the problem is that after Independence in 1947, some of the ethnic regiments went into the jungle. From then on, General Ne Win dissolved the ethnic regiments separately. But now, those ethnic armed groups are calling for a federal army composed of such ethnic regiments, to march together.

ANON: Every ethnic army fights for their own race, but in the Kachin area, the Arakan Army is fighting for Kachin State as well. They are fighting for an area, not for an ethnicity. And in Shan State, there are at least five to ten prominent ethnic groups still inside it. They come to realize that ethnicity-based ideas are not working well enough. They want their own independence and want to make a deal for economic rights, social rights, and political rights. For leverage, they're fighting the central government. They are not fighting for certain ethnic people or the area.

They want rights. Partly it's the idea of the leaders to hold on to the power they have now.

"We're trying to elevate their way
of thinking as much as we can."

ALAN CLEMENTS: Ko Ko Gyi: Where do you find hope today? What gets you out of bed every day to serve your people? And do you firmly believe that it's possible to bring true democracy to Burma?

KO KO GYI: Our country first embraced democracy after independence in 1947. After five decades of authoritarianism, we are trying to revitalize democracy again in our country. So, one of the main issues is democratic practice and another key problem is poverty. Our people are getting poorer and poorer. That's why more and more individuals are not only not thinking for themselves but also losing their community bonds. We need to focus on development issues, and on basic education. We're trying to elevate their way of thinking as much as we can, because people are very frustrated about the present situation.

ANON: See, we expected a lot after the change from total military power to a civilian power. Everyone expected things to change abruptly. But, it has been much less than what everyone expected. The frustration is with leadership. The incapacity of leaders. People have started to notice that things can be done, but it doesn't happen. Only after three years did people begin to realize the truth of situation, what should be done and what cannot be done. And now, there is no other way but to be patient. We cannot expect anything to happen abruptly, nor do we see any miracles coming any time soon. Meanwhile, we must live on and keep trying. Many people feel it will take ten years or more.

AC: But Daw Aung San Suu Kyi and her government never made promises they could not keep, did they?

ANON: Yes, of course. They did a lot, but that's natural. Nor was she prepared for what was to come. Frankly speaking, she doesn't know who to appoint as ministers, or even the president and vice president. Decisions were made in the last minute. There was nothing prepared, and when choices were made, they turned out to be bad choices. So, it's very reasonable that we cannot achieve anything any time soon. But there is no alternative but to carry on and try harder. As I said, we cannot expect any miracles at this point, but neither are we depressed.

AC: What are the greatest hardships that your people face today?

ANON: Lack of security—all kinds of security. Financial; day-to-day. It's even dangerous to go out at night-time these days because of crime. It's rising rapidly.

KKG: Food security; social security; everything. Everything is compromised. People are struggling.

ANON: Yes. Food security is one of the biggest threats. But overall, the complications are more due to a lack of rule of law. There's bribery and corruption everywhere. There's no real system; you cannot see any system working. The only thing we can say is that we can now complain if we like, but nothing will happen. Still, you have a right to say something. We didn't have that in the past. We couldn't talk to each other freely. Now we can talk, unless you are in the military. It will progress gradually, I hope.

AC: You know, when struggle becomes desperate, people take to the streets.

ANON: That can happen in the future. There could be an uprising.

KKG: Another point is polarization. The NLD has the popular support. That's a reason, very clearly, to vote for the NLD. The other thing is just to protest the USDP—that's a signal to vote for the NLD. The previous government we could openly criticize—people cheer a lot. But now, many of our activists dare not criticize the government, because many of the supporters for the NLD say, "Oh, only for two years; we need more time. How can we solve 50 years of problems in such a short period of time?"

AC: That's a common argument?

ANON: For the NLD insiders. Actually, these people are "yes men" and there is no real transparency inside the NLD. That is one of the biggest problems.

KKG: That's why, with the media itself, many of the journals, they dare not touch the NLD too much.

AC: Why?

KKG: Their circulation will be compromised. And another problem is social media.

AC: Say more about that, please.

KKG: Many people use a fake name. For example, one person may be using nine or ten or more Facebook accounts, lobbying for or against each other. That's a common practice here.

AC: Am I right to say that we cannot, in this democracy, openly criticize the government? We can't criticize the NLD?

ANON: You can criticize, but nothing that is seen as demeaning. You can criticize if they consider it constructive criticism.

AC: That's vitalizing for democracy and freedom of speech, to say what's true for you.

ANON: Yes. But if they are suspicious of you then it will become a problem, and sometimes, if you use the wrong words, you may be sued. There are around a hundred cases of people being sued due to writings on Facebook.

AC: Although truthful and motivated by *mettā*—love in the heart—there are wrong words? What are some of the words?

ANON: Sometimes a personal attack. Name calling, or if you give wrong information about Parliament then they consider that as inciting other people.

AC: Are you saying people are going to jail because of their posts on Facebook?

ANON: Yes. By using Article 66(d). There's no bail. You will go directly to jail, and without bail you have to face the charges.

AC: This is identical to the dark days of dictatorship.

ANON: In some way, yes.

KKG: And another problem is how easily the label sticks—"Oh, you criticized the government, therefore you are on the side of the USDP or army." That criticism sticks fast. And then, if you're talking about the Rakhine issue, some of them call you a nationalist or racist. And to form a nationalist group, it's easy to stick the label "minions of the Western countries."

AC: You'd think there would be an encouragement that the people, after all these years of suppression of free speech, that they would celebrate—"This is good news that you're speaking out. It's good of you that you're speaking out; finally, use your mind, use your conscience, use your thought," right? What are they afraid of? What is going on that people are so sensitive to do the very thing that they fought against and went to prison for?

ANON: The first thing is that the civilian government is not confident, they're insecure. That's because they were not prepared for the job. Also, they consider the army and USDP to be behind the many activities to defame them. They think they will lose votes in the next election. Whoever criticizes them, they scrutinize the intention. Whether it's right or wrong isn't the problem; is their intention to lose them votes in the next election? That's what they fear most. Once the vote is cast, you can stay easily for five years, you don't need to worry. But that's not what's happening, because they have a lot of insecurity—they believe they are not qualified.

AC: Back to the possibility of an uprising. People are talking? Do you hear it among people on the street?

ANON: It won't happen unless someone organizes it. Frustrations are everywhere, but they won't make these unrests happen, because it will hurt everyone. People don't want it to happen. But if someone organizes it intentionally, it could happen.

AC: Well, back in '88, you were a group of dissidents. Is there such group in Burma today that is fed up and frustrated?

ANON: There was a group but no real leader. See, people were talking like this on August 8th, that it could happen, but there was no plan. Suddenly a group came up and everyone was expecting there must be certain changes to change the totalitarianism. No one believed that it would happen on that day, but then, at this rally, everyone joined, everyone followed.

AC: What happened was that no one really believed it, but the small group came out, and then everyone came out?

ANON: Yes.

AC: So, the same thing could happen now?

ANON: This time, people do not want any kind of unrest.

AC: Unless the suffering becomes so acute that they have nothing to lose?

ANON: During that time, we had a totalitarian government. This time, if you can wait, in three years' time you can vote for an alternative.

AC: I've been in Yangon for a considerable amount of time. Personally speaking, I find it challenging. I walk the streets day and night. I'm in cars, here there and everywhere. I talk to people in tea shops. I ask questions, trying to get a feel for life today, post dictatorship. Meanwhile, the air quality in Yangon is so comprised. And the traffic is mostly gridlock. Massive T-cranes dot the skyline with condominiums, hotels, and mega-malls going up everywhere. It's somewhat toxic, loud, and disturbing. Meanwhile, people the world over are talking about the certainty of economic and environmental collapse. Surely, there is an awareness of the bigger picture in government? Does anyone notice the environmental denigration of Yangon as democracy is born?

ANON: People will survive. That's their mentality.

AC: The other day, I was in rush hour traffic, and as you know it was bumper to bumper all the way from University Avenue to Sule Pagoda— four miles of gridlock in 105-degree heat, no less. Every light, every car was stopped. And the taxi driver said to me matter-of-factly, "Every day is like this. How can it go on? How can I live? I have just enough money if I drive 12 hours a day, to feed my family of four rice and a curry, and to breathe some of most toxic air in any city in the world." What would you say to him?

ANON: You are not alone. When I was in Bangkok recently, people asked, "How will your country survive such a catastrophic situation?"

AC: And what do you say to them?

ANON: All our lives, we've survived like this. The after-smell of dictatorship is terrible, but we're used to it, so we don't complain.

AC: Freedom has its costs?

ANON: There's a chance today to be involved with politics, and to make a change. Everyone, if they want, can get involved. In the past, no one had the right. Not even to talk. So, to change the system was out of the question. Now, if you dare, you can go and do whatever you like, or write a book.

AC: But it's very selective, right? There's only a small margin of what you can say?

ANON: I don't accept what the NLD people say, but only after three years did we start to realize it cannot go on like this.

AC: These decisions to persecute people are from the NLD? They're the ones censoring Facebook, they're the ones who are saying, "Go straight to jail, you cannot criticize."

ANON: There is no real censorship organization, it is generally someone who complains.

KKG: Now, Parliament is trying to amend the existing law. Previously, you are the first person, I am the second person. So, I'm talking about you in the wrong way, and a third person or more can sue you, or me. That's a third person, that's what the problem is. In a defamation case, a third person can claim.

AC: On what grounds? What right do you have to sue me? You're not harmed.

ANON: If you are not involved in that conversation but if I assume it is affecting the government or the country or the laws or defaming someone else, the third person can sue on the grounds that you are affecting a certain person.

KKG: To be quite clear, to be obvious, say I'm talking about The Lady—Daw Aung San Suu Kyi; her defender, her supporter, can sue me for defamation.

AC: That's called "the long arm of dictatorship," isn't it?

ANON: A bit like that but there is no real organized institution to do that at the moment.

AC: In a way, what Bill Richardson did, openly in the press, if he was Burmese, he could be put in prison.

ANON: Certainly, yes.

AC: In a way, he defamed her in his comments: "lacking moral leadership."

ANON: He was accused of attacking the government, defaming the government, not The Lady.

AC: Defaming the government; calling her panel a cheerleading squad. "Whitewashing" the issue in Rakhine State—pretty defaming. It's so dizzying, so complicated. You know, Ko Ko Gyi, let's go back to you again, and we'll conclude with this. Are you going to run for high office or for Parliament? What will be your ambition, your vision for yourself in the upcoming elections? What is the best-case scenario for you?

KKG: According to the existing political system, you need to run for the parliamentary seat for a particular township. After that, as a cabinet member, any president, or whoever wins from the election, can then appoint cabinet members, whether they are MPs or not. So, the first thing is to contest in the elections. Otherwise, I'm just a party boss, and my people, my guys, run in the elections and lead the cabinet. But now, I have to say something about the 2020 elections. Now we are learning about the organizational process. We've opened offices in the Irrawaddy delta, Bagu, Magwe division, and Shan State. Next month we'll open offices both in Mandalay and Mon State.

AC: When in 2020 are the elections?

KKG: Overall, it's not easy to speculate on the 2020 situation. Generally speaking, in the ethnic areas, they're more active than before, because of the 2015 elections. They know how to prepare for the coming election. That's why four Kachin parties are trying to marge together, and likewise, some other Mon parties, Karen parties and Chin parties as well. That's why, for the 2020 elections, generally speaking, the ethnic political parties will be more active than in 2015 elections.

AC: I wish you much success in serving your people. Your life is a great example of nonviolence in action. You chose prison rather than armed resistance. That's ethically courageous. Thank you.

KKG: And thank you for serving our people and for the betterment of our world.

CHAPTER 19

CONVERSATION *with* MIN KO NAING

April 2015

- "Although these things have happened in the past, we must be careful not to let them steal our future."
- "To the leaders of the world I'd say they must not forget mainstream politics."

Interview with Min Ko Naing, artist, activist, political prisoner of 20 years and one of the most prominent student leaders who spearheaded the 8-8-88 uprising. Min Ko Naing is one of the most well-known and well-respected pro-democracy activists in Burma, an inspiration to Burma's youth and perhaps one of the most important student activists in the world. *The New York Times* described him as Burma's 'most influential opposition figure after Daw Aung San Suu Kyi.' Min Ko Naing built the student underground into the All Burma Federation Students Union, and founded the '88 Generation Peace & Open Society, organizing peaceful demonstrations and nationwide campaigns against rising fuel prices that sparked the Saffron Revolution of 2007. In this interview, Min Ko Naing shares the inspiration behind his activism, and how he survived two decades of brutality in prison, using the *Dharma* principles of compassion towards his captors. With his humor intact, this inspirational leader embodies the practices and principles at the foundation of a successful transition to democracy.

> *"Although these things have happened in the past,*
> *we must be careful not to let them steal our future."*

ALAN CLEMENTS: Thank you for taking the time to speak to the world through our set of books about your country's nonviolent struggle titled, *Burma's Voices of Freedom*. My questions are meant for those who want to understand what you stand for and what you've done, especially in regard to peaceful revolution and the conscience and courage required to stand up for universal human rights, regardless of the consequences.

You were the key leader in the 8.8.88 uprising. At the time, the world was riveted to the marches and, tragically, the thousands killed by the military. This was, of course, almost a year before China's Tiananmen Square Protest and the subsequent massacre. As the main person at the heart of your country's struggle for freedom, what moved you to inspire your fellow students to challenge the military dictatorship? What was in your heart?

MIN KO NAING: It was inspired by the previous student movements in our country, by other student leaders who'd taken the same route before me. I was simply following in their footsteps. In 1962, the military regime took power; then again in '67 and '70, and in '74 when there was the U Thant Crisis, and again in '76, but at that time, the students could not make change.

AC: You were imprisoned, in total, for over 20 years for your revolution-ary acts of conscience. Is there a single most important lesson you have learned as a leader of nonviolent revolution?

MKN: I don't think of it as hardship, just life experience—food for thought, really! *(Laughs)*.

AC: Let me ask you this way: all over the world we see oppression. All over the world there is injustice. Many young activists, both today and in years to come, want to use their voices, their hearts, and their minds to challenge corporate and military greed, and the injustice of denigrating life now and in the future. They may look to you and think, 'This man was a courageous nonviolent activist who was willing to go to prison for his conscience.' What advice might you give them to fulfill their activist vision, whatever it may be?

MKN: In Buddhism, as you may well know, we have the concept *loka-dhamma*. The *loka-dhammas* point to the inevitable ups and downs of life, such as gain and loss, honor and dishonor, happiness and misery, and praise and blame. Like waves on the surface of the ocean that rise and fall, these worldly waves, these *loka-dhammas*, go up and down by nature and often out of our control. If you are rich, sometimes you suddenly become poor. When healthy and happy, suddenly you can become ill and miser-able. At times you are celebrated and other times you are reviled. When you accept that life's experiences, these *loka-dhammas*, always go up and down, you find some balance in facing all these waves, and in time you live with as much non-attachment as possible, and with a peaceful heart.

Although I was in prison for 20 years, it was just another aspect of life that I faced. Whether inside or outside, I felt the same. The difficulties I faced inside—I believe I would also have had to face them if I'd spent all those years outside. If I was outside, I would have faced the same thing as inside. So, for me, inside and outside were not so different. I could bare the situation inside despite being confined to a small cell for 20 years.

Also, while most imprisoned activists were tortured physically, they didn't torture me physically. They tortured me mentally. They put me in a very narrow cell, and in solitary confinement. The first time I was impris-oned for nearly 16 years. There was no human contact. No conversation. No reading. No writing. I had to face extreme loneliness. I was starved of human contact. I had no human contact at all for 16 years. The loneliness was so pervasive that for the first 10 years I didn't even know what was missing. I'd spent so long alone I'd forgotten what I'd lost. But then one day, after 10 years, they transferred me to Sittwe Prison in Rakhine Division, and, on the way, I heard the sound of a child crying. Then I realized, suddenly, what was missing—everything. I missed the whole world.

AC: Truly unthinkable. How did you mentally survive?

MKN: There were three things that allowed me to survive long-term imprisonment. The first was the *Dhamma* teachings of Buddha. The second was a firm belief in our cause. The third was a sense of humor! *(Laughs).*

AC: I dare ask, you had no one to laugh with; how did you bring humor to solitary confinement?

MKN: In my interrogations, the interrogators tried to break me, to make me surrender. But I didn't react. I just relaxed. I learned to bend like a cane. A cane can bend easily but does not break. So, I learned to relax and bend. I became very flexible. *(Laughs).*

AC: My God. *Dhamma yoga* for the mind. Did you meditate in prison?

MKN: Oh, yeah. But not during the first two years. After two years, I resolved on developing my *citta-mind*—I made a determination to meditate every day, without fail. And I continued with my meditation practice for the rest of my prison terms, the next 18 years.

AC: People all over the world have come to know your country's nonviolent struggle for democracy as a "Revolution of the Spirit," a concept first brought forth by Daw Aung San Suu Kyi. In 1988 it meant one thing. In 2007, at the time of the monk-led Saffron Revolution, it meant something different. Today, you, as a political prisoner, have been released. Many of your colleagues are free, but many people I speak to harbor *dosa* (anger).

MKN: Ah-ha, yes! I know.

AC: Blame: 'The regime has stolen my years...'

MKN: Mhmm... *(chuckling).*

AC: '...they took my home, killed my brother...'

MKN: Yes, yes...

AC: May I ask, how do you encourage former political prisoners to deal with their anger, their fear and blame?

MKN: I would say that although these things have happened in the past, we must be careful not to let them steal our future.

AC: Do you also advise them to meditate? Do a silent mindfulness meditation retreat?

MKN: Well, in truth, let me clarify something: I didn't call my practice in prison meditation, in the classical Buddhist sense, that is. It was a concentration practice. In classical *Vipassanā* meditation there are stages of development or stages of insight, as you know, that arise. But that's not the way I did it in prison. I concentrated on *anapana*. I bypassed enlightenment! *(Laughs)*.

AC: *(Laughs)* Awareness of the light air at the tip of the nose?

MKN: *(Laughs)* Yes, only concentration. I was practicing peace of mind. I'd close my eyes, sit on the floor and practice *anapanasati*. When the superintendent of the prison came in and saw me, he was impressed! *(Laughs)*. But I admitted, honestly, 'No, no, I'm not meditating, I'm just practicing concentration.' In fact, I was composing a lot of songs in my mind at the time and writing novels and essays in my head! *(Laughs)*.

AC: Because they didn't allow paper?

MKN: No! They never allowed that. Nothing. No books. Nothing. An empty space. If they found a pencil, they'd beat you until they broke your ribs! *(Laughs)*. Over a pencil, no less. They'd kick you until your ribs broke. But I wrote in the secrecy of my mind: secret essays, novels, poems and songs. I couldn't stop composing them, continually reading them in my mind and going over them until they were complete.

AC: Did you receive any news or information about the status of your country's struggle for freedom? Did you hear about your colleagues, where they were, how they were doing?

MKN: The only information I got was from the thin filter wrapped around Cheroots, our Burmese cigars. Cheroot filters have a one ply tiny piece of newspaper wrapped within them. That's the only information I could get.

AC: So, you were able to smoke in prison?

MKN: Yeah, and whether or not you smoked, most of the prisoners had them. After smoking you could dip them in water, peel off the piece of newspaper and read the scrap.

AC: What about your mother and father? Your brothers and sisters? Did you see them?

MKN: They didn't allow me visitors for the first three years, but after that I was allowed to meet them twice a month, but only briefly.

AC: And when you were released, how did they tell you? One day they just came to your cell?

MKN: No, first they punished me with a 15-year sentence, when I'd already been in prison for three years. So, I thought at the time, 'Okay, 15 years minus 3 years is 12 years.' I thought I would only have to serve another 12 years, but they explained to me, 'No, the 15 years starts from today'! *(Laughs).* The first three years was just a detention period, not a prison term. They didn't count towards my prison term. They were legally allowed to renew the detention period every six months for up to three years, so I was detained for three years without any charges. Only after three years did they charge me and sentence me to 15 years, and it started only after three years of solitary confinement.

See, the authorities had announced that all prisoners would have their terms reduced to 10 years maximum. It was because of that, because they feared I would only serve 10 years, that the superintendent told me, 'Today is your release day, but the government has accused you again'! *(Laughing).* I laughed loudly! I immediately responded, 'Okay, just what I thought!' I just said, 'Oh, fantastic!' There was the 10-year amnesty declaration, when all sentences were reduced to 10 years, whether the original sentence was 20 years or even 50 years. So, here was their excuse—10 years' imprisonment, and then, on the day the term was fulfilled, the superintendent comes to tell me the government has charged me with another term. They would extend my detention by six months at a time. After six months the superintendent came back to announce the new decision, and as I saw him, I'd say to myself, 'Oh look, here come the authorities again, just to tell me 'Another extension, six months, enjoy.''

AC: Min Ko Naing, how do you not harbor anger towards these men?

MKN: *(Laughing)* Because the anger would burn me first! The *dosa* will burn me first. I know this, this is my understanding. I'll tell you a story. At that time, the director in charge of Military Intelligence came to review my situation. He came and studied me twice a year, and he'd talk with me, saying, 'Hello, how are you?' And my response would always be the same, 'I'm still not mad!' *(Laughs).* Then, of all things, this madman, the head of vicious interrogations and torturing people, ended up in my cell-ward as a prisoner! Yeah, that's right! This cruel human being had been arrested and imprisoned. And here he was next to me curled and cowering like scared dog. He must have been tortured. He was totally broken. This is what I mean about *loka-dhammas*—the waves of life. You never know the twists of fate in this ocean of life. In fact, most of the military intelligence persons were also arrested and put into prison.

AC: Your interrogator and captor was arrested, tortured and put into prison with you?

MKN: That's right. And I didn't bear any grudge at all. In fact, I hosted him and encouraged him and helped him in every way I could. Yes. The very man in charge of my case became a prisoner. But no matter what I did, and how I helped him, he degenerated quickly. He had no inner reserves. He had no *silā* to draw upon. He seemed be devoid of *Dhamma*. He had no place of refuge. He was a broken man.

AC: Why did they put him in prison? Was it Khin Nyunt?

MKN: The one in charge of his case was Colonel San Pwint, assistant to Khin Nyunt.

AC: The Prince of Evil.

MKN: He was the second-in-command in Military Intelligence. I also met San Pwint in prison. He was the one who arrested me and had me tried in court. We met again as prisoners at the Thayet Prison. At one point, I had some special food that I gave to him. Then, in the end we were freed together, on the same day! *(Laughs)*. I greeted him warmly. But he was full of guilt and sorrow. When reporters and journalists came to do interviews, he refused. 'No, no, no,' he said, 'I am no one. You must meet Min Ko Naing—he is the great one!' *(Laughs)*.

AC: What a lesson. Min Ko Naing, most everyone in the world would be interested in knowing how a nonviolent freedom fighter kept hope alive in prison, especially in solitary confinement. Besides creating songs and writings and poems in the silence of your heart and mind, when the going gets tough, really, really dark—and I'm projecting that such times exist—what do you draw upon to face another hour, another day, another month of unbroken isolation?

MKN: I believed that when it comes to *Dhamma* and *adhamma*—bad people and good people, bad will and goodwill—in the end, goodwill wins. That I believe. Although we don't know when, I believe that ultimately the good will wins. That kept me alive in prison. That got me through the most difficult times.

AC: Almost everyone I have spoken with says that the dictator, former General Than Shwe, is the ongoing leader of Burma, from behind the scenes. I would assume that if he had said, "Take Min Ko Naing out of prison," you would have been released on the spot. People today also say that he's reading books on *Dhamma* in his mansion in Naypyidaw. I've even heard that he has closed circuit TV access to Parliament. He may very well read this book as well. I'm also hoping he will agree to an interview for the book. Regardless, if he were in the room with us today and asked you to be open and frank with him and share your innermost truth what would you say? Of course, he's ordered torture. He's ordered mass killings. Some say he's ordered ethnic cleansing. The prisons have been filled based on his orders. You had the "Open Heart Campaign" to encourage your people to express their feelings to him. What would you like to say to him?

MKN: Personally, I have no feelings of revenge towards him. I regret nothing, and I can forgive. But, for the other people who have suffered—it's up to them. I won't deny them their feelings. But that doesn't mean they should take physical revenge. What I do think is that they have a right to their suffering, and they should be financially compensated for their anguish. But they should seek compensation rather than hurting someone else.

Our people must have justice. Than Shwe must, at the very least, listen to the people who have suffered, how they suffered, and why they suffered. I want him to listen and to understand the colossal suffering he caused for our people. But the main reason I do not accept revenge as a response to the suffering, is because I don't accept that the stronger person should harm the weaker one. That's how revenge works. That I cannot accept. The people who become stronger should not hurt the weaker ones. People need to be educated so that they understand such values. It's a shameful thing to hurt someone. People should instead have their revenge by helping someone who needs help. But Than Shwe must know that such suffering is not acceptable in our society. Although he may live a long time, he will not be accepted by our society. That is, unless he apologizes publicly and financially compensates those individuals who have suffered.

"To the leaders of the world I'd say
they must not forget mainstream politics."

ALAN CLEMENTS: We're on the cusp of your country's national election; there are reforms—some see them as stalled, some see them as insincere, others see them as better than the way it was before, when there was persecution, torture, and killing. Min Ko Naing, you're highly respected throughout the whole of your own country. What would you like to say to your people at this time that might inspire them to move Myanmar forward towards true and lasting democracy?

MIN KO NAING: First I would like to say that there have been two major elections in my life, and both times I went to prison. So, in a way, I'm afraid of the coming election!

AC: It could happen again, you're saying?

MKN: Yes, it could happen again for next election! *(Laughs).* I suspect some division with some leaders. Well, I'm not really afraid, but I am aware that it could happen, according to my previous experiences.

AC: Let me ask you this: What would you like to say to those men who would be the ones who could possibly put you back in prison?

MKN: I want to say to them, "Do not do anything wrong in the course of this election. Do not use the elections as an incentive to make arrests. Do not exploit the elections for personal benefit." I would ask them not to use the election as an excuse to make arrests. They may do something like that. But people are not addressing that because they are afraid that they might lose the election. They want the election to happen, so they may have to ignore other abuses of the government during that time.

AC: And, to the leaders of the world—the President of the United States, members of the EU, the United Nations, Australia, all leaders of the world—what would you like to say to those people to advise them on how best to relate to your country? How best to understand, and how best to support, true freedom here? True freedom, not corporate interests. What do you want them to know?

MKN: There are mainstream politics happening, but issues that come up every now and then dominate the mainstream and it becomes diverted or derailed due to these issues; I worry that these issues will come up and divert the mainstream. I mean, the mainstream political issue is the amendment of the Constitution and to build a federal democratic union. But I think most of the issues you hear of day to day come from the media and journals that are monopolized by ex-generals. I think they intentionally use propaganda to stir up nationalism and to obscure the mainstream dialogue. The international community should highlight our mainstream politics and our main cause.

AC: Your country has numerous 5-star hotels being built as we speak, major corporations are coming in every month along with international banking; the streets are clogged with Land Rovers and massive SUVs while millions of people are languishing in squalor. Tourists: five million of them are said to be coming to Myanmar this year. My question: How would you want these international tourists to relate to the people of your country and supporting them in establishing a high regard for universal human rights? And what do you want them to know about the real Burma?

MKN: First of all, to the leaders of the world, I'd say they must not forget mainstream politics, the basic requirement to amend the Constitution— constitutional reform and federalism. The government and other world leaders must not forget the mainstream and be distracted by lesser issues. At present, CSOs are strongest, which also made the issue base stronger. That's what's happening at present.

Secondly, I want the tourists to notice that the government does not allow them to visit many ethnic areas and conflict zones. It is not only for security reasons, but because they have many things they want to hide. Tourists must notice that what they're seeing in the central area is not all that is happening. They should notice that many other areas are covered up and forbidden. In Manila for example, when world leaders visited, all the beggars were arrested and sent somewhere else. That's a government cover-up. They're doing the same thing in our country. The tourists need to understand that these things are still going on. Our people are very hospitable, and will accept all kinds of foreigners, wherever they come from. But there are some religious conflicts going on. Foreigners must understand that these religious conflicts are at a dangerous stage, and they should let other people know there is religious conflict happening in our country. Yet, although conflicts are happening, it's not because our people are hostile. Actually, they are hospitable—you can see it in their eyes. These conflicts are the result of manipulation by those in power. They are the main culprits. The tourists should not misunderstand our people.

AC: Is there anything else that you would like to share?

MKN: I like your questions very much. I've never had such an interview.

AC: Thank you. You are a great inspiration to me. The honor is mine. I have a final question, regarding your colleagues. There's close to 10,000 former prisoners of conscience. I hear that many of them are depressed and out of work. What I hear that many of them have been marginalized and run the risk of being forgotten. How can your comrades best be helped? And what can we do, as outsiders?

MKN: The outside world should meet ordinary political prisoners who are otherwise anonymous, and unseen. No one will know them, and no one will recognize them, unless good people go out of their way to meet them. They should also have a voice. At present, most of them are anonymous. They have suffered but no one hears them. I can speak whenever I want, make my voice heard, but many of my revolutionary brothers and sisters are anonymous. So, please let the world know about these anonymous people, how they feel, how they suffered and how they continue to suffer. They are beautiful people. They have beautiful stories. They are beautiful minds.

AC: I will do that.

MKN: Let these political prisoners also know that their voices are already heard by the world. Let them know. What people want is recognition. Everyone. So please let them be recognized.

AC: I will do this, happily. Thank you. Thank you very much.

MKN: Thank you.

CHAPTER 20

CONVERSATIONS *with* SAYADAW U PANDITA

February 2016

CONTENTS

Introduction

For the last thirty-seven years of his life, Sayadaw U Pandita was my spiritual teacher, my life mentor, and my friend. In the early years of that period, I was a monk living at the Mahasi Thathana Yeiktha, the monastery in Yangon which had been founded by Mahasi Sayadaw in 1947 and which had been Sayadaw U Pandita's home since 1954. He later moved to his own monastery, Panditarama, where I visited him in the months before he died. It was here that I was privileged to have nine nights of profound conversations with him. These were among his final teachings. He died forty-five days later on April 16, 2016 at the age of ninety-five. This book is the edited record of those conversations, his offering on the way of reconciliation for a troubled world.

By the time of his passing, he had been in the monastic order within Burma for eighty-three years, having ordained as a novice monk as an orphan at the age of twelve. During his years at Mahasi Thathana Yeiktha he became a senior meditation teacher and founded an annual four-week Buddhist Culture course specifically for children in the development of "mindful intelligence." When Mahasi Sayadaw passed away in 1982 Sayadaw U Pandita was appointed the Ovadcariya Sayadaw (Head Monk) of the monastery. As the senior teacher, he was for many years the spiritual advisor to Aung San Suu Kyi and other leaders in Burma's democracy movement and had been influential in honing their strategies of nonviolence. Over the years, he also became the *Dhamma* teacher to many thousands of Asian and Western students worldwide.

I met Sayadaw U Pandita within a few months of my arrival at Mahasi Thathana Yeiktha in 1979. He was already a senior teacher at that time, and on our first meeting we talked well into the night. Despite not having traveled much at that point, he had a vast knowledge of science, literature, culture, art, and, of course, classical Buddhist teachings and in particular, *Vipassanā* (mindfulness practice). He spoke several languages and could quote at will from, say, Tolstoy to an obscure Buddhist text from the 1920s. Often in the middle of a discussion he would cheerfully pull a passage from one of the thousands of books in his greeting room at the monastery. A great conversationalist, he also had a natural curiosity about his young western guest and wanted to know all about my life growing up in America: what were my interests as a child, my difficulties, my education. Thus began a cross-cultural understanding that was to deepen over the decades. Perhaps we educated each other in the differences of how eastern and western minds are conditioned.

I was dazzled by his brilliance and his kindness to me, and I think he found in me a novice in need of direction. I asked for and was granted permission for him to be my primary teacher there in that exotic land of Burma in which I found myself, eager to come to terms with my mind, living as a monk in a monastery far from home.

Eventually, I made my way back to my own homeland but Sayadaw U Pandita and I never lost touch. I organized his first trips to America and Australia and I went regularly back to Burma to visit him and to continue our exploration of the deeper streams of life. His wisdom and intellect only grew with time.

Although these nine nights of conversation cover a wide range of subjects, in the end Sayadaw U Pandita's passion was to convey the importance of finding ways to live in harmony with each other. He could see the trends in the world and their potential for political and social strife. As someone who had lived through world war II along with the more recent troubles in Burma, he also knew the limits of force, hatred, and abuse of power. His lifelong message was that peace is only possible through communication and understanding. Thus, he spent some of his last moments on earth emphasizing these ideals in the art of dialogue, which was his particular genius.

Alan Clements
SEPTEMBER 18, 2018

Biography

Ashin Paṇḍitābhivaṃsa, the Panditarama Shwe Taung Gon Meditation Center Sayadawgyi, was born on Thursday, July 28, 1921 in the Shwebo Su quarter of Tadah Kalei Village in Yangon. His parents were U Hpe and Daw Chit Su. He was the ninth of ten children. When he was four years old, his mother passed away. When he was ten, his father passed away.

At age seven he began his *Dhamma* education under the tutelage of Sayadaw U Jāgara in the village monastery of Kaw Che, Bago Division. As a schoolboy he passed the Pahtama Ngay and Pahtama Lat oral examinations in Buddhist scripture held by the Dakkhinayone Shwe Kyin Daik in Kawa Township. At age twelve, he ordained as a novice monk under the supervision of Sayadaw U Jāgara.

At age eighteen, he went to study under the great Sayadaw Ashin Kelasa of the Mahabodhi Forest Monastery in the village of Kyauk in Bago Township. There he passed the Kyauk Tan Mahabodhi Forest Monastery Oral Scriptural examinations for the Pahtama Kyi level.

When he reached twenty years of age, on the eighth waning day of Dapou Dweh in 1302 (1941), he became a fully ordained monk with the sponsorship of U Bo Han and Daw Thaung of Kyauk Tan in the Khanda Sima hall of the Mahabodhi Forest Monastery. His preceptor was Mahabodhi Sayadaw U Kelasa.

During World War II, he was an assistant teacher at the Kyaikkasan New Shwe Kyin Daik Study Center in Thinghan Kyun Township. During that period, in 1308 at the age of 26, he passed the examinations for Pahtama Lat in the first ever Pali Pahtama Pyan Examinations.[1] He passed the Pahtama Kyi examinations in 1309 as well as the Cetiyangana Pariyatti examinations[2] for students.

In 1311 at the age of 28 he went to Mandalay to study at the new Mahavisuddhayone Study Center under the guidance of Zi Pin Sayadaw Ashin Sujatatthera. He studied the Pali, Commentaries and Subcommentaries related to the Dhammacariya level of study under many excellent teachers. He also studied in Yangon under Saya-gyi U Aung Myat at the Phaya Kyi Daik and with Ashin Vasetthabhivamsa of the Than Lyin Thapyaykan Dhammikarama Study Center. In 1313, at the age of 30, he passed the Siripavara Dhammacariya and Sasanadhaja Siripavara Dhammacariya exams. The following year, he passed the Cetiyangana Teaching Level Examination, taking first place.

While living at Kyaikkasan Shwe Kyin Monastery, he studied English with Saya-gyi U Hpe Thin. They made an agreement that whoever saw the *Dhamma* first would tell the other. Saya-gyi went to Mahasi Sasana Yeiktha in Yangon, practiced, and became satisfied and inspired. He then went to the Shwe-Taung Gon Sayadaw-to-be and urged him to practice

---

1 These are Pali examinations sponsored by the government. Pali examinations were held in the days of the kings, under the British and are also held today. Nowadays there are exams sponsored by the government as well as exams sponsored by associations. The exams can be oral or written. The government degree is the standard qualification.

2 The Cetiyangana examinations are sponsored by an organization.

under the guidance of Mahasi Sayadaw. Therefore, in 1312, at the age of 29, he approached Mahasi Sayadaw and receiving his instructions, began the practice of Satipaṭṭhāna under the tutelage of Ashin Vicāra. He became firmly convinced that only when Pariyatti is followed by practical experience would he gain a firm footing in the teachings of the Buddha. After he practiced, the intention arose in him to spread the *Dhamma* to the whole world, beginning with his close relatives and companions.

He had the desire for others to know and experience the taste of the *Dhamma*, which is many times better than all the other tastes of the world, and for others to beautify their lives and develop their virtues with the *Dhamma*. In 1316, at age 33, while he was teaching Pali, he participated in the Sixth Great Sangha Council as both Reciter and Corrector of Pali.

In the following year, he went to Mahasi Sayadaw to continue his work of Vipassana and carried out the responsibility given to him by Mahasi Sayadaw.

In 1320, at the age of 37, he accompanied Mahasi Sayadaw to Colombo, Sri Lanka, for the opening of a new meditation center. He taught the *Dhamma* there in accordance with the instructions of Mahasi Sayadaw for nearly three years before returning to Myanmar due to poor health. In Myanmar he studied profound scripture and practice under the direct guidance of Mahasi Sayadaw, and during that time also instructed yogis who came to practice according to the Mahasi method.

In 1340, or 1979, at the age of 57 he was appointed Nayaka Sayadaw and in 1982, after the passing away of the most Venerable Mahasi Sayadaw, he was appointed sole Ovadacariya of Mahasi Sasana Yeiktha, a post he held for eight years. In 1990, at the age of 68, he founded Panditarama Shwe Taung Gon Sasana Yeiktha in Yangon. With a broad vision that included the Sasana of the future, he worked tirelessly to preach the *Dhamma* of the Buddha in accordance with the instructions of Mahasi Sayadaw, encompassing both scripture and practice so that neither is omitted.

There are many yogis, both foreign and local, who have had the chance to take shelter under the shade of Panditarama Sayadawgyi's Sila, Samadhi and Panna, and to absorb the nourishment of the *Dhamma*, having come to see its virtues through Sayadawgyi's great Metta and keen determination.

Following heart surgery in 2007 at age 86, the momentum of Sayadawgyi's teaching increased in a manner inconsistent with his age. In addition to holding an annual 60-day special retreat at the Panditarama Hse Main Gone Forest Center, he travelled on *Dhamma* missions to the United States, Taiwan, Nepal and Singapore.

Within Myanmar, centers are now located in Yangon, Bago, Than Lyin, Mawlamyaing, Kywe Khyan, Pyin Oo Lwin, Htauk Kyant and Hle

Gu. Overseas centers are located in Nepal, Australia, Korea, England, USA, Canada, Malaysia, Singapore and Taiwan. These spread the light of the *Dhamma* far and wide.

All the centers work hand in hand to spread the Sasana of Practice which includes Scripture and the Sasana of Scripture which includes Practice, in accordance with the high-level desire of their benefactor, the Panditarama Shwe Taung on Sayadawgyi. Starting from 2010, an annual Dhamma Family Gathering has been held so that all the centers, both within Myanmar and abroad, can listen to Sayadaw-gyi's guidance together in order to carry out their projects uniformly and so that Sāsanā work can continue long into the future. 2016 marked the 7th annual Gathering.

While putting all his energy into promoting the Sāsanā, Practice intertwined with Scripture and Scripture intertwined with Practice, Sayadawgyi passed away on Saturday, the 9th waxing day of Dagu, 1377 (16 April 2016) at 7:35 a.m. at the age of 95 years, 75 vassas.

"Requisites for Reconciliation"

ALAN CLEMENTS: Allow me to start by saying how grateful I am for the opportunity to speak with you. My intention in speaking with you is rooted in *Dhamma*, seeking your wisdom in illuminating the way beyond fear, anger, and delusion. I have known you for thirty-seven years and have known you to only speak what is true and beneficial. It is for that reason that I seek your advice and insights into what is most beneficial for the people of your country as well as everyone in the world.

My first question: For anyone who has been violated, it is common to react with hurt, anger, even outrage, and at times, seek revenge. As we know, many millions of people in your country have been oppressed for over fifty years by a succession of dictatorships. What advice can you offer the oppressed, especially those harboring feelings of hostility and retribution? How to overcome those feelings of anger and revenge and restrain from acting on them?

VENERABLE SAYADAW U PANDITA: Forbearance is the best. It is what the Buddha taught. Social problems are sure to happen in human society. There are things one likes and things one doesn't like. One smiles at what one likes and scowls at what one doesn't like. It is important to have forbearance—the ability to withstand these swings. Forbearance should be developed from the start, before problems occur. One should make it strong.

In this country we say, "Khanti is the highest austerity." In the human world, we are certain to encounter things we do not like. If every time one encounters such things, there is no forbearance and one retaliates, there will be no end to human problems. There will only be quarrels.

To be patient and forbear fully, there must be the ability to logically reason. Without forbearance, a fight occurs, both sides get hurt and there's no relief. And many wrongs are done. When one can forbear, the quarrel quiets. This is the benefit gained.

In this, one needs to add mettā, the desire for another's welfare. When the desire for the welfare of others becomes strong, one can be patient and forbearing. When harmed one can forgive, one can give up one's own benefit and make sacrifices. Problems occur because people are not able to have this attitude of mettā, the desire for another's welfare.

AC: To end the cycle of conflict, first neutralize one's reaction?

SUP: There are two kinds of enemies or danger: the danger of *akusala* and the danger in the form of a person. *Akusala* are the unwholesome deeds which occur when *lobha* (desire, selfishness), *dosa* (anger, cruelty, hatred) and *moha* (delusion, stupidity) are extreme. These are called the internal enemy. They are also called the nearest danger. Danger in the form of a person is also an enemy: someone who is hostile to us. The Buddha practiced to gradually weaken the internal enemies until they disappeared.

If one cares for oneself and can reason, "When the danger of akusala, unwholesome deeds based on lobha, dosa, and moha occurs, there's no end to human problems—there's no relief, neither for myself nor for others. Therefore, one should control oneself." If one restrains oneself and comes to understand the benefit of doing so, when one's forbearance becomes strong, problems are naturally resolved. Since it's important to resolve social problems, the main quality needed to do this is forbearance. And in order to have forbearance, one must have mettā as well as compassion.

AC: What is the basis, the spiritual or moral motivation, to restrain *akusala*?

SUP: One should be disgusted by *akusala* as if it were excrement. And one should shrink from doing *akusala* just as one would shrink from picking up a red-hot coal. With a healthy disgust and fear, understanding that *akusala* gives us trouble, one can refrain from wrong-doing.

Further, there should be consideration for others. One should spare others because one understands how they would feel if harmed. That is important. Hirī and ottappa [moral shame and moral fear] and consideration for others are the qualities which motivate one to refrain from doing akusala, unwholesome deeds.

If *lobha* (greed) and *dosa* (anger) arise in us, one will easily break one's *sīla* (moral integrity). One should be disgusted by breaking *sīla*, just as one would be disgusted by excrement. One should be disgusted by the lack of shame and the lack of fear, just as if these were feces. Being without shame and fear, one becomes brash. One should fear being without moral shame and moral fear as one would fear touching a red-hot coal. When one possesses moral shame and moral fear, who would pick up excrement? Who would pick up a red-hot coal? It would burn one. These are the first mental attitudes to arise.

To explain this in material terms, if one wears white clothing in the hot sun, it won't absorb heat. It will reflect the rays of the sun. If one wears black clothing, it will be hot. Lack of moral shame and fear is like wearing black in the sun. These qualities absorb base actions, speech, and mental attitudes. Hirī and ottappa, like the color white, repel unwholesomeness. People need to know this.

They are also called the Deva Dhammas. Deva dhamma means dhammas (practices or trainings) which make virtues brilliant. When one lacks these, one's human virtues fade. The quality of behaving like a human being, being able to keep one's mentality humane, having human intelligence, being able to develop special human knowledge—all these human virtues fade without hirī and ottappa. When one has these qualities, one's virtues become bright. They are the dhammas that make human virtues shine.

They are also called the loka pāla dhammas. Loka pāla means the 'Guardians of the World.' They preserve the world, keep it from being destroyed. What's important here is one's own individual world as well as the world around one. These qualities preserve one's own individual world so that it is not destroyed. The stronger they are, the more secure one's own world is, and equally, one no longer harms the world around one. The world around one is peaceful.

AC: Allow me to ask: Here in Myanmar, the newly elected leaders along with the vast majority of citizens, have stated their desire for "National Reconciliation" —societal harmony based on a policy of loving-kindness, non-hostility, and non-retribution. You have advised how the oppressed can do their part to both heal themselves and society. What role can the oppressors play in healing the nation, in moving forward towards a safer, more peaceful and prosperous future, with respect for rule of law, democratic principles, and universal human rights?

SUP: Only if there is no selfish desire for oneself or for one's own group will there be the attitude of wanting good things for the people of this country.

Wanting to have the best only for oneself or for one's group is lobha, or greed—extreme greed. If extreme greed is forceful, then mettā-karuṇā, or loving kindness and compassion, will dry up. Only if there is mettā and karuṇā will one be happy to see another's welfare. One will want others to be well, just like oneself. One should also develop muditā, or joy at seeing another's good situation. If there is no mettā and karuṇā, there will be no muditā. There will only be envy and miserliness.

Those who have done wrong should correct it by Dhamma means, just like when a monk commits a monastic offense. They should make an honest admission: 'This act and that act were wrong. I ask your forgiveness.' No matter how great the fault, about half [the people] would be satisfied with this. They will have mettā (loving-kindness) [for those who confess their wrong].

A hero, a person who is courageous, has the courage to admit one's mistakes, one's faults. Such a person also has the courage to do things that are beneficial for society. The most effective way to create peace among the people is for the oppressors to courageously admit their faults and reconcile with the oppressed. That is the best.

AC: Is there any further advice you might offer the oppressors to begin this essential process of national reconciliation and peacebuilding?

SUP: One should understand: wrongs done because of selfish greed and devoid of *mettā* and *karuṇā,* bring only bad results. On the other hand, tasks done without selfishness, and with *mettā* and *karuṇā* present, bring only good results. One should understand the nature of good and bad results. Due to extreme *lobha* and *dosa*, neither knowing the bad results of lacking *mettā* and *karuṇā* nor the good results with *mettā* and *karuṇā* at the forefront, there is blind stupidity. There is darkness. And with darkness, one can't see. As long as this understanding is absent, one lacks moral shame and moral fear.

AC: And the cycle of oppression continues?

SUP: Without *hirī* and *ottappa*, there is *akusala* (unwholesome actions). With *hirī* and *ottappa* (moral shame and moral fear) there is pure clean *kusala* (wholesome actions). That is important.

What should one do to prevent problems from occurring in the world? There should be both control and preservation, so that one's personal world is not destroyed and the world outside one is protected from harm. And if there were a great number of people who kept their own individual world from being destroyed (by restraining unwholesome thoughts, speech and actions), the world would become peaceful.

Another way to foster self-restraint is to have consideration for others. When thoughts, speech and actions are strong enough to cause suffering, reflect: just as I do not wish to suffer, neither do others wish to suffer. As such, one avoids doing harm. Being able to put oneself in another's place is very important.

AC: What is the word for this?

SUP: Empathy: reflecting on yourself and knowing that just as you like happiness, so too others like happiness. This is important for human beings. Having moral shame and moral fear, if one avoids doing wrong due to not wanting to defile oneself, not only are one's actions and speech clean, but others are not harmed. Alternatively, out of consideration, one protects others so as not to harm them or make them suffer mentally or physically. By protecting others, one keeps oneself from doing wrong. This two-fold protection is essential.

AC: Your country has been ruled for decades by corrupt leaders, and those leaders had support, "cronies," as you call them here in Myanmar— friends, family members, colleagues, business acquaintances, subordin- ates—who were corrupted, and in turn, corrupted others. And through this collusion, the country functioned as a cycle of corruption. The entire apparatus of dictatorship, as I understand it, was a lucrative business based upon a culture of corruption. What single piece of *Dhamma* advice can you offer to transform Myanmar's corruption?

SUP: When an infant lacked breast milk and has already grown up mal- nourished, scrawny and stunted, with poor physical stamina, one can no longer give breast milk. One can't give baby food to correct this anymore. It is only important to develop a new generation. One has to simply focus on that.

AC: Is there a cure for the older generation?

SUP: For them, the best way is to practice the *Dhamma*. This is my ex- perience. There were some officers who came to practice after they were fired [during the U Ne Win period]. When they came to see the nature of the *Dhamma* due to their practice, they came to know that *Dhamma* is the most important thing. They gained firm ground on which to stand. It wasn't possible to teach them starting from the basics. Therefore, the best thing for them was to come and practice. For those people, that is the best method for becoming a good person.

AC: The meditation cure?

SUP: Firstly, one must gain victory over oneself. One has to gain victory over one's own bad habits. More important than victory over external enemies is to first gain internal victory. The Buddha taught how to over- come the internal enemy.

Starting from the age a child can speak, just as one nurses an infant and feeds him or her baby food, parents who know their duties should teach their children well. That is the most basic plan. The children taught according to this plan become cultured and obedient. If they marry a person with the same upbringing, the child they bear will have a good early start. After the child is born, the parents teach the child good habits. Later, before marriage, when the child practices meditation, he or she gains practical experience. Overall, one needs to have a plan to provide children with the initial seed of Buddhism, to develop good habits and gain practical experience of the Dhamma.

Because people try to conquer others instead of gaining victory over themselves, there are problems. The Buddha taught that one should simply gain victory over oneself. He taught the method for gaining complete self-victory. If one conquers oneself, the good devas (celestial beings) won't sit still. They will protect that person. If one doesn't master oneself but gives up and commits immoral deeds, the devas will never come and help.

If one has been born a human being, there are rules. Like driving a car, one should understand the rules of the road. In America, they drive on the right. One should drive the proper speed and be careful. If the light is green, go forward. If it's red, stop. Life can be likened to driving a car. If one follows the rules then one doesn't suffer due to mistakes, and one doesn't hurt others either. But one can still suffer when others are in the wrong. So, one must be careful about this too.

Human beings have rules and duties. If one follows the rules and fulfills one's responsibilities, then one is not at fault. The five precepts (1. not killing. 2. not stealing. 3. refraining from sexual misconduct. 4. refraining from telling lies 5. refraining from the use of intoxicating substances) are the basic rules of for human beings. And to help others when it is beneficial and suitable is a human duty. The five precepts are not only to be kept by Buddhists. All human beings, if they want to be truly human, should keep them. Not knowing this is to be blind and stupid. One's beliefs go the wrong way and one commits acts of violence.

AC: Speaking of *devas*, with the human world fraught with extreme struggles, from famines to world wars and far too many genocides, dangers everywhere, inside and outside, why not dedicate one's everyday *Dhamma* practice to becoming a *deva* and carrying on in a higher plane of existence, where, I assume, it's far easier to attain higher stages of awakening?

SUP: Much more important than wishing to become a *deva* is to practice the *Dhamma* to completion while in the human world. If one goes to a *deva* world without having developed the *Dhamma* to completion, when one gets there one forgets about *kusala* (wholesome deeds).

Better than the deva realms or the human realms, is to just have one lifetime. When the Buddha-to-be was born in the deva realms with a very long lifespan, he wasn't able to fulfill pāramī (the work of someone who is an excellent person). He performed adhimutti-kāla-kiriyā, or a sort of deva-suicide. Before the end of his lifespan, he let go of that existence, because in it he had no opportunity to fulfill the pāramīs.

The human world is the best for fulfilling pāramī (the ten perfections: 1. Dāna pāramī: generosity; 2. Sīla pāramī: virtue, morality; 3. Nikkhama pāramī: renunciation; 4. Paññā pāramī: liberating wisdom, insight; 5. Viriya pāramī: energy, effort; 6. Khanti pāramī: patient forbearance; 7. Sacca pāramī: truthfulness, honesty; 8. Adhiṭṭhāna pāramī: determination, resolution; 9. Mettā pāramī: loving-kindness; 10. Upekkhā pāramī: equanimity).

The human world is a place where if you can live free of fault, you go up. If you are a stupid fool, you go down. That is the human world.

AC: May I ask what evidence you have of rebirth?

SUP: I am a disciple of the Buddha, therefore I follow the path of the Buddha. According to the *Paticca Sammuppāda* [the teaching of Dependent Origination,] cause and effect continue.

AC: What is the motivation to become a Buddha?

SUP: Look at the *Bodhisattva's* motivation to become the *Buddha Gotama*. When he met *Buddha Dipankara*, he had the potential to cut off any further lifetimes. But he also wanted to help beings who were not yet free of the dangers of old age, sickness and death. Without help, they would suffer. With that vision and compassion, he relinquished the opportunity he had at hand to realize the fruition knowledge of an *arahant* (a fully enlightened being). As such, he had to endure suffering. One must say that the basis for this was reasoning power and compassion.

The Bodhisattva's reasoning power showed him the way to start fulfilling the pāramīs in order to become a Buddha. He reflected that if one doesn't know the true Dhamma oneself, it won't be possible to teach it to others. In order to master the true Dhamma one needs to fulfil the pāramīs beginning with dāna (generosity). After fulfilling the pāramīs, the Buddha practiced satipaṭṭhāna (the four foundations of mindfulness) and put an end to the kilesas (unwholesome states of mind). When the kilesas were dried up, delusion (moha) or ignorance (avijjā) was included. Because avijjā was eliminated, when the Buddha reflected, he could know whatever was to be known. For the Buddha to assist others, he knew that it was essential to first be complete with self-knowledge. If one wants to give food and clothing to those who are poor, it is only possible when one has something to give. One has to work to gain that something.

Further, only if one has compassion will one want to help. There are four kinds of people: The person who knows for him or herself but is unable to give that knowledge to others. The one who doesn't know for himself but tries to teach others. The one who first practices himself and teaches that to others. The one who neither practices nor gives the practice to others. The Buddha was the type of person who first practiced and then gave the method of practice to others. He was that type of person, the one who worked first to know for himself.

AC: Do you have hope for real change here in Burma?

SUP: Resistance power is important for everyone. People work to develop physical resistance to withstand heat, cold, and fatigue. For the most part, people give priority to developing physical resistance. There's little concern for developing mental resistance. Of course, mental powers are also important. Nothing can be substituted for them. They can't be achieved by listening or reflecting alone. One has to work to develop them, to put focused energy into one's mind. When one has developed mental resistance power, one can withstand the ups and downs one encounters. When one encounters suffering, one can stand it. When one encounters happiness, one can stand it. Every time one experiences something good or bad, one doesn't get elated nor depressed. There is spiritual resistance, the strength to control one's mind. This is needed by everyone. It is weak in the world today. With the correct method it can be developed.

There are spiritual faculties which bring self-control, self-mastery. These need to be developed in order to have spiritual resistance. They are called indriya or bala in Pali. For developing these faculties, the path of satipaṭṭhāna (practicing the four foundations of mindfulness) is best. One can't do this by meditating for just a short time. If one meditates meticulously, with real desire, one can gain these spiritual faculties. These faculties can be called spiritual multi-vitamins – similar to the multi-vitamins we take for physical health. When one develops the mind with satipaṭṭhāna meditation, this is like taking spiritual multi-vitamins. If half the world would possess these spiritual faculties in themselves the world would become peaceful.

"The Dhamma Protects those who Protect the Dhamma."

ALAN CLEMENTS: Let's talk about extremism and religion in Myanmar. A short introduction to the question: Burma has been in the world's eye for some years, and especially now with the transfer of power to the new "National Reconciliation" government, as the National League for Democracy (NLD) calls it. The world is watching. They are celebrating, cautiously, as are the people of Burma. But, from all indications, it looks as though there is a miracle occurring, albeit a hard-earned one and only the first stage of a long and perhaps arduous process of reform.

So that the world will not think little of the Buddha Sāsanā in Myanmar, as an Elder in the Sangha (monastic order), what advice might you give to your fellow Buddhist monks, if they were in the room with us right now?

VENERABLE SAYADAW U PANDITA: What was your objective when you became a monk? The life of a monk is for liberation from the suffering of *Saṃsāra* (the beginning-less cycle of repeated birth, existence and dying again that all beings pass through). Just that. This objective should not be lost. If this objective isn't lost, you can do your work and carry out your duties. Is that objective being lost?

Self-protection is very important. A monk must make his ability to defend himself sturdy. He must practice to build his defense in advance.

There are two kinds protection: internal protection by means of internal suppression and external protection by means of external suppression.

The first kind of protection—inner protection—is to defend oneself against lobha (desire, selfishness), dosa (anger, cruelty, hatred) and moha (delusion, stupidity). These arise within one's being. If one gives in to these, under their influence one no longer behaves like a true human being. One cannot keep one's mentality humane. And although human, one loses one's basic human intelligence. This happens because one lacks the internal protection needed to overcome lobha, dosa and moha that arise from within. One should give priority to this internal protection.

One must make one's internal protection strong and sharp. One does this with the three trainings of sīla (moral integrity), samādhi (concentration) and paññā (liberating wisdom).3 When one's internal protection becomes strong due to repeated practice, one will cherish their morality. The more one values their sīla, the more one will not allow it to weaken. One's ability to preserve it and make it strong will increase and become even stronger.

If the number of people who practice sīla, samādhi and paññā becomes large, the Dhamma which they protect will protect them in return. In this way, there will be freedom from disturbances. When the

---

3 The three trainings of sīla, samādhi and paññā, or morality, concentration and wisdom comprise the Dhamma, the teachings of the Buddha.

practice of Dhamma is not maintained, how can the Dhamma protect a person?

In order to increase the number of people who practice sīla, samādhi and paññā, one must spread knowledge of the correct practice. During the time of the Buddha, people who professed the doctrine of self were the majority. The Buddha became enlightened in that environment. The Buddha understood for himself the doctrine of non-self, that there is no self, and taught the practical method for coming to understand this.

When there were more people like this, the disturbances they had didn't amount to much. And the devas gave their protection. They protect those who are doing good work.

Even our Buddha arose during a period when only one quarter of the people are good. This period is called kali yūga.4 It is a time when peoples' behavior is for the most part quite immoral. Now, it has been more than 2,500 years since the passing away of the Buddha and the teachings of the Buddha has become very weak.

AC: You are aware that terrorism is an increasing problem all over the world. In my country of America, pretty much any western country for that matter, there's a deep and increasing fear of terrorism, whatever its ideological basis may be. My question: What advice might you offer to defeat radical extremism, that, I might add, in most cases considers success not only in the death of those whom they attack but in their own death, as well?

SUP: The best way is avoidance. Don't go to a place where there is fire. But if you can't avoid it, be prepared. Reasoning power is important. Reasoning power means there is *sātthaka sampajañña* and *sappāya sampajañña* (two of the four kinds of clear comprehension). The ability to weigh whether something one is about to do or say is beneficial or not is called *sātthaka sampajañña* (clear comprehension of benefit). One shouldn't do what is unbeneficial. Further, one should look to see if it is suitable or not. This is called *sappāya sampajañña* (clear comprehension of suitability). If something is both beneficial and suitable one should do it. Only then will one succeed. When one has reflected before acting or speaking many times, this knowledge becomes mature. Then it is easy in practice to avoid doing what is unbeneficial and unsuitable. This mature knowledge is called *pariharika*

---

4 There are four periods in time described in the texts. The worst is called kali yuga. Kali yuga means 'a period of many faults', a time where beings do many things wrong. If we look at the human population in the world and divide it into four parts, it is the period in time where only one part is good.

paññā (the wisdom to carry out what is both beneficial and suitable).[5] One becomes courageous about doing what is beneficial and suitable. When one avoids doing what is unbeneficial and unsuitable, then there is no detriment to oneself. And in doing what is beneficial and suitable, good results come.

For example, people need to consider before eating something, "Is this good for me or not? Is this suitable for me or not?" If it is suitable, when the time is right one should eat it. This is pariharika paññā: avoiding what is unbeneficial or unsuitable and carrying out what is both beneficial and suitable. This is very important for everyone. It is lacking in the world today.

AC: I was speaking with the American Ambassador not long ago about his views on the possible spread of violent extremism from abroad into Myanmar, and how disastrous that would be if it occurred. According to an alarming piece I read in a recent edition of the New Yorker Magazine, such ISIS-inspired activities are going on in neighboring Dhaka. What's required to raise the quality of governance in Burma to counter such a potential threat?

SUP: There are two programs for the country—a short-term program and a long-term program. The short-term program is to gather together as many elders and young adults as possible who know and have faith in the basic virtues of the *Buddha*, *Dhamma* and the *Sangha*, and are of good moral character. The long-term program is to train the children in basic Buddhist culture so that they will have good moral character as well as a good education. That is the long-term program for the country to become good again.

The long-term program is something like the example set by King Ashoka who ruled India in the 3rd century BC. At first, he was violent and cruel. He ruled by the sword. He was hated by the people because he oppressed them. After meeting Buddhist monks who corrected him, he put down the sword and his cruelty and ruled by the Dhamma.

He studied the Buddhist texts. He understood the precepts of a king, how to have mettā (loving-kindness) for the people and to handle things with foresight. Having studied the texts, he understood how to govern the people and how to support the teachings. Acting according to his understanding, during his reign the country became peaceful and the teachings

---

5   Pariharika paññā is the combination of two of the four kinds of clear comprehension, clear comprehension of benefit and clear comprehension of suitability [Sātthaka sampajañña and sappaāya *sampajañña]*. Sampajañña, or clear comprehension and sampajāno, someone who is clearly comprehending, are terms found in the Mahā Satipaṭṭhāna Sutta.

flourished. He used the term Dhamma vijaya, or "one who has gained personal victory with the Dhamma and the discipline."

He drew the conclusion that when the number of people who gain victory over themselves with the Dhamma becomes large, it is easy to govern. That is the Asoka program. Later, so there would continue to be generations of good people, he built monasteries for learning the Buddhist scriptures and for practicing meditation. That is creating new generations.

'Dhamma vijaya' is the way to conquer oneself. If you conquer yourself, will you break your sīla? Or harm others?

The children who have been learning basic Buddhist culture at the centre are taught both theoretically and practically about the teachings of the Buddha. They also try to gain practical experience by meditating. The young people who have finished this program have formed a group called the Dhamma Vijaya youth group. These young people are using the method of King Asoka, even though they don't have his abilities yet. In the future they will be capable of good governance. This is the plan established for the long-term.

AC: Playing the devil's advocate, it's no longer just protecting ourselves from our inner enemies. In the world today there are real and lethal external dangers. So my question: Do you see something required here to protect both the people and the *sāsana*, other than just mindfulness of one's own mind and one's protection against one's inner enemies?

SUP: There should be protection prepared in advance. It must be established. Combining theory and practice, one has to work to develop a large population with a firm commitment to the *Dhamma*. Further, unity and harmony are very important.

One has to work to make oneself and one's group good. When one's group or community is good there will not be injustice towards others. When that attitude becomes mature, as it is said, Dhammo have rakkhati dhammacārī—the Dhamma protects one who protects the Dhamma, so as not to encounter danger nor to decline.

It's important to be able to defend oneself. In the Parābhava Sutta, the Buddha said, "Dhammakāmo bhavaṃ hoti, Dhammadessī parābhavo." This means, 'One who learns the teaching and puts it into practice prospers. One who despises the teaching and the discipline declines.' When teaching the principles of Buddhist culture according to the instruction from the Parābhava Sutta, it is important for teachers, from elder Sayadaws on down to parents and schoolteachers, not just to teach the texts but to teach how theory is put into practice.

The teaching of the Buddha encourages self-protection by making SQ (spiritual intelligence or one's capacity for moral integrity, concentration, and wisdom) strong. If one can control oneself and gain self-victory, one will not feel troubled by others.

Which is more important, protection against external enemies or protection against internal enemies? Is it more important to conquer the external enemy, or the internal enemy?

AC: Well, it would depend on the circumstances. But I would say, the internal enemy. Even so, are you concerned that people of other religions will overwhelm Burma?

SUP: It can happen. People of other religions overwhelmed India, the place where Buddhism arose. When scriptural knowledge is not put into practice, a person doesn't know the benefits of the *Dhamma*. Not knowing its benefits, he doesn't value it. Not placing a value on the *Dhamma*, he won't try to preserve it, to keep it from disappearing. This is what is happening. A person needs to look at himself to see if the *Dhamma* has been lost or not. One has to work so that doesn't happen.

AC: In America, a pluralistic nation, there are many religions and spiritual faiths, as in Europe, Canada, Australia, and other democratic countries around the world. And the same here in Burma—all the major religions and faiths co-exist, albeit with stress and occasional bursts of violence. But what you're saying is that you think Burma will go the way of ancient India and lose its Buddhist culture?

SUP: If we can teach Buddhist cultural principles starting at a young age, the culture will take root in our children and become firm and strong. We have to take care with regard to preserving our own culture. But in preserving our culture, we must be careful not to harm others.

A plan needs to be established and carried out. If not, then within 50 years, at the very most 100 or 150 years, the teachings of the Buddha will leave the country of Myanmar.

AC: Some people have criticized Daw Aung San Suu Kyi for not defending Buddhism sufficiently enough here in Burma. When I have been asked about this in the media, I have, at times, pointed out that Daw Aung San Suu Kyi actively defends Buddhism, first, by being a nonviolent, *silā*-endowed practicing Buddhist who spent nearly 17 years under detention for her beliefs, both spiritual and political. But more to the point, when you look at the persecution of people here in Burma, the majority have been Buddhists. Of the thousands of people said to have been killed during the 1988 pro-democracy uprising, the vast majority were Buddhists. Of the additional 10,000 or more political prisoners that suffered in Burma's prisons, all but a few are Buddhists. Those tens-of-thousands forced into labor and portering for the military were mostly Buddhist. At the time of the Saffron Revolution here back in 2007, the military regime primarily focused on attacking Buddhist monks and monasteries and subsequently imprisoning and torturing many members of the *Saṅgha*. Overall, the Buddhists in Burma were the ones under siege by the former regime, by fellow Buddhists, at least, that's what they claim to be. And of course, the Karen and Kachin Christians and the Shans have also been under attack for many years.

SUP: Although they are nominally Buddhists, their understanding of the qualities of the *Buddha*, *Dhamma* and *Sangha* is vague, weak, deformed, without substance and totally uninformed. People who know nothing don't understand how to keep morality and the benefits of doing so. They don't understand the drawbacks incurred by immoral behavior. Thus they are not afraid to be immoral, commit misdeeds and be cruel. The good they do—making donations—has nothing to do with moral behavior.

AC: Few people know that you are Daw Aung San Suu Kyi's *Dhamma* teacher. She looks to you for *Dhamma* advice and guidance. If I am not mistaken, she learned meditation under house arrest from your book, *In This Very Life*. You receive her regularly. Her office often posts photographs on Facebook of your meetings; she's been here to Panditarama too many times to count. She's practiced meditation here. As such, you've paid a price for the association; from interrogation by MI (military intelligence); having the monastery's internet and electricity cut at times; being denied building permits and land use permits for branch monasteries; and many other ways as well. Throughout it, you have remained unscathed and steadfast, loyal in your association. You even have an NLD calendar featuring a large photograph of Daw Suu on the wall here in your meeting room. With that said, would you care to comment about the criticisms leveled at her?

SUP: I can't be everywhere, going after all those people. "What you do is the work at hand, where you get to [at night] is where you make camp." When planting rice or beans, farmers choose a place with fertile soil. Only then will their work be worthwhile. If one ignores the workable land one has and goes and plants on untilled, virgin land, what good will it do? One should do what works.

I ask you. To whom would you give priority, if both were to approach you at the same time: a person with good potential or a person with little potential?

AC: The first person.

SUP: Right. Choosing is important.

It is no good to try to become a hero by means that don't pacify hatred but only increase it. Daw Aung San Suu Kyi has become a heroine by pacifying quarrels according to the way of the Buddha. She didn't try to become a heroine, but she has become one naturally.

There is a Burmese saying, "follow the example of Asoka." We spoke about him earlier. King Asoka ruled in India more than 2,000 years ago. Wielding the power of the sword, he ruled with cruelty so that people had no room to move. They had no freedom. And the people hated him. He was known as "Cruel Asoka." Later, when he put down the sword and ruled according to the *Dhamma*, he became successful.

Government can only work after one has gained victory over oneself by means of the *Dhamma*. King Asoka was the first to use the term, '*Dhamma vijaya*,' or '*victory by means of the Dhamma.*'

In particular, the people at all levels of government, if their administration is to be effective, should conquer themselves by means of the *Dhamma*, not just superficially but with right practice. Asoka also worked to enable the people to gain *Dhamma* victory for themselves. He became very successful. H. G. Wells said much in praise of Asoka, saying there had never been anyone like him before. ("... the name of Asoka shines, and shines almost alone, a star." The Outline of History, 1920.)

When he ruled by the sword, he was known as 'Cruel Asoka,' but after he put down the sword and began to rule by the *Dhamma*, he became very successful and was known as 'Righteous Asoka [*Dhammasoka*].' Those who govern should always look back at history.

If you can't overcome the internal enemies, they not only give you trouble but give others trouble too. And in future lives they also give trouble. An ordinary, external enemy can't debase you. If he or she kills you, it's only in one lifetime. The internal enemies kill a being lifetime after lifetime. They also degrade one. They are quite frightening.

AC: Thank you Sir.

The Dhamma of Reconciliation and the SQ Revolution

ALAN CLEMENTS: I would like to follow up with the issue of "National Reconciliation"—the centrepiece of (Myanmar State Counsellor) Daw Aung San Suu Kyi and her government's vision of a peaceful and prosperous Burma. Obviously, this is an epic challenge. Would you share your thoughts on overcoming those forces within oneself—those defilements— that prevent genuine reconciliation with those who have harmed us? Your guidance would not only be a gift to the people of your country but the world over. As we know, conflicts are everywhere, and if we expect to over-come them, we need urgent wise leadership. We need both a moral compass and the ethical courage, and the "spiritual intelligence" or the mindful intelligence, to make real on Daw Aung San Suu Kyi's hope of a healed nation. What happens here may serve as a model for peace everywhere.

What is the Dhamma of reconciliation?

VENERABLE SAYADAW U PANDITA: As far as Daw Aung San Suu Kyi's side goes, they are ready. The previous government abused our country and the people. They are at fault, and if they admit those acts, everything will work out. As I said before, just as monks do when they commit a monastic offense, if they admit honestly and bravely, "We simply acted according to how we saw things, but, as everyone knows, this is what came about; we take full responsibility, these acts are our fault," then everything will work out.

Human beings should have the courage to avoid doing what is wrong and the courage to do and to say what is beneficial. If one does something wrong, whether deliberately or out of carelessness, one needs to have the courage to admit one's mistake.

The Pali word vīriya means the courage to avoid doing things that are wrong, the courage to do what is right and if one errs, the courage to admit it. That is called vīriya. When taking such a moral risk, one must bear the suffering encountered. Such courage must be nurtured. It does not come quickly. You must develop it gradually.

When the courage to refrain from doing wrong becomes strong, one will understand that they are free of fault. One will also have the courage to do things that are good. When one does good things, good results will come. When one knows what is beneficial and free of fault, one will value the ability to take risks. When the attitude of valuing courage arises in the mind, one won't allow one's courage to decline.

Firstly, there must be honesty. The difficulty is that few people are honest. Because of dishonesty, there's much deceit.

You were formerly a monk. When you commit an offense, what must you do?

AC: Admit it openly in front of the *Saṅgha*.

SUP: Right, you have to admit it. First of all, you have to avoid committing an offense, but if you know you have committed one, you must confess it.

In the realm of *Dhamma*, whether one is a monk, nun, or a lay person, there are rules and responsibilities. Lay people have their rules and responsibilities, monks have their rules and duties, and nuns have theirs. When one knows these rules and duties and acts accordingly, it's like keeping to your lane when traveling. One automatically goes in the right direction.

It won't do to learn these duties and responsibilities only when one becomes an adult. They need to be learned from a young age. Just as one must try to make one's IQ good, at the same time one must also try to make one's SQ (spiritual intelligence) good. It won't do to make SQ good only after one's IQ has become good. It's just like feeding a child appropriately. You must first nurse the baby and then all along the way, gradually, feed the child appropriately, taking into account the child's age, size, growth and of course, both the quantity and quality of the food. Good health has many considerations. But you must feed the child appropriately starting from a young age.

Parents have the first duty to teach the child and after them, teachers have their duty to teach them. In the world there are many parents and many teachers who do not fulfill their duties. This is, in large part, why the world is in such conflict and being destroyed. Have you thought about it?

AC: I have, especially as a parent.

SUP: For the world to be peaceful, parents are crucial because they are a child's first teachers. Even in Myanmar where Buddhism flourishes, because there are so many people who are ill-equipped to be parents, the *Dhamma* has declined. Because I knew that many parents were not fulfilling their responsibilities, since the days of Mahasi Yeiktha I've tried to teach children about Buddhist culture both in theory and practice, so that a new generation could emerge. This was a priority and remains so.

AC: Can you say more about nurturing courage?

SUP: Parents have to explain this to their children so that they develop the courage to avoid doing what is wrong. An analogy is that parents should explain the bad results of eating what is unsuitable for them. To avoid eating food which is not suitable requires courage. When one courageously avoids unsuitable food, one doesn't suffer.

Similarly, parents should explain the benefits of eating suitable and appropriate food. Eating suitable food also requires courage. If one has courage, one gains benefits such as good digestion, physical energy, healthiness, and so on.

Parents should explain the value of having courage to avoid doing wrong and to do what is right by using comparisons like this that children can understand. This will only come about through establishing a specific plan. It can't be done without one.

In America, a country where science and technology flourish, education or IQ has been given great emphasis, whereas moral behavior and emotional intelligence or EQ have been ignored. Proceeding in this way, children gain a worldly education but there are many teenagers who have become immoral. Searching for the cause, one can draw the conclusion that it is because moral behavior is being ignored.

In a research study it was found that a person's success was due to IQ in only 25 percent of the people studied, while EQ was crucial to success in 75 percent of those studied. Afterwards, EQ became the first priority and IQ the second.

Because our country is doing the same as America, emphasizing IQ over moral behavior, teenagers are becoming immoral. Therefore, in our (Dhamma) courses for children I emphasize SQ (spiritual intelligence) in order to strengthen it in them. I use the term SQ in place of EQ. SQ (spiritual intelligence) stands for sīla (ethical intelligence) and sikkhā for training6. And the highest is satipaṭṭhāna (cultivating the four foundations of mindfulness). All three words begin with 'S.'

When Daniel Goleman, who popularized the term EQ (emotional intelligence), came to speak with me, I told him I prefer to use the term 'SQ' (spiritual intelligence). He agreed and concluded that people with good SQ are able to skilfully assess themselves. They know what sort of person they are. That's the first quality. They are able to control their impulses.

In America, there is a lot of tension, stress, and depression. People with good SQ are able to control these feelings. They are able to maintain their discipline. In SQ, this refers to the five precepts. Further, they have compassion for others. They also feel gladdened by others' good characteristics. They aren't jealous or envious. When something must be done, they have the intelligence to evaluate whether it is beneficial or not and whether it is suitable or not.

We should give priority to SQ and de-emphasize IQ. This is in keeping with the teaching of the Buddha, to teach children right from wrong, then provide an education.

It's been more than 50 years that I have been teaching this program to the children, since my days at Mahasi Yeiktha. This program is the basic Buddhist culture course for children. It's a training in SQ. In essence, the children are taught, "Those things are bad and they bring bad results." Knowing that something is wrong, one shouldn't fail in one's duty to avoid it. "Those things are good." Knowing what is good, one shouldn't fail in one's duty to undertake them. Not neglecting to avoid what should

6   The three-fold training in higher virtue (adhisīla-sikkhā), higher mind (adhicitta-sikkhā), and higher wisdom (adhipaññā-sikkhā).

be avoided and doing what should be done. That is called appamāda, or heedfulness.

AC: Then the question arises, how to get parents to wake up and bring their children to Panditarama, and to understand the value of SQ?

SUP: Parents have woken up—they know and they accept that their own children know more than they do about the teachings of the Buddha. They are alert to this. Over the last 50 years [in Myanmar], most parents failed in their duties to their children. Teachers, for the most part, failed in their duties to their students. They have come to realize their failure. But it's just a small oasis in a vast, burning desert. And in comparison with the whole world, it's a tiny spot.

AC: To actualize reconciliation and abide in clear conscience, you speak of the necessity of having the courage to honestly admit one's mistakes. But as a former monk, before ordination, I was aware of the rules expected of me and agreed to follow them. And if I failed to keep any one of them, I also agreed—out of self-honor and respect for the *Saṅgha,* as well as the lay people who supported us—to openly admit my failings.

In Myanmar and her quest for National Reconciliation, we have people—the oppressors, the old guard—who have made no such commitment to a moral code of conduct or rule of law. To the contrary, the majority of them, perhaps all of them, so it seems, think they've done the right thing for the country. So the idea of admitting a mistake when they in fact think their actions were not only justified but were for the betterment of the people, blind as that may be, is essentially asking one to admit to something they do not see in themselves. Or do they, and they are pretending? Of course, only they know.

Regardless, if courage is required to admit one's wrongdoing, how to get someone, who doesn't see that what they did was wrong, to actually admit that what they did violated others? In other words, how to overcome self-deception?

SUP: Just look back on your own life and the things you do every day, whether doing something for yourself or for others. It's never perfect. There are times when something is missing, when something is lacking or especially when something is wrong. The Buddha talked about these three things: the gaps, the things that are needed and the things that are off, incorrect. He also talked about how to fill in the gaps, how to complete the parts that are incomplete, and how to make things correct. It's very important to be able to look back and see that. When you look at your own life and then you see, "Oh! This is missing," that's admitting your error. You ask, "Is there something lacking here, in this task?" When you recognize that something is lacking, that's admitting your fault. "I did these things incorrectly, they're not right—I missed the mark." One has to understand that. If there is an error, one has to look for the reason and correct it.

A person's life is like driving a car. When driving one must stay in one's lane, right? If one starts to swerve out of one's lane, one has to correct this and straighten out. To be able to steer is essential. This ability to steer is called yoniso manasikāra (wise consideration).

The same can be said with a boat, you always have to control the rudder. And in order to steer well, you must learn how. But for the most part, people cannot control their own lives. They're without the ability to steer. Although they have a rudder, they can't steer. Do you think that's true?

AC: Sure, there's chaos everywhere. It's rather maddening, frankly. But this madness has become normalized, in many ways. And often, those who point out this madness—those who can't steer, as you know from having lived under totalitarian regimes for over fifty years—are often considered mad and scapegoated, vilified, even imprisoned. As was Daw Aung San Suu Kyi and many of her NLD colleagues, and for decades. What was lacking in their oppressors, besides being unable to properly steer their lives?

SUP: When they were young, their parents didn't teach them properly.

AC: Bad parenting?

SUP: That's right. Because the parents were lacking, because they did not fulfill their responsibilities. Look at the *Singālovāda Sutta*, in the *Pātika Vagga* of the *Dīgha Nikāya*. This explains six sets of human relationships in society and shows what responsibilities or duties people have to each other, how they should relate to each other.

AC: You mentioned, 'when one takes risks, one must be able to bear the suffering encountered.' Would you shed light on how to ignite one's conscience to say something as radical as, "I ordered the killing of your brother, I ordered the torture of your daughter, I steered our country down a road of ruin and created an authoritarian state. And in so doing, I amassed an enormous amount of wealth and at your expense. And I did it because I was driven by fear and extreme selfish greed. Now, I humbly stand before you with shame. How can I make my wrongs right?"

SUP: First of all, there has to be the courage to avoid doing wrong. Daw Aung San Suu Kyi has this. If she does something wrong, she knows it. People who always have mindfulness know, "I've made a mistake," when they have erred. When correct, they know that too. When in error, they correct the mistake. When correct, they simply keep on going straight ahead. Like driving a car.

AC: That's for oneself, but what about for others?

SUP: If one can control oneself, others are automatically preserved, because one doesn't do harm. She understands that too. Self-control is not just for one's own benefit. It's not just for one's own physical, verbal and mental behavior. To the extent one controls oneself, one no longer harms others and one protects others so that they aren't harmed. There are two methods for this. There is self-control because one has moral shame and moral fear of doing wrong, and self-control because one understands how others would feel if harmed. However, it may be, both sides benefit. The difficulty is that most people do not have these qualities.

AC: For decades, the previous regimes did not see their errors. When people don't see their faults how can there be National Reconciliation and a peaceful, united country?

SUP: They're like a boat, the bow of which is broken and can't be maneuvered. So instead of trying to fix them, the only thing to do is gather people together who are in agreement and work to make yourself and the country good. If one pays attention to those people, how will anything be accomplished?

AC: Unify like minds?

SUP: It's very important to get the work done.

AC: How would you define the 'work' to be done?

SUP: Human beings have what are called moral behavior and duty. First and most important is moral behavior and after that, duty or responsibility. It's very important to fulfill these two. If one has been born a human being, then one should have the courage to ask, "What morals do I need to be a true human being?" If one investigates, one will come to understand morality. Next, you must put it into practice. If one doesn't know one's duties, one needs to learn them and fulfill them. When those two things are fulfilled—good moral behavior and our human responsibilities—one becomes a true human being.

It's also important to keep your mind humane, to keep your mind like a human's mind should be. You can't just look at what benefits you. You've got to look at what's good for others, too. You have to do what is good for others as much as possible, and do it with an attitude of goodwill.

One should also have compassion, the feeling of wanting to respond to the needs of others. When there is a basic attitude of *mettā* (goodwill) and *karunā* (compassion) there won't be envy for others' good circumstances. Rather, there will be the desire for others to enjoy the good circumstances one has for oneself; *muditā* (sympathetic joy) will arise. These are basic mental attitudes of a true human being.

Further, human beings encounter two kinds of things: good and bad. We experience good things and bad things. We encounter things that we like and we encounter things that we do not like. Things which are depressing and things to be happy about. In the face of these things, we shouldn't react. We should nurture equanimity, or balance of mind. The more we nurture this attitude, every time we encounter something good or bad, we won't respond with liking or rejection, but will remain balanced, in equanimity.

For this, *sātthaka sampajañña* and *sappāya sampajañña*, or reasoning power which is able to consider whether something is beneficial or unbeneficial, and suitable or unsuitable, is very important.

In particular, when one practices the *Dhamma* consistently and knows the true *Dhamma* to a large extent, the mind matures. When the mind matures, it has resistance power. Physical stamina is the ability to withstand the punishment of heat, cold, fatigue, and so on. When the mind gains knowledge, it becomes mature. Due to being mature, although the mind encounters something good, it doesn't feel elated. Similarly, when encountering something bad, it doesn't get depressed. It is able to stay balanced in between elation and depression. This is called equanimity. It's important to gain this ability.

Look at your own life. Before you practiced meditation, before you gained knowledge of the *Dhamma*, what was your life like? And after practicing, what was your life like then? Do you see the changes before and after practicing?

AC: Yes, I've seen dramatic changes; nothing short of miraculous.

SUP: This is like being reborn in this very life.

AC: Beautiful!

SUP: This is the only way to be reborn without dying. One's life changes for the better due to the practice, not for the worse.

AC: Yes, meditation changed my life.

SUP: When something is this valuable, why do so few people pursue it?

AC: Well, you have to be smart. You have to see life and death and the limitations of sense pleasure and the emptiness of desire. You must become weary of the ego and tired of the *kilesas*, attachment, addictions, and fear. And even if you have wealth or success, you have to be smart enough to see them as a house of cards or a sandcastle; conditions beyond your control and changing all the time. And further, it takes a lot of effort to turn inward, to seek a higher inner refuge, a higher freedom born from insight into *Dhamma*.

SUP: When you want something valuable, you have to pay the price. Faith, effort, mindfulness and concentration, or *saddhā, viriya, sati,* and *samādhi,* are the price.

AC: Earlier, you encouraged reconciliation through cultivating the compassion practice of putting oneself into another person's place and feeling how they might be feeling. Would you share more on this process? I think most good people would like to be more compassionate: abandon egoism, discrimination, any hint of apartheid.

SUP: Has it ever happened that someone yelled at you, cursed you?

AC: Yes. I've encountered my fair share of abusive people.

SUP: Can you bear it? And do you like it?

AC: I did not like it. I found it revolting.

SUP: What you don't like, others wouldn't like either. The ability to put ourselves in another person's place is based upon the ability to reason. It's called empathy, or consideration for others. People who are selfish do not have that ability to reason, to reflect like that.

AC: What is this state of consciousness, the ability to reflect?

SUP: Reasoning power, or what is called clear comprehension of benefit and suitability (*sātthaka sampajañña* and *sappāya sampajañña*). It's what we discussed earlier. People do not have the ability to think about what is beneficial and suitable for others if they are only thinking about themselves.

AC: Consideration for others, the requisite of a great leader?

SUP: Yes, it's important for a leader to have that quality.

AC: If there's reconciliation and harmony in Parliament, there'll be harmony in the country. Maybe it should be advocated, that there should be an SQ retreat. Should the PMs go on retreat?

SUP: That would be the best.

AC: And maybe for the military as well.

SUP: In India, at the time of the Buddha, King Bimbisāra ruled the country after becoming a *sotāpanna* (the first stage of enlightenment). And, while continuing his *Dhamma* practice under the Buddha's guidance, he also continued to fulfil the duties of his office. The world cannot be ruled by weapons and administrative power alone. There must be this justice of the *Dhamma* to rule the world. That's why, in the old days when kings ruled their countries, they were known as '*Dhammiko*,' a *Dhamma* person or '*Dhammarājā*,' a king who rules with *Dhamma*.

AC: This is the military version of SQ?

SUP: There should never be unjust killing or oppression. But a person who leads the country needs to be precise in following the laws. That is the ruler's duty.

AC: Sayadaw-gyi, I appreciate your reasoning power, your discerning wisdom, your warrior-like expression of spiritual intelligence. And I pray that your *Dhamma* advice serves to facilitate reconciliation and peacebuilding both here in Myanmar and around the world. I am honored that you share it. Thank you.

SUP: This is just the way the Buddha taught.

'Looking for the Dhamma You Find it in Yourself.'

ALAN CLEMENTS: I would like to thank you once again for taking the time to share your wisdom, both for the people of your country and others around the world. Tonight, I would like to follow up with issues raised in our previous conversations. You have shared quite a lot on the reconciling process. You've also touched upon SQ (spiritual intelligence) as foundational wisdom for enacting that process. We've talked about healing the wounds between the oppressed and the oppressors as a means of fostering peace and harmony among the people. We've also talked about good parenting—the importance of parents knowing their duties to their children and doing them well.

My question: Burma is the newest born democracy on earth. We have several hundred new Members of Parliament, Cabinet Members, Ministers, a new President and Vice Presidents, and most of them have never before been in positions of high leadership. In fact, many of them spent the majority of the past two decades as prisoners of conscience, here in their own country.

Would you speak about the Dhamma qualities of good leadership?

VENERABLE SAYADAW U PANDITA: In order to understand what qualities a good leader needs to have in terms of the *Dhamma*, first of all, we have to look at the qualities of a good friend, a *kalyāṇa mitta*. There are six qualities this person should have:

- *Piya*—to have good personal behavior, not just pretending. When one has good personal behavior, one is loved by those around one. This is the first quality that needs to be mentioned.
- Not only does the person have good personal behavior, they have a good mental attitude and are able to help others. Due to this, the person receives the respect of others. There must also be this quality of being respected, called *garu*.
- These two qualities combined lead to *bhāvaniya*, which means to be the recipient of others' *mettā* (loving-kindness).
- The next quality is *vattā*, which means when there is something to be said that is beneficial and true, the person can speak frankly.
- Further, when they receive criticism from others, they can accept it. This is called *vacanakkhama*.
- And the last quality is that they do not use those who depend on them inappropriately—*no c'aṭṭhāne niyujjako*. This means not urging people who depend on you to do things for your benefit that aren't good for them to do; not to use people for your own selfish means.

A person who possesses these six qualities is a good friend, or kalyāṇa mitta. One has to start by understanding this. That is what the Buddha taught. If a person possesses these qualities, one could choose that person as a friend, mentor or a teacher.

AC: These six qualities of a *kalyāṇa mitta* also apply to good leadership?

SUP: Yes. It's important to possess the qualities of a good friend.

AC: How can one know and trust that a person has these attributes?

SUP: In human society, if someone has good morality, or good personal behavior, those around that person will come to perceive this. Associate and you'll know. Throughout time, one comes to know through association with another whether they have a bad character or a good character. But, one can't find this out in a short time. One must take time to choose a good person.

There are six other qualities of a good leader. First of all, leaders must be patient (*khamā*), in all ways. They must be able to bear heat, cold, suffering, and blame from others. That's important. Second, *jāgariya*: they must be watchful, vigilant and prompt to act. And *utthāna*, they must be active. Fourth, *samvibhāga*: they should share what they have with friends and associates, and not just keep things for themselves. Five, they should have compassion for others (*karuṇā*). Six, *ikkhana* or foresight: they should be able to assess a situation accurately. If a person has these six qualities, one could choose that person as a good friend, a teacher or a leader. Here, the text refers to a leader of the *Saṅgha*, but anyone who is a leader of an organization or association should have these qualities.

AC: What is another word for foresight?

SUP: Foresight can also be called reasoning power; when there is something to be done, it is the ability to consider whether that task is beneficial or not. If it is beneficial, then to consider further whether it is suitable or not. And whether or not the time is right to do it. What is important is that one's actions should not be detrimental for oneself or for others. Even though you may not be able to help, you can control yourself so that you don't bother others. There is a Burmese proverb, "If you can't help, let it be, but don't make trouble."

AC: In reference to having consideration for another and then through reasoning power determining what would be beneficial or harmful to that person, and from there, acting appropriately, what if 'the other' is not yet born—we are going forward here a generation or two; can you speak to that type of future-reaching foresight, or multi-generational compassion, that exchanges self for others not yet born?

This question is more relevant today than ever, as many leaders in our world have not had the foresight nor the compassion to see the effects of what looked to be a wise decision in their day, but as it turned out, was detrimental to future generations. For example, nuclear power and nuclear weapons have placed life in jeopardy; they hold all life hostage. In addition, we have a 'homicidal economy' fueled by obsessive consumption and the blind burning of fossil fuels, that has led to global warming, runaway climate change, and with it, the melting of the polar caps and the release of toxic methane, and the acidification of the oceans, habitat loss and disruption of food supplies, and the possibility of extinction, perhaps much sooner than we think. All based on human ignorance, the absence of reasoning and the obsession with "self, progress, and stuff." And all done, for the most part, by so-called educated leaders trying their best to do what was right for the people. But it's been the very opposite of foresight and far-reaching compassion. Few people were able to think that far ahead; few people were able to put themselves in the shoes of the unborn and determine what was best for them.

The question: How to really know what it means to put oneself in the mind of Life not yet conceived? What does it mean to embody future generations and have the foresight to care for those life-forms, the animals, the birds, the trees, the water, the people, all life, known and unknown? This is an essential question, in part, because Burma is the latest birth of democracy on the planet and the learning that has gone on in older democracies could be made here with good intentions, yet without the foresight to sustain in the long term.

Translator: Alan is saying that because some of the present leaders of the world don't have vision or foresight, for example, the destruction of species, the destruction of forests, the natural disasters that are now occurring, the disruption of the order of things, cutting down forests to an extreme, extreme use of petroleum, are things that were done because of a lack of reasoning and foresight. Due to this, there are all kinds of problems in the world now. The extinction of species, about 200 a day, for example. At present, they are even trying to find types of fuel other than petroleum, ways to avoid global warming and pollution. Because of a lack of vision, all over the world people are encountering all sorts of problems. If the leaders of the future were to have this type of vision regarding future generations, how would you advise them, in terms of *Dhamma*?

SUP: That would be difficult. When there is selfishness, when people are self-centered, and all that matters is getting what they want, or what their group wants, when people are oppressed by greed, then *mettā* and *karunā* have dried up. One no longer cares for the welfare of others. One no longer knows how to have love and compassion for others, whether presently alive or future generations. As a result, their duties as humans are left unfulfilled.

In the world today, selfishness—a lack of mettā and a lack of karuṇā—are thick. People are human in form, but not truly human. And there is no truth, no foresight, no compassion, no ability to truly see what is beneficial for others and have the courage to do what is right and refrain from what is wrong. People no longer know there is truth, and that they should stand by what is true.

AC: Standing by the truth?

SUP: What this means is that there is a correct, straight path: 'That's right.' If one approaches a *kalyāṇa mitta* and has the ability to weigh whether something is beneficial or not, whether something is suitable or not, the quality of being upright and pure, *uju*, arises. Because one comes to know what is beneficial and correct, the quality of being upright, or *uju*, comes to be. Then people are able to keep their own discipline, they are able to keep their *sīla*. People should be moral and fulfill their duties. This is important. If one doesn't keep basic morality and doesn't perform the duties and responsibilities that one should perform, because of no longer understanding the benefits of doing this, then the upright, pure mind will not arise. Therefore, one must explain to others the importance of morality as well encourage an understanding of their social responsibilities. Then one must be watchful to see if they do as explained. Do they keep their morality or not? Do they fulfill their duties or not?

As one waits and sees, if they do things sincerely, is there benefit or not? When people can see that they are gaining benefit, then restraint will follow. People will feel, "Because we respect this path, things are peaceful and beneficial. When our morality is good and we fulfill our duties and responsibilities, good things come." Because they understand the benefits, they are sure to follow straight along this path.

There are people who kill others, who steal, who commit adultery or other sexual offenses, who lie, who take drugs and intoxicants and go wild because of them. One realizes that it is good to avoid these actions. One realizes, "If I avoid doing these things, my behavior becomes clean, my morality is intact and other people are not harmed because of what I do." This is an upright mental attitude. When one really looks at this, one comes to realize that it's peaceful. One's morality is intact, and it's good for others too. When one sees this, one doesn't want to lose the benefits one has developed. One is sure to walk along this straight path.

When people who initially don't know anything about the *Dhamma* practice and come to know the nature of the *Dhamma*, what happens? Is their mind the same after they practice, as it was before? It's not the same anymore, it changes, doesn't it? It's like that.

If one hasn't yet made oneself upright with correct means, then one does not have any confidence in doing it because the results haven't yet appeared. In that case, one will just keep going along one's way. One's path won't be straight. But when one realizes the benefits, one will go straight.

In essence, one has to first learn the method for developing self-control so one doesn't follow the wrong path, so that one can keep from doing things that are wrong. When one has a reliable method, one simply follows that correct path. Following the correct path, one reaches a safe place. Because one has learned the method for self-control and one knows the benefits of gaining self-control, as well as the faults of not gaining self-control, one will surely control oneself. And being free of fault, one experiences good results. When one can restrain oneself, problems are sure to be solved.

For solving these problems, in order to get the best answer, now and for the future, practice *satipaṭṭhāna* to a satisfactory level. Before practicing *satipaṭṭhāna* and after practicing *satipaṭṭhāna*, how did your life change?

AC: In every way.

SUP: Was it a good change? Did you gain self-mastery?

AC: I certainly improved, nothing short of miraculous.

SUP: So, you have the answer.

AC: On the subject of *satipaṭṭhāna*, this next question is universal, in that it applies to everyone and has the potential to benefit all beings in this world, now and in the future. I think it was Burma's first Prime Minister, U Nu, who was, as you know, one of the founders of Mahasi Yeiktha here in Yangon—where the worldwide mass lay mindfulness movement began—who said, over fifty or so years ago, that Burma's number one export was mindfulness.

Prophetically, he was right. Mindfulness is now a global phenomenon and a lucrative one as well. Fortune Magazine recently reported it to be a $1-billion-dollar industry. And I'm sure you are aware that mindfulness training is being applied in numerous multi-billion-dollar corporations; Ford, Google, American Express, to name just a few.

Pro-athletes espouse it as the basis of their expertise. We see it being taught in prisons. In hospitals. Colleges. Highs schools. Even children, as in Burma, are seeing its tremendous benefits; increasing their ability to focus, reduce their stress and anxiety, and better able to manage negative emotions.

We also see mindfulness being used in the military. I'm not sure how deep into the military it's applied, but when we use the word military, we generally mean both defense and offense. So it's probably being used anywhere from combat, to stress management in highly volatile areas and I wouldn't be surprised if it's used by those who pilot drones from a safe distance that strike thousands of miles away and either kill their intended targets and or kill innocent civilians.

At 95 years old you are perhaps the most Elder Buddhist monk in Myanmar. Having ordained at age of 12, with a tremendous knowledge, both theoretically and experientially, of the satipaṭṭhāna dhamma, you are perhaps the senior-most teacher of mindfulness in the world, with tens of thousands of students both in Myanmar and worldwide.

I think it is fair to say, that the majority of people who currently practice it and guide others in it, have little idea that its origins are rooted in Buddhism and Dhamma, or, perhaps, that there's an entire culture here in Myanmar that has been practicing sati (mindfulness) for centuries.

My question: Would you care to offer a few points of guidance to anyone interested in pursuing the practice of mindfulness or more specifically the practice of satipaṭṭhāna, especially as it becomes more embedded worldwide?

SUP: What's most important is to find a good spiritual friend, a *kalyāṇa mitta* and practice meditation. There are seven qualities that a good spiritual friend must have as explained in the *Visuddhimagga*, which quotes what the Buddha taught. The seven qualities are: being loved (*piya*), being respected (*garu*), being the object of others' *mettā* (*bhāvaniya*), being able to say frankly to the students what they need to hear (*vattā*), being able to take it when others criticize them (*vacanakkhama*), being able to speak about the deep *Dhamma* because of both practice and understanding the theory (*gambhirañca kathaṃ kattā*), and not using one's students in inappropriate ways, for one's own benefit (*no c'aṭṭhāne niyujjako*).

The qualities of piya, garu, bhāvaniya and so on are resultant qualities. In order to possess them, one must possess the causal qualities: saddhā, sīla, sūta, cāga, vīriya, sati, samādhi and paññā (faith, morality, learning, generosity, effort, mindfulness, concentration and wisdom). When a person has these causal qualities, they don't have to say, "May others love me." It automatically happens that such people are loved and that they're also worthy of respect. People have the feeling of wanting such a person to be well and happy. A person with such qualities is brave enough to speak when there's something that needs to be said, and when other people criticize them, they can forbear and be patient. Because one has practiced the Dhamma of satipaṭṭhāna to a satisfactory level one is able to speak about the profound Dhamma. And possessing the courage to avoid doing what is wrong and to undertake what is correct, one doesn't use one's students inappropriately.

This is how to look at a teacher, in terms of those qualities. You should examine if a person is a true kalyāṇa mitta, a good spiritual friend possessed of these qualities. This is what the Buddha taught. Why? Because one has to choose a good guide in order to take the right path. Only then will one go the right way.

The Buddha said that sati (mindfulness) is needed everywhere. He acknowledged this in the word sabbatthika—sati is needed everywhere, like fresh air. We need air every second, don't we? If we breathe polluted air, immediately we feel tight and tense and if we breathe air that contains poison we can die immediately. Sati is needed everywhere. It's like fresh air. Think about it.

People usually don't think breathing fresh air is important. Or it's not a big deal. But if you think about it, it's not only important, it's essential. And it's something we must do immediately, right now. If we don't breathe we die.

You have to do it right now; you have to do it repeatedly; you have to do it in time; and you need to breathe fresh air. That is why people may not necessarily think that breathing fresh air is important or don't even think about breathing as something that's important because it's happening all the time. But you have to do it yourself. You have to do it right away, right now. You have to do it regularly. And if you do that, the results are good for you. These four aspects are important.

In the same way one applies mindfulness. You need to do it yourself; you have to do it right now; you have to do it regularly; and the results will be beneficial. Every important thing that a person does has these four characteristics. You can look at anything in terms of those four points and if it has those four characteristics, you know it is one of the most important things you can do: that you cannot not do it, you have to do it yourself, you have to do it regularly and in time, and it is very beneficial.

AC: What are your thoughts about teaching *sati* (mindfulness) removed from *satipaṭṭhāna*? Is it still effective? Can you be deluded about thinking it's effective? And are there dangers in teaching from that separation?

What I mean by 'separation' is removing the Buddhist context from *sati*, removing the ontological eco-system from the root concept of mindfulness. In other words, teaching mindfulness without reference to *Dhamma*, Buddhism, *nāma-rūpa*, the five aggregates, the progress of insight, awareness of *anicca*, *anatta* and *dukkha*, or the four foundations of mindfulness, or the eight-fold path, or the four noble truths, or the seven factors of enlightenment or *nibbāna;* purposely removing the key transformational constructs of the *Dhamma*, the Buddha's teaching, from it. So by removing the *Dhamma* from *sati*, I'm assuming one is removing *satipaṭṭhāna* from it and teaching mindfulness as a stand-alone state of mind.

Further, there's a tremendous debate in the West and perhaps the world, on what the 'mindful' state of mind really is. There doesn't seem to be a clear consensus on the true nature of mindfulness.

SUP: As the Buddha said, "*Sati* is needed everywhere." In the olden days, there was a monk who was given the instruction to rub a small piece of cloth—just to keep on rubbing it with awareness. While rubbing the cloth, *vīriya* (energy), *sati* (mindfulness), and *samādhi* (concentration) arose, and he became enlightened.

If we look at this from a modern-day perspective, it seems laughable—not something an adult would do. But as the monk was rubbing, his mind became concentrated. At first, insight-knowledge didn't arise. But later, he came to know 'touching.' He rubbed, and knew the 'rubbing.' Samādhi arose, then there was touching, and knowing the touching. These moments of touching and knowing arose and then disappeared. He came to know the arising and passing away (of the mental and physical phenomena). Vipassanā (insight) knowledge arose. None of the teachings of the Buddha were mentioned, just to rub the cloth—the 'doctrine' of rubbing.

AC: So, mindfulness is sufficient in itself to free the mind? That when practiced rightly, mindfulness reveals reality, and as such, awakens insight into the arising and passing of phenomena, and freedom follows?

SUP: It is not a matter of 'practicing mindfulness rightly.' Reality is revealed when there is focus on the object, *sati* becomes steadfast and doesn't separate from the object but always stays with it.

AC: And what stays with the object is mindfulness? What is the object—seeing, hearing, smelling and so on?

SUP: It could be any of these, as long as one is observing real mental and physical qualities as they arise.

A person learning to shoot at a target must aim. There's a target with a bull's eye. One has to aim and then shoot. So that mental defilements, *kilesas*, won't arise, we aim at the arising object. When *sati* is established on the object it doesn't give *kilesas* the chance to arise. When I am sitting in a chair that is big enough for only one person, no one else can sit here. It's the same when *sati* is established on the object.

If *kilesas* do arise, then what to do? Note them accurately and in a focused way.

This is like prevention and cure. One protects against the enemy, but if the enemy comes one notes it immediately. So, when the object arises, we need effort and aiming, or *vīriya* and *vitakka*. Aiming is like placing the object in our sight and effort is like pulling the trigger.

We note the main object of the rising and falling of the abdomen, don't we? We put our mind on the abdomen, like waiting to greet a visitor. As soon as the abdomen rises, the observing mind must be there. We must have ardent effort (*ātāpa*) as well as accurate aim. These, first of all, are the most important things. Because when they are present *sati* and *samādhi* are sure to follow. There's no need to do anything. Later, when one gets good at practice one doesn't need to aim any longer. One can just look at the target and shoot.

AC: In other words, mindfulness isn't the lead quality? Other qualities lead it?

SUP: When we practice *satipaṭṭhāna* meditation, only when *vīriya*, *vitakka* and *vicāra* are developed does *sati* arise. So *vīriya* or ardent energy, the application of effort, and *vitakka*, aiming or focusing must be there in order for *sati* to arise in practice. This is what happens when we practice *satipaṭṭhāna*.

This is not ordinary vīriya. This is called ātāpa—ardent energy which is not cool, not sluggish but always wakeful, alert, active. When I was young, I played marbles and when learning how to shoot I found that when there was too much effort, when I used too much energy, the marble would go off, go past the marble I wanted to hit. And when there was too little energy it wouldn't be effective either. So the effort had to be just right. This is what the quality of aiming does: it makes our quality of effort just right.

When there's ardent effort and application of aiming, then the marble connects with the marble you're trying to hit. There's vicāra, the quality of rubbing that occurs when it connects just right with the marble, and then joy arises, pīti. This is what happens in satipaṭṭhāna practice.

The *sati* that arises in practice behaves the way a stone does when dropped into water. When dropped in water, the stone sinks on the spot. The characteristic of *sati* is that it doesn't skim the surface of an object. It goes right into the object, like a stone dropped in water. Think of it like that.

The function of *sati* is to not lose sight of the object. It keeps the object in sight at all times. It also penetrates the object. *Sati* is non-superficiality. It does not allow the object to go out of sight. It brings the observing mind face to face with the arising object. When the mind is face to face with the object, then *kilesas* (greed, anger, and ignorance) have no opportunity to enter the mind. This is how *sati* manifests—as protecting the mind, guarding it from *kilesas*.

When *sati* is steadfast, the mind stays present, right there. It doesn't scatter. This is *samādhi*, when the mind is collected on the object. *Sati* brings *samādhi* with it. So when one applies ardent effort to observe the arising object again and again and again, along with the *jhānic* factor of aiming, then *sati* becomes steadfast and *samādhi* arises. When this happens, in fact, if you look at the amount of energy that is involved in one moment like that, it's nothing much, but if you have one moment of consciousness after another without a gap so that they are contiguous, one occurring right after the other, then amazing energy is generated. This is because this clean mind has the same nature, one following another, the things are of the same nature, that's how the energy can be built. The mind with *viriya*, *vitakka*, *sati* and *samādhi* is pure and clean; this occurs again and again and again without a gap, so that they are contiguous.

AC: In other words, when *right effort* is made in this way, knowledge naturally follows?

SUP: The nature of energy is that when the clear mind occurs just once, it's not strong. But when that clear clean mind—which in itself is not strong—arises continuously, then it automatically becomes very strong because each occurrence has the same nature and there is no gap between them.

Present at the same time is vitakka—the mind accurately placed on the object, and momentary concentration, the mind falling collectedly on the object. What happens is that when the mind observes the rising of the abdomen (when one inhales) and knows the qualities such as stiffness or tension—the mind sees true nature. And the same with the falling sensation of the abdomen (when one exhales)—one perceives movement and possibly other objects as well, and as such, one knows the true nature that is present at that moment. This is paññā (wisdom or insight knowledge). This is knowing correctly. And it's knowing completely and for oneself.

Here we are talking about sampajañña (clear comprehension). This knowing, the way one knows, is not confused, not mixed up; one thing and another are not mixed up. One sees clearly. There's stiffness and knowing of it. There's tension and knowing of it. So one sees the different phenomena as being distinct, not mixed up, one and the other.

This type of knowledge is far better than the type of knowledge gained from reading or from thinking about things. For this type of knowledge, the Buddha used the word sampajañña. We touched upon this earlier. The Buddha used the word sampajāno to mean 'one who knows in this way,' one who 'clearly comprehends.' The noun, knowledge, is sampajañña. So when we study satipatthana we know this; and when we practice satipatthana we understand it.

The Buddha talked about how what we come to know in practice is like what we know when we eat food; when we chew the food we know what it tastes like and we know very clearly what that taste is. And the characteristics that make up what we could call true nature, sabhāva. They are also called sarasa, because they are like the flavors that we find in food. And when we practice, as when we eat food, we know the flavors for ourselves. This is knowing for oneself.

Mind and matter, nāma and rūpa, each have their own individual characteristics. One is not the same as the other. When we start to practice, this is the first thing we come to know, that mind is one thing and matter is another. When we continue to observe true nature, when we continue to practice and our knowledge of the true nature becomes mature, when we are able to see it more deeply, then we come to see what things have in common.

So we come to see that hearing, seeing, smelling, touching, tasting, hot, cold and so on, all these things appear and disappear, they arise and then pass away, and in arising and passing away, all the things we experience are the same. This is called vipassana knowledge. So whatever it is, if we want to know true nature, if we want to know how things truly are, we must observe what is there when it happens. We have to observe what happens when it happens. This is known as *anupassanā*, repeated observation.

Anupassanā is a word found in the Satipatthāna Sutta. It is something you have to work to develop. You have to practice to develop the skill to observe. The way the word anupassī is explained in the Commentary is that first one practices: tries again and again to develop the ability to observe with mindfulness. Second, by continually developing the ability, one gains the skill to dwell seeing, dwell observing with mindfulness. That observation is called anupassanā.

To re-cap, anupassī is explained in two ways: anupassanā-sīlo, developing the ability to observe, and anupassamāno, meaning one can just do it, one can keep on dwelling with mindfulness.

The process of coming to know true nature or developing this ability to observe with mindfulness is like looking at something from a distance and then coming closer and closer to it. Like a line of ants, when seen from a distance, appears to be a rope or stick—we mistake reality. We see something but we see it wrongly, as a rope or stick. And as we move closer and closer, finally we see it rightly as a procession of ants. Coming even closer, we see that each ant is moving in a different way.

First of all, you have to practice to develop this skill and then when you practice enough, you gain the skill. Practice makes perfect. This is what's involved in meditation. If you don't practice, without working to develop the skill, you're never going to know. Knowledge without practice is merely reflection. Practice brings experiential knowledge.

For example, someone puts a bowl of sugar in front of you and says, "sugar is sweet." You see the sugar cubes and hear "sugar is sweet." That's one way of knowing that sugar is sweet. But when you take the sugar cube and place it on your tongue, you come to know the true nature of sugar as sweet. So how are these two different?

AC: One is direct experience of course, and one is imagination.

SUP: *Sūta-maya-ñāṇa* is what you read or hear, *cinta-maya-ñāṇa* is what you know by reflecting, and *bhāvanā-maya-ñāṇa* is knowledge born of meditation.

Take for example, while sitting there: when you clench your fist what do you find? There are three levels on which you can see: the form, the manner, and the true nature. The form: the shape of the hand. Manner or position is how it's clenched: in a fist. But these aren't true nature. At the start of practice, one's mind goes to the form or the manner, the way its clenched. These aren't true nature, but because the mind isn't going anywhere else it's still good. Later, when one continues to observe, one's mind becomes collected and one starts to know. When the mind is mindful of stiffness, it knows the stiffness. If the mind falls on tightness, one knows the tightness. One can also know the uncomfortable feeling. All these things are true nature.

At the start, we see things mixed up with either the manner or the form, but as we keep going we come to see just the true nature, only the true nature and nothing else. When your hand becomes hot, don't you want to open it again? That's because it's uncomfortable. Because there is the intention to open the hand, you release the hand. By releasing it ... opening it feels comfortable. And the fingers have to be released one by one. You have to move them slowly, very, very slowly, bit by bit, observing one moment after another. Slowly! Very slowly!

So how do you feel right now?

AC: I feel relieved, as I imagine everyone in this country will feel through the process of reconciliation, by mindfully opening their hearts and minds, and releasing the clenched fist of anger.

SUP: Looking for the *Dhamma* you find it in yourself, that's all. You come to see how change takes place, the old being replaced by the new.

AC: Sayadawgyi, as a monk who has trained for many decades in the Buddhist scriptures as well as in practice, you have explained, combining theory and practice, how *sati*—mindfulness—develops. Mindfulness is everywhere today, and in some circles among those who guide others in mindfulness, they are somewhat proud that they are not teaching it through the lens of Buddhism. In fact, some feel they are doing a service to humanity to have removed the *Buddha, Dhamma* and *Sangha*—all those so called "cultural and religious trappings"—from the essence, pure mindfulness. And in so doing, mindfulness is often taught as a tool for effectiveness, productivity, efficiency, mind-state management, and so on. I'm not saying this in a negative sense, but the argument goes: when mindfulness is so powerful on its own, why bring religion and culture into it?

SUP: Such work is not grounded. That means, it has no foundation. One has to start with the basics. The basics are to know the qualities of the *Buddha, Dhamma* and *Sangha*. After that, one should continue with morality and the duties of a human being, going hand in hand. These basics are missing.

AC: What about the argument that *sīla*—Right Speech and Right Action—refraining from stealing, slander and intoxicants and so on, are universal ethics and not owned by Buddhism? Why can't one practice mindfulness with basic ethical intelligence as the basis and still proceed wisely and confidently along the journey of life? Why does one have to be a Buddhist?

SUP: Inherently, the teaching of the Buddha is not a religion. Religion has faith as its base and is accomplished only through faith. If one wants to know the *Dhamma* experientially, the best way is to practice.

"If one does good, one will get a good result. If one does bad, there will be a bad result." This is like understanding that when one eats nutritious food, one can digest it and gain strength; the knowledge that eating what is poisonous or unsuitable for one brings harm. This basic intelligence is needed. There are pure and clean actions, speech, and mentality, and unwholesome actions, speech, and mentality. Pure and clean actions, speech and thought bring good results. Unwholesome actions, speech and thought bring bad results. If one has that basic knowledge, one can meditate.

AC: That's basic *Dhamma* intelligence?

SUP: That knowledge as a base is enough to be able to practice. The base is very important. When constructing a building, only if the foundation is firm will the building last long. Some kinds of earth require one to place pilings to make a good foundation. If the fundamental practice is missing, it's not possible to go on to the higher practice.

AC: Is *sati*—mindfulness—always a wholesome state? Always? It's never wrong? Or are there instances when you can practice wrong mindfulness? In other words, we are familiar with the terms Right Speech and Wrong Speech; Right View and Wrong View; and so on. Then we come to Right *Sati*, or Right Mindfulness. Is there such a thing as Wrong *sati?* Wrong mindfulness? Or is *sati* always Right?

SUP: More important than having *sati* is *yoniso manasikāra. Manasikāra* means aim or objective. Whatever one is doing, one should aim to make errors minimal and makes things correct. Like when driving, steering correctly to get to our desired destination. One must follow the road. It's like that. More than *sati*, one's aim or objective is important.

AC: Will you please give an example of a wrong objective—steering in the right and the wrong way?

SUP: For example, if you go to a dangerous place, you should prepare whatever is needed to remain free of trouble. That sort of thing. So that danger doesn't occur, on your side, you need good protection. You make preparations so that you won't err. This is steering in the right way. You have to drive within your lane, according to the rules of the road. You can't straddle the line, driving in between the lanes.

AC: Allow me to ask the question another way: What if I were a president, a cabinet minister, the speaker of the house, an MP here in Myanmar, or even a general and I trained my military in mindfulness. I trained them to exercise mindfully, speaking and eating mindfully, and I even had them undergo mindful target training.

In addition, as King Bimbisara did, I had them believing that the enemy was out to kill us and that they wanted to disturb our peace and tranquility, harm our families and take our land. Worse yet, convert us to their religion. And as 'loyal soldiers, mindful soldiers,' we believed that we were defending our homeland, our peace and values. But it turned out to be a lie, a hoax. It was a manipulation by the top leaders to accumulate more wealth and power. Call this basic dictatorship. It may even be basic democracy in the Western world. Regardless, is that the wrong application of sati? Wrong mindfulness? Because the goal is wrong?

SUP: One's objective is important. There are two kinds of *sati*: *sammāsati* and *micchāsati*. *Sammāsati* (right *sati*) is involved in work that is pure and clean. *Micchāsati* is involved in *akusala*, unwholesome deeds. That is called *micchāsati* or wrong sati.

Sammāsati follows a clean objective. Micchāsati arises when one has an impure objective. When harming others or causing them pain, the awareness involved is not right sati. It is wrong mindfulness. One has to develop awareness in a blameless way.

AC: A final question for today, if I may: It seems that much of what you share, your *Dhamma* advice, is about recognizing that 'we are all in this together,' that no one lives in isolation, no one is an island. In other words, we need each other to survive, to learn from, and grow—children with parents, students with teachers, citizens and leaders, so many essential relationships to wisely consider. In the South African culture, they have the concept of *ubuntu*, which means, "I cannot be who I am without you."

Translator: We have it here in Burma too.

AC: How interesting. Because, the issue you speak of, that 'of exchanging ourselves for others,' seems to be closely linked or essentially the same as *ubuntu*. And if we could truly learn how to '*ubuntify*' ourselves, so to speak, the qualities of *mettā*, *karunā* and *muditā*, along with most every other beautiful state of mind, would develop, naturally. And if we could merge foresight—our future-oriented compassionate open eyes—into *ubuntu*, we may well preserve life, survive as a species, and prevent a sixth extinction; maybe.

My question: Is there a Pali Buddhist word for this ubuntification of being? Again, the meaning of ubuntu, as I understand it, is that 'I am who

I am because of you.' Or, 'I become human through my relationships.' In other words, 'no one can become free in a vacuum.' Is there a Pali word for this idea, for the idea of how we become free and human through each other?

SUP: There is a worldly saying, not a Pali one. It goes like this, "If he's not part of it, it can't be done. But he alone can't do it. If you aren't part of it, it can't be done, but you alone can't do it. Without me, it can't be done. But I alone can't do it. Only when he, you, and I are part of it can everything be done." This is a Burmese saying.

AC: Beautiful. This points to our inherent mutuality, our inter-relatedness with all things. Do you use this concept in your *Dhamma* teachings? And does this concept have significance or have a corollary concept for a *Bodhisattva* (one who has made a vow to become a Buddha)? Because, as I understand it, a *Bodhisattva* cannot accomplish the development of *pāramī* without others. Is this essentially the same concept?

SUP: It is not possible to fulfill *pāramīs* by oneself, alone.

Pāramī can be fulfilled in a constructive way. Things to one's liking. And they can also be fulfilled in a destructive way, by having to endure something done against one. Either way, pāramī is fulfilled.

In the case of Devadatta (the Buddha's nemesis), in his previous lives he helped the Buddha to fulfill pāramī in a destructive way. But the Buddha-to-be endured all these destructive actions, knowing that it is only through encountering people who oppose one that the pāramī of khanti, or patient forbearance, can be accomplished. Because of his forbearance in the face of destructive actions, starting from his first life as a Bodhisattva up until his last existence when he became the Buddha, Devas and humans understood how great his patience was and revered him.

AC: It strikes me that this concept could have great importance within the development of SQ in leadership.

SUP: When there is a difference of viewpoints, SQ is important for people to be reunited. People who have good SQ are straightforward, they automatically go the right way.

AC: Would you illuminate the meaning of the word *pāramī* more fully? In addition, how can *pāramī* be embraced by leaders as the basis of *ubuntu* and compassion, and therefore, develop high-quality SQ-based leadership?

SUP: I rarely use the word *pāramī*, but in my *Dhamma* teachings, my encouragement amounts to developing *pāramī*.

The word pāramī means, with a basic good mental attitude, doing things for others and at the same time making oneself great. Only a high-level person, an excellent person, can do that type of work. Therefore, the literal meaning of pāramī is that which makes a person excellent. It is how they become excellent.

When a person does not think of his or her own benefit but works for the benefit of others, how will people feel when they see this? They will feel that person is really good, truly superior—this idea arises in their minds. That is how the word *parama* arises. *Parama* in Pali means superior, excellent. What makes you perceive that person as excellent, or *parama*, is *pāramī*, the cause for that person to be perceived as excellent.

This word *pāramī* does not refer to the work done by people who only think of themselves and lack *mettā* and *karuṇā*. Only what is done with great *mettā* and *karuṇā* for the welfare and benefit of others is true *pāramī*. That is why the word *pāramī* is explained as 'the work of someone who is an excellent person.' It is the cause for a person to be called 'good.' Or, it is what an excellent person does. That is called *pāramī*.

When we speak about the *Dhamma*, although we don't use the word *pāramī*, we are talking about how excellent people behave, what things they carry out: "If you follow this path, your status in life becomes excellent." That's what we say. Although the word *pāramī* is not used, it is the work of *pāramī*, every day.

Doing things solely for one's own benefit with no *mettā*, no *karuṇā* is not *pāramī*. For example, if you give somebody something, you shouldn't have any expectations, such as, "He'll be indebted to me, he'll love me, he'll be friendly to me." That is not *pāramī*. Your personal benefit is involved. But when you give something and think, "May this person be happy because they have this thing to use," you are giving so that the other person will be happy. Or thinking, "May what they lack be fulfilled." One is working in order to solve the problem of not having enough, to make the other person feel happy. This is *pāramī*.

When one puts one's own interest at the forefront and does things to help others, that is not *pāramī*. When one puts others' interest at the forefront, instead of self-interest, whatever one does for the benefit of others is *pāramī*. People think that this word *pāramī* means something very great.

And it is a great word. It means the work of excellent people. This work in itself is great. It isn't the work of ordinary people.

AC: What is the relationship of practicing *satipaṭṭhāna* and the development of *pāramī*?

SUP: When you practice *satipaṭṭhāna*, *sīla* is involved, as well as *samādhi* and *paññā*. One's physical, verbal, and mental behavior all become purified.

One doesn't make trouble for anybody else. Although one is doing this for oneself, because one doesn't cause trouble for anyone, it is *pāramī*.

Letting go of your own personal benefit and working for the benefit of others without expectation of return is pāramī. When one keeps sīla purely for the benefit of one's own liberation from the suffering of existence, when one practices to develop good samādhi, when one works to develop knowledge, when one practices satipaṭṭhāna meditation, this is pāramī for one's own benefit. One doesn't trouble anyone else, and one works for one's own benefit.

The word pāramī has two meanings: the cause for people to be excellent (paramānaṃ bhāvo pāramī in Pāli) and the work of excellent people (paramānaṃ kammaṃ pāramī). When one carries out work for others' benefit in an honest way, that causes others to see that person as excellent, superior, or parama in Pali. Therefore, it is said, paramānaṃ bhāvo pāramī. The work they are doing is the cause for the knowledge to arise in the viewer's mind that "this person is really excellent (parama)." Therefore, the work that they are doing is called pāramī. A person who is excellent like that will only do things that are blameless and pure. That blameless, pure work is the work of excellent people. That is why the word pāramī is also defined as paramānaṃ kammaṃ—the work of excellent people.

AC: Thank you, sir. And may the good leaders of your country and those in other countries as well, embrace the consciousness of *ubuntu* and the action of striving for excellence through *pāramī*.

It's Important To Be a True Human Being

ALAN CLEMENTS: This will be the conclusion of our series of conversations titled, "Wisdom for the World and Dhamma Advice to My Nation" to also be published in the forthcoming book *Burma's Voices of Freedom*.

Tonight I would like to ask you for your Dhamma advice to the people outside of Myanmar, those foreigners who will visit your country in the years to come, as well as all others worldwide with their eyes on Myanmar, watching the developments, with the birth of democracy, respect for human rights, and a vision of national reconciliation.

My question: What advice would you care to offer the good people who will either visit your country or those who are attentive, looking for ways to understand and possibly help the people of Myanmar? I might add, there are close to a million foreigners in Burma right now. The hotels are filled, often months in advance. Temples are packed with visitors. And millions more are on their way. I would not be surprised if your meditation center and Mahasi Yeitkha as well, become filled with eager foreigners wanting to practice *satipaṭṭhāna* at the epicenter of where the worldwide mass lay-mindfulness movement began some 70 years ago. And each one of these visitors will bring a little piece of their own democracy here, their own unique experience of freedom.

It's an exciting time for Daw Aung San Kyi and the people of your country. It has been a 27-year long nonviolent 'revolution of the spirit,' and now the next phase of that revolution has begun; call it "the reconciliation revolution" through *mettā* and *karuṇā* or, in your language, "the SQ revolution."

What might you wish to share with these good people?

VENERABLE SAYADAW U PANDITA: It's natural for people to help each other, and this should be done without self-interest. One shouldn't want to get something out of it, and one should help with *mettā* and *karuṇā*. This is correct, to help in this way, to discard selfish interest and to help with loving kindness and compassion. When you give to another, whether it's giving to an individual or giving to a group, whether you give a material thing or whether you give advice or whatever it is that's needed, it should be done with the attitude "may the person receiving this be happy to have it." One should not have an expectation of return for oneself. If one wants to profit from it for oneself, that's not truly helping. One must not boast to the world, "My country, my people, can help." Only when help is pure and true does it truly help. It should be help offered without *lobha*, without greed, without selfish interest.

Further, when you help people who are limited or lacking in some way, giving them what they need, fulfilling what is missing or lacking for them, then you should do so with the wish, "May they be well, may they be happy," and this attitude should permeate your mind so that the mind is fresh and moist with this feeling. Just as one should have this wish for the welfare of those one is helping—this attitude of pure mettā—so too, when one sees that people are lacking what they need, one should cultivate the attitude, "May they not suffer," and then go about trying to remove their suffering, relieving them from their struggle. The attitude of compassion, karuṇā, is very important.

When we give, when we help others while free of self-interest and with a basis of loving kindness and compassion, then we'll be happy with the results. One won't have envy for the recipients in seeing their good situation. One will be joyous to see their good situation. And because one has helped with an attitude of wanting their welfare, selflessly, then one doesn't feel jealous, one doesn't feel that they wish they hadn't given. The quality of happiness for another's good situation is *muditā*. This is based on *mettā* and *karunā*. Without a basis of true loving kindness and compassion, this *muditā* will not arise.

Further, both the giver and the receiver, although separated by different countries, should have the attitude they are related; one should have the attitude that one is helping one's relatives. Asia is one of the continents of the world and Asians are related to each other as relatives on the Asian continent. And the people of the world are all the same in being human. So we're related as world relatives.

People from other continents are related to each other although their continent is different; they're not related as continental relatives but as world relatives. And according to the Buddha, the people of the world have lived countless lifetimes before this one. We've all been related in one way or another, as father and son or brother and sister and so on. In countless ways we've been related to everyone. This is what is said in the texts and one should try to have this attitude.

In addition to this way of being—related on two or three levels—the Buddha taught so that people can become related by the way of *Dhamma*, related by *Dhamma* blood. The *Dhamma* is that which bears the *Dhamma* bearer, the one who knows the correct method and puts it into practice. It lifts one up so that one doesn't go down into the four lower realms of *Apāya* and so that one doesn't wander a long time in *Saṃsāra*.

This *Dhamma* is what the Buddha searched for and found. People who have faith in the *Dhamma*—relatives—practice it, and through this practice are able to live happily in this very life as well as become free of existential suffering. People who reach this level of developing the *Dhamma* blood within themselves become related by *Dhamma* blood. Between them there is mutual understanding, trust and friendliness.

So, think about your own life, as you ask this question. Before the practice, how was it? And after practice, learning about the *Dhamma*, how was it?

The Buddha taught the *Dhamma* so that people who were related in worldly ways automatically would become related by *Dhamma*. And those who practice and develop the *Dhamma* blood don't make distinctions about nationality. They don't have this attitude that "I am this," or "I am this or that." We're all the same.

For us monks, whatever foreigner comes here to practice, if he or she practices the *Dhamma* with respect and care, they become close, a *Dhamma* relative. So think about that—when you practiced, did this type of feeling arise in you? Did you feel connected?

AC: Deeply, sir, like family.

SUP: People of the world are related in three worldly ways, but this is not enough to solve the complex problems that exist in society now. They will continue to exist. Only if people become related through *Dhamma* blood will social problems gradually become weaker and weaker until finally people can gain peace.

AC: The people of your country have suffered, greatly. Equally, they have inspired many of us in the world to become more courageous in transforming our own sufferings and, moreover, putting ourselves in the mind and body of others, to feel and to act compassionately. What would you like to leave us as a final statement, to your people, and to everyone in the world?

SUP: If one is born a human, it's important to be a true human being, and it's important to have a humane mentality. And one should also search for a way to come to know what is true, to know the true *Dhamma*, and to walk the path of *Dhamma*. One should walk this straight path because if one walks it one will reach a safe destination. This is what's really important, these three things.

In this regard, in the time of the Buddha there was a *deva* (a celestial being) who came to see the Buddha, and he said that the beings of the world are tangled up in a tangle, both inside and outside; who is it that can untangle this tangle?

The Buddha's reply was very simple. With *sīla* or morality as a basis, if one works to develop *samādhi* and *paññā*, or concentration and wisdom, to completion then social problems will be resolved. That's the essence.

Many people lack basic morality and no longer fulfill their duties as humans in society. Without morality and not performing their duties, their minds are no longer upright. Such people are crooked, and because of that social problems have arisen which are nearly impossible to solve. But if people learn to keep basic *sīla* and fulfill their human duties, when they start to get the benefits from this and they recognize these benefits, then they will follow this path, realizing it is good. They will follow this path honestly. They will no longer want to get the better of others. They won't want to make a profit at the expense of others.

When people keep morality, fulfill their human duties and understand the benefits, they become honest and upright. Then our existence in society becomes one of interdependence, like the Burmese saying, "The island depends on the grass and the grass depends on the island." When there is grass growing on the shore, the island can withstand the water striking it. When a wave comes in, what happens? It doesn't erode the shore. The grass protects the shore. And the shore holds the grasses so they can grow. If there were this kind of mutual preservation in society, the world would become fresh and peaceful again. This is called in Pāli *aññoññanissita,* or 'each relying on the other'—interdependence. Without morality, without fulfilling social duties and without honesty, then interdependence or mutual preservation cannot occur. Only with these as a basis can these occur.

When people don't have basic morality and don't fulfill their duties or responsibilities in society, what happens between people? There is immorality and people's character is not upright. But if both self and others keep morality and fulfill their responsibilities, then their character is sure to become upright. If that thrives within society then there will be mindful interdependence. If that happens, the world will become a happy place.

AC: *Sādhu, sādhu, sādhu.* Thank you, from my heart.

SUP: Thank the Buddha, they are the Buddha's teachings.

AC: *Sādhu* to the Buddha. *Sādhu* to the *Dhamma. Sādhu* to the Sangha. *Sādhu* to you, Sir. *Sādhu* to Daw Aung San Suu Kyi and the National League for Democracy, and all the courageous people of your country too. *Sādhu* to the people who sacrificed their lives for this birth of freedom. *Sādhu* to everyone on having the moral courage to admit their mistakes, reconciling with each other, and bringing peace and harmony to your beloved Myanmar. And beyond, to the people around the world. May we all take greater risks to put ourselves into the shoes of each other, and the unborn, and to act compassionately, now and forever.

With good will for the entire cosmos,
cultivate a limitless heart:
Above, below, & all around,
unobstructed, without hostility or hate.

SUTTA NIPĀTA 1.150

CHAPTER 21

CONVERSATION *with* SITTIGU SAYADAW

2013

Sittigu Sayadaw, the meditation master and Buddhist scholar known as Burma's Dalai Lama, has written more than 100 books and received five honorary doctorates. He is a champion of 'socially engaged Buddhism' whose charitable works are world-renowned. In this chapter, he talks about the contrast between *Dharma* as the 'middle way' and religious extremism as a corruption. A strong advocate of interfaith dialogue, he explores the common ground between all faiths, and points to the universal virtues of compassion and tolerance that create the foundation for freedom, exploring the Buddhist practices of *silā*, *samādhi* and *paññā* as a means of preventing unwholesome action.

"Buddhists, true Buddhists, are never extremist."

ALAN CLEMENTS: Greetings, sir. We've never met before. My name is Alan Clements. Many years ago, I ordained as a Buddhist monk at the Mahasi Sasana Yeiktha here in Yangon. Mahasi Sayadaw Payagyi was my preceptor. I was ordained for four *vassa*. In 1984, I was told to leave Burma by Ne Win's authorities, with no reason given. This had happened a few times before, so I decided to disrobe and leave the monastic *Saṅgha*. In 1995, I came back to Burma, soon after Daw Aung San Suu Kyi was released from house arrest. At that time, my close friend and mentor, former General U Tin Oo, introduced me to Daw Aung San Suu Kyi, and this led to a series of conversations with her over the next six months. These conversations were taped and smuggled out of the country and published as *The Voice of Hope*—a title that her husband, Michael Aris, chose. The book was translated into many languages and made available worldwide. Because of this book, and perhaps a few others before that as well, I was banned from entering Burma for the next 17 years. Only recently did President Thein Sein un-blacklist me.

SITTIGU SAYADAW: Where are you from, originally? Which country do you live?

AC: I'm from America, sir, from Boston, Massachusetts. I grew up in a military family until my father retired and we settled near to Washington, DC. I attended the University of Virginia and quit near the end of my second year to pursue my desire to be an artist. This eventually led me to meditation. My partner and I then went to India to pursue the *Dhamma*, and this led to Burma where we met Mahasi Sayadaw.

SS: What is your purpose to come here?

AC: I am back in Burma again to meet with as many people as possible for the purpose of bringing the innermost truths of your country's ongoing nonviolent revolution of the spirit to the world. I intend to publish an updated edition of my book, titled, *Burma's Voices of Freedom: Conversations with Alan Clements.* Because I have a great love of Myanmar, a great love of *Dhamma,* and knowing that you are a highly respected Sayadaw, having met the Dalai Lama, the Pope, and many other dignitaries, and revered by thousands of people here in your own country, I would like to respectfully invite you, sir, to be included in the book as one of your country's voices of freedom.

SS: You're from the media? A journalist?

AC: Not formally from the media. But I have every intention of making this book known to the world through the media. Nor am I a journalist, per se. I'm an independent activist studying your country's transition from dictatorship to democracy, primarily from the perspective of the *Sāsana* (doctrine), and what we can learn from nonviolent struggle. I am most concerned about the role of the *Dhamma* and its intersection with political and spiritual freedom, with democracy, human rights, rule of law, justice, responsibility, accountability, forgiveness and reconciliation.

If acceptable, sir, please allow me to ask you: How should the world understand the best way to relate to the allegations that Buddhism—more specifically some elements of the monastic Saṅgha (community)—has become an extremist movement here in Myanmar?

SS: Buddhism has never been extremist. Buddhism is that of going the middle way, not extremist. But incidents may occur in our country sometimes. Most religious leaders, they understand neutralism, they follow neutralism, they are teaching neutralism. They want to establish a mutual understanding between every religion and Buddhism. But sometimes, some incidents—some unexpected, uncontrolled evil, some violence—have taken place in Myanmar. And some very stupid politician, some stupid opportunists, exploit these incidents. Therefore, we must control and maintain the stability of our country. We must try to establish mutual understanding and social tradition between every nation. This is my policy.

Let me be clear: Buddhists, true Buddhists, are never extremist. According to religion, religious leaders and religious teachings, we are of the middle way. My policy, the policy of our Buddhist religion, is great tolerance. This is Buddhist policy; this is called *pāramī,* a way to nobility. When the *Bodhisattva* (the Buddha to be) searched for 'the way,' how to become Buddha, he discovered ten perfections, ten *pāramī,* ten codes of nobility.

If someone wants to become the perfect human, they must follow the ten codes of perfection. I delivered the ten codes in an address to the United Nations. So, great tolerance, regardless of a good situation or bad situation, whether attached to a good situation, a pleasant situation, or whether detached from an unpleasant situation, we shall go through and follow the middle way.

We must control our hatred and our anger. This is our policy. We can say this is the policy of Buddhism; tolerance, and then forgiveness, and then forget the other's mistake: 'forget-ness,' and then 'self'-forget-ness. We must try to benefit others. We shall not be self-'ish-ness.' Always appreciate others, this is my policy for all nations. Whether discrimination occurs because of color and creed, I always say it this way: tolerance, forgiveness, and then forget the other's mistakes, the other's wrongdoing. And then self-forget. Whatever I do, I try to benefit all others without discrimination because of color and creed. This is how I wish to establish peace, harmony and good existence for all people in this land of Myanmar. I always try to establish universal citizenship; whether Islam, Christian, Hindu, Buddhist, these are just labels. I believe Jesus also taught love and compassion. I also believe Mohammed taught love and compassion and tolerance. Even people who are worshipping the spirit, for example, in northern, southern, western Burma, in Shan State and Kachin State, they worship the spirit—deity. These deities also, if they teach, will teach tolerance, compassion and loving kindness. These qualities are universal. They belong to no one religion. They are common to all. And this is our common ground. And we are called upon to live it together peacefully, happily, with great tolerance. I always teach like this. This is my main objective.

I don't want to fight any other religion. Islamic people, they can go to the mosque and worship their god Allah. But they must follow tolerance, loving kindness and compassion. Christian people, they can to the church Saturday and Sunday, and worship their God and Jesus. But they should follow the teachings of Jesus—that of love, compassion, and wisdom. Yes, including wisdom. Pray to have it. Our Buddhist people also, going to the Shwedagon Pagoda, or any other pagoda, or a meditation center, they must try very hard to control their mind. Not to do any violence. Not to do any evil. Not to speak any evil. This is the Buddhist discipline. It's universal. Everyone can follow this practice. If you are Christian, go to the church, but practice this *Dhamma*. If you are Islamic, go to the mosque, but practice and follow this *Dhamma*. *Dhamma* is universal.

In this *Dhamma*, briefly, only three things are included: *sila*, *samādhi* and *paññā*. *Sila* means discipline; to control bodily action. Not to do any evil. Not to speak any evil. To control verbal action. This is *sila*, in brief, the basic principal for all—anyone can practice it. For example, this is water, but, in Burma, you are American, and you can drink it to feel cool and peaceful—the water. Made in Burma, made in a Buddhist country, this water. In the mosque, I can offer it in the mosque; they can drink it and they will feel the cool, right? *Dhamma* is like water. Everyone can use it for peace and to purify. So, *Dhamma* is very powerful.

The way to purification of life, the way to cool, to calm, and to create peace in life, is in this *Dhamma—silā*; the basic discipline not to do any evil, speak any evil. And the second stage: to control mental action, mental activity. Everyone must control mental activity; not to think any evil—greed and hatred. Delusions are the motivation to think evil, to speak evil, to do evil. Therefore, in a meditation course, we can learn to control our mental activity, to let it subside. Christian, Islam, Hindu, Muslim; anyone. They are all human beings. They can practice and learn to control mental activity. Therefore, meditation is very powerful, to control mental action. It's non-religious, non-sectarian. It's universal. Islamic people going to the mosque must control their mind under the guidance of meditation.

So, *Dhamma* is very powerful. *Silā;* discipline to control body and speech. *Samādhi;* to control mental activities. *Paññā;* understanding ourselves—"What am I?" If you are Christian, you must learn for yourself, "What am I? Where am I? What I have to do?" Therefore, everyone should be the peacemaker. Everyone shall be the benefactor of humankind. Everyone who is born in this land must learn not to be an enemy of anyone. Everyone must be friends of all people. This is how I live. I am always trying to be friends with all.

AC: If someone has committed misdeeds, what is the best thing for them to do to correct their misdeed, to whom they've done it to and to redeem themselves, inside of themselves?

SS: The three stages are essential. *Silā*: discipline to control body and speech. *Samādhi:* discipline to control the mind. *Paññā:* mindful reasoning, understanding; this is right or wrong, this is good or bad, this is the benefit or detriment for all beings. Everyone should have such basic wisdom, according to Buddhist word *paññā*, translated sometimes as 'knowledge,' sometimes as 'understanding,' sometimes as 'wisdom.' Whatever the interpretation, I have to say that wisdom means 'eye of the mind.' Everyone must have the eye of wisdom.

Buddha said, "The whole world is blind." Most people don't have wisdom, which is being able to reason what is right or wrong, beneficial or unbeneficial, peaceful or violent. They cannot decide, therefore we must upgrade the world to be educated through wisdom. On the other hand, every country needs to re-balance education and ethics into a *Dhamma* education. Basic education and religious education must be balanced. Nowadays, moral, spiritual, intellectual, religious engagements are mostly poor in every country. So, more than education, *Dhamma* education must be practiced in every country. In this way, every leader of a nation should consider reforming their educational infrastructure, for the long future. This is very important.

Sometimes, in the United States, and other countries too, you see very young boys shoot guns. Many friends, many students, dying on the spot; 20, 40, 50. The gunman is so happy, thinking that "My name is known to the world." They want to become known to the world, they want to become famous in the world, therefore shoot and kill as many people as possible. They do not understand the difference between famous and notorious: this is the lack of basic education. These mass killings are happening more and more frequently, in the USA, the EU, Africa, the Middle East. I'm sure you have heard of these atrocities. And so many more. They happen everywhere and have happened all throughout history as well. Therefore, the Buddha said, 'the whole world is blind.'

So, in conclusion, we must upgrade education and infrastructure. Education and moral education must be in balance. Most young people, especially in western countries, do not understand the difference between notorious and famous. So, *paññā*, the eye of wisdom, is very important. In Buddhism: *silā, samādhi, paññā. Silā*: morality, discipline to control body and speech; *samādhi*: to control the mind and mental action, not to be easily angered, not to be immediately angered, control of anger, hatred, delusion, illusion, and then, under the power of insight meditation, to remove, totally, such kinds of evil. This is my policy. Every religious person should learn about *paññā*.

AC: For someone who has violated others, how do they heal themselves and possibly help heal the people they harmed? How does a leader redeem herself or himself?

SS: It goes back to wisdom or the lack of wisdom. This is the basic issue. This is very important point. Jesus always taught forgiveness. Most people who violate others do not want to confess their transgressions. Yet, truly honest people, never forget. That is why they are respected. They have conscience. They are honest. They are moral. They are open. They confess. And to confess they must have an education in right and wrong. They must have wisdom. If they have done wrong, they must confess openly and honestly. It is the way to peace. If they can confess, generally speaking, other people are ready to forgive. As long as they cannot confess, the other side finds it difficult to forgive. Forgiveness and confessions must be given together. It's beneficial to do this for the peace of the world. So, we must foster common ground; tolerance, compassion, forgiveness, 'forget-ness,' and self-forget-ness is most important. "I am; I am," please forget.

AC: Sadhu, Sadhu, Sadhu. Thank you, sir.

CHAPTER 22

CONVERSATION *with* CARDINAL CHARLES BO

March 2013

- "It was a mistake on the part of Prime Minister U Nu to officially declare Buddhism the state religion."
- "Many of the children would think that life here in Myanmar is normal everywhere else in the world."
- "We hope that everyone is aware that each person is responsible for nation building—every Buddhist, every Catholic, everybody."
- "When we refuse to forgive, we become a prisoner in a prison we've built ourselves."

Charles Bo, Archbishop of Yangon and Burma's first cardinal, heads a Roman Catholic order of 450,000 in the country's capital. A prominent advocate of democratic reform, peace, justice and sustainable ecology, Cardinal Bo is known around the world as a voice of freedom. In this candid interview, he addresses the topical subject of Burma's historical ethnic diversity and its relationship to ethnic violence since the time of Burma's independence in 1948, specifically addressing the intercommunal violence between Buddhists and Muslims in Rakhine State, and his stance towards reconciliation as a senior clergyman. He talks of corruption and the erosion of moral values after independence, and of his role in being an outspoken advocate of democratic reform, offering guidance on interfaith dialogue and the nature of spirituality in an ethnically diverse and violent climate.

"It was a mistake on the part of Prime Minister U Nu to officially declare Buddhism the state religion."

ALAN CLEMENTS: Greetings, sir. An honor to meet you. Thank you for taking the time to speak with me about the state of affairs in your country and sharing your views on transforming the mindset of society from dictatorship to democracy. You are the Archbishop here at Saint Mary's Cathedral in Yangon. How long have you been in the Catholic order?

ARCHBISHOP CHARLES BO: This June I'll be completing ten years. Previously I was the bishop of Pathein, in the Delta, for seven years. Before that, I was a bishop in Lashio in the Shan State for an additional ten years. So, ten years in Lashio, seven years in Pathein and another ten years as archbishop here.

AC: You've immersed yourself in Burma's diverse ethnicities.

ACB: Yes. In Lashio, most of the ethnic groups are there: Kachin, Shan, Lisu, Lahu, Chinese and Wa. A most diverse people there.

AC: How many languages are there in Burma?

ACB: Main languages, over 100. But, of course, the language of Burmese, or Myanmar, is the official one, which is spoken by 70 to 80 percent of people, except in some remote areas where there are some people who can't understand Burmese.

AC: The term 'multi-faith' is commonly used today as an entry point into understanding unity and respectful co-existence within diversity. May I ask, what might you say about the meaning of 'multi-faith' within Burma today?

ACB: In Burma, the most predominant faith is Buddhism. It's been here practically all throughout our history, and, of course, the last regime, for 50 years, has been insistent on 'Burmese Buddhists.'

AC: Insistent?

ACB: Yes. Burma is also Christian, Muslim and Hindu. The reality is, according to our history—from the time we got independence from the British in 1948—it was a mistake on the part of Prime Minister U Nu to officially declare Buddhism the state religion. That was the beginning of the different ethnic groups starting civil war. They became rebels. If we look at history, Myanmar has been diverse, a rainbow nation, but, from the time of our independence up to now, I think there's never been a single year where we've had no internal conflict.

AC: A 65-year history of overlapping civil wars? Why?

ACB: Yes, constant conflict up to today. See, Burmese people are nice, but at the same time, regarding politics, especially among certain ethnic groups and the central government, conflict has always been a problem.

AC: Former Prime Minster U Nu's declaration of Burma as a Buddhist nation was decidedly wrong? Why?

ACB: It was very wrong! In fact, recently I asked a minister from religious affairs whether the government would again declare Buddhism the state religion, and he said that they learned their lesson. They'll never do it again.

AC: Civil war based on religious hierarchy? Buddhism imposed on others?

ACB: Take for example the conflict in Rakhine State. The Rakhines are nearly 100 percent Buddhist. Now the problem is the Rakhines and the

Rohingyas. The Rohingyas are practically 100 percent Muslim and the Rakhines nearly 100 percent Buddhist.

AC: As the leader of a major religion here in Burma, if you would please explain in simple terms what's going on in Rakhine State? And why is there conflict between the Buddhists and Muslims?

ACB: With regard to Rakhine State, originally it was not a religious conflict. It was about citizenship and the migrant issue. The Rohingya are supposed to have entered Burma 40 or 50 years ago, and up to now, many of them have not received a citizenship card. But at the same time, just recently, there are difficulties with some of them entering from Bangladesh. So, they've been under strict surveillance from local authorities.

I myself visited there about two years ago, and even going to a market or to the nearest town they needed permission from the local authorities to move from their own villages. It's true that restrictions are there, and at the same time, many of them have been entering Burma from Bangladesh. And now, they're asking for their own separate region—a Muslim region.

I've said that although it started with these migrant issues, since practically 100 percent of the Rohingya's are Muslim and the other 100 percent of the Rakhines are Buddhist, it came to be seen as something to do with religious issues. Thus, the conflict.

Personally, I think that some Buddhist monks are trying to excite the people. Of course, they're concerned because the number of people in some of the Rohingya villages are increasing every year, as are the number of children, quite conspicuously. They're afraid Muslims will overpower Buddhists and Buddhism. So, it's difficult for the government to decide whether to give citizenship to all these people. There's almost a million of them in Rakhine. It's a difficult situation both for the government and the Rohingyas.

AC: As a Catholic, what do you think?

ACB: I met some Catholic bishops from Bangladesh while these things were happening. As it turns out, the Rohingyas are not wanted in Bangladesh. This is a major dilemma.

Another issue is the KNA, the Kachins and the government. Of course, there are many reasons for this conflict between the government and the Kachins. The Kachins also feel that during the past 10 to 15 years of ceasefire, their natural resources have not been respected and were taken over by government authorities. There's also the issue of this very close relationship between the government and China. They feel they've been exploited and that most of their resources have gone to China. Then again, among the Kachins, seldom do you find a Buddhist. Most are

Baptist or Catholic. So, it could also be said that the conflict is between the Christians and the government. But in truth, it's not that. It's more to do with ethnic issues.

Also, the Kachins are worried about their place, especially as the natural resources are rich there, with jade, teak, gold and everything. So, the Kachins want these resources for themselves. At the same time, so does the government. Much of this conflict is over natural resources.

"Many of the children would think that life here
in Myanmar is normal everywhere else in the world."

ALAN CLEMENTS: Sir, as an Archbishop of a large cathedral here in Yangon, you have a unique role among the people. Members of your congregation confess to you.

ARCHBISHOP CHARLES BO: Yes, in church we have the sacramental confession.

AC: As such, you've had a unique window into the soul of Myanmar citizen, so to speak, and for decades, and in many areas of the country. You've come to know intimate things about their inner life—their concerns, their fears, their aberrations, their immoralities, their transgressions. And, I hope it is not too personal to ask, what are the main issues that ordinary Burmese citizens have struggled with under decades of dictatorship?

ACB: During these five decades under military rule many people lost their facilities and privileges. Four generations have been unable to develop their capacities. Opportunities have been denied. Some have become prisoners of silence, controlled by military intelligence. Five decades where many young people, and older people too, feel numb. They don't know of a world outside of their own enclosed space. Many children think that life in Myanmar is normal everywhere else in the world. They don't see the world outside and they don't see opportunities.

Then again, I think Buddhism, somewhat, gives direction to the minds of the people. Our Burmese people, when I have a conversation with them, you hear that our present life is because of what we've done in a previous life. So, the present situation, the poverty here and the situation with the government, the political situation, is because of what we have done in a previous life. And if we are to have a better life next time we'd better bear up, have patience with the government, with the situation, to have a happier life with promoted status—women to become men, men to become all these angels or what have you.

These past years, because of the situation since 1965 when all the schools were internationalized, there are things like cheating. Before that there were missionary schools and other schools where children were given a moral education for character formation. After internationalization, these past 40 years, the moral classes, the character formation, has gone. It's been replaced by cheating and stealing and doing whatever you want, provided you are not caught. These transgressions are common at every level.

AC: At every level?

ACB: At every level. Government officials accept bribery and all its trappings. It's happening everywhere, even in our Catholic church. For example, all these years we've been restricted; we can't build a church or a convent or clergy house. Or when we want to have a celebration, it's banned, and we have to appeal. To get permission bribery comes in.

AC: Even for you?

ACB: Yes, we have to give extra money as bribery even for a celebration. When we have a big celebration with a procession going into town, then we also have to bribe the local authorities. Bribery is the culture at every level.

AC: Corruption from top to bottom, bottom to top? It's a way of life?

ACB: It's a way of life. Money says everything. Money solves everything. That happens in the religions—of course, I'm not sure about the Buddhists, because the generals try to protect whatever projects they have, the pagodas or the monasteries. High ranking people donate. But for us, these past years, we've felt a lot of discrimination.

AC: Towards the church?

ACB: Towards the church, and with the Buddhists. Although, personally, I would say that there is no direct persecution.

AC: Have you had threats of closure, where authorities say, 'Listen, Archbishop, we like you but if you speak in your mass using the words 'Daw Aung San Suu Kyi' or 'democracy' we're going to close you down,' anything like that?

ACB: These past two years I've spoken very freely, it's ok. Before that, even 10 years ago, I would sometimes jokingly or indirectly say many things, even about the current situation of the country or what the government authorities were doing. I would mention it.

AC: You're outspoken?

ACB: Quite outspoken. Sometimes I make my books public, like on parent's day, on subjects on what parents should do. So, in the family you have the father, mother and children. In religion you have the priest, pastors and followers. Then in government, you have ministers and you have civilians. I'm outspoken about what is the right attitude—we should have dialogue, this understanding, this type of listening. I'd make those three points, but in between, I would say there's actually just one man, one show and one policy. But so far there's no threat, nor any questions from any of the authorities.

I first became a bishop in 1985, in Lashio, and from then to now, so far, the authorities have never asked me anything about what I'm up to or about my concern with any of the political issues. They've never asked me anything about financial matters, either—nothing.

Of course, on my part, I'm careful to follow the guidance from the social teachings of the church, like in 1988, in the nationwide demonstration, and in 2007, with the Saffron Revolution. I always explain to my people, "For ordinary Catholics, ordinary Christians, you have the right, if you have the desire, to join a demonstration and to choose any political party."

AC: You would say that "It's your right to demonstrate"?

ACB: Yes. It's your right to demonstrate, you can choose political parties.

AC: You're an activist priest.

ACB: As a bishop, or a priest, or sister or a nun, according to our religion, you may give guidance to the people. Not yourself going into the streets to demonstrate. It's against that.

AC: Helping people gain the confidence to make a choice for themselves?

ACB: Personally, we cannot choose any party, we can just give general guidance on what has happened in the past and our standing now. Also, when you vote, you can see which party gives you real freedom and progress for the country. You can choose. On our part, we cannot mention 'choose this' or 'choose that.'

> *"We hope that everyone is aware that each person*
> *is responsible for nation building—every Buddhist,*
> *every Catholic, everybody."*

ALAN CLEMENTS: How does the church and the Christian tradition, as you know it from your life, intersect with global human rights?

ARCHBISHOP CHARLES BO: Regarding human justice and equality—our approach is holistic. We don't separate what is spiritual and what
is material. We don't separate the present moment and our next life in
heaven. We don't separate our human person, what is body and what is
soul—it's integrated. We don't distinguish between religion and culture.
We don't separate, for example, our religion, our spirituality, from justice
and peace. It's all integrated.

The church is very strong in advocating for justice and peace, and
for ecology and climate change. We are concerned. We're also concerned
with poverty, with human development, livelihood, education, health—
for us, it's just one thing. Although as a Christian or Catholic we believe
in Jesus Christ, our personal encounter with Jesus, at the same time, we
embrace the whole of humanity, with it's good, as well as its difficulties.

AC: Yesterday, Pope Francis passionately pledged to support the poorest
of the poor, the weakest of the weak, the least recognized on earth. He
also pledged, in this time of destruction and death, to give hope. How do
you give hope to your congregation, to your people? What should they be
hopeful for? And what is the living essence of this hope?

ACB: Hope for a better communion with all religions and all races here
in Myanmar. For that, all things must start with the leaders. We also hope
that everyone is aware that each person is responsible for nation building—every Buddhist, every Catholic, everybody.

What's happening is that since all chances and privileges have
been denied these past years, now that a new dawn has come, everybody
is fighting for their own rights. All the races are shouting for their own
rights, and any religion, and all the townships, are saying, 'We want this,
we want that.' That's what Aung San Suu Kyi said when we had the memorial service for her mother last December (there were about 20 of us
religious leaders there): "Now, in this era, it's a little free and everyone's
shouting 'my right, my right,' when instead each one should think about
how they can contribute to nation building. Instead of shouting for rights,
ask, 'What is my duty for the building of the nation?'"

Of course, there are many issues, but people feel free now, psychologically. There's no more suspicion or fear of anybody following you. Now,
people speak freely, and at the same time we have many concerns as well.
Although there are many positive sides, at the same time, there's anxiety.
So, with President Thein Sein for example, we're saying, "Ok, he's trying
his best" but asking, "What will be the role of Aung San Suu Kyi?" And
she's an icon but at the same time some people are asking questions, as in
the case of the copper mine, where some villagers were blocking her, not

allowing her to enter the village. They were questioning the strength of the NLD, and Aung San Suu Kyi herself.

AC: What are your thoughts on Daw Aung San Suu Kyi?

ACB: I've met her several times. After 1995, then in 2000, when it was a very dangerous time to meet her, before her release even. I met her three or four times, and I also knew her husband personally, before he passed away in England. She's full of integrity, and her character lends a special personal quality to her style of leadership, as does the influence of her father, the name and prestige of Bogyoke Aung San, who fought for independence. Although she was under house arrest for over 15 years, she really managed to keep herself disciplined with daily meditation and work. I asked her what she was doing during those years and she said she prayed, meditated, exercised, and at the same time, she had a transistor radio and was studying world news.

My concern is with the NLD and her followers. Some of them might be okay, but she needs more professional people around her that lead the country with her. For example, last time I met her I said, "Daw Suu, there are people in the country, and also from abroad, who have tried to contact you yet you have no professional people near you to arrange such meetings or appointments." She said, "I don't want to have any professionals. I like to have only a few good people near me whom I can trust. For the time being this is enough."

AC: I like that. She's clear.

ACB: But she cannot stand alone. She needs her group.

AC: A stronger, more professional center?

ACB: A strong center. On her part, she has said she is interested in gaining or getting into power, saying, "Only then will I be able to change the country." As it is, she has no authority to rule the country.

Of course, there are other people who comment that she shouldn't have created a party, things like that, that she should be away from any party and have a general sort of guidance for the whole of Myanmar to move towards democracy.

AC: Speaking of guidance; when it comes to the issue of national reconciliation, we still have a military dominated country, with decades of violently enforced totalitarian authority. Obedience is embedded into culture. These men in uniform, and some women too, have committed grave violations. You know them much better than I; a number of governments, NGOs and human rights organizations have documented them in detail.

My question: What guidance might you offer on how to change the psychology of those who committed such violations, in order for such violations not to reoccur in the future? How to change the mind of a torturer to cease torturing? How, as a religious leader, does one get to the very roots of these destructive human impulses that seem to be common to the very soul of humanity, within the psyche of all life? What would you advise, as an ethical spiritual leader to the violators, the perpetrators of such crimes? Burma has five decades of totalitarian psychology. How do we get people to stop torturing? Stop oppressing? Stop raping? Stop ethnic cleansing? What's needed? And how to change the mindset of dictatorship, itself?

ACB: It's a universal question. Basically, we must go back to one's conscience, one's own heart. If there's peace in one's heart, then this peace will be contagious towards others. But if there is no peace in one's own heart, then all these violations and atrocities and wars will happen.

The First World War and Second World War started because there was no peace in the mind of a few generals that had power. To re-educate such a mindset would not be an easy matter. But, of course, we also must embrace justice for the victims. Then forgiveness, and all that comes with it, may come to be, and of course, healing of the memories of trauma, both from those who committed the atrocities and the victims of it. Of course, healing and finding the heart beyond violence is not an easy thing.

For the past 50 years there is so much fear. We live in a culture of fear; fear among the people; fear among the generals; fear within the companies that have bullied our people, victimizing farmers, victimizing the weak, and victimizing the poor.

I think both sides must work it out. Aung San Suu Kyi made it clear that to build the nation, to rebuild Myanmar, we need our religious leaders. They have the moral influence over the people, within religion, with awareness of God—a compassionate God—whether Buddhism, Christianity, Hinduism or Islam. Last month in Jakarta we had a conference of Muslim and Christian leaders over a small incident. By the end, we came to the same belief, I think, a love of God—a God with one heart—and the importance of loving one's neighbor. Our tensions and our points of view may be different, but at the end of the day, all people on both sides, whether victims or aggressors, came to the same conclusion—the necessity to love.

AC: Allow me, sir, to ask you a challenging question: Say, hypothetically, the retired senior general and former dictator Than Shwe came to your mass one Sunday. Moreover, he's so moved by your sermon that he comes to confessional where he asks you the question in total privacy, "Archbishop Charles Bo, you're a religious leader; how can I learn to love my neighbors? My neighbors, sir, are the whole of our country. How can I learn to love them? Because as it is, I don't love them, and can't love them, nor do I trust them—especially the ones wanting democracy." What would you say to him?

Before you answer, please allow me to provide context for those who do not know him. He has been a misguided tyrant here in Burma, and the military under his command became the machinery for his tyranny. Okay, let's take it off of him at the moment; in my own country of America, we have a long history of tyranny and violent conquest. We are for the most part a predator nation. Let's say our very own US President is also in that confessional booth. But he asks you, "Sir, how can I love my Muslim terrorist neighbors? How do I love the Taliban? How do I love ISIS? How do I love that which frightens me? How do I love those neighbors that I perceive to threaten my people, my country, the free world itself?" How to love thy neighbor when you perceive them as a threat to your perception of peace security and stability? And, coming back to Myanmar, what would you say to U Than Shwe kneeling in your confessional booth?

ACB: In the scripture itself it says we must "love thy neighbor as yourself." You put yourself in the shoes of your neighbor, of other people. Whether a Buddhist, or a Christian, or a Muslim, if they are sincere, every day they should spend 10 to 15 minutes meditating and reflecting on whether they followed the Buddha's teachings or Christ's gospel teachings or Mohammad's teachings. One must reflect on oneself, on how one can love thy neighbor. Whatever the religion, I believe the Holy Spirit is in each and every one of us. It's the spirit that will animate and guide us.

So, how to love thy neighbor? Personally, when I have a problem or conflict with anybody, maybe that's just natural. When you have two or three people arguing their opinions, when there's conflict or disagreement, what I do after that is go to a quiet place to reflect: how did this conflict bring good for me? So, love thy neighbor as thyself? If one is really serious about this life, then try to reflect. With that meditation, when the mind is really sincere, then I think one's behavior and thoughts will also be sincere.

Last Christmas, when we had a joint Christmas here with other religious ministers, I was asked to give a Christmas message. I was talking about the changes here, how we have come to dawn after being in prison for 50 years, saying these changes are coming around, so we thank God for that. We thank God, but at the same time we thank those people who made these changes possible. So, I was about to publish an article on that, thanking Than Shwe—actually, he's still in power, and he can still destroy the country, but even then, he allows these conversations to happen. So, I said, "We must also give thanks and appreciation for what he has done."

We are not praising what he has done in the past, all the mischief, but the fact that he allows the country to be as it is now. It is because he allows and gives permission, although he has the power to take it away. Normally, a dictator stops because they die or because of bloodshed and revolution. But in this case, no. Not his death, and no bloodshed taking place with these changes. So, perhaps instead of putting all these negative notes and accusations and penalties on him, offer him appreciation. I always say that whatever happens you must have gratitude for the past.

AC: In other words, "No future without forgiveness." Reinforce the intention of doing good? You think the nation should say, "Dear Than Shwe, thank you for having the moral courage—a moment of conscience, for your *hiri* and *ottappa,* your moral shame and regret—to free the nation of your tyranny?"

ACB: Yes. We are telling the truth, not blaming him or approving of what he has done in the past, but, here, currently, he is to be esteemed and given honor where honor is due.

"When we refuse to forgive we become
a prisoner in a prison we've built ourselves."

ALAN CLEMENTS: A final question. Archbishop Desmond Tutu was here recently...

ARCHBISHOP CHARLES BO: Yes, I missed him *(laughs)*. I was away, in Jakarta, but he emailed me.

AC: As we know, he was the chairman of the Truth and Reconciliation Commission in South Africa. My question is about reconciliation, and, I may add, I've asked this question in a variety of ways to numerous former political prisoners, and no one has said what you just said, about thanking Than Shwe. They've all said, by and large, "We want him to address the nation and apologize." It's not about forgiveness; it's about accountability. People throughout your country want to hear him say, "I did wrong. I know that. I was misguided. I was led astray by *lobha, dosa* and *moha*, by greed, anger and delusion." How does honoring him for his moment of conscience and accountability for his atrocities come together?

ACB: You're speaking about Than Shwe?

AC: Yes, Sir, I am. And frankly, not just him but every other senior commander of Burma's military that also did wrong by the people of your country. Your people, by and large, want to hear a public confessional, at the least. They want to hear an acknowledgement of having done wrong—a very human thing. They want to say, "You've raped our daughters, you've killed our sons, you've forced labor upon children, you've imprisoned and tortured many thousands simply for their belief in freedom and truth and the right to live free of fear. All these rights and more have been violated. Yet, we haven't heard you acknowledge any wrongdoing. Please excuse the language, but we have not heard you acknowledge the hell you've put us through."

He's human—we're all human; maybe he's too proud at the moment, maybe his heart's softening; Desmond Tutu listened for four years to that council, to men and women who made the leap of faith to sit in front of that council, in front of those families, and sincerely communicate what they did, why they did it, and seek reconciliation. Sincerity about admitting one's wrongdoing was the key to avoid imprisonment, as I understood it.

You hear confessions all the time, but there's a whole world of people out there who want to but can't quite get to it, because of some fear, some stigma, some loss of strength or character or position. How do you encourage someone who's just at the edge—"I'm a member of the Third Reich, I committed hell for Jews and others"—how do you get them to feel conscious and empowered enough to say, "I'm genuinely sorry" and mean it? What's required of the human heart to rise up and see it as a strength rather than a weakness to confess one's wrongdoings? How can we get someone to tell the truth and to say they're sorry?

ACB: I will not be able to answer in his place. Normally, even as a religious leader, even the blessed John Paul II, in the jubilee year, was apologizing to Jews, as well as many people; he was apologizing to different Christian denominations and others, in the name of the Holy Church; he was apologizing for the wrong that the Catholic church has done in the past. Personally, if I have done wrong, in order to liberate myself to get real freedom, I would apologize.

AC: To liberate myself from fear and shame?

ACB: At the same time, while you're talking about Than Shwe and my message to him, I want to address the other side, the majority of the citizens. I want to give them a message also. For example, if somebody, in the name of a group or the whole nation, wants to retaliate or demands justice and tries to put him in the judgement seat while saying we cannot forgive all those violations, then who becomes the prisoner? It's the unforgiving heart that is the prisoner. If one forgives, you release the prisoner that is yourself. An unforgiving heart is the one that builds its own prison then puts itself inside. On the side of the people, of course, there are issues of justice, but on our side, whether Christian or Buddhist, we must realize that, when we refuse to forgive, we become a prisoner in a prison we've built ourselves. To soften a heart, this eye for an eye, tooth for a tooth, does not help. We may ultimately punish someone like Than Shwe but we will never soften our hearts that way. He has been our leader and our president, and if there are people who have access to him and could genuinely convince him, maybe a Buddhist monk, if we try to understand him, I think one thing the people would like to hear is an apology. But force will not do that. Only love. Only love will conquer.

AC: Well, if so, he would certainly be nominated for the Nobel Peace Prize. Sir, thank you for your time. It has been an honor speaking with you.

ACB: Thank you. And thank you for the chance to meet. I've heard your name for some years, and about your book of conversations with Aung San Suu Kyi.

AC: I thank you for your honesty, your wisdom, your moral courage. Your words are priceless, they heal.

CHAPTER 23

CONVERSATIONS *with*
AL HAJJ NYUNT MAUNG SHEIN

March 2013

- "They don't want Muslims in Myanmar."
- "This is the way of the destruction, to devalue democracy."
- "We don't know if they're real monks or not."
- "If action was taken by law and order on the spot the troubles would not have spread."
- "These events are not instigated by Muslims and Buddhist neighbors."

A Conversation with Al. Hajj Nyunt Maung Shein, president of the Islamic Religious Affairs Council Myanmar who works closely with the government. In this interview, he discusses in detail his views on Burma's five decades of dictatorship, focusing on the country's Islamic culture, its history, and the current intercommunal violence, exploring myths and misconceptions while highlighting common ground in the context of dictatorship. He serves as the voice of Burma's Muslim population, a voice of freedom from across the sectarian divide.

"They don't want Muslims in Myanmar."

ALAN CLEMENTS: Greetings, sir. An honor to meet you as an essential voice to be included in our forthcoming book titled, *Burma's Voices of Freedom*. Rather than starting with a question, may I invite you to openly share whatever you wish.

AL. HAJJ NYUNT MAUNG SHIEN: Good to meet you as well. Upper Burma is my native land. Meiktila is my native home. My brothers, sisters, and relatives are there, and they are helpless, surrounded by Buddhist extremists. They'll be tortured, punished, killed. This morning we met the adviser to the secretary in the government and they informed us that almost all people in Meiktila are facing a very dangerous situation. There's no help, no security. From here in Yangon we cannot do anything. And almost all Muslim homes are burning in Meiktila; still, at this very moment, they're burning.

AC: Tragic. If we can, let us get into the details of this most unfortunate circumstance. Now, you, sir, are the president of the Islamic Religious Affairs Council in Myanmar?

NMS: That's right. In Myanmar, we are one of five religious organizations recognized by the government, working in collaboration with the Ministry of Religious Affairs, concerning the religious affairs of Muslims in Myanmar.

AC: If you would, again, please explain what's going on in Meiktila?

NMS: In Meiktila, on the 20th of this month—two days ago—a seller came to a goldsmith shop and a buyer looked to buy a gold piece. The buyer bargained. In that bargaining they did not reach an agreement and quarreled. As a result of that quarrel, a mob gathered, and quickly the destruction of Muslim houses started. It started at about 9:30 in the morning. The mob destroyed the shop, and after that all nearby shops were destroyed. They beat Muslim men and women. Tortured them. After that, they destroyed an Islamic mosque.

Since Meiktila is a Muslim populated area there are 12 mosques. We've received news that seven or eight mosques collapsed. Most people have run away, leaving their homes and possessions behind. Hundreds of others are gathered outside the town on a football ground, and 250 or so others are living in a police compound. There's no water, no food, no shelter, no medicine.

Whenever the surrounding towns, like Mandalay, sent food, drinks, and water, they were blocked at the gate. They could not pass these items to the victims. Muslims are in danger.

AC: What's at the root of this crisis? Burmese seem so tolerant, for the most part.

NMS: Actually, Burmese people are good natured. They are tolerant and harmonious. But this is their plot, their conspiracy, to damage Muslim land, to damage Muslims throughout the country. We have information, and put it to the government, that these monks, in their religious sermons, are lecturing that they're going to damage Muslims, Muslim houses, Muslim belongings. We're hearing religious sermons saying this. This is widespread and well organized. It's nationwide.

AC: And what does the government tell you?

NMS: The government doesn't tell us anything; they are doing it their own way. This is our democratic way of life. They are going about things freely, and the problem is that they are given freedom.

AC: I'm not sure I understand what you're saying. How does freedom, democracy, and violence towards Muslims connect?

NMS: Burma has been ruled by a military dictatorship for nearly five and a half decades. But now the people are free, the government has changed, it's democratic. And now they want to wage an anti-Muslim campaign. Why? They don't want Muslims in Myanmar. It started with the Rohingya-Rakhine conflict. And now, at this very moment, the campaign in central Burma is happening, and after that they'll continue by targeting Muslims all throughout Myanmar.

AC: When you say, 'they don't want Muslims,' who are 'they'?

NMS: Buddhists, Rakhine Buddhists. They do not want Muslims.

AC: What about Burman Buddhists, do they not want Muslims in Myanmar as well?

NMS: Burman Buddhists are separate. This crisis is the instigation of Rakhine Buddhists. And in Meiktila, it started with the instigation of the monks in their religious sermons—an anti-Muslim campaign was started.

AC: Do we know the names of these monks?

NMS: Yes, we know their names and personal history. There's a full record with the state.

AC: Just a few, or many?

NMS: So many; 50, 60, or 70, like that.

AC: So, you're saying there is a war on Muslims in Myanmar, and Muslims will die?

NMS: Yes! They will kill!

AC: Where does this hatred come from? Is it from decades of suppressed hate of military authority and dictatorship?

NMS: I think it's from extremists, opportunists, those who want to interfere in society.

*"This is the way of the destruction,
to devalue democracy."*

ALAN CLEMENTS: Are you talking about extremist monks?

AL. HAJJ NYUNT MAUNG SHIEN: Yes. The instigation is mainly from Buddhist monks.

AC: But the military shot the monks during the Saffron Revolution in 2007.

NMS: They shot the monks before we got democracy.

AC: What do Rakhine Buddhists dislike about Muslims? And what do these 50, 60 or 70 monks say in their sermons?

NMS: Their message is difficult to mention. Actually, the Burman Buddhists, also do not want Muslims. But it is not the whole community of monks. It's those monks who are linked with politics—the monks who are linked with the politicians, and the monks who are connected with the Rakhine people. The monks who are interested in politics are doing the harm. They're creating the misunderstanding between Muslims and Buddhists, everywhere in Myanmar.

AC: What's their motive?

NMS: Their motivation is this: they do not want Islam in Burma.

AC: Is there a deeper motivation?

NMS: They want to return to a military regime.

AC: So, it's politically motivated?

NMS: Yes, it's politically motivated.

AC: And you have evidence of this?

NMS: Yes, yes. You can see it. Without any purpose, who will do this damage from one society to another?

AC: Who is doing?

NMS: They—the Rakhine Buddhists.

AC: Who do the Rakhine Buddhists get their orders from?

NMS: From Rakhine society, the same political party—the Rakhine government.

AC: And they take orders from Naypyidaw?

NMS: Yes!

AC: Who in Naypyidaw gives the orders?

NMS: Naypyidaw is the central government. Rakhine is a divisional government, but that divisional government is playing tricks.

AC: This is a ploy to maintain dictatorship? That's what you're saying?

NMS: Yes. They're moving to go back to dictatorship. See, this is the way of destruction, to devalue democracy. It's reckless and worthless—a ploy so they can say that 'democracy is not fit for you.'

AC: What must happen to prevent a return to dictatorship?

NMS: We must advise the government, the president in the government, to implement constitutional changes first, and to practice full democracy very quickly.

There are many disturbances in Myanmar, in politics, in democracy, in society. The country is wavering. Our government is good—they're leaning toward democracy. But destruction is occurring. An anti-Muslim campaign has started, and with it, how can we move towards democracy, when one society lacks privileges, all rights, and all is lost? How can we as Muslims participate in this kind of democracy?

AC: What is the Muslim population in Myanmar?

NMS: The government says it's four million, but there are four million in Rakhine division alone. Our assumption is that the overall population of Muslims in Myanmar is 12.5 million. See, in Myanmar there are nearly 60 million people. It's majority Buddhist, and second is Christian. Third is Muslim. And fourth is Hindu. And the other is animist.

So, how can I express better why some Buddhists hate Muslims? We have lived for thousands of years together hand-in-hand. It is not the enmity that comes from the Burmese Buddhists. It is the enmity of the politicians and the motivators and mischief makers who want to ruin society.

AC: Correct me if I'm wrong; what I hear you saying is that it's not really a Buddhist issue. Rather it's a political one? A political issue, used through the filter of Buddhism?

NMS: Yes! Right, right, right; yes.

AC: Military backed?

NMS: Yes.

AC: Than Shwe-backed? With the agenda of continuing dictatorship?

NMS: Yes, that's right. Of course.

AC: You want the world to know that? You're telling the world that Than Shwe is behind the violence? That's what you're saying?

NMS: Yes. They purposely created this conspiracy against Muslims, so as to change the image of the political landscape in Myanmar.

AC: How far will it go?

NMS: You must remember that the Rakhine conflict started in the year 2012, on August 28th, and up and down the country it hasn't ended. It will go on. Rakhine is a small place, Meiktila is a big one. It will go on.

AC: And get bigger?

NMS: Yes, bigger.

AC: This has nothing to do with true animosity towards Muslim people?

NMS: No. It's not about that. None of that.

"We don't know if they're real monks or not."

ALAN CLEMENTS: When I've asked a Buddhist from Myanmar, "What, if anything, you do not find acceptable about Muslims, as you know them," many of have stated: 'Well, now that you ask, I don't like it that they force their Muslim faith upon their wives. Nor do I like that they marry two, three, or four women. I also don't like that they sacrifice cows…'

AL. HAJJ NYUNT MAUNG SHIEN: Yes, yes. We sacrifice cows, animals, in the name of Allah.

AC: How would you respond to these criticisms by some Buddhists in Myanmar?

NMS: Actually; they are claiming that Muslims are marrying four wives. Please show me an example. In a hundred people, there will be no 10 persons marrying four wives.

AC: Less than 10 percent?

NMS: Yes, less than 10. In one hundred people, please show me that 10 people are marrying four wives. There's nothing to show this.

AC: How many Muslim men marry one woman?

NMS: Only, maybe, for two or three.

AC: Two or three wives per one man?

NMS: Two or three wives. Not four. But they are creating this grudge, this enmity, this hatred of Muslims. They refer to our prophet Mohammed allowing 60 wives. Actually, in Islamic society, it is recognized that he married 11 wives, and out of that, only one was a virgin, and the rest, the other 10, were widowers. Why? To take responsibility for the security of the people, for those who are suffering from hunger, from the destruction of society. The prophet had to take those widowed ladies as his wives for those reasons. What is her age? 50. What is her age? 60. What is her age? 45. How will he enjoy life—45, 50, 60-year-old widows. Will that man be able to enjoy life with that lady? Almost all 10 women that the prophet

Mohammed married were widows. Those widows are with two or three husbands in due course.

AC: So, let me be clear: Muslim men can marry up to four women, although few do, less than 10 percent? But 90 percent or more often have two or three wives?

NMS: True.

AC: Let me ask you this: say I'm a Muslim, and I marry a Christian woman—she then must become Muslim?

NMS: Muslims and Christians are the same. All Abrahamic faith—Islam, Christianity, and Judaism—all these belong to one god, Allah. The same God, the same bible, the same scripture. We believe Abraham, you believe Abraham, and all these religions believe the same. Muslims, Christians and Jews are brothers and sisters. All the Abrahamic faith. One god. And we can marry Christian women. It is allowed.

AC: She can stay Christian?

NMS: Yes! Because she's got the bible. The bible is the message of Allah. That is why we can marry a Christian lady without changing her religion. But, if we marry a Buddhist girl, she must come into our religion, that is, after reading the Koran, establishing faith, and stating that she believes in Allah as the messenger of God.

AC: I see. A Christian woman can stay Christian, but a Buddhist woman must convert to Islam. What is the logic of that? Why one and not the other? Are Buddhists considered outside the fold of a true God-based Allah-worshipping religion? And before you answer, as I understand it, beyond respecting the global human right of being able to choose one's own religion, the Burmese Buddhist girl, the woman, is sacred to the family here in Myanmar, right? She is sacred to society in that she brings forth life. She is also sacred in furthering Buddhism. So, when you take a young Buddhist village girl and she's forced to become Muslim, you're not just violating her human right, you are in away, excuse the language, raping the soul of the collective Myanmar Buddhist culture. Of course, this is not grounds to persecute and to kill Muslims at large. But it definitely infuriates, if not violates the cultural and religious fabric of decency and respect. I'm just being a journalist trying to get to a deeper place of understanding. I do not mean to offend you. Your thoughts?

NMS: Brother, what about the Muslim girls marrying Buddhists? There are many!

AC: What would you like to say about that, please, openly?

NMS: It's the same! So many Muslim girls fall in love with young Buddhist men. They are changing their religion. Why? And there are so many Christian ladies in love with Buddhists, and they are changing. Why?

AC: But in such cases, the women are not forced to convert to Buddhism or Christianity. Whereas, as you said, a Buddhist woman marrying a Muslim man must convert to Islam, and if he happens to be in the less than 10 percent category of Muslim men who marry four wives, he has four Buddhist women convert to Islam, times two children from each wife or more and we have a total of 12 new Muslims and four less Buddhists, plus their children. I am simply trying to understand the existential threat many Buddhists tell me that they feel from the spread of Islam in Myanmar.

NMS: Muslims have lived in Myanmar for thousands of years. There was no hatred and enmity in the history of our country. Once in a blue moon something would happen, but it's only now surfacing with emergence of democracy, and of course, with the Rakhine Buddhists who are given freedom. And they grow up and want to exceed the Rohingya people, the Bengalese.

AC: What is the solution to the intolerance, to the fear and hatred?

NMS: Just yesterday we talked about this problem, Muslim leaders with Buddhist monks, in front of local authorities of the Rangoon government. I said, "To calm these tensions we must negotiate side by side. So," I said, "brother, what are the things that you do not want from the Muslim side? Please tell us. We will try to change these things, if we can. You tell us." Sacrifice is not the problem—it's only once a year. And divorce is not the problem. Taking four wives is not the problem. And what about our Muslim and Christian girls marrying your Buddhists? What is that?

AC: The solution?

NMS: The solution is that we must sit side by side and discuss who is at fault, who shall change this fault, what are the things they do not like, what are the things we do not like. What they don't want from the Muslim side—we must openly discuss. And make the changes that we can make. And the same with the other side. We must work this out together.

AC: What do the Buddhist monks tell you that they do not like? What is their list of grievances?

NMS: Most of the monks have good hearts. They have no discrimination. They have nothing against Muslims. They have no hatred. All the monks at the meeting said this. But those other monks participating in the riots are foolish monks. Almost all head monks are good and kind-hearted.

AC: How to control the foolish monks?

NMS: They cannot be controlled.

AC: Why?

NMS: Maybe they are real monks or imitation monks. We don't know for sure.

AC: Whether they are imitation monks or real monks, who is pulling their strings? Are they puppets of the military, the government? Who is controlling them? And why can't they be controlled?

NMS: They are stooges of the government. And when monks wear their gown, we cannot differentiate whether he is real or not.

AC: Why not ask him? Investigate? Photograph them and trace their history? Hold them accountable. Insist on rule of law.

NMS: It is not our concern. Nor do we have the authority to ask.

AC: Up in Meiktila, how many monks were party--

NMS: Oh, so many. But we don't know if they're real monks or not, whether they're staying in a monastery or not, whether they're practicing their Buddhist rituals or not. But they are wearing the monk's gown and participating in the crisis.

AC: What about getting on national television, a leading monk says--

NMS: Yes, you can see this on the news on TV.

AC: What are they saying?

NMS: I will give you videotapes tomorrow. This is a nationwide crisis, and one that is escalating. From Meiktila to Mandalay. And it will go on! From here to there, they are manipulating everything.

AC: And what you're saying is that Muslims are at threat of dying from lack of water and food? The situation is critical?

NMS: Yes. At this moment.

AC: Who's going to feed them? Who's going to give them water?

NMS: People who are near Mandalay division sent trucks with edibles and water, but they were blocked at the gate by the military.

AC: What's the reason for blocking these provisions for their survival? It doesn't make sense.

NMS: There's no security, and in crisis where there is no law, a 1(144), a curfew was issued. We are not allowed to go in because of the curfew. But that deters all people trying to get in.

AC: So, as a result, many may starve to death?

NMS: Many people are already dead. The corpses are there, unburied.

AC: I'm so sorry to hear this.

NMS: Yes, it's terrible.

AC: And what's really painful is that the majority of people in your country are good, and Daw Aung San Suu Kyi, and many, many others near her and in the NLD, are good.

NMS: Yes. Actually, in society, and among the Buddhist people, they are good. They are kind-hearted and broad minded. But everyone is not like this. Those people who are bad, who are ill mannered, extremists and opportunists, who want to make problems, are doing these horrible things. The Rakhine monks and Rakhine Buddhists are the ones instigating the problem.

"If action was taken by law and order on the spot the troubles would not have spread."

ALAN CLEMENTS: How can the international community assist?

AL. HAJJ NYUNT MAUNG SHIEN: Please spread these details internationally: Myanmar is in crisis and all Islamic countries should help. Please look after Muslims in Myanmar; please help the government and the people in danger. That is my request.

AC: What might you want Daw Aung San Suu Kyi to do to assist your people? Or to potentially quiet the crisis?

NMS: In Meiktila, Aung San Suu Kyi's party gained a seat in Parliament through the Muslim vote.

AC: Muslims voted for U Win Htein?

NMS: Yes, we recommended Daw Aung San Suu Kyi's party and Captain U Win Htein was selected as the electorate of that area. It was the Muslim vote that got him elected. That's why so much hate has come to Muslims in Meiktila— "Why have you Muslims, who were not intending to vote, then vote for the NLD?" That is also a source of hatred, that Muslims are furthering the power of the NLD.

AC: Meaning, that this is another reason why you think the military is behind this crisis?

NMS: Yes. We think this government is good, but their background motive is unknown to us. We are not politicians. We are religious persons. And though they are embarking on the democratic life, some extremists and some attached to the military, are attempting to turn things backwards. That's the problem—and they are targeting the Muslim majority.

AC: What level of control do you have with Muslims throughout the entire country?

NMS: The authority that we have is found within the five organizations of Muslim leaders and it is but one request that we have for our people— do not engage in excess, do not go to extremes. Live in line with law and order. This is how we advise them.

AC: You are the most trusted leader of the many millions of Muslims in Myanmar. What's required to establish peace among all religious groups in the country?

NMS: Two things are lacking in Myanmar. One is that between each faith group there is no link—no link between Muslims, Buddhists, Christians and Hindus. There is only a very narrow link to understand each other. That narrowness creates misunderstanding. If there is no connection and togetherness with these diverse faith groups, there will be no misunderstanding. This conflict comes from misunderstanding and misinformation.

For example, the sale of gold rings at the shop in Meiktila, the case of a buyer and seller quarrelling. If action were taken on the spot by the authorities and law and order handled properly, the troubles would not have spread. If there is no law and order and no security, no immediate action taken, then a crisis spreads and easily turns into a mob.

The main point is that we need two things here in Myanmar, among the faith groups. Buddhists, Christians, Muslims, and Hindus must come together to exchange their rituals, traditions, customs and cultures. As it is, there is a narrow communication between the faiths, a very narrow interfaith message. Even on the government's side, and on the civil society side, there is a narrow connection. This narrowness results in unwanted situations.

AC: So, it's the same problem that we saw under military rule—blind authoritarianism, no regard for rule of law and no regard for open dialogue?

NMS: Yes. No rule of law and dialogue! And the same thing is happening within the religious sector. And as I said, if a crisis occurs, action must be taken immediately. If they don't, if it's too late, it becomes a crisis, a mob develops with shouting and unrest. These two things are missing, and as a result of this neglect, all these unsatisfactory things happened. So, there's no peace. If these two things are rectified, among government and civil society and the faith groups, there will be no problem.

AC: How do you propose the different religious groups start to speak with each other?

NMS: A ministry of multi-faith. And the minister of religious affairs came to this place and said he will appoint one person to talk about inter-faith dialogue with other faith groups in the ministry and keep rotating this so that everyone heard from everyone. And we should also encourage them to suggest that we have interfaith dialogues broadcast from the state level throughout the country, to the grass roots level. In this way, every-one hears everything that is going on. We've told the minister of religious affairs this very thing many times. Even before the start of the Rakhine crisis we told him such and such kinds of crisis will occur. We suggested to the government beforehand, but they did not take action. We put it to the president. I wrote him a letter. No action was taken.

AC: Your suggestions are good ones, yet they are falling upon deaf ears. Why?

NMS: They ignore it. I don't know why. All five of our Islamic organiza-tions, in written reports to the president of the country, advised that such kinds of unnecessary things will happen—'Please take action!'

AC: Should this plea also come from the NLD? Maybe from the Maha Sangha Council of Senior Monks as well? Maybe from senior politicians, from the Archbishop, from Hindu leaders, from everyone with a stake in peace and democracy?

NMS: Yes. Yes. Yes.

AC: How to inspire the people in power to let them know that it's in their best interests to act wisely and in a timely way? How to create a radical sense of urgency? How to communicate that the house is on fire? What's required to snap someone out of this trance of inertia, apathy or denial and to take action to avert a national disaster? Must it come from Daw Aung San Suu Kyi in a televised address to the nation? From the leading monks in Myanmar? Since your pleas have gone unanswered, now what?

NMS: Yes, it is especially the duty of political organizations. Take it to Parliament. Wipe out all unnecessary obstacles. Everyone must work together in a unified way. And they must do it now!

AC: If you could address Parliament this very day, what would say?

NMS: If I was allowed to speak to the Parliament, I would say that each and every person here and throughout the entire country is responsible for peace-making. Each and every person must act for the welfare of others—create peace and security and respect for law and order. A Buddhist person must know Islam, and a Muslim must know Buddhism, and Christians and Hindus must know each other, and they must know Buddhists and Muslims too. Everyone must understand everyone else. And we must commit ourselves to peaceful co-existence. If we feel disagreements, something sets us apart or against a religion, or against the culture of another, we must discuss these disagreements face-to-face. There must be tolerance, forgiveness, kindness, and equality. If these things are missing, there will be problems.

There will only be peace if I respect Buddhism and Buddhism respects Islam, and the same with Christians and Hindus alike. We should all work and live in peace together. Until we are together, in heart and in practice, everything will be in vain. We cannot become a democratic country through lip service. We must desire learning about each other and learn tolerance and practice kindness, to respect our differences.

AC: What's at stake if the government doesn't act as you are suggesting?

NMS: The government is in fact trying to act according to law and order, but still it's in vain. Still it is not the action that is needed. It's trying to practice law and order according to a democratic way of life, but still the monks and the civil society are not following according to law and order.

"These events are not instigated by the
neighbor Muslims and neighbor Buddhists."

ALAN CLEMENTS: There's been seven or eight mosques raised to the ground, hundreds of families displaced, many killed and others living in terror. There must be enormous hatred within the Muslim community towards their violators. How are they dealing with it? How are you advising them?

AL. HAJJ NYUNT MAUNG SHIEN: Actually, this hatred is not a hatred of Buddhist society as a whole. This is not the hatred of all Muslims towards all Buddhists, or towards all Christians or all Hindus. It is only a very small portion of Muslim society holding this hatred towards just those instigating this misunderstanding and misbehavior.

AC: I was in the former Yugoslavia during the final year of their conflict, and as I understand it, when it broke apart as one country, it wasn't long before there were religious tensions that were brought up, real or imagined. We saw Milosevic from Serbia instigate discrimination towards Bosnian Muslims. They had no weapons, and, suddenly, weapons started coming in from Islamic countries. Over the years, tragically, it became a three-way war, an overlapping convulsion of ethnic cleansing. My question: Can you imagine weapons being smuggled into Myanmar? Obviously, there's weapons in the long-standing civil wars in Kachin state, Karen state, Shan state, and they have high value weapons at that. Attack helicopters, rocket grenade launchers, automatic rifles, land mines. Could you imagine Islamic countries funneling in top-of-the-line weapons to Muslim rebels in Myanmar, if such a faction appeared?

NMS: No, no. Islamic countries are not doing this, nor will they do it. And Islamic countries are not concerned with Myanmar. No guns, no ammunition, no support.

AC: None?

NMS: None.

AC: What kind of weapons are being used in the riots?

NMS: Local hand-made weapons. Handmade guns that we find in Rakhine state. Not imported from other countries, but handmade.

AC: You can't imagine an underground Muslim-inspired insurgency starting here in Myanmar? It happened in Bosnia. It has happened in almost every border state of your country. Why not with Muslims in Rakhine or even in Meiktila?

NMS: No, no.

AC: And you do not foresee some kind of Muslim terrorist reprisal-action towards Buddhist communities?

NMS: No, no, no. Further, almost all the guns and weapons we see are handmade. Not foreign made. There is no support from other countries, and certainly no support at all from Islamic countries.

AC: What is your next plan of action?

NMS: In reality, you see, if there's no tolerance and understanding from the people and no law and order from the government, if these developments are not undertaken in a practical way, everything is vain. The government must also be tolerant and sympathize with civil society, and civil society must try and understand law and order, and all these things that I have presented to you within the framework of religions, cultures, customs and relationships.

AC: Is there anything additional that you would like the world to know about the plight of your people?

NMS: Muslims in Myanmar lack security, and local administrative authorities ignores their security. After their homes were burned in Meiktila, a prayer house was burned, and violence repeated continuously from August 28th, 2012. After three days, all Muslims were running from their homes. It was a criminal case that was not handled by the police and local authorities. They ignored the situation. They did not take action in time. And legal action must be taken according to laws and regulations—and it must be taken on the spot. But they ignored it. Justice was ignored. That's why the violence repeated as it did.

But somebody was behind these events, with well-thought-out-guided plans. It's not only my opinion, but it was written in the Myanmar Times that 'Well-Trained Terrorists Behind Meiktila, [Say] 88 Generation.' They revealed the underlying facts, that there must be well-trained terrorists behind the violence. Min Ko Naing and Ko Ko Gyi (two main leaders of '88 Generation) explained the matter to the press in that way. These events were not instigated by Muslim and Buddhist neighbors. A third party must have come in from somewhere foreign—from where we do not know. They came as groups. One group entered houses and killed every man and woman, old and young, even pregnant women. All killed. Half an hour later they left, and another group came and looted the homes. And after that, they left, and another group came in. They burned the houses. Almost every act of violence followed in this same sequence. That is why we say they must have been trained terrorists. But we do not know exactly, because we're civilians. But the government must know.

So to the world, I want to convey this is what is happening in Myanmar. And who is responsible for it, who will identify who is doing this damage? It must come from the government sector, from local authorities, that is why I want to convey my message to the international community, that in Myanmar, in each and every case of violence, there is no immediate action taken according to law and order. There's no immediate action to guard the Muslims who are suffering. We are in a helpless position. We have no arms. We are not rebels. We are good citizens, but we've lost everything. We have lived here for thousands of years, hand-to-hand and mouth-to-mouth, as brothers and sisters, with authentic history referring to Muslims as citizens of Myanmar since a thousand years ago—but they are still telling us that we are guests, coming from abroad. We are not guests. We are native here. We are born and brought up here. We will die here. We have no authority, no other country to go to. Bangladesh, India, Pakistan, they are not our countries. There are Muslims living there, but we are ethnic Muslims of Myanmar.

AC: You're the president of the Muslim Federation of Myanmar. You have your mind and heart, your conscience and compassion, focused on the millions of Muslims in your country. How would you describe the collective psychology and the most predominant emotions of your people today?

NMS: They are depressed and afraid. They don't know what to do. They don't know their future with such repeated persecution and violence occurring. We have no fault—we do not *know* our fault. Actually, our men, our Muslim men and women, they have not committed any crime, and now they don't know whether in the future they will be able to carry on their lives in Myanmar or not. They have to consider, that if such killing and persecution continues, it will become unbearable for them.

For the next generation, how can we have interfaith dialogues and expect them to be harmonious if these killings are done by monks? The Buddhist law, the Buddha's religion, doesn't allow monks to participate in violence. And neither are Muslim clergy permitted to engage in violence, and neither are Christian clergy. Bishops also, they are not allowed to participate in such violence. That is not their way. But some head monks are bringing in this violence. These are Buddhist monks! Head monks! There's one—his name is Wirathu. This monk is the one leading anti-Muslim campaigns in the whole of Burma.

AC: When I interviewed Wirathu as well as other senior Buddhist monks here in Myanmar, each of them said, in their own way, paraphrasing here, that historically, Buddhism, Buddhist monks and nuns and monasteries, have been destroyed by Muslim invaders...

NMS: Where?

AC: They said in India. Pakistan. Afghanistan. Indonesia. Bangladesh. Malaysia. All former Buddhist countries. India, the home of the Buddha, as you know. I was told that, was it in the 12th Century, Muslim Moguls mercilessly destroyed Buddhist monasteries, slaughtered monks, and pretty much wiped out Buddhism in India. And there is the belief, I hear, that with all the mosques that are coming up in Burma, that Myanmar is the next country to be decimated by Islam. What is your response?

NMS: My response is that Islam cannot be depicted in this way in Myanmar, today, tomorrow, and for the future. It cannot be. Muslims have no such intentions.

AC: They explained that it happened in the past, so I ask you, what's to prevent it happening today or in the future? Muslims clearly have had a historic hatred of Buddhists.

NMS: Maybe in history. But I do not think it was right. In fact, maybe history was wrong. History can be wrong, that is, if the writers are wrong, if those who note the history are wrong. Recognized and authentic historians who write this one as a good point of view, maybe it is acceptable—maybe there's some right and wrong history in each and every country.

Still, you have been to India and there are Muslims and Hindus living their together. Not vanished. The Hindu population has not vanished, and the Muslim population has not vanished. If there is any problem or violence in India, all Muslims must be wiped out?

AC: Of course not. All I'm saying is that Buddhism was almost completely wiped out in ancient India and history has it that it was decimated by Muslim invaders. In saying that, I'm trying to understand the deeper roots of what may be motivating the crisis here in Myanmar, at least in part. Let me say it another way: a lot of what U Wirathu and other monks and nuns in this country feel is that there's a strong history, like, for example, the Jews suffered dramatically under the Nazi Germans that resulted in mass extermination—a holocaust. It's both a very fresh wound and a historical and systemic collective trauma. Many Buddhists in Myanmar and the world at large, feel that Islam has been to Buddhists as the Nazi Germans were to the Jews; I don't mean to compare something like the holocaust with the annihilation of Buddhist culture throughout South Asia and Indian subcontinent, but the fact remains that historically the Muslims have been radically violent towards Buddhists. And so, this furthers Wirathu's position, that if Buddhists don't stand strong, they might be the next country to be decapitated like the heads of Buddha statues were severed from their bodies in Band-e Amir in Afghanistan. And so, I'm not saying that's what's going to happen, I'm just saying that maybe there's something psychology to appreciate here, that some Buddhists are terribly afraid. How can you quiet their fears?

NMS: I think that if this feeling is really in their minds, why are they not considering the past thousand years. A thousand years of us living hand-to-hand and mouth-to-mouth and home to home together here in Myanmar. History is telling us this fact. That harmony and coexistence is what we have done here in Myanmar for a thousand years or more. And that the government also issued a presidential speech to that effect—you can read it. We have lived harmoniously, with tolerance for so long together. So why this problem now? Why create this problem now?

Wirathu is referring to the history of India—but this is Burma, not Afghanistan or Indonesia. The people are taking the same religion but relating it to different people. Naturally, we are different from those people living in Afghanistan, Bangladesh, India, Pakistan. We are traditionally different; our background is Burma—Burma has nice people. They have no right to refer the Muslims with the Muslims of others, though our religion is the same. You are a Christian: he has no authority to compare Christians of America, Christians of the UK and Christians of Germany. He has no right. These are different things. You say about your history— why do you ignore this, that since thousands of years ago we have lived harmoniously? Why do you not confess this? Why does this problem come up? Where is the problem? Say the problem! Not by adding the words that is on the sign board and saying that we will take over the universe! It is impossible. Even in Islamic countries it cannot be considered that in the 21st century Muslims will be dominating the world. Can it be, sir? May I ask you? Can it be?

AC: I cannot say no with any conviction. I have ISIS, Al Qaeda and 9/11 fresh in my mind. Terrorism is real and, frankly, no religion is exempt.

NMS: There is no way Muslims will overrun this country, sir. You may write, and you may convey this message. May I ask you: can 57 Muslim countries take over, capture, the whole universe in the 21st century? Muslims in Burma, we have no arms, no rebellions, no army, no nothing. We are killed, we are homeless, our mosques are damaged, we are being killed day by day! How can we be accused as those who will be retaining authority in the 21st century? They are fools! Those who are saying this, are fools! There's no wisdom according to the voice of our Buddhist monks. This is the fact: we must make peace with each other. We must be harmonious with each other. We must coexist. We must be tolerant, we must be nonviolent, we must forgive and co-exist harmoniously.

AC: May it be so, sir. May the violence cease. Thank you for your time, courage, passion, and honesty. And may your vision of peaceful co-existence of all religious groups as well as all ethnicities in Burma, come to be, and soon.

CHAPTER 24

PREFACE *to* BURMA'S SAFFRON REVOLUTION

*We outside Burma cannot look away and ignore the plight
of Burma's peoples. Our religious and philosophical teachings
tell us that human suffering anywhere must be
accepted as our own suffering. And our worldly experience
convinces us that only practical political action can help end
that suffering.*

—ARCHBISHOP DESMOND TUTU

Václav Havel, leader of the nonviolent Velvet Revolution of Czechoslovakia, says of his first becoming a political activist, "I stopped waiting for the world to improve and exercised my right to intervene in that world, or at least to express my opinion about it." Howard Zinn, the great American author and human rights advocate, reminds us that "at many of the key moments in history some of the bravest and most effective political acts were the sounds of the human voice itself."

From Burma we now hear and see a powerful expression of these values: the power of the powerless and the activism of the human voice, the sound of conscience itself. In this predominantly Buddhist nation of 50 million people, many, at this very moment, risk their lives for the right to choose their destiny—freedom from the most brutal military regime in the world.

The Voice of Hope reveals one of the most politically ravaged, yet spiritually vibrant societies on Earth. In conversation, Aung San Suu Kyi illuminates one of the most awe-inspiring, nonviolent revolutions in modern times. As Burma's democratically elected leader she remains, to this day, imprisoned by the violent military junta.

I first met this formidable human being in 1995, a few weeks after her release from six years of house arrest. Two additional long periods of incarceration were still to come. She told me, "Nothing has changed since my release....Let the world know that we are still prisoners in our own country."

Twelve years have passed since the first publication of this book.

Has anything changed in Burma?

On October 24, 2007, Aung San Suu Kyi entered her twelfth year of detention since her initial arrest on July 20, 1989. Several thousand other prisoners of conscience remain incarcerated in Burmese prisons. Relentless ethnic cleansing—the murder, torture, and rape of minorities there—has left more than 3,000 villages destroyed. Nearly 1 million refugees have fled the country, and 1 million more are internally displaced, subsisting in primitive, malaria-infested jungle conditions. Hundreds of thousands of Burmese citizens are enslaved as forced laborers building roads, bridges, dams, and monuments for tourism. Millions more are tyrannized by one of the largest standing armies in the world. Dictator Senior General Than Shwe commands 400,000 rank and file soldiers. As many as 70,000 of them are children, some as young as eleven years old.

In its totalitarian terror, Burma is an Orwellian nightmare. There is no regard for human rights. None. Burma remains a land of 50 million hostages—prisoners in their own country.

Has anything changed over twelve years?

There is one notable difference: the voices of hope are multiplying, fast.

Aung San Suu Kyi, in her own words, offers insight into the courage of the Burmese people. Despite her silence and isolation, both her voice and her presence infuse them with strength and a vision of freedom. "Those of us who decided to work for democracy in Burma," she explains, "made our choice in the conviction that the danger of standing up for basic human rights in a repressive society was preferable to the safety of a quiescent life in servitude. Ours is a nonviolent movement that depends on faith in the human predilection for fair play and compassion. Some would insist that man is primarily an economic animal interested only in his material well-being. This is too narrow a view of a species which has produced numberless brave men and women who are prepared to undergo relentless persecution to uphold deeply held beliefs and principles. It is my pride and inspiration that such men and women exist in my country today."

The protests in Burma between August 19 and October 2 of 2007 confirm a nation's unrelenting resistance to dictatorship. Their moral bravery stands as a new benchmark of nonviolent spiritual activism in the world. I, like millions of others, watched on television as robed monks risked their lives in hopes the world would help. Tens of thousands of Buddhist monks and nuns marched peacefully in the streets of their nation's major cities. Infused with the moral authority of an unwavering belief in freedom, they demanded an end to decades of tyranny, deprivation, and slavery.

For that moment in time the world stood still, enraptured by the elegance of nationwide, spiritually led revolution. An archetypal confrontation of opposing forces rose up—Buddhist monks chanting prayers of loving kindness towards rows of armed soldiers with their rifles poised to kill. The power of this vision continues to ripple around the world, spilling its message into our own lives. On September 21, at the peak of the protests, five hundred monks defied the regime's threat of a crackdown. They marched past Aung San Suu

Kyi's home in Rangoon, chanting a sacred Buddhist prayer for "sending loving kindness towards all sentient beings." To the surprise of the world, their democratically elected leader and the only incarcerated Nobel Peace Laureate somehow managed to briefly leave her home. She was seen crying at the gate of her walled compound as she reverentially lowered her head in prayer towards the monks. This was the first sighting of the imprisoned Aung San Suu Kyi since her 2003 reentry into house arrest.

Over the next few days international headlines told a grim tale:

Soldiers Fire on Peaceful Protesters, Killing and Arresting Monks.
The Killing Continues as the Regime Attacks Monasteries Nationwide.
Rangoon is Locked Down, Streets Silent, Monasteries Emptied.
Mass Arrests Continue Nightly, Reports of Torture Widespread.

Awed. Saddened. Repulsed. Outraged. These are just a few of the emotions reflected in the media. World leaders echoed dismay. Millions of us remained fixated on the trickle of pictures, footage, and commentaries of the regime's brutal assault on the monks and other protesters.

As smoke from the automatic rifles and tear gas lifted, the city streets emptied. Soldiers poised on almost every corner, the monks had disappeared.

Shari Villarosa, the chief diplomat at the United States Embassy in Burma, issued a statement asserting, "We have pictures where whole monasteries have been trashed," and "at least fifteen monasteries in Rangoon alone have been totally emptied." In another report, a dissident group stated that thousands of monks had been imprisoned in the north of the country. Monasteries emptied. In some, only broken glass and bloodstains remained.

International outcry has resulted in little change. Numerous monasteries remain barricaded or under armed surveillance. Arrests continue nightly. Reports of torture and imprisonment persist. Many monks hide in the countryside, or remain missing. Countrywide, the state-run papers print propaganda, restrict Internet access, jail journalists, harass photographers, censor writers, and ban publications, making it impossible to know how many monks and protesters have been killed and are being tortured and detained. No one believes the regime's official body count of fifteen dead. The Norway-based Democratic Voice of Burma puts the death toll so far at 138. Many hundreds, perhaps thousands more are injured, eerily reminiscent of the regime's bloody response to the peaceful pro-democracy marches in 1988.

Mahatma Gandhi once said, "When I despair, I remember that all through history the ways of truth and love have always won. There have been tyrants, and murderers, and for a time they can seem invincible, but in the end they always fall. Think of it—always."

Is there hope, really?

On the one hand, the travesty in Burma elicits easy comparisons to China's brutal suppression of democracy at Tiananmen Square. Or further to the horrors of Darfur. Or that of Pinochet's murderous reign of terror in Chile. On the other hand, Burma's "revolution of the spirit," as Aung San Suu Kyi often refers to her country's struggle for democracy, offers an opportunity like "the miracle in South Africa," or the lightning-speed fall of Romania's Nicolae Ceausescu. Or Havel's Velvet Revolution. Or the mass pro-democracy demonstrations that flooded Belgrade and eventually delivered Slobadon

Miloševi´c to the War Crime's Tribunal.

Yes, there is hope.

This is how I see it.

At the heart of Burma's revolution is a life-transforming metaphor, a candle of hope illuminating this totalitarian darkness. Its unrelenting flicker, when expanded to a blaze, offers the power to ignite the thunder-flame of conscience in everyone. It reveals an invitation to rise in spirit and take action—an invitation to support not just Burma and Aung San Suu Kyi, but the message of freedom and the belief in hope.

Thus, may we join what is perhaps the most courageous and the most compelling spiritually inspired, nonviolent revolution the world has ever seen. "Feel always free," Aung San Suu Kyi encourages everyone who dares to enter the revolution. "Nobody can detain [your] mind, though they can detain [your] body . . . master your mind [and] nobody can abuse you. We need to remember this. . . . Feel always free."

How to accept this invitation to be free?

How to join Burma's revolution of the spirit?

Meeting Aung San Suu Kyi was one of the most memorable experiences of my life. I had many questions. One of the first questions I asked was, what core quality could make your country's revolution successful when confronted by such overwhelming military might? Without equivocation she answered, "Courage! You were outside on the street when I spoke to the people. There were Buddhists in the crowd, as well as Hindus, Christians, and Muslims. All of them want the same thing: Freedom. They risk long prison terms, even torture, to participate. That takes courage."

She told me about the nature of courage. "It takes courage to lift one's eyes up from their own needs and to see the truth of the world around them, a truth, such as Burma, where there are no human rights. It takes even more courage not to turn away, to make excuses for non-involvement, or to be corrupted by fear. It takes courage to feel the truth, to feel one's conscience. Because once you do you must engage your fundamental purpose for being alive. You can't just expect to sit idly by and have freedom handed to you. Liberation will not be achieved this way. Our revolution will be successful only when everyone realizes they can do their part. In this regard, courage is threefold: The courage to see. The courage to feel. And the courage to act. If all three domains are realized our revolution will succeed."

Throughout years of persecution, Aung San Suu Kyi has continually stressed the importance of everyday revolution—the art and activism of expressing liberation through living. "Love is an action, not just a mind state," Aung San Suu Kyi told me. "It is not enough to just sit there and send thoughts of loving-kindness. One must put that love into action."

My experiences in Burma showed me what is possible when conscience is stirred, when good people care deeply enough to act on behalf of the greater good. Years later, watching these most recent monk-led uprisings, I realize that Burma's struggle for democratic freedom is in fact a microcosm of the larger picture—the world's struggle to overcome tyranny, to end violence, and to establish free societies.

I realize that continuing to hope is in fact an act of tremendous resistance. All these years of growing and nurturing a revolution have brought Burma closer and closer to a democratic country—one that is more benevolent and compassionate. This is expressed in the countless daily acts of courage that help to preserve self-respect and human dignity over the many long years under the tyranny of oppression.

Aung San Suu Kyi's nonviolent revolution of the spirit offers us—the global community—an awe-inspiring model of how to peacefully engage complexity and tyranny. It offers the potential to bring about true social and political change. It is my firm belief that through innovative expressions of nonviolent activism—our own unique expressions of everyday revolution—the world will be a much safer and better place to live. And we will see a liberated Burma, a freed Aung San Suu Kyi, and a nation offering the world community a new, more enlightened expression of democracy. This democracy will have a human face, one that embodies dialogue over domination, kindness over cruelty, and compassion over killing.

Ultimately, the revolution in Burma is a directional challenge to us all: the voice of democratic decency everywhere versus the machinery of repression. It is a message for our planet.

How can we make Burma's revolution of the spirit our personal revolution? The answer is in our own, insistent voice of hope.

Together with Aung San Suu Kyi, I pray that one day we will live in a world that celebrates a liberated Burma.

Alan Clements

NOVEMBER 2007

We have faith in the power to change what needs to be changed but we are under no illusion that the transition from dictatorship to liberal democracy will be easy, or that democratic government will mean the end of all our problems. We know that our greatest challenges lie ahead of us and that our struggle to establish a stable, democratic society will continue beyond our own life span. But we know that we are not alone. The cause of liberty and justice finds sympathetic responses around the world. Thinking and feeling people everywhere, regardless of color or creed, understand the deeply rooted human need for a meaningful existence that goes beyond the mere gratification of material desires. Those fortunate enough to live in societies where they are entitled to full political rights can reach out to help their less fortunate brethren in other areas of our troubled planet.

—AUNG SAN SUU KYI

CHAPTER 25

CONVERSATIONS *with* U GAMBIRA

2007 & 2013

Burma's Revolution of Conscience

The following interview is the result of a three-way communication over a number of days in October 2007 between author Alan Clements; Dr Ashin Nayaka, a Buddhist monk and visiting scholar at Columbia University in New York who served as translator; and U Gambira, a leader of the All-Burma Monks Alliance that spearheaded the nationwide protests in Burma in September 2007. Twenty-nine-year-old U Gambira became a fugitive following the deadly September 26-27 crackdown on pro-democracy protesters in Burma. Shortly after this interview took place, on November 4, he was arrested by military police in Sagaign (upper Burma) was charged with treason, a capital punishment in Burma. If convicted, U Gambira will very possibly face execution. It is believed that he is being held at Rangoon's Insein Prison and is in grave danger of torture. The regime's security forces also arrested a number of U Gambira's family members, including two brothers and a sister. Sources close to the family say U Gambira's father and another sister are on the run.

ALAN CLEMENTS: Word has it that as many as 1,000 monks in Rangoon alone have been taken to Rangoon's notorious Insein Prison. The security forces raided 50 monasteries. They're cutting phone lines, seizing computers and mobile phones, and ransacking the grounds during their raids.

I am also told that there is a nationwide manhunt for you and that you are fugitive on the run, avoiding arrest by going from home to home, sometimes every few hours. Given the dire urgency of the situation, since my first question may be our last one, if you are arrested, what do you want to tell the world on behalf of your country's monk-led anti-government uprisings and for the future of freedom in Burma itself?

U GAMBIRA: People the world over have witnessed for themselves the disastrous and wicked system of the dictatorship imposed upon us. They have seen, through media, the brutality. The military regime has killed peaceful demonstrators. They have killed monks. They have emptied monasteries. They have forcibly disrobed monks. Beaten them, assaulted them very badly. Even tortured them. Jailed them. Many others are missing. Others are running and hiding. I am hiding. They want to butcher me. My situation is not good. I have slept outside for two nights now. I am not very well.

The dictatorship has committed crimes against humanity. This is a great tragedy for our people and for the Buddhadhamma (the teachings of the Buddha) in our long history of monastic Buddhism. This wicked regime committed these atrocities in full view of the world. They are shameless, seeking only to systematically oppress us for decades to come.

What I wish to say is this: The spiritual authority of Burma resides in the *Dhamma*. The *Dhamma* in Burma is both protected and practiced primarily in the minds and hearts of the monks and nuns in my country. Of course, the lay people too practice *Dhamma*. But the symbol of hope in our society is the *Sangha* (the order of monastics).

At present the *Sangha* is the enemy of the regime. If this continues unaddressed, further bloody confrontation is unavoidable. Our spiritual obligation is to freedom, not to silence or submission. So, we the *Sangha* of Burma will not stop until the goal is reached. To reach our goal we invite everyone in the world who cares about freedom to enter our struggle with us. Find a way to help us that suits you and then please take that action.

AC: There are 400,000 rank and file soldiers under the dictator in Burma. Most of these young men are devout Buddhists. Many of them have at some point in their childhoods ordained as novice monks and lived in monasteries studying the basic teachings of the Buddha. Yet they are being commanded by their superiors in the military to murder monks, to attack the *Sangha*, to shoot at the most sacred institution in their own country. This is like asking someone to put a bullet through their own conscience, a type of moral suicide.

Why do these Buddhist soldiers follow orders to kill Buddhist monks? Why don't they throw down their weapons, walk off the job en masse and say, "No, we refuse to follow your sick orders?"

UG: We too are shocked. We never thought that our own soldiers would open fire on us. We trusted that the soldiers had some degree of *sadha* (faith) in the *Sangha* (community). And that *sadha* would prevent them from following any orders to harm us, or arrest us, or kill us should they be ordered to do these wicked acts towards the *Sangha*.

We have learned that if the soldiers do not follow orders they will be arrested or killed. We have no doubt that the soldiers know that by assaulting the monks, they are assaulting the Triple Gem, the Buddha, *Dhamma*, and *Sangha*. And to assault the Triple Gem is, according to Buddhist scriptures, the greatest crime one could make in one's life. It is likened to killing one's parents or killing one's own children. It is unthinkable.

According to our Buddhist beliefs, we believe in *kamma* and *vipaka* (the law of cause and effect). We also believe in *lokiya* (different dimensions in the universe). We believe that life is not confined to just this earth. And even here on earth there are many forms of life: animals, insects, birds, dogs. With *kamma* and *vipaka*, these heinous actions that they have committed will lead them to the *apaya lokas* (or the lower worlds), where suffering is very intense. You call this hell in English. We call it *apaya*. And *apaya* is something similar to what we hear about in Sudan.

But there were other soldiers who acted differently. We saw tears in some of the soldier's eyes. When they came closer, we could see tears.

We could also see they were tormented inside. If they were to lay down their guns there would be no place for them to go, no safe passage for them to flee the country or find safe haven inside the country.

We are certain that the majority of soldiers under the dictator are very sympathetic to our *Dhamma* message of love, kindness and compassion. After all, although they wear uniforms, they are Buddhists at heart. And as Buddhists they know what is right from wrong. They too want freedom from tyranny. They too want democracy. It's the dictator Than Shwe and his senior generals who must be stopped. Once they are stopped, we are confident the soldiers will come to our side.

AC: Burma's Supreme Military Dictator Senior General Than Shwe and his leading Generals claim to be devout Buddhists. They proudly visit monasteries, pay their respects to the abbots, offer large donations and, in turn, recite basic Buddhist prayers for offering these gifts (a Burmese Buddhist custom of sharing the merit from one's offerings for the "betterment of all sentient beings.")

My question is this: I want to know how these generals think—how do they talk to themselves? How do they justify in their own mind not only the murdering of monks but the murdering of them in the name of "harmlessness and basic human goodness"—the two most salient features of the Buddha's teachings? These are teachings that they openly and proudly claim to hold.

Of course, one could simply say they are hypocrites. Or they are pathologically mind-blind. What do you think? Do they actually believe what they are saying and doing is in accordance with the *Dhamma*? For that matter, does anyone in Burma believe them?

UG: It's very simple: they are talking Buddhist talk, but not walking Buddha's walk. We see this level of hypocrisy and perversity almost everywhere in the world. It is the norm, not the exception. We see it among all walks of life, from ordinary citizens to political leaders, human beings who by and large do not know themselves. They cannot distinguish what they think. They do not know what they feel. They cannot differentiate states of consciousness, mistaking one state for another state.

In English, I think you call this mental blindness, or ignorance or stupidity. In *Abhidhamma*, or Buddhist psychology, we call it by the Buddhist Pali word: *moha* or *avijja*. It's a type of mental perversity that mistakes reality. Killing monks is not only wrong, it is insane. This expression of perversity is what we call a gross and wicked level of *moha*.

If you are asking whether Than Shwe and his generals think killing monks is compassionate and beneficial for the "stability of the nation" then they may be psychopaths. There's good reason to believe they are. But because we are Buddhists, deep down inside of us, we believe in redemption and therefore do not think they are beyond hope.

They are scared. They kill because they are scared. Violence is an act of weakness. Violence is not a sign of strength. They must know this. There is some place in them that must know this.

On their state-run television you can see the generals visiting certain monasteries with their soldiers. Yet, the generals are seen still carrying pistols in their holsters. To bring a gun into a monastery is unimaginable. Our monasteries are sanctuaries of peace. They violate that sanctity because their fright is stronger than their faith, or their commitment to *Dhamma*.

The question I ask, that we all ask, is whether they have a conscience. And if so, can their conscience be activated?

It was our belief that the monk-led protesting would stir their conscience. Maybe it did. Maybe they are not yet aware of it. Maybe in a quiet moment, when Than Shwe or any of the others are alone with themselves, they may feel a deep uneasiness in their hearts. In Buddhism we call this uneasiness of the heart *hiri* (moral shame) and *ottappa* (moral remorse). These two states of mind are what you would call conscience.

If they feel this uneasiness, that would be the greatest good for them and the future of our country. That would be the only true road to reconciliation. And it is reconciliation that we want. We want peace.

Every human must conquer their own heart. No one can subdue the forces of tyranny latent in the hearts of us all. "Only by oneself can these forces be confronted," the Buddha has instructed us. And it starts with feeling *hiri* and *ottappa*. Those two qualities of consciousness are what will save this country and bring true and lasting peace.

For that to happen, Than Shwe and others in his ranks must enter their hearts and feel the terrible transgressions they have committed. This is one of the gravest acts of self-delusion we have seen in modern Burma. They believe it is to their own benefit to force countless sufferings on the people. But they can change this at any time. That is, if they change themselves.

Our message to them is this: raise your consciousness, increase your ethical integrity, and align yourselves in reality to the principles of Buddhism. That means to conquer your own fear, put down your weapons, and do what is right for the people. They can do this at any time.

Buddhism is a compassionate teaching. It is firmly rooted in forgiveness and redemption. There are numerous examples of great transformations of consciousness in the traditional Buddhist texts.

Other monks are being arrested at this very moment. I, too, may be arrested today. Still, the uprisings are not going away. They may kill or arrest or torture us, but the uprisings will continue. Like bamboo that is rooted deeply in the soil, no matter how much you try to cut the bamboo back, it sprouts up here and then over there and then everywhere at once. We the people of Burma are determined to keep rising up everywhere until the land is free to grow our democracy and end their dictatorship.

AC: What change of mind is needed for the regime to truly understand that for the betterment of the country, for true peace and security of the entire population, including themselves and their families, they must open a meaningful dialogue with Aung San Suu Kyi and other members of her political party?

Why is dialogue so difficult for the Generals to understand as a means to settle one's differences? What are they afraid of? Loss of power? Fear of persecution? Fear of losing their wealth? Fear of a Truth Council? Fear that China would betray them and not grant them asylum if they were to flee?

Is it that they are uneducated military men trained on decades of dictatorship and blind obedience to absolute power and have become totalitarian robots? Can you shed some light on the core psychology of what drives the dictator and his killing machine?

UG: We monks asked the regime to face up to the real world and find peace and national reconciliation—to do what is best for the people and the country. We realize this presents challenges, and risks. The monks did not ask the generals to give up their power. As Aung San Suu Kyi has said many times, we need our military. We need it as part of the solution to achieve peace and tranquility in our county. But these men know that they have done wrong. They have blood on their hands. They have committed crimes against humanity. Crimes against the *Sangha*. Crimes against the *Dhamma*. Crimes against the Buddha. How could they not fear the people's power? Perhaps they are afraid of their own hearts. This is why I said they must "conquer their own hearts." Conquer their fears.

If they conquer their fears and open a dialogue of real value, they will quickly come to see that their future in Burma is much more secure under a democracy than under a dictatorship. Under democracy they would be able to enjoy the inner prosperity of a nation at peace with itself rather than command frightened soldiers to kill peaceful monks.

Fear. It's all about fear. They must realize that we do not wish them harm. We are monks. We are Buddhists. We are tolerant. But the people can only take so much, and I think we have reached that point. The bamboo will begin sprouting everywhere. Wait and see.

AC: During the war in Vietnam we witnessed Buddhist monks and some nuns immolate themselves as a form of revolutionary protest. These immolations shocked the world. In most cases, the horror of it ignited a worldwide sense of conscience that forced us to feel the gross level of atrocities committed by the US forces upon the people of Vietnam. Some historians say that those televised images of monks burning were the beginning of the end of the war.

In Burma, has a monk or nun ever immolated him or herself? And, if so, who was he or she, and under what circumstance did it occur? Also, during the current monk-led protests, has there been any discussion of such an action by any of the monks or nuns? And if so, what was said? And if not, how do you feel about self-immolation as a form of revolutionary political protest?

Ashin Nayaka and U Gambira: As monks applying ourselves to revolutionary actions for the greater good of the people, we restrain from two extremes: self-indulgence and self-mortification. Immolation is not our way. Peaceful protests are a preferred expression. Before we began our protests, we discussed what we thought would be the response of the military regime. Would we face arrest? Would we face torture? Would we face life in prison? Would we face death? We discussed this in great detail. We concluded that whatever the consequences, we were unafraid. We also concluded that we would remain peaceful under all circumstances. It remains our firm belief that our commitment to the *Dhamma* will overthrow these unjust rulers in Burma. We also hope that by them seeing the *Dhamma* power of the monks and the people, they may find faith in themselves to seek a higher way, to seek their own *Dhamma* power and let us all come together in the spirit of freedom.

AC: Along those lines, what revolutionary action would you like to see right now either inside Burma or outside the country, to bring up a change in government? Would it be armed intervention? Would it be a mass stopwork by the people? Would it be America bombing the new capital where the generals are bunkered? Please, openly, what would you like to see?

Ashin Nayaka and U Gambira: Let me read a message that I have prepared. It is a message to the United Nations Special Envoy Ibrahim Gambari, and to the United States President George Bush. And it is also a message to the world:

"Please do something effective for Burma. Measures such
as economic sanctions and arms embargos will take time to
achieve a political solution. What is most important is today.
Please tell Mr. Gambari that I am grateful for his participation in
Burmese affairs. I have a tremendous respect for him. But please
tell him to implement effective practical measures in Burma. Please
try. Please send U.N. representatives to Burma to carry out various
ways and means to get political results for us right now. For today."

"To Buddhists all over the world and activists and supporters of our
Burmese movement, please help to liberate the people of Burma from
this oppressive and wicked system. To the six billion people of the
world, to those who are sympathetic to the suffering of the Burmese
people, please help us to be free from this evil system. Many people
are being killed, imprisoned, tortured, and sent to forced labour camps.
I hereby sincerely ask the international community to do something
to stop these atrocities. My chances of survival are very slim now.
But I have not given up, and I will try my best."

AC: Burma is a land of 50 million prisoners, enslaved, if you will, by a
military force acting more like a terrorist organization than a noble institution meant to support and defend the aspirations of the people. Since
your struggle is a nonviolent one, rather than only marching for peace,
have you encouraged the people to engage in acts of civil disobedience?

Let me offer a quote from Henry David Thoreau's manifesto,
"Resistance to Civil Government," that he wrote in 1849.

He states: "Under a government which imprisons unjustly, the true
place for a just man is also a prison, where the State places those who are
not with her, but against her, the only house in a slave State in which a
free man can abide with honor....A minority is powerless while it conforms
to the majority; it is not even a minority then; but it is irresistible when it
clogs by its whole weight.

"If the alternative is to keep all just men in prison, or give up war and
slavery, the State will not hesitate which to choose. If a thousand men were
not to pay their tax bills this year, that would not be as violent and bloody
a measure as it would be to pay them, and enable the State to commit
violence and shed innocent blood. This is, in fact, the definition of a peace-
able revolution, if any such is possible."

My question is this: Why not encourage all monks, nuns and lay
people in Burma to stop working for the dictatorship? Or encourage them
to all march and fill the prisons full until the only ones not in prison are
the generals and their soldiers?

In other words, what methods are you and the other monk leaders encouraging the people of Burma to follow in order to bring change besides marching?

Ashin Nayaka and U Gambira: The regime has made Burma into a country of slaves and prisoners. Yet our message remains the same: change through compassion, not killing. And compassionate forms of civil disobedience are the only way to put an end to this hell we are living under. But it is difficult to convince all the people not to cooperate with the regime, especially the soldiers whose lives are at risk if they defect.

Since the nonviolent approach is our way, we firmly believe the people will find more and more courage to defy the rules of this regime. It may be gradual, but change cannot be denied. It will happen.

We know what we will do on the inside but what about the outside? Will it come through international pressure or international bloodshed?

AC: This book will be inevitably smuggled into Burma, and may I invite you to speak to the people of your country and to Aung San Suu Kyi herself. What do you wish to say?

Ashin Nayaka and U Gambira: Change is the law of life. Those who look only to the past or the present are certain to miss the future. We really believe in this opinion. We constantly search ahead to meet the challenges of the future with greater determination. We have the potential to transform our country into a dynamic democratic state, one that can hold its head high in the world as a nation of insight and compassion.

I am confident that with courage, endeavor, and wisdom we can apply ourselves to the exciting task of rebuilding our country, and creating institutions built upon foundations of dignity.

We hope that all freedom loving people across the world, particularly in Burma, including our own armed forces, will join with us in our struggle for freedom. This way, the promise of the saffron revolution - a united and liberated Burma - will come true.

Hold your heads high in honor of your courage and character to defy the world's most brutal regime. Let us honor the heroic monks who paid the ultimate sacrifice for the cause of peace and freedom in our country. Your deeds for the people of Burma will not be in vain but held in the memory of the sacred *Dhamma* passed from generation to generation.

We cannot live without admiration for the character, the courage, and the strength of spirit of Daw Aung San Suu Kyi. She is deeply infused with the Buddha's teachings on patience, kindness, and forgiveness. Despite the military regime's incessant false accusations against her, she stands firmly as an ethical guide to all who desire freedom in the world. And she represents our own voice of hope here in Burma.

These important and difficult issues ask us to call upon our deepest inner resources. We are obliged to join the revolution and to stand up for freedom.

Let us remain steadfast in our commitment to the freedom in our country and the freedom in our own hearts. Let us not forget that we are one as a species. We are together. From unity we can create lives of dignity, freedom, and peace.

To our fallen heroes over the many years of the struggle, let us bow our heads. They paid the ultimate price so that we can move closer and closer to true peace and true freedom.

Freedom for the people of Burma is near. The cost of that freedom is the only question. We are at a critical moment in history. The light of the *Dhamma* is your guide in this revolution. The light of your dignity and your commitment to nonviolence is your source of strength. Remember: The future of Burma rests in our power of forgiveness and our commitment to unity. We must reconcile even with our enemies. Trust that compassion is a more powerful weapon than guns.

AC: Thank you, Venerable Sir. May your revolution of the heart become one that inspires the hearts of many millions around the world. May we one day celebrate a liberated Burma.

Thank you, and thank you to the people of your country for their breathtaking courage, and for showing us all such a profound expression of spiritual revolution.

U Gambira at Traders Hotel, Min Yan Naing translating, April 2nd, 2013

> *"Some activists are very famous,*
> *but many people nobody knows."*

ALAN CLEMENTS: U Gambira, you were a very prominent monk during the Saffron Revolution. How long was the period from the start of the revolution to your arrest?

U GAMBIRA: After the Saffron Revolution, I was arrested on November 4th, 2007. At the time I'd escaped to Mandalay. My family were arrested sometime between the 10th and 15th of October.

AC: Why did you demonstrate?

UG: I demonstrated because I wanted to remove the military dictatorship from our country, because I wanted to transition to democracy by leading the monks.

AC: But the dictatorship didn't violate monasteries nor obstruct the monks, so why did you want to lead the monks to challenge dictatorship?

UG: I'm now a civilian, and act as a civilian of this country, but the monks should protect the people. I believe the monks have that responsibility, particularly as the regime affects the lives of all 60 million civilians in Burma. That's how I see it as a civilian, and that's why I feel responsible for this work. I started to organize things with the monks in 2003 through the Sangha Organization.

AC: Is it right to say that you were the leader of the Saffron Revolution? Or were there many leaders?

UG: In 2003/2004 I started to organize a small group. All of the states and divisions were organizing their own small groups. At the time I didn't try to mix the groups, but in 2006 I started to merge each group and make connections. In early 2007, between April and June, I was making connections between each group. At the same time, the military started to make arrests and to attack our organization. That's why, in September 2007, I organized all the groups, my organization and other alliance groups, and announced a statement that our organization is the All-Burma Monks Association, a small union of monks and other alliances through which we made an alliance group.

The reason I tried to make this alliance is that I was not satisfied with the restrictions that prevented us from mixing together. I wanted to show that alliances in our country can't be made through arms, that armed struggle is not safe and can't forge alliances. I wanted to show our solidarity, the solidarity of the monkhood, and started to make an alliance between the different groups. I was leading the Young Monks Union (Yangon) and I was organizing the Young Monks Union in both Upper and Lower Burma, and many other unions also. At midnight on September 7th, 2007, I started to create the All-Burma Monks Alliance. We wanted to start organizing other people. But this only included monks, not nuns. That's why I couldn't call it the All-Burma Sangha Alliance. I started to organize this on September 7th, 2007, and I wanted to include the nuns, who I see as our best friends, but they didn't come, they were too afraid. That's why they weren't included, and I couldn't organize an All-Burma Sangha Alliance.

AC: What was your life like in prison?

UG: They tortured me mentally and physically. I have mental trauma. Physically, I was handcuff and shackled.

AC: The whole time?

UG: The whole time. They bound my hands with a kind of string that cut my hands. They had to feed me so I could eat. The criminal prisoners had to assist me. My hands were tied behind my back, for months. And my ankles, the cuts were even deeper. And the mental trauma created many problems. That's why I tried to heal through *Dhamma*. But because I endured severe torture my trauma was so great.

AC: Do you have any regrets about what you've done?

UG: In truth, I feel bad about many things. During the revolution, some monks were killed. I have great regret for that. And after the amnesty, and my release from prison, the assistance for political prisoners was weak. The support structures for their care are weak. Some activists are famous, and many others unknown. They cannot get help from anyone or any organization.

Another thing is I can no longer organize my group, which makes me sad. If I could continue to organize during the current situation with these religious conflicts, I could lend help to these religious problems, these ethnic problems. I could assist and things may not be happening like they are. That also makes me sad.

In Myanmar, most of the people only lend their support to the famous activists. Many others suffer in bad situations. Their life is difficult. This is not only happening to former political prisoners, but to their families as well. The military government not only destroys the lives of activists, but they also destroy their families. And support structures are weak.

"You must have your own truth,
and be committed to it."

ALAN CLEMENTS: You're a well-known revolutionary; why is a nonviolent approach better than armed resistance?

U GAMBIRA: My beliefs concern nonviolence. But armed struggle is also important to this military dictatorship—that's one point. It's just that I have a strong belief in nonviolence. In my view, nonviolence is a win-win situation. That's the positive view. But another thing is that one must have goals, one's own objectives—you must have your own truth, and be committed to it, and act accordingly. Nonviolence also means that less people are fighting and killing each other. Nonviolence has less blood. But the nonviolent way takes time. And we need more resistance. We need stronger resistance. We support for the nonviolent way. It takes a strong person.

AC: If I may ask a difficult question: how did you practice *Dhamma* in prison when tortured?

UG: I practiced many techniques. Buddhist meditation. Meditation in the Christian way. I also practiced Tibetan Buddhism, the Mahayana way. Overall, I practiced while being tortured and after to remove the trauma from my torture.

AC: You practiced the *Dhamma* in prison in such a way to remove the torture, and to remove the trauma; if there's one lesson you've learned from your years in prison, what would that lesson be?

UG: The main lesson I learned is to be capable of love, of *mettā* and forgiveness, and to be confident about what you know, your wisdom. You must draw upon these things over and over again in prison.

AC: Have you any feelings of revenge?

UG: Establishing and promoting democracy in our country, to me that's my revenge. Freedom is the best revenge, not an eye for an eye. If you don't like this system, you need to develop democracy. Gandhi said if you take an eye for an eye the whole world will go blind, and there are things that are far more important than revenge, like establishing rule of law and transitioning to democracy. I don't want revenge, but, in the future, we need a better system of justice. I don't want revenge, but I worry that if we don't establish the rule of law and a better system of justice then a new dictatorship will arise in the future. That's why justice is so important. More so than revenge.

AC: Thank you for your bravery, your moral courage and conscience.

UG: Thank you for your work on behalf of our people.

PHOTOGRAPHIC
SECTION

1996, Rangoon. Aung San Suu Kyi, flanked by (NLD Chairman) U Tin Oo (left) and (former Vice-Chairman) U Kyi Maung (right) speaking to the public gathering on the nature of freedom and universal human rights.

Credit: Burma Project USA Archives

1996, Rangoon. The National League for Democracy's (NLD) Executive Committee Members.

Credit: Burma Project USA Archives

Aung San Suu Kyi giving a talk in front of her home in Rangoon in 1995 with "students for a democratic Burma" lined in front of her.

Credit: Burma Project USA Archives

1940s. General Aung San – Aung San Suu Kyi's father – speaking to the people of his country. Many years later his daughter Aung San Suu Kyi, continues his work for democracy and a unified nation stating: "After all it was my father who founded the Burmese army and I do have a sense of warmth towards the Burmese army."

1988, Rangoon. U Tin Oo, Aung San Suu Kyi and Burma's first Prime Minister U Nu.

Credit: Burma Project USA Archives

1989, Rangoon. Aung San Suu Kyi tirelessly encouraged the people of her country to stand in solidarity and to never let their fears prevent them from doing what they know is right.

Credit: Burma Project USA Archives

Aung San and Daw Khin Kyi (Aung San Suu Kyi's parents) on their wedding day, 1942.

Credit: Burma Project USA Archives.

Aung San Suu Kyi addressing members of her NLD party at their Yangon office on Martyrs' Day July 19, 2011. Martyrs' Day is a national holiday to commemorate Gen. Aung San (Aung San Suu Kyi's father) and seven other leaders of the pre-independence interim government, and one bodyguard —Thakin Mya, Ba Cho, Abdul Razak, Ba Win, Mahn Ba Khaing, Sao San Tun, Ohn Maung and Ko Htwe—all of whom were assassinated July 19, 1947.

Credit: Burma Project USA Archives Courtesy National League for Democracy

1995. Aung San Suu Kyi, at her home in Rangoon, where she spent 15 years in detention due to nonviolently calling for an end to military dictatorship and the rise of democracy.

Credit: Burma Project USA Archives

Burma is an ancient land of 55 million people, with over 130 ethnicities and languages.

Credit: Burma Project USA Archives
Courtesy of Henri Cartier-Bresson

Aung San Suu Kyi offers food to a procession of young Burmese Buddhist nuns on traditional alms rounds in Yangon.

Credit: Burma Project USA Archives Courtesy National League for Democracy

Co-founders of the NLD, former General U Tin Oo and Aung San Suu Kyi, in Yangon.

Credit: Burma Project USA Archives Courtesy National League for Democracy

Aung San Suu Kyi offers dana – a morning meal – to her meditation teacher and Dhamma (spiritual) advisor the late Venerable Sayadaw U Pandita at her home in Yangon.

Credit: Burma Project USA Archives Courtesy National League for Democracy

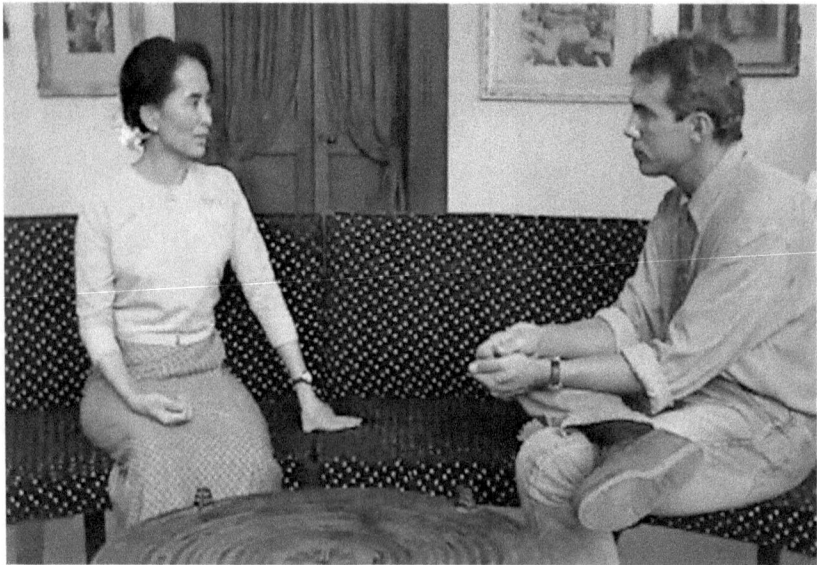

Aung San Suu Kyi and Alan Clements in conversation over a six month period at her Rangoon home in 1995 and 1996, for the book they co-authored titled, *The Voice of Hope*.

Credit: Burma Project USA Archives

January 4, 1996. Union Day Celebration at Aung San Suu Kyi's Rangoon home, attended by hundred's of courageous democracy activists who defied the military dictatorship and risked imprisonment in order to honor freedom and nationwide democracy and respect for universal human rights.

Credit: Burma Project USA Archives

As the basis of democracy Aung San Suu Kyi reminds the people of her country: "My priority is for people to understand that they have the power to change things themselves."

Credit: Burma Project USA Archives
Courtesy National League for
Democracy

353

The NLD flag of the dancing peacock – the party symbol adopted from the Myanmar Student Union flag – displayed in the stairway of Aung San Suu Kyi's home in Rangoon during her years of detention.

Credit: Burma Project USA Archives

The National League for Democracy's Executive Committee Members on Union Day January 4, 1996 when members of all ethnic groups throughout the country celebrated unity and freedom at Aung San Suu Kyi's Rangoon home.

Credit: Burma Project USA Archives

Alan Clements at the front gate of Aung San Suu Kyi's Yangon home at 54 University Avenue.

Credit: Burma Project USA Archives

From behind Aung San Suu Kyi's residence overlooking Inya Lake and one of the many luxury hotels that were under construction at that time (in 1995), and remained vacant or closed for years due to the international boycott of travel to Burma in support of Aung San Suu Kyi and the peoples' desire for freedom and democracy.

Credit: Burma Project USA Archives

August 8, 1988, Rangoon. A non-violent uprising takes place nationwide, led by university students, seeking the end of totalitarian rule and the emergence of a multi-party democracy.

Credit: Burma Project USA Archives Courtesy of Steve Lehman

August 8, 1988. Prodemocracy demonstrations in front of the US Embassy in Rangoon, seeking support for the nonviolent struggle that quickly gathered momentum and spread nationwide.

Credit: Burma Project USA Archives Courtesy of Steve Lehman

Pro-democracy student demonstrators August 1988.

Credit: Burma Project USA Archives Courtesy of Steve Lehman

"Human beings the world over need freedom and security that they may be able to realize their full potential." Aung San Suu Kyi

Credit: Burma Project USA Archives Courtesy of Steve Lehman

Student demonstrators carry a poster of Aung San, Burma's national hero, and Aung San Suu Kyi's father.

Credit: Burma Project USA Archives
Courtesy Alain Evrard

Freedom-loving students exhausted from growing up under the debilitating plague of military totalitarianism were at the forefront of the mass pro-democracy protests in August 1988.

Credit: Burma Project USA Archives Courtesy of Tom Lubin

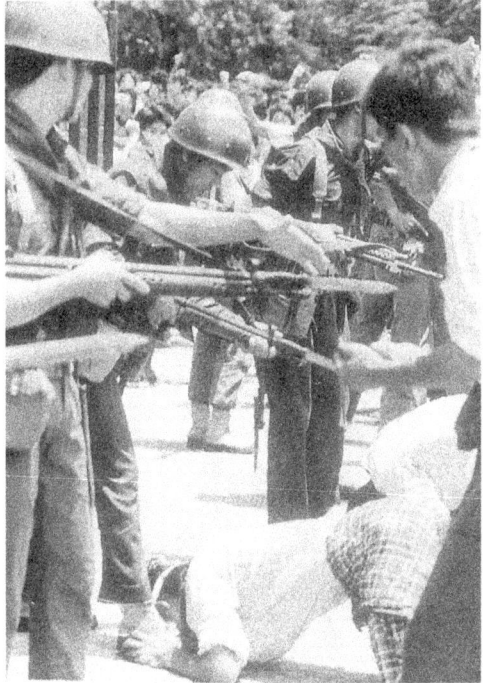

A student kissing the boot of a soldier blinded by his loyalty to the dictatorship during the prodemocracy demonstrations in Rangoon, August 1988.

Credit: Burma Project USA Archives
Courtesy Ryo Takeda

Soldiers loyal to the dictatorship poised to kill during the 8.8.88 uprising for democracy. Aung San Suu Kyi later states, "It is often in the name of cultural integrity as well as social stability and national security that democratic reforms based on human rights are [violently] resisted by authoritarian governments.

Credit: Burma Project USA Archives

Ne Win – Burma's maniacal dictator operating from behind the scenes – ordered his army to attack, and they did—ruthlessly shooting and bayoneting thousands of unarmed demonstrators over a two month period (August and September 1988).

Credit: Burma Project USA Archives Courtesy Alain Evrard

Aung San Suu Kyi speaking with the people shortly before her arrest and first six years of detention in 1989: "A revolution simply means great change, significant change, great change for the better, brought about through non-violent means.'

Credit: Burma Project USA Archives

Students on hunger strike demanding freedom, democracy and an end to one party rule, city center, Rangoon. 1988

Credit: Burma Project USA Archives Courtesy of Zunetta Liddell

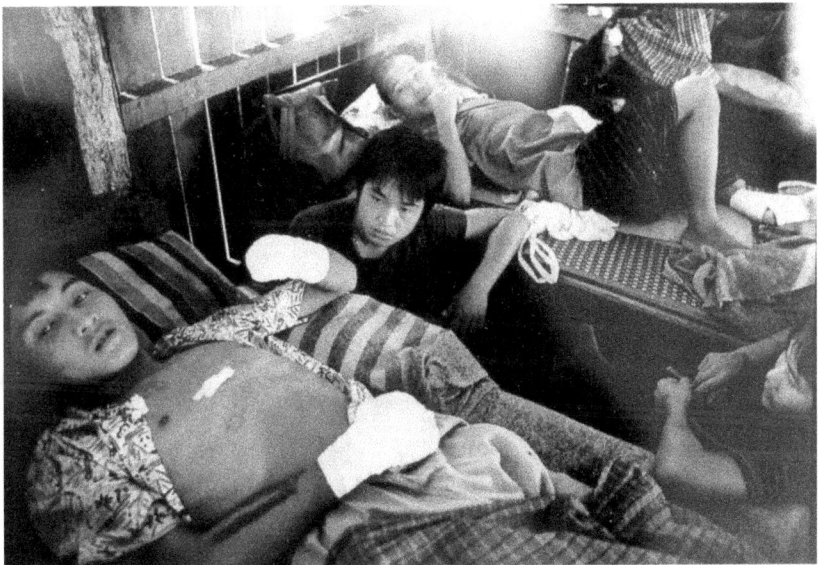

By mid-2008, nearly one million refugees had fled Burma into neighboring countries and make-shift camps along the Burmese border. During their journeys, refugees were often maimed by land mines, suffered and died from malaria and other diseases, and were enslaved by army sol-dier's loyal to the dictator.

Credit: Burma Project USA Archives

Aung San Suu Kyi was awarded the Nobel Peace Prize in 1991, while under house arrest, for her non-violent struggle for democracy and human rights. Her sons Alexander and Kim Aris and her husband Michael received the award on her behalf in Oslo.

Credit: Burma Project USA Archives Courtesy National League for Democracy

Aung San Suu Kyi, flanked by (NLD Chairman) U Tin Oo (left) and (former Vice-Chairman) U Kyi Maung (right) and Alan Clements (far left) on Union Day January 4, 1996 at Aung San Suu Kyi's home in Rangoon.

Credit: Burma Project USA Archives

1996, Rangoon. Alan Clements with Aung San Suu Kyi and U Tin Oo at her home during the making of their book of conversations, "The Voice of Hope." Every meeting was framed as "our first and potentially last," as she and colleagues were subject to rearrest at any moment. Aung San Suu Kyi states, "The only real prison is fear and the only real freedom is freedom from fear."

Credit: Burma Project USA Archives

The army ruthlessly attacked — killing thousands of unarmed demonstrators during August 1988.

Credit: Burma Project USA Archives Courtesy Alain Evrard

A victim of the street massacres in Rangoon August 1988. Thousands more were killed in the demonstrations, offering tragic wisdom to Aung San Suu Kyi's statement: "War is not the only arena where peace is done to death."

Credit: Burma Project USA Archives

Medics risked their own lives to rescue comrades dead and wounded in Rangoon during the '8.8.88' uprising.

Credit: Burma Project USA Archives

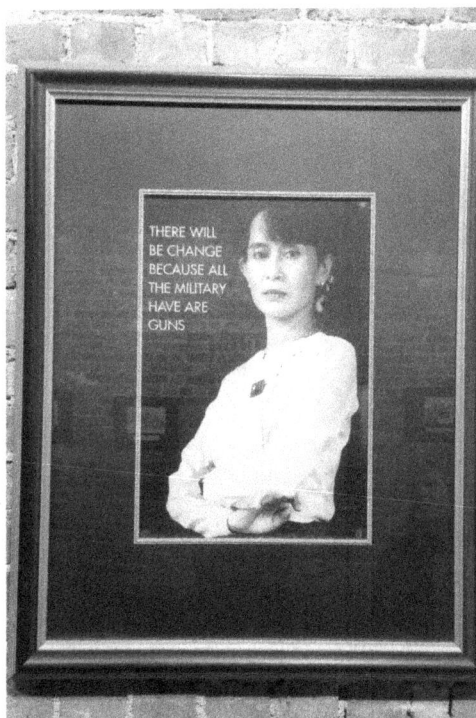

THERE WILL
BE CHANGE
BECAUSE ALL
THE MILITARY
HAVE ARE
GUNS

Aung San Suu Kyi spent 15 years under house arrest due to nonviolently calling for an end to dictatorship and the establishment of an open democratic society.

Credit: Burma Project USA Archives

Fleeing persecution by soldiers loyal to the dictatorship, Burmese students carry a wounded comrade across the Moei River into Thailand. 1988

Credit: Burma Project USA Archives
Courtesy Bettman Library

Aung San Suu Kyi writes, "My attitude to peace is based on the Burmese definition of peace – meaning, removing all the negative factors that destroy peace in this world. So peace does not mean just putting an end to violence or to war, but to all other factors that threaten peace, such as discrimination, inequality, and poverty."

Credit: Burma Project USA Archives

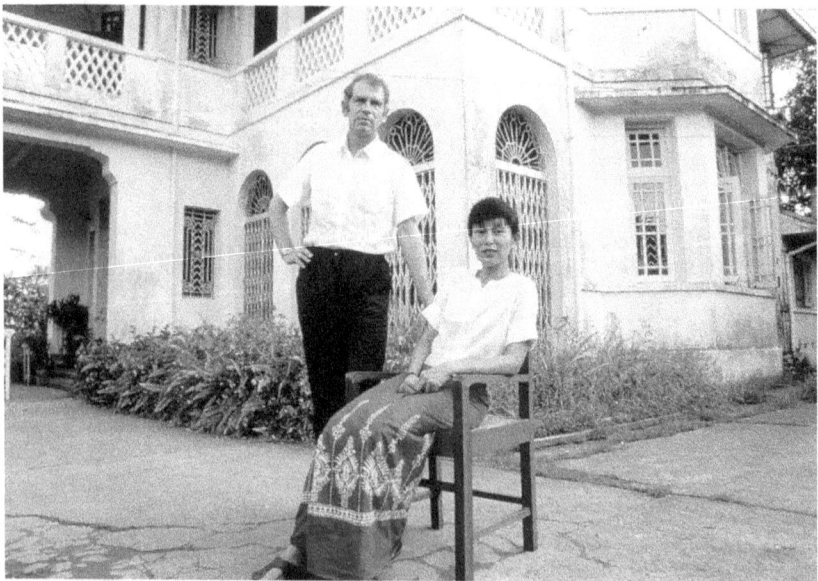

Aung San Suu Kyi and her (late) husband, Dr. Michael Aris, in front of their Rangoon home, 1996

Credit: Burma Project USA Archives

Any achievement that is based on widespread fear can hardly be a desirable one, and an 'order' that has for its basis the coercive apparatus of the State, and cannot exist without it, is more like a military occupation than civil rule... it was the duty of the...State to preserve...dharma and abhaya – righteousness and absence of fear. Law was something more than mere law, and order was the fear-

One of the many scrolls Aung San Suu Kyi wrote and posted on the walls of her downstairs foyer during her first six year period of house arrest. The passage is a quotation from the writings of Jawaharlal Nehru, India's first Prime Minister.

Credit: Burma Project USA Archives

On 27 January 1947, General Aung San (Aung San Suu Kyi's father) and the British Prime Minister Clement Attlee signed an agreement in London guaranteeing Burma's independence within a year; Aung San had been responsible for its negotiation. At a press conference during a stopover in Delhi, he stated that the Burmese wanted "complete independence" and not dominion status, and that they had "no inhibitions of any kind" about "contemplating a violent or non-violent struggle or both" in order to achieve it. He concluded that he hoped for the best, but was prepared for the worst.

Credit: Burma Project USA Archives

Aung San Suu Kyi paying homage to her father's memorial in Yangon. On July 19, 1947, a gang of armed paramilitaries of former Prime Minister U Saw broke into the Secretariat Building in downtown Rangoon during a meeting of the Executive Council and assassinated Aung San and six of his cabinet ministers, including his elder brother Ba Win, along with a cabinet secretary and a bodyguard.

Credit: Burma Project USA Archives Courtesy National League for Democracy

For his independence struggle from the British and uniting the country as a single entity, General Aung San is revered as the architect of modern Burma and a national hero.

Credit: Burma Project USA Archives

Ne Win was a Burmese politician and military commander who served as Prime Minister of Burma from 1958 to 1960 and 1962 to 1974. Ne Win was also Burma's military dictator during the Socialist Burma period of 1962 to 1988. His maniacal rule was characterized by political violence, isolationism, cronyism, xenophobia, totalitarianism, economic collapse, and is credited with turning Burma into one of the poorest and least developed countries in the world. Ne Win resigned in July 1988 in response to the 8888 Uprising that overthrew his party and was replaced by the military junta of the State Law and Order Restoration Council (SLORC) and with it a succession of military dictators.

Credit: Burma Project USA Archives

Aung San Suu Kyi's father General Aung San – regarded as Myanmar's independence hero – was a personal friend of Jawaharlal Nehru (November 14, 1889 – May 27, 1964 – an Indian independence activist, and subsequently, the first Prime Minister of India). Aung San Suu Kyi has said that many of the challenges faced by Gandhi and Nehru along the path to India's independence were the ones her movement had been facing over the course of its struggle.

Credit: Burma Project USA Archives

Daw Khin Kyi, wife of General Aung San, who was assassinated when their daughter Aung San Suu Kyi was two years old, served as her political and cultural mentor. She was appointed Burmese ambassador to India and Nepal in 1960, and Aung San Suu Kyi followed her there. She studied in the Convent of Jesus and Mary School in New Delhi, and graduated from Lady Shri Ram College, a constituent college of the University of Delhi, with a degree in politics in 1964.

Credit: Burma Project USA Archives

A family photo in the 1940s of General Aung San and his wife Daw Khin Kyi – Aung San Suu Kyi's father and mother, along with her brothers, in Rangoon.

Credit: Burma Project USA Archives

With her sons, Alexander (left) and Kim, May 1993—a rare photo of Aung San Suu Kyi while under house arrest.

Credit: Burma Project USA Archives

Aung San Suu Kyi, flanked by (NLD Chairman) U Tin Oo seated (left) and (former Vice-Chairman) U Kyi Maung (seated right). 1996

Credit: Burma Project USA Archive

On 19 September 1964 U Tin Oo became Commander of Central Regional Military Command. He was then promoted to the rank of Brigadier General and became Deputy Chief of Staff of the Tatmadaw (military) on April 20, 1972. On March 8, 1974 he was promoted to the rank of General and became Commander in Chief of the Tatmadaw. After his forced retirement in 1976, he was accused of high treason against the armed forces, the party (BSPP) and the state. He was subsequently arrested and tried for the alleged withholding of information concerning a failed coup-d'état against General Ne Win. On January 11, 1977, he was sentenced to his first 7 of 19 years imprisonment (and house arrest). He is co-founder of the NLD.

Credit: Burma Project USA Archive

Aung San Suu Kyi, at about seven years of age.

Credit: Burma Project USA Archives

Burma's Tatmadaw on parade – a 400,000 strong army started by Aung San Suu Kyi's father, Aung San. "The democracy process provides for political and social change without violence," she states.

Credit: Burma Project USA Archives

Aung San Suu Kyi with the international media during a photo session at her residence a few days after her release from house arrest in July 1995.

Credit: Burma Project USA Archives Courtesy Yamamoto Munesuke

(former) Dictator (now retired) General Than Shwe and other generals. Aung San Suu Kyi states, "My opinion is the greatest reward that any government could get is the approval of the people. If the people are happy and the people are at peace and the government has done something for them, that's the greatest reward I think any government could hope for.

Credit: Burma Project USA

Chained "forced laborers" in Burma, estimated to be in the hundreds of thousands, used by the military regime to build bridges, roads, dams, and tourist attractions.

Credit: Burma Project USA Archives
Courtesy Peter Conrad

Former General and Dictator Than Shwe and his wife Daw Khaing Khaing paying their respects to a Buddhist shrine somewhere near their mansion in the capital, where they are protected by a round-the-clock contingent of armed guards.

Credit: Burma Project USA

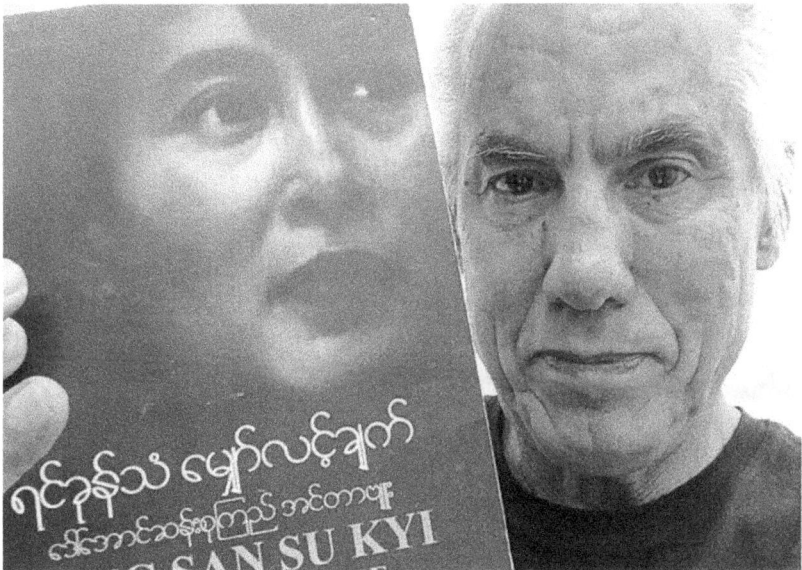

2012 Yangon. Alan Clements, co-author with Aung San Suu Kyi of the book, *The Voice of Hope*, with a Burmese copy of the book in a Yangon bookstore, that for the previous 15 years was an imprisonable crime to have in one's possession.

Credit: Burma Project USA

Aung San Suu Kyi outside her front gate on the day of her release from house arrest, July 10, 1995.

Credit: Burma Project USA Archives Courtesy Stuart Isett

Aung San Suu Kyi with U Kyi Maung at her Rangoon residence, 1995.

Credit: Burma Project USA Archives

Aung San Suu Kyi in discussion with U Win Htein, one of her longest most respected friends and confidants during her decades in Burma, and one of the principle leaders of Burma's non-violent struggle for democracy.

Credit: Burma Project USA Archives

In 1995 and 1996, crowds defied the dictatorship's threat of imprisonment and gathered at Aung San Suu Kyi's gate on weekends to listen to her talks on democracy – to rise up in solidarity for the ongoing struggle for freedom.

Credit: Burma Project USA Archives

The pubic pro-democracy gatherings were stopped by Burma's military dictatorship in late 1996 and Aung San Suu Kyi was placed back under house arrest, and almost all of her NLD colleagues were re-imprisoned.

Credit: Burma Project USA Archives

1989 Rangoon. Aung San Suu Kyi with U Par Lay – Burma's pree-minent spoken word satirist and comedian after his performance on Independence Day at Aung San Suu Kyi's compound. He was rearrested days later and sentenced to 7 years in prison with hard labor (in addi-tion to the six years he had already spent in prison, also with hard labor, chained, pounding rocks 20 hours a day).

Credit: Burma Project USA Archives
Courtesy National League for Democracy

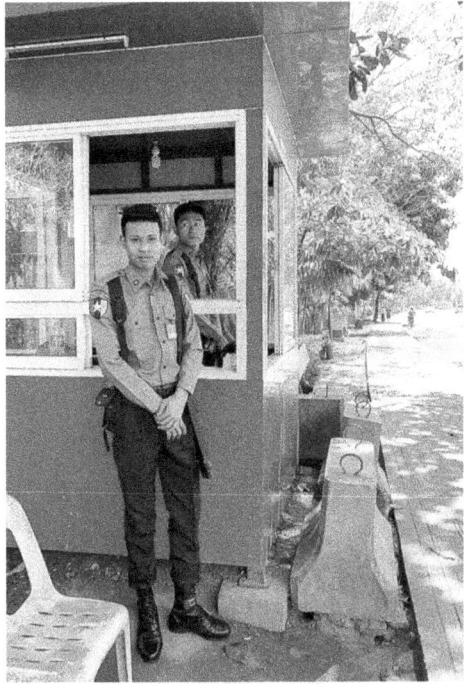

A police guard placed outside Aung San Suu Kyi's home at 54 University Avenue, Yangon, Myanmar.

Credit: Burma Project USA Archives

Rangoon University student leader at the time of the 8.8.88 Uprising Min Ko Naing, at a press conference for "88 Generation" in Yangon, April 2012. Having spent 19 years in prison, he is one of Burma's great revolutionary democracy dissidents and is the recipient of numerous human rights awards. The New York Times has described him as Burma's "most influential opposition figure after Daw Aung San Suu Kyi."

Credit: Burma Project USA Archives Courtesy of Kirsten Duell

Alan Clements interviewing Mon Mon Myat, a leading Burmese author, intellectual and dissident. She is cofounder of the prestigious International Human Rights and Human Dignity Film Festival.

Credit: Burma Project USA Archives

Alan Clements in conversation with U Win Htein discussing his 20 years as a prisoner of conscience, and on becoming an honorable member of parliament and a tireless voice for unity and national reconciliation.

Credit: Burma Project USA Archives

On September 23, 2008, U Win Tin (March 12, 1929 – April 21, 2014) is released after 19 years in prison in solitary confinement. As a prominent journalist and politician he co-founded the National League for Democracy (NLD). After his release from prison he refused to remove his blue prison-issued shirt as an act of conscience to remain in solidarity with the remaining political prisoners in Burma until they too were freed.

Credit: Burma Project USA Archive Courtesy National League for Democracy

November 13, 2010. Aung San Suu Kyi appears at her front gate after being released from house arrest by Burma's military dictator Than Shwe. She vowed to carry on the nonviolent struggle for democracy.

Credit: Burma Project USA Archives Courtesy National League for Democracy

U Thant was a Burmese diplomat and the third Secretary-General of the United Nations from 1961 to 1971. "As a devout Buddhist he said, "I was trained to be tolerant of everything except intolerance." He was the recipient of the Jawaharlal Nehru Award for International Understanding.

Credit: Burma Project USA Archives Courtesy U Thant org

Thakin Nu, a leading Burmese statesman and political figure who was the first Prime Minister of Burma under the provisions of the 1947 Constitution of the Union of Burma, from January 4, 1948 to June 12, 1956, again from February 28, 1957 to October 28, 1958, and finally from April 4, 1960 to March 2, 1962.

Daw Than Than Nu, daughter of Thakin Nu, She is the founder and director of the philanthropic organization – U Nu Daw Mya Ni Foundation (her beloved parents).

Credit: Burma Project USA Archives

NLD co-founder and Chairman U Tin Oo, honoring his beloved revolutionary colleague and friend, U Win Tin, also co-founder of the National League for Democracy, on the anniversary of his passing away April 21, 2014

Credit: Burma Project USA Archives Courtesy National League for Democracy

The second major crackdown came in September and October 2007, when Burma's army, under the dictator, General Than Shwe, brutally and mercilessly crushed the Buddhist monk-led pro-democracy Saffron Revolution.

Credit: Burma Project USA Archives

One of the regime's numerous "relocation camps," forced on people living in areas of strong support for Aung San Suu Kyi and the democracy movement. A New York Times article titled, "Burma: Horror Story of Mass Re locations," from March 20, 1990, stated "at least 500,000 Burmese are being forced to move from [most major] cities to new, ill-prepared outlying towns where malaria and hepatitis are rampant."

Credit: Burma Project USA Archives

Aung San Suu Kyi showing her respect (in a traditional Burmese Buddhist manner) to monks she invited to her home in 1996 to offer them a pre-noon meal.

Credit: Burma Project USA Archives

Dictator General Than Shwe on parade. Aung San Kyi and the government have consistently sought national reconciliation. In her words, "a regime is made up of people, so I do put faces to regimes and governments, [and in so doing] I feel that all human beings have the right to be given the benefit of the doubt, and they also have to be given the right to try to redeem themselves if they so wish.

Credit: Burma Project USA Archives

1995. Alan Clements with U Aung Ko, the male lead actor in John Boorman's celebrated feature film, Beyond Rangoon, depicting Burma's nonviolent struggle for freedom, based in part, on Alan's ground breaking book,"Burma: The Next Killing Fields?," with a foreword by the Dalai Lama. Alan was the script revisionist and principle advisor on the film.

Credit: Burma Project USA Archives

Chairman of the National League for Democracy (NLD), U Tin Oo, who has spent a total of eleven years in solitary confinement and five years under house arrest, with Alan Clements.

Credit: Burma Project USA Archives

Aung San Suu Kyi: "We want to empower our people; we want to strengthen them; we want to provide them with the kind of qualifications that will enable them to build up their own country themselves."

Credit: Burma Project USA Archives Courtesy National League for Democracy

Aung San Suu Kyi on the 25th anniversary of the nationwide democracy uprising of August 8, 1988, honoring the courageous leaders (Min Ko Naing, Ko Ko Gyi and so many others) along with the hundreds of thousands additional dissidents, as well as the 1000's killed by the unconscionable military crackdown that tried to end it.

Credit: Burma Project USA Archives Courtesy National League for Democracy

November 18, 2012. US President Obama and Secretary of State Hillary Clinton met with Aung San Suu Kyi at her home in Yangon, after being under house arrest for the better part of two decades, offering their dedicated support for her peoples unfinished non-violent struggle for democracy and human rights.

Credit: Burma Project USA Archives Courtesy National League for Democracy

Spiritual leader of Tibet and fellow Nobel Peace laureate, the Dalai Lama greets Aung San Suu Kyi, as reported in the Tibet Post International November 16, 2015.

Credit: Burma Project USA Archives Courtesy Tibet Post International

March 2020. The once banned and criminalized Headquarters of the National League for Democracy (NLD) at 97B West Shwegondine Road, Bahan Township, Yangon, Myanmar.

Credit: Burma Project USA Archives

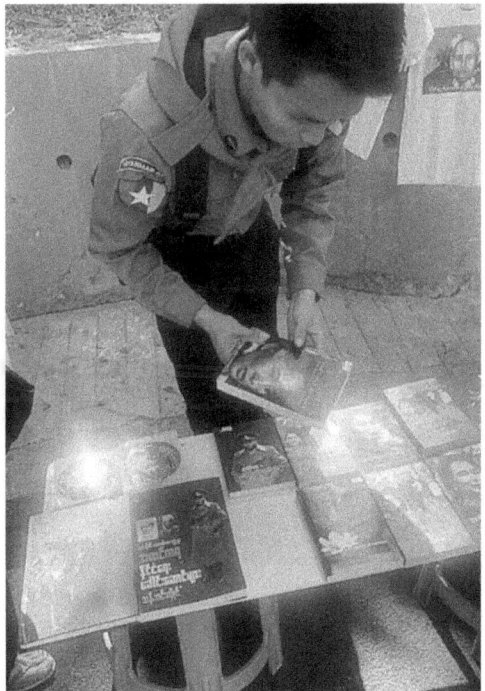

February 2020, Yangon. A policeman looks at Alan Clements' book of conversations with Aung San Suu Kyi (*The Voice of Hope*) previously banned in Burma since 1996 and an imprisonable crime if caught with a copy.

Credit: Burma Project USA Archives

Aung San Suu Kyi meeting Senior General Min Aung Hlaing, who has frequently stated in her speeches "that if you want to bring an end to long-standing conflict, you have to be prepared to compromise." This is the heart, so to speak, of her government's long standing desire of achieving national reconciliation.

Credit: Burma Project USA Archives
Courtesy National League for Democracy

The famed Shwedagon Pagoda in Yangon, over 300 feet high and nearly 2500 years old, is the unifying symbol of harmlessness and peace among Burmese Buddhists both inside Burma and worldwide.

Credit: Burma Project USA Archives

Aung San Suu Kyi states: "The struggle for democracy and human rights in Burma is a struggle for life and dignity. It is a struggle that encompasses our political, social and economic aspirations."

Credit: Burma Project USA Archives

Aung San Suu Kyi paying her respects to Buddhist monks on the anniversary of the August 8, 1988 Uprising.

Credit: Burma Project USA Archives Courtesy National League for Democracy

Aung San Suu Kyi paying her respects to her slain father at The Martyrs' Mausoleum in Yangon, located near the northern gate of Shwedagon Pagoda. The mausoleum is dedicated to Aung San and other leaders of the pre-independence interim government, all of whom were assassinated on July 19, 1947 and now designated as Martyrs' Day, a highly revered public holiday in Myanmar.

Credit: Burma Project USA Archives Courtesy National League for Democracy

2012. Alan Clements with his long time dear friend, and NLD parliament member, U Win Htein, in his office in Meiktila, central Burma.

Credit: Burma Project USA Archives

Aung San Suu Kyi states: "I think I should be active politically. Because I look upon myself as a politician. That's not a dirty work you know. Some people think that there are something wrong with politicians. Of course, something is wrong with some politicians."

Credit: Burma Project USA Archives Courtesy National League for Democracy

Venerable Sayadaw U Pandita and his long time attendant and translator, U Khin Hlaing in March 2016 during one of nine nights of conversations with Alan Clements (his long time student and friend). This was the Venerable Sayadaw's final Dhamma teachings for a world audience before he passed away a few weeks later.

Credit: Burma Project USA Archives

September 2012, San Francisco, CA. Aung San Suu Kyi is honored with the Vaclav Havel Award for Creative Dissent, with Alan Clements, his daughter Sahra Bella Clements Earl, and her Mother, Lorinda Earl. This was the first time Alan and Aung San Suu Kyi had spoken in 17 years, after he was banned from Burma in 1996 and she was placed back under detention.

Credit: Burma Project USA Archives

Deep in Karen State in 1990 where Burma's army had a scorched earth take no prisoner alive policy.

Credit: Burma Project USA Archives

The many thousands of Burmese students who fled the country's major cities after the 1988 uprisings were brutally crushed by the military regime, gathered in jungle enclaves along the Thai border where they formed the All Burma Students Democratic Front (ABSDF). The flag is the symbol of Burma's struggle for freedom.

Credit: Burma Project USA Archives

Alan Clements travelling the Moei River on the Thai Burma border after two months in Mannerplaw and surrounding areas in 1990, that resulted in the seminal book, Burma: The Next Killing Fields?

Credit: Burma Project USA Archives

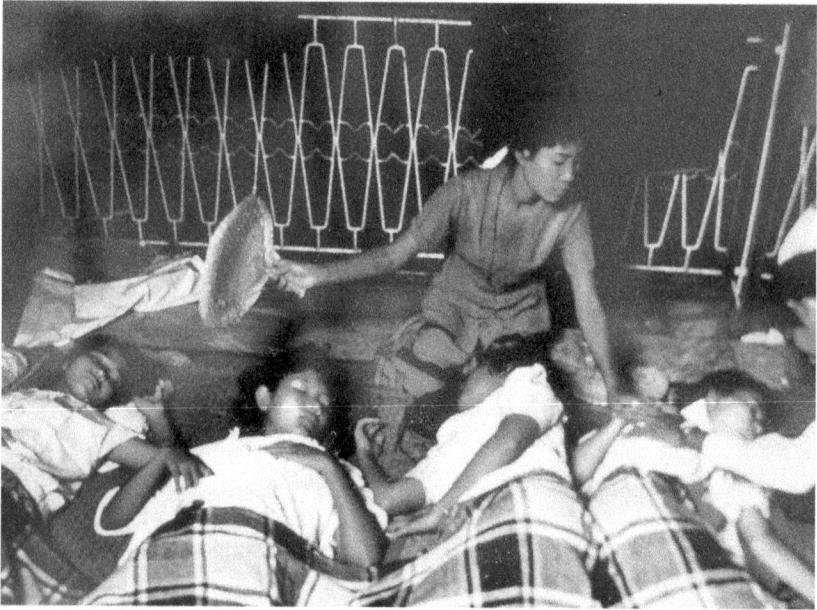

Burmese students suffering from typhoid and malaria in a refugee camp along the Thai border, 1990.

Credit: Burma Project USA Archives

Alan Clements with Tibet's spiritual leader, the Dalai Lama, who wrote a forward to his book, Burma: The Next Killing Fields? in 1990.

Credit: Burma Project USA Archives

Alan Clements – co-author of The Voice of Hope: Conversations with Aung San Suu Kyi – upon returning to Paris after meeting with Aung San Suu Kyi for six months in Burma, 1996.

Credit: Burma Project USA Archives

Mahāsī Sayādaw U Sobhana (July 29, 1904 – August 14, 1982) was a Burmese Theravada Buddhist monk and meditation master who is widely considered to be the father of the modern day mass lay mindfulness meditation movement that began at his Rangoon Mahasi Sasana Yeiktha Meditation Center (MSY) in 1947 under the invitation of Burma's first Prime Minister U Nu and Sir U Thwin. There are now 660 branch centers in Burma and over 100 more worldwide. Many leading politicians and government leaders over the decades have practiced meditation at MSY or with teachers trained at the center. Mahāsī Sayādaw was the chief questioner and final editor at the Sixth Great Buddhist Council in Yangon Burma in 1954.

Credit: Burma Project USA Archives

1979. Alan Clements, one of the first Westerners to ordain as a Buddhist monk under the guidance of the Venerable Mahasi Sayadaw at the Mahasi Sasana Yeiktha Meditation Center in Rangoon, Burma, where he lived and trained in vipassana (insight) meditation and Buddhist psychology for several years.

Credit: Burma Project USA Archives

Soon after the Venerable Mahasi Sayadaw passed away on August 14, 1982, Venerable Sayadaw U Pandita (on the right) became the Ovadacariya Nayaka (the Head Monk and main teacher) at the Mahasi Meditation Center Rangoon. Here he is seen paying his final respects to Mahasi Sayadaw, along with U Aggacitta (left) – Sayadaw U Pandita's student and main English translator at the time.

Credit: Burma Project USA Archives

At the Venerable Mahasi Sayadaw funeral procession in Rangoon, August 1982.

Credit: Burma Project USA Archives

After being expelled from Burma several times by the dictator Ne Win, Alan Clements disrobed as a Buddhist monk and left the monastic life in 1984 and remained under the guidance of Sayadaw U Pandita, who became his teacher after Mahasi Sayadaw passed away.

Credit: Burma Project USA Archives

Venerable Sayadaw U Pandita, Yangon. Aung San Suu Kyi writes, "My husband gave me a copy of Sayadaw U Pandita's book (while under house arrest), In this Very Life, the Liberation Teachings of the Buddha. "By studying this book carefully, I learned how to overcome difficulties of meditation and to realize its benefits...and how it increased mindfulness in every day life."

Credit: Burma Project USA Archives

December 2019. Denying that Myanmar had genocidal intent in its treatment of the Rohingya people, Aung San Suu Kyi urged the International Court of Justice in The Hague to let her country's justice system run its course. "Can there be genocidal intent on the part of a state that actively investigates, prosecutes and punishes soldiers and officers who are accused of wrong-doing?" she asked at the world court, while presenting her opening statement on the second day of public hearings related to Gambia's lawsuit alleging that Myanmar had breached the 1948 Convention on the Prevention and Punishment of the Crime of Genocide.

Credit: Burma Project USA Archives Courtesy National League for Democracy

By late 2017, an estimated 650,000 Rohingya refugees from Rakhine, Myanmar, had crossed the border into Bangladesh, fleeing the persecution of Burma's army, in large part, provoked by ARSA – the Islamic terrorist group. According to Amnesty International May 22, 2018 "Myanmar: New evidence reveals Rohingya armed group massacred scores in Rakhine State" "[ARSA] A Rohingya armed group brandishing guns and swords is responsible for at least one, and potentially a second, massacre of up to 99 Hindu women, men, and children as well as additional unlawful killings and abductions of Hindu villagers in August 2017," Amnesty International revealed today after carrying out a detailed investigation inside Myanmar's Rakhine State. The plight of the Rohingya refugees is a humanitarian tragedy.

Credit: Burma Project USA Archives Courtesy National League for Democracy

In conjunction with the Buddha Sasana Nuggaha Organization (BSNO) of Myanmar, the Buddha Sasana Foundation of America, co-founded by Alan Clements and Dr Ingrid Jordt in 1984, and co-directed by Dr Jeannine Davies, organize an annual Wisdom of Mindfulness ten day meditation retreat at the Mahasi Sasana Yeiktha (MSY) meditation center for English speaking yogis worldwide to come to Myanmar to practice mindfulness at this renowned center and in context to the sacred country of Burma.

Credit: Burma Project USA Archives

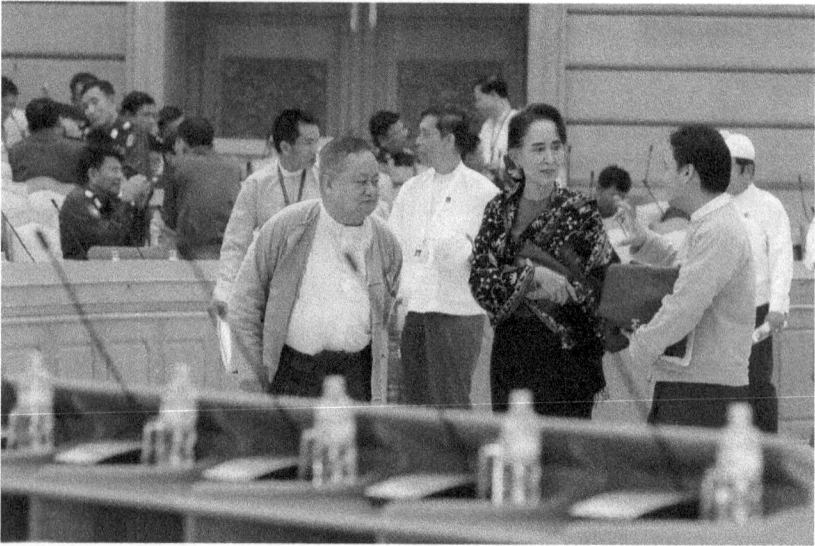

Aung San Suu Kyi in Parliament in Naypyidaw – the capital of Myanmar – with long standing advisor U Win Htein (left) and Zeya Thaw (former hip hop singer in the band ACID and co-founder of the activist group Generation Wave) and NLD Parliament member and her assistant.

Credit: Burma Project USA Archives Courtesy National League for Democracy

March 2020. Burma's parliament rejects a constitutional amendment to reduce military political power. The NLD, headed by State Counsellor Aung San Suu Kyi, was unsuccessful in reducing the role of the military in Myanmar's parliament. The NLD proposed amendments to the 2008 (undemocratic) constitution, which requires more than 75% of members of parliament to pass constitutional amendments while giving the military 25 % of the seats under Article 436. This allows the military to veto any proposed constitutional amendments. Senior General Min Aung Hlaing of the military opposition claims that the military "has … taken those seats as a measure to ensure national stability" while the country transitions into democracy.

Credit: Burma Project USA Archives Courtesy National League for Democracy

Senior General Min Aung Hlaing on Armed Forces Day. Aung San Suu Kyi has repeatedly called for dialogue and reconciliation. "I don't want to see the military failing. I want to see the military rising to dignified heights of professionalism and true patriotism."

Credit: Burma Project USA Archives

Aung San Suu Kyi with the late Venerable Sayadaw U Pandita at Panditarama – his monastery and meditation center in Bahan, Golden Valley, Yangon, shortly before his passing away in April 2016.

Credit: Burma Project USA Archives

Buddhist nuns paying homage to their Dhamma teacher the late Venerable Sayadaw U Pandita at Panditarama Meditation Center in Yangon. He was the meditation teacher to tens of thousands of yogis from numerous countries around the world, as well as spiritual advisor to Aung San Suu Kyi.

Credit: Burma Project USA Archives Courtesy of Panditarama Meditation Center Yangon Myanmar

NLD Chairman U Tin Oo, paying his final respects to his long time spiritual advisor and meditation teacher, Venerable Sayadaw U Pandita, days after the 95 year old Elder Buddhist monk passed away in Burma on April 16, 2016.

Credit: Burma Project USA Archives Courtesy of Panditarama Meditation Center Yangon Myanmar

March 2020, Yangon. Nayaka (senior most) Member of the NLD, Saya U Tin Oo, 93 years old, who, despite having had a stroke and unable to speak, understands fully everything that is said. He's one of the most respected revolutionary heroes in the history of modern Burma.

Credit: Burma Project USA Archives

About Alan Clements

Boston born Alan Clements, after dropping out of the University of Virginia in his second year, went to the East and become one of the first Westerners to ordain as a Buddhist monk in Myanmar (formerly known as Burma). He lived in Yangon (formerly Rangoon) at the Mahasi Sasana Yeiktha (MSY) Mindfulness Meditation Centre for nearly four years, training in both the practice and teaching of Satipatthana Vipassana (insight) meditation and Buddhist psychology (Abhidhamma), under the guidance of his preceptor the Venerable Mahasi Sayadaw, and his successor Sayadaw U Pandita.

In 1984, forced to leave the country by Burma's dictator Ne Win, with no reason given, Clements returned to the West and through invitation, lectured widely on the "wisdom of mindfulness," in addition to leading numerous mindfulness-based meditation retreats and trainings throughout the US, Australia, and Canada, including assisting a three month mindfulness teacher training with Sayadaw U Pandita, at the Insight Meditation Society (IMS), in Massachusetts.

In 1988, Alan integrated into his classical Buddhist training an awareness that included universal human rights, social injustices, environmental sanity, political activism, the study of propaganda and mind control in both democratic and totalitarian societies, and the preciousness of everyday freedom. His efforts working on behalf of oppressed peoples led a former director of Amnesty International to call Alan "one of the most important and compelling voices of our times."

As an investigative journalist Alan has lived in some of the most highly volatile areas of the world. In the jungles of Burma, in 1990, he was one of the first eye-witnesses to document the mass oppression of ethnic minorities by Burma's military, which resulted in his first book, "Burma: The Next Killing Fields?" (with a foreword by the Dalai Lama).

Shortly thereafter, Alan was invited to the former-Yugoslavia by a senior officer for the United Nations, where, based in Zagreb during the final year of the war, he wrote the film "Burning" while consulting with

NGO's and the United Nation's on the "vital role of consciousness in understanding human rights, freedom, and peace."

In 1995, a French publisher asked Alan to attempt reentering Burma for the purpose of meeting Aung San Suu Kyi, the leader of her country's pro-democracy movement and the recipient of the Nobel Peace Prize in 1991. Just released after six years of incarceration, Alan invited Aung San Suu Kyi to tell her courageous story to the world, thus illuminating the philosophical and spiritual underpinnings of Burma's nonviolent struggle for freedom, known as a "revolution of the spirit."

The transcripts of their five months of conversations were smuggled out of the country and became the book "The Voice of Hope." Translated into numerous languages, *The Voice of Hope* offers insight into the nature of totalitarianism, freedom and nonviolent revolution. Said the London Observer: "Clements is the perfect interlocutor....whatever the future of Burma, a possible future for politics itself is illuminated by these conversations."

Clements is also the co-author with (New York Times bestselling author) Leslie Kean and a contributing photographer to "Burma's Revolution of the Spirit" Aperture, NY) – a large format photographic tribute to Burma's nonviolent struggle for democracy, with a foreword by the Dalai Lama and essays by eight Nobel Peace laureates. In addition, Clements was the script revisionist and principal adviser for *Beyond Rangoon* (Castle Rock Entertainment), a feature film depicting Burma's struggle for freedom, directed by John Boorman.

In 1999, Alan founded World Dharma, a nonsectarian, trans-traditional organization of self-styled seekers, artists, rebels, writers, scholars, journalists, and activists dedicated to a trans-religious, independent approach to personal and planetary transformation through the integration of global human rights, meditation and the experiential study of consciousness, with one's life expression through the arts, media, activism, and service.

In 2002 Alan wrote "Instinct for Freedom – Finding Liberation Through Living" (New World Library & World Dharma Publications), a memoir about his years in Burma that chronicles his mindfulness meditation training and dharma-informed activism, while illuminating the framework of the World Dharma vision. In 2003 he co-founded with his colleague, Dr. Jeannine Davies, the World Dharma Online Institute (WDOI) that offers an evolving video master course based on his life's work.

Instinct for Freedom was nominated for the best spiritual teaching/ memoir by the National Spiritual Booksellers Association in 2003 and has been translated into numerous languages.

Alan's two most recent books, "Wisdom the for the World –

The Requisites or Reconciliation: Alan Clements in Conversation with Venerable Sayadaw U Pandita of Burma," and "A Future to Believe In – 108 Reflections on the Art and Activism of Freedom," inspired by and dedicated to his daughter Sahra, has received distinguished praise from numerous leaders and activists, including Dr. Helen Caldicott, Joanna Macy, Dr. Vandana Shiva, Bill McKibben, Paul Hawkin, and Derrick Jensen (the environmental poet laureate) who wrote:

> "This culture is killing the planet. If we are to have
> any future at all, we must unlearn everything the culture
> has taught us and begin to listen to the planet, to listen
> to life – the core intelligence of nature and the human
> heart. This book not only helps us with the unlearning
> process – the greatest challenge humankind has ever
> faced – it provides the essential wisdom, the spiritual in-
> telligence, to open ourselves to finally start to hear."

In addition, Alan has presented to such organizations as Mikhail Gorbachev's State of The World Forum, The Soros Foundation, United Nations Association of San Francisco, the universities of California, Toronto, Sydney, and many others, including a keynote address at the John Ford Theater for Amnesty International's 30th year anniversary. More recently, Alan was a presenter at the Touché Global Consciousness Conference 2019 in Bali.

In conjunction with the Buddha Sasana Nuggaha Organization (BSNO) of Myanmar and the Center's Nayaka Sayadaws (Senior Meditation Teachers), Alan conducts with Dr Ingrid Jordt and Dr Jeannine Davies an annual Ten Day Wisdom of Mindfulness Retreat for English speaking participants at the Mahasi Sasana Yeiktha Yangon (MSY), Myanmar. For more information, please visit: AlanClements.com or WorldDharma.com

ALSO BY ALAN CLEMENTS

A Future to Believe In
108 Reflections on the Art and Activism of Freedom

"This book is the music of wisdom, a dance with the finest places of the human heart. It is also like a walk with your favorite friends, mentors and teachers as they point out the beauties of the journey. You will want to keep this timeless treasure within reach, so you can open it to any page, and let a paragraph or a line ignite you again to the truth of your own being."

—JOANNA MACY, AUTHOR OF *WORLD AS LOVER, WORLD AS SELF*

"Distilling the essence of world religions, cultures, politics, and spiritual traditions, Alan Clements' magnificent, timely book provides a courageous and intelligent compass personifying our aspirations for freedom and wisdom, and in so doing, offers insights on how to actively shape a future that gives life hope. With our planet in peril, it is imperative that we act now to provide a secure future for our children and future generations. Make this book your guide, mentor and friend."

—DR HELEN CALDICOTT, AUTHOR OF *NUCLEAR POWER IS NOT THE ANSWER* AND *IF YOU LOVE THIS PLANET*; FOUNDING PRESIDENT PHYSICIANS FOR SOCIAL RESPONSIBILITY

"In this radiant book is a new consciousness."

—LOWRY BURGESS, ARTIST, PROFESSOR, CREATOR OF THE FIRST OFFICIAL NON-SCIENTIFIC ART PAYLOAD TAKEN INTO OUTER SPACE BY NASA IN 1989

"*A Future to Believe In* is a treasure, not a mere book."

—PAUL HAWKEN, AUTHOR OF *BLESSED UNREST*

"This transformational treasure is more relevant now than ever before, and perhaps the most important book available to face the global crisis head on and transform our lives and the planet for the better. Please join the revolution, and share word of this masterpiece of 'mindful intelligence' and compassion with the world."

—MARCIA JACOBS - PSYCHOTHERAPIST SPECIALIZING IN WORK WITH VICTIMS OF WAR, RAPE AND TRAUMA. A SENIOR STAFF MEMBER OF THE UN AND OTHER HUMANITARIAN AGENCIES FROM 1993 - 2005, WORKING WITH REFUGEES AND OTHER WAR-TRAUMATIZED POPULATIONS

"At a time when the contemporary spiritual landscape has become dangerously gentrified and domesticated, Alan Clements restores us to our senses — wild and elemental. He summons the voices of those who, along side him, have not traded their souls for the market-driven need to be tame or acceptable, and points us to the wilderness of true, engaged, fiercely authentic awakening. This is why we are alive — to set freedom free, in ourselves and for others, in every aspect of our lives from the most mundane daily task, to the most profound political act."

—KELLY WENDORF, AUTHOR AND EDITOR *STORIES OF BELONGING*

"*A Future To Believe In* provides us with a standing wave of insight, a perpetually central pivot pertaining eminently to private and political spheres, inextricable, afterall. This book should be made mandatory world-wide for all heads of state."

—LISSA WOLSAK, AUTHOR OF *IN DEFENSE OF BEING, SQUEEZED LIGHT* AND *PEN CHANTS*

"We live in times that spread greed, violence, fear and hopelessness. We live in times when consumerism enslaves us while offering pseudo-freedom. Alan Clements labor of love, "A Future to Believe In: A Guide to Revolution, Environmental Sanity, and the Universal Right to Be Free," brings us reflections that inspire us to be free and fearless."

—DR. VANDANA SHIVA, AUTHOR OF, *EARTH DEMOCRACY; JUSTICE, SUSTAINABILITY, AND PEACE, SOIL, NOT OIL, AND STAYING ALIVE*

Instinct for Freedom: Finding Liberation Through

"During an era when a spate of shallow, narcissistic fiction has found a niche as 'sacred literature' Alan's work is a wonderful relief and reminder that the heart of spirituality still is, and will always be, compassion."

—BO LOZOFF, FOUNDER OF THE PRISON ASHRAM PROJECT AND HUMAN KINDNESS FOUNDATION AND AUTHOR OF *WE'RE ALL DOING TIME* AND *IT'S A MEANINGFUL LIFE*

"Rarely has a book touched me as deeply and personally as *Instinct for Freedom*. This profound work is a call to action, a spiritual force for change. May the beauty of Alan's writing and the power of his personal journey compel you to be true to your own heart so that we may all experience the gift of freedom in its purest form."

—CHERYL RICHARDSON, AUTHOR OF *STAND UP FOR YOUR LIFE*

"This superbly written, profound, and moving work addresses head-on the central question of our time: how to put meditation into action and so transform the real conditions of the real world. Its honesty and passion are liberating, and its message both timeless and acutely timely."

—ANDREW HARVEY, AUTHOR OF *THE DIRECT PATH* AND *SACRED ACTIVISM*

"Courageous and compelling, *Instinct for Freedom* is a vivid account of how one man's renunciation gave way to his own love and desire. This is a haunting and beautiful story, one full of teachings for seekers of all persuasions."

—MARK EPSTEIN, M.D., AUTHOR OF *GOING TO PIECES WITHOUT FALLING APART*

MEDIA AND SPEAKING INQUIRES FOR
ALAN CLEMENTS

contact@**WorldDharma**.com

"How to describe Alan's presentations? A tall order. Love poems/riffs/odes/ chants to the goddesses of compassion, deeply inscribed with the blood of Burmese slaves, soldiers in Iraq, Palestinian children, freedom fighters anywhere. A momentary entry into an internal tête-à-tête, ad infinitum; a glimpse at all that inner discursive dialog which marks us unequivocally as members of the human race. Just in case we get too spiritual, let's not forget that we are required to, by nature, include everything. To paraphrase the Vietnamese monk Thich Nhat Hahn's poem, "Please Call Me by My True Names," I am both the 12-year-old raped girl and the pirate who raped her. It is difficult to reconcile seeming opposites, and it takes the heart of a poet. Thich Nhat Hahn is a poet; Alan is one as well."
—MARCIA JACOBS, A PSYCHOTHERAPIST SPECIALIZING IN VICTIMS OF WAR, RAPE, AND TRAUMA; A SENIOR U.N. REPRESENTATIVE FOR REFUGEES IN BOSNIA AND CROATIA, 1993–1997; AND A FORMER OFFICER OF THE INTERNATIONAL WAR CRIMES TRIBUNAL

"Alan's life is material for a legend. An intellectual artist, freedom fighter, former Buddhist monk, he shares his insights and experience with a passion rarely seen and even more rarely lived. He'll make you think and feel in ways that challenge your entire way of being."
—CATHERINE INGRAM, *IN THE FOOTSTEPS OF GANDHI, PASSIONATE PRESENCE* AND *FACING EXTINCTION*

"I have known Alan for close to three decades. He is my first call when I seek insight and candor concerning personal and professional advice. As a speaker, his eloquence moves audiences to ask the questions behind questions about how we live, why we work, and how it fits together. Alan's presence—his remarkable ability to engage an audience, connect with their heart—stands alongside the best talent I have seen in the world."
—ROBERT CHARTOFF, PRODUCER OF ROCKY, THE RIGHT STUFF, AND RAGING BULL

"One of the most important and compelling voices of our times . . . Alan Clements is a riveting communicator — challenging and inspiring. He articulates the essentials of courage and leadership in a way that can stir people from all sectors of society into action; his voice is not only a great contribution during these changeful times, it is a needed one."
—JACK HEALY, FORMER DIRECTOR OF AMNESTY INTERNATIONAL, AND FOUNDER OF THE HUMAN RIGHTS ACTION CENTER

FERGUS HARLOW first "met" Alan Clements through Robert Anton Wilson's online Maybe Logic Academy in 2004, where Clements was conducting a course based on his book *"Instinct for Freedom"*. Harlow went on to become a key member of Clements' World Dharma Online Institute (WDOI) in 2007, and Clements has been a friend and mentor ever since.

From early 2013, Fergus has been Alan's personal assistant and colleague, working closely with him on producing all aspects of his World Dharma vision, including producing all aspects of these volumes; from initial fundraising efforts, to research, editing, and writing. Harlow compiled the Aung San Suu Kyi sections, as well as the latter part of the chronology, and transcribed and co-edited all of the interviews.

A keen student of yoga and the Dhamma, previous to this work he had been living and volunteering at various spiritual and retreat centres in the UK. He currently resides in Edinburgh, Scotland, where he is pursuing his own creative writing projects.